Healthcare Safety and Security

Safety and security are important issues both for hospital staff members and their patients. Written by healthcare gurus, Charles Schnabolk and Ben Scaglione, this book is an expose on the current state of healthcare and the dangers and risks associated with being a patient navigating within the healthcare environment. The authors address the risks and threats hospitals and healthcare staff endure while treating patients and working in the healthcare field. They discuss the potential hazards associated with patient treatment and care. From wrong-site surgeries to acquired infections, the book includes some of the top patient risks as outlined by the Joint Commission's National Patient Safety Goals and discusses other less acknowledged risks, ones not immediately known to the public, like loss of personal property, sexual assault, and the physical as well as mental abuse that patients may suffer while housed or visiting within the healthcare environment.

Also included is a discussion of newer hazards brought on by current technology like cyber security. The authors describe the challenges hospitals have associated with hackers and staff who wish to destroy or steal medical records. Hackers who hold hospitals hostage and seek monies in return for stolen access to medical records captured during a hack into the hospital's virtual network. Staff who steal medical record information which they look to sell to the highest bidder on the dark web for use in compromising the financial information of those patients who use hospital's services. Most hospitals in the U.S. have a long list of procedures, rules, and regulations to keep staff and patients safe including, but not limited to staff assaults, abuse, and bullying. The violence staff has endured while working within hospitals, clinics, and the Emergency Department has been increasing over the years peaking post- Covid-19 to levels never seen before.

The book discusses the violence that has plagued healthcare for decades. According to the Joint Commission, healthcare workers are around four times as likely to experience workplace violence compared to workers in other industries. Talking about the unknown abuse that occurs between nurses and doctors in the care of patients during surgeries and medical treatments. The authors address these issues and many more while providing current information on each topic and suggesting resolutions and mitigation strategies that assist in reducing the potential for the identified risks from occurring again.

Dedication

This book is dedicated to Charles Schnabolk, a brilliant mind and mentor. Charlie started his career as a writer and author publishing articles in local newspapers, even getting as far as the New York Times. Educated as an engineer, Charlie's security career took off when he won the bid to design the security systems for the World Trade Center in New York. Subsequently, he went on to design security systems for schools, churches, hotels, and hospitals. His innovative designs were way ahead of the times, often creating controversy throughout his career, but bolstered the pioneering security design in the New York City, tri-state area. Charlie was the first to use magnetic locks with a time delay on exit doors in schools and hospitals which saved thousands of lives. He was the first to obtain New York City Building Department approval for these locks within the Maternity unit in hospitals and schools, dramatically reducing the potential of infant abduction in hospitals and violence in schools.

Throughout his career, he has mentored many people within the security field including myself and provided inspiration and guidance enabling others to look outside of the box in the design and operation of security systems and operational programs. Having written many books, Charlie's passion has always been in healthcare. Providing innovative solutions while being a critic of the way healthcare provides its services. Always looking to improve how healthcare can provide better care and treatment for patients.

This book is dedicated to Charlie, whose passion for healthcare has created this book. As Charlie has done throughout his career, he has authored this book in his own unique style, with my assistance, to challenge the healthcare industry to look at itself to improve its culture, patient care, effectiveness, and efficiencies.

Contents

About the Authors

Charles Schnabolk, P.E. – Consulting Engineer, Inventor, Author, University Lecturer, and a pioneer in security technology since 1970 when he designed the security system for the original World Trade Center. He is consulted on the security design of hundreds of complex facilities, including schools, banks, retail stores, hotels, and in many of the nation's major hospitals and medical care facilities.

Bernard J. (Ben) Scaglione, CPP, CHPA, CHSP, is principal of The Secure Hospital a blogging and resource management site. Ben is author of the book, *Security Management for Healthcare: Proactive Event Prevention and Effective Resolution.* He has a master's degree from Rutgers University School of Criminal Justice and has served as a security director for more than 25 years in New York City area hospitals, including New York Presbyterian, Bellevue, and Atlantic Health System. Ben has served in multiple capacities for International Association for Healthcare Security and Safety (IAHSS) over the past 10 years, including several councils, committees, and the IAHSS Board of Directors. He is former Chairman of the ASIS International Healthcare Council and past President of the New York City Metropolitan Healthcare Safety and Security Directors Association. Ben is a past columnist for Security Magazine and a frequent contributor to the *Journal of Healthcare Protection Management.* He has served as an adjunct faculty member at Pratt Institute, Interboro Institute, New Jersey City University, and John Jay College Peace Officer Academy.

Challenges in Hospital Operations

The growing healthcare field, and the many disciplines that comprise this complex industry, present complex and difficult challenges for security professionals. The legion of federal laws, along with the copious codes and regulations mandated by governmental agencies, makes it difficult for a physician to focus on treating the sick and infirm. Healthcare security extends not only to physicians and hospital staff but to equipment designers/-CARE manufacturers, surveillance-system installers, architects, and consultants – all offering guidance to overwhelmed hospital security staff and administrators.

While the healthcare available in the nation's 6,120 hospitals is the best in the world, it is also the most expensive. As an example, the average hospital stay in the U.S. costs $5,220 per day – compared to just $765 in Australia.[*] Overall, according to the *American Journal of Medicine*, the U.S. spends $3.5 trillion on health care per year. This huge difference has created a new industry in which travel agencies offer complete packages to foreign countries for treatment, using doctors trained in the U.S. and hotel and meals for one-third the cost of a similar experience in local U.S. hospitals. A well-publicized story that appeared in 2020 involved an employee of a major corporation arranging for a knee replacement to be paid by the company insurance plan. The cost for the three-day hospital stay and the doctor's fee

[*] Fast Facts on U.S. Hospitals, 2024, American Hospital Association Website.

was $23,000. The patient chose to have the procedure done in a Cancun, Mexico hospital for $7,500 that included a basic package:

- Air flight
- Hotel stay for four nights
- Hospital for five days

Additional costs were the R/T flights for a well-known MD specialist from a first-class American hospital in the patient's hometown, including an overnight accommodation in a hotel and the fee for the operation. The total cost for the entire procedure was $8,500 and was paid by the insurance company, which included the approximate $5,000 fee for the doctor to fly back to his hometown city the afternoon following the operation. It is said that the insurance company then paid a bonus of $3,000 for an extra week's vacation in Cancun for the patient's family.

Introduction

My name is Ben Scaglione, and I have been working within the Healthcare field for over 30 years. Early in my career, I had the distinct pleasure of meeting Charlie Schnabolk. I first met Charlie when he came into my office one day extolling the virtues of his magnetic exit locks, a technology still ahead of the fire code. He delivered on a promise to get building variance approval, and we installed the locks – effectively reducing unauthorized access to the hospital where I worked. His ability to get the New York City Building Department to agree to installing the locks provided a safe and secure environment within the hospital. Later, we installed his devices in a Hospital's Maternity and Pediatric units – again, getting city approval to lock both entry and exit portals, restricting access into and out of those high-security units.

Recognized as an expert in the security and healthcare field, Charlie Schnabolk is not only a pioneer; he is the pioneer and innovator in all aspects of modern physical security. His writing within this book gives readers an in-depth look at the healthcare field. With over fifty years of experience in the healthcare field, Charlie provides insights not normally observed by the average person.

Charlie's knowledge of healthcare institutions, security services, and expertise in fire code translated into a secure treatment environment – and more importantly, saved lives. His ability to create out-of-the-box solutions is reflected in the writings within this book. With my assistance, together we have put together a book on healthcare insights not normally expressed. Our decades of experience in healthcare have provided us with unique perspectives in hospitals and the healthcare profession overall.

So, with my experience and literary support, prepare yourself for Charlie's exceptional insight on how hospitals work and how to keep yourself and others safe. Enjoy the read!

Chapter 1

Strategies and Security Challenges

Security Is a Reaction – Not a Prevention

Even before the coronavirus pandemic took the attention and most of the resources in the healthcare industry, hospitals spent hundreds of thousands of dollars on questionable systems to comply with codes and privacy regulations intended to treat patients and keep staff safe. Some of the goals involved preventing the kidnapping of newborns, but systems must also protect against the hacking of medical data, Medicare fraud, equipment theft (regulators), trespasses, and other crimes indigenous to a healthcare facility. Securing the healthcare community means protecting millions of patients. Among fast-growing industries in the Health Care and Social Assistance sector: General Medical and Surgical Hospitals, which gained the most annual payroll, up $13.8 billion between 2017 and 2018 to $364.2 billion; Home Health Care Services, which added the most employees between 2017 and 2018, up 72,255 to 1.5 million; and Individual and Family Services, which added the most establishments between 2017 and 2018, up 4,915 to 80,577.[1] In some of the nation's major cities, medical facilities are the largest employers in the private sector – outnumbered only by civil servants in the municipal agencies.

Medical facilities also labor under safety and fire codes. This is an obligation of the emergency second responder in the event of a terrorist attack or a novel coronavirus rampage. Healthcare employment accounts for 9.3% of total employment.[2] This ever-expanding field now comprises about

DOI: 10.4324/9781032630670-1

17.3% of the U.S. gross domestic product.[3] With the introduction of universal healthcare in 2014, continues its rapid growth. Miracle drugs and life-extension technology will see this trend continue – with significant growth in hospital and nursing home capacity. In 2023, there were approximately 1.3 million seniors in the nation's 15,683 nursing homes.[4] This number is expected to increase by three million in 2024 and even more in the future. Security is an essential part of a facility's operation, but many administrators view security as a financial burden – since it is often considered an unnecessary, non-revenue producing overhead.

The 2020 virus rampage overwhelmed the entire industry, even in the facilities that had strong security planning. Hospitals could not handle the sudden and unexpected large numbers of COVID-19 patients, and thousands died when the injured or infected were rushed to a hospital or emergency treatment center. Those in charge have little experience in crisis intervention planning within the healthcare facility itself. Even though hospitals and the related healthcare industry are the largest buyers of security systems, they were unable to adequately protect patients and staff from the virus attack. There are many reasons for the inability to protect patients and staff; however, operating a facility with 24/7 public access is the primary handicap. Healthcare/emergency activities require rapid responses in already critical emergency situations. The training of the security staff and the selection of the security system are unlike that of any other public facility. While there is no perfect solution, much can and must be done to upgrade security in locations where evolving strategies threaten to overwhelm healthcare administrators.

Hackers Target Medical Record Data

A national survey reveals 83% of 1,300 physician practices surveyed already have experienced a cyberattack – increasing the need to better support medical practices.[5] This situation became uncontrollable during the coronavirus pandemic because more employees switched to working at home – causing terminals to become easy targets for cybercrimes. Some data storage facilities experienced a doubling of attempted hacking – specifically phishing emails, hunting for someone on the staff who would innocently click on a malicious link that allows malware to enter into the health system's network.

The reason for the increased interest in global cybercrime is money, which is estimated to be in the billions of dollars a year. This enormous amount of money exceeds the amount of money obtained illegally from credit card theft.

Stealing a credit card number has a life cycle of one or two days until the person realizes that the card is missing and cancels the card. An electronic medical record is far more valuable. The FBI considers a stolen credit card or social security number to be worth just $1 on the black market, while an electronic health record (once hacked) could be worth much more if it belongs to a celebrity or an elected official. Hackers based in China and Russia have broken into computer networks on a regular basis and stolen personal information of between four and six million patients in an average year. Security experts say cyber criminals are increasingly targeting the $4.5 trillion U.S. healthcare industry,[6] which has many companies still reliant on aging computer systems that do not use the latest security features.

Hospitals have had low security, so it's relatively easy for individual hackers or those working for foreign countries to get a large amount of personal data used for medical fraud or ransom. The data for sale includes names, birth dates, policy numbers, diagnosis codes, and billing information. Fraudsters use this data to create fake IDs to buy medical equipment or drugs that can be resold, or they combine a patient number with a false provider number and file made-up claims with insurers, according to experts who have investigated cyberattacks on healthcare organizations.

Medical identity theft is often not immediately identified by a patient or their provider, which gives criminals years to milk such credentials. Stolen health credentials can sell for a larger fee, which can go up to about ten or twenty times the value of a U.S. credit card number. Healthcare providers and insurers must publicly disclose data breaches affecting more than 500 people, but there are no laws requiring criminal prosecution. As a result, the total cost of cyberattacks on the healthcare system is difficult to pin down. Insurance industry experts say these are one of many expenses ultimately passed onto Americans as part of rising health insurance premiums. Consumers sometimes discover their credentials have been stolen only after fraudsters use their personal medical ID to impersonate them and purchase high-value consumables like cars, consumer electronics, healthcare services, and other expensive items. When the unpaid bills are sent to debt collectors, they track down the frauded victim and seek payment.

The government's efforts to combat Medicare fraud have focused on traditional types of scams that involve provider billing and overbilling. Fraud involving the Medicare program totaled more than $60 billion in the last two years, according to a Coalition Against Insurance Fraud report issued by Insurancefraud.org.

Physical Threats

With the establishment of controversial universal healthcare programs (Obamacare), the increase in the number of newly insured patients could make the security situation in a hospital environment almost unmanageable. NHE grew 4.1% to $4.5 trillion in 2022, or $13,493 per person, and accounted for 17.3% of Gross Domestic Product (GDP).[7] With all the attention focused on the nation's healthcare infrastructure, the United States still lags behind most other Western nations in the quality of medical treatment issues – despite being the most technologically advanced nation in the world.

- *Juvenile fatalities*: The United States spends twice as much on medical care as many European nations. Yet, American children are twice as likely to die before the age of five compared to Czech children.
- *Childbirth*: American women are eleven times more likely to die in childbirth compared to Irish women.
- *Infant deaths*: Thirty-three countries have lower infant death rates than the United States.
- *Doctor ratio*: More than forty countries have more physicians per capita than are found in America.
- *Life expectancy:* Men in twenty-seven countries live longer than the average American male.

Watchdog federal agencies have forced hospitals to be more cost-conscious, which usually translates into reducing the security budget. Hospital administrators have a traditional reluctance to spend money on security. The administrators consider that expenditure is a low priority, since it is a non-revenue generating expense. Security systems and the salaries for a uniformed security officer are always the first items eliminated by cost-cutting measures.

However, one important justification for maintaining the security budget is savings. Providing adequate security limits liability exposure – and the threat of malpractice suits from seminal events, such as infant kidnapping, physical attacks on nursing staff, and violence in the emergency room and psychiatric ward. The liability exposure and penalties for lax hospital security can jeopardize the very existence of a facility due to high jury awards. A successful infant kidnapping can cost a facility tens of millions of dollars in jury awards. Such a penalty might force a hospital to close its nursery or even bankrupt the entire facility.

The Best and Most Expensive Medical Care

High-profile patients from all over the world have followed in the footsteps of tens of thousands of patients who come to the United States for medical treatment every year. They choose American hospitals and doctors because, despite its flaws, the U.S. healthcare system still provides the highest quality care in the world. Whether the disease is cancer, pneumonia, heart disease, or AIDS, the chances of a patient surviving are far higher in the United States than in other countries. This nation is responsible for much of the world's research on health-related matters, and eighteen of the last twenty-five winners of the Nobel Prize in medicine are either U.S. citizens or work in an American laboratory or research center. U.S. companies developed more than half of all new major medicines introduced worldwide over the past twenty years, and Americans have played a key role in the most important non-pharmaceutical medical advances over the past forty years. This includes the cure for malaria and polio, the development of Prozac, and the discovery of Viagra. The healthcare system may not be perfect – and is possibly too costly – but it is the best in the world and is only getting better.

The President of the United States signed into law the most comprehensive changes to the healthcare system in American history in 2010, which directly affected the size of the patient pool and increased the need for upgrading security systems to handle the changes in procedures that hospitals had to make in order to accommodate the new demand for medical care. The added costs to implement the provisions listed below will involve billions more than ten years ago. Some provisions of the new healthcare policy include the following, but subsequent legislation has modified some of these items:

- Provides coverage for an additional thirty-two million people, or 95% of Americans.
- Requires everyone to get insurance or face fines.
- Fines for the uninsured.
- Expands Medicaid to cover everyone with an income less than $30,000 for a family of four.
- Allows young people to stay on parents' health plans up to age twenty-six.
- Denies coverage for illegal immigrants.
- Cannot deny coverage for pre-existing conditions.

Traditional responsibility in approximately 5,300 of the nation's full-service hospitals (with approximately 4,200 operating with newborn nurseries and obstetrics/gynecology departments) are focused on maintaining a haven for the sick, the infirm, and even the mentally ill. Gradually, the healthcare community has faced new tasks and responsibilities since the mid-1980s that were, at one time, inconceivable, including:

- *Kidnapping*: protecting more than the approximately 4,000,000 babies born each year within birthing centers and nurseries.
- *Epidemics*: preparing for flu-type contagious diseases, including pandemics.
- *Catastrophes*: being designated as the second responder in case of catastrophe (including terrorist attacks and natural disasters).

Regulations and constantly changing rules and oversight regulations add many woes.

- *Accreditation*: achieving accreditation adds new responsibilities to an already overwhelmed healthcare community.
- *Emergency Room*: one in five Americans will visit the emergency room in an average year.

Healthcare institutions are also a source of restricted and controlled substances, as they dispense many so-called controlled drugs desired by drug dealers and addicts. Hospitals are often associated with notoriously undersupervised pharmacies and undetected medical staff theft (doctors, nurses, and others). Drug abuse among physicians is difficult to estimate due to the lack of oversight, responsibility, or recordkeeping. Doctors are rarely reprimanded, challenged, or searched by the intimidated security staff – making it easy for the medical staff to remove controlled drugs from the premises.

Prescription form creation and distribution have been newly safeguarded, with some state health departments mandating blank prescriptions being kept in a secured cabinet, locked desk, or storage closet. The printer on which blank prescription forms are printed now must be locked or otherwise safeguarded. Regardless of the security measures adopted by the hospital pharmacy, no solution can completely safeguard drugs within the healthcare environment. Surveys indicate that more than 10% of obstetricians, gynecologists, and psychiatrists have some dependency on alcohol and dangerous drugs, and addicts seriously compromise security.

With its renown in healthcare, the United States pays dearly for its accomplishments in producing most of the world's prescription drugs, medical technologies, and Nobel laureates in medicine. In 2022, the most recent year for which comparative data on multiple countries was available, U.S. healthcare expenditures accounted for 16.6% of its economy and remain substantially higher than its peer countries.[8] If the United States cannot get its healthcare costs more in line with those in other industrialized nations, America may rapidly lose its competitive advantage – and all those Nobel laureates will be small compensation.

Room Décor with Butlers and Chefs

With the rising costs for many of the more premium hospitals throughout the nation, private rooms are being recreated to resemble a suite in a five-star hotel. Hospitals must compete with each other along with other foreign cities (like Singapore and London) for a select clientele that demands first-class accommodations and will pay for a room and special services with cash – no insurance forms to fill out. According to a 2021 study from the Kaiser Family Foundation (KFF), the average cost of a hospital stay per day in the United States was $2,883. The challenge in attracting expectant parents, celebrities, and foreign potentates is very competitive – and hospitals are forced to spend millions of dollars on renovating their nurseries, lobbies, patient rooms, bathrooms, and patient treatment rooms to resemble the presidential suites in the best hotels. Bedrooms are no longer filled with plain, IKEA-style furniture. Medical facilities that do not upgrade the appearance of their facilities will be forced to close their nurseries first, followed by other floors scattered throughout the entire building. Many facilities have installed whirlpool baths, saunas, luxurious "labor and delivery" areas, and recovery suites with 54-inch flat-screen TVs to remain competitive.

Hospitals often upgrade their rooms to resemble a Las Vegas luxurious suite, reserved for high rollers. Interior decorators design patients' rooms to meet the cultural needs of rich kings, high-profile celebrities, and even new mothers. Some provide food at a certain temperature and even offer masseuses or doulas to help in the birthing process. Midwives who assist in the delivery go back into the community and tell other women about the care and extra frills, which can seem more appealing than the skills of the presiding physician. Hospitals schedule tours of the birthing facility weeks before the due date and then provide a postpartum expert to instruct new mothers on infant care. The last thing a hospital wants to cope with, besides a successful abduction, is an unhappy mother.

Recently, entire floors in several of the nation's best-known medical facilities were completely renovated, with the walls between rooms removed to create 2,000 square foot living spaces. Conventional bathroom fixtures were replaced with gold faucets to accommodate the requests of people such as the King of Saudi Arabia and his 150-people entourage, including his private chef. The two private planes that brought the sick king to New York City in 2011 required a two-mile-long caravan of forty limousines to take the servants and guards, along with special furniture (mattresses and heated toilet seats, and so forth), to the hospital. The cost for the thirty-day stay exceeded $4 million, and the entourage rented presidential suites at nearby four-star hotels, which added another $2 million to the king's total bill. Hollywood actors are not quite as outlandish in their demands as potentates, but many of the bigger stars take up half the nursery area when they reserve the maternity ward (meaning the entire nursery ward) for the birth of their child with a funny first name. Hospitals compete for these types of eccentric and affluent patients, none of whom use insurance plans to pay for their first-class treatment. Plus, they pay with cash.

The fancy accommodations are no longer limited to royalty and celebrities. Ordinary patients now wake up after surgery in suites with beds covered with high thread-count sheets and bathrooms gleaming with polished marble. Instead of normal attention from the floor nurse, a patient is greeted by a man in a black vest and tie proffering an elaborate menu and introducing himself as the on-demand butler. Catering to the conspicuously rich can be a little tricky and requires a competent public relations staff. However, with cutbacks on medical subsidies by the government, these high-priced suites are necessary, and the trend has not abated. More and more hospitals are offering a floor with VIP amenities, including a dedicated chef and lavish service. From Johns Hopkins to Cedars-Sinai Medical Center in Los Angeles and the Presbyterian Hospitals in New York City, all promise the grandest in pampering with lush maternity suites. These services necessarily engender additional security challenges.

The rise of medical tourism to glittering hospitals in far-off places, such as Singapore and Thailand, has turned coddling and elegance into a marketing necessity. The demand for elaborate suites and gourmet menus has grown every year. Some doctors believe that, within the next few years, people will be calling the hospital catering facilities to reserve a table at the commissary for the evening meal. No one makes fun of "hospital food" any longer.

Red-Blanket Patient

A growing trend for hospitals is to provide extra comforts to rich patients who are willing to pay for special VIP treatment while recuperating in a healthcare facility. Once the patient is identified for special care, some hospitals provide these individuals with a red blanket to cover themselves, instead of the plain white blankets issued to all the other patients. Of the nation's top fifteen hospitals, as ranked by U.S. News and World Report, at least ten offer luxury-treatment options. These options include paying extra to stay in private, hotel-like rooms on the top floor, which come with gourmet food, plush bathrobes, and small business centers. Some physicians suggest that VIP services are a harmless way to raise money. A wealthy patient can pay more than $4,000 a night for deluxe rooms, and if they receive good service, they might make a big donation.

Some doctors worry that the red-blanket patient may receive worse care than one with a white blanket – as elite patients often receive unnecessary tests or are treated with medications unlikely to be helpful, because a physician may feel pressure to appease them. The special treatment to a select few may seem unethical since it may result in some patients being labeled "important", causing a doctor to consider others as less important. Regardless of the controversy, it appears that VIP treatment will be adopted by more hospitals in their competitive drive to attract richer patients. These institutions need more money to pay their executives more than $1 million a year, a figure that is becoming common in large teaching hospitals and special care healthcare centers.

Healing Power of Paintings

Studies show that paintings and other works of art help patients and families in the healing process while convalescing in a hospital room. These studies indicate a direct link between the content of images and the brain's reaction to pain, stress, and anxiety. Hospitals are considering and choosing artwork based on this evidence and considering it of higher importance than merely decorations for sterile rooms and corridors. Hospitals spend millions on artists who create original art to support optimism, vitality, and energy as an attempt to overcome white coat syndrome (the term for what occurs when visitors and patients become nervous when they see a doctor about a health issue).

Close to half of hospitals have instituted some type of art program – which includes art therapy classes and musical performances, reports the Arts and Health Alliance. Studies show that nature images helped calm restless behavior and noise levels in the emergency waiting rooms. Other findings indicated that images of fearful or angry faces, as well as a lack of realism and sharp contours, elicited negative emotional responses in the brain and should be avoided. The goal of the paintings in the hospital environment is to take the patient's mind away from the disease and replace time lost in the hospital with moments and memories of enjoyable beauty. Studies have found that beside paintings, patients in a room with a view of nature recovered faster from surgery than those who faced a brick wall. Even rooms with more sunlight are associated with decreased patient stress. All of these factors influence how a patient's room should be designed. Architects can no longer ignore the environment, as it heavily influences patient recovery.

Obsolete Traditions – Regulatory Laws

Since 9/11, the Hurricane Katrina response of 2005, and the 2008 terrorist attack in an Indian hospital, the public has become aware that security in healthcare facilities must be upgraded, redefined, and properly funded. A hospital, unlike other large public facilities, does not close on holidays or in bad weather. Nor do these facilities have the option of locking their entrances at 9:00 P.M. on workdays and after 5:00 P.M. on weekends. Hospitals are "public facilities" that must remain open 24/7, just like hotels – except hotels do not have to admit the physically sick, the mentally challenged, and the destitute. Hospitals aren't allowed to cancel reservations because they are "more than booked," either. Hospitals have the biggest payrolls in major cities and have to deal with problems that are unique to these facilities.

In New York City, the largest healthcare network is also the largest private-sector employer, with about 53,000 employees. Municipal agencies make up the only organization with more employees.

The healthcare community now must be prepared for events such as anthrax threats, bioterrorism attacks, and other Armageddon-type scenarios resulting from violent actions – not only from patients and terrorists, but from natural disasters as well. Since 2000, the nation has suffered eight of the ten worst catastrophes in our nation's history. What once was considered unimaginable is now accepted as inevitable. The response efforts of hospitals and their personnel are crucial in such disasters. Other responsibilities added to a hospital's expanded list of responsibilities include preventing infant abduction and following the many new patient information privacy laws. There is the always-present dread of an impending Joint Commission on Accreditation of Hospitals (JCAHO) survey plus impractical regulations from the Occupational Safety and Health Administration (OSHA) in addition to the Health Insurance Portability and Accountability Act (HIPAA), plus compliance with the National Fire Protection Association (NFPA) fire codes. As a result of all these mandates, rules, and regulations focused specifically on the healthcare community, once-considered "safe havens" have grudgingly become the largest purchasers of complex security systems in the nation. These institutions have had to double the security staff to comply with the various regulations, which have upgraded the duties of the security department and its staff.

Adding to long-established problems along with new regulations confronting healthcare facilities is the enormous task of supervising and monitoring the almost 120 million visitors in the approximately 4,000 emergency rooms nationwide. These visits can not only overwhelm the medical staff but also create a new set of challenges for the usually underpaid and understaffed members of the hospital security department. No other category of the institution meets the same level of regulation as healthcare. The growing responsibilities that hospitals and other patient-care facilities are forced to follow can challenge the resources of the most efficient security department, and the results are not very encouraging. A summary of the most important codes and regulations that now define the expanding responsibilities of healthcare facilities show that they are often conflicting, redundant, and even a little impractical – especially in the areas related to medical record security.

Patient Privacy Law – HIPAA

The well-known acronym HIPAA refers to the federal law – the Health Insurance Portability and Accountability Act – which every healthcare worker recognizes. It is the first attempt by the government to establish a "Notice of Privacy Practices". This law mandates procedures to protect an individual's right to decide who, when, and how their health information is disclosed. It also mandates the need to maintain confidentiality when exchanging medical information between healthcare-related facilities. Few members within the healthcare community realize that HIPAA, passed in 1996, was not as concerned about privacy as it was about ensuring the ability to immediately qualify for comparable health insurance coverage when employees changed jobs (so their health insurance would not be denied). While HIPAA regulations were introduced to reform insurance, the regulations evolved to become the guiding force in keeping patient information from being distributed without proper authorization. The current HIPAA goals now affect far more individuals than the original law intended.

An example of the far-reaching effect on patient privacy is seen in HIPAA guidelines require that baby photos be protected, no less so than a medical chart or birth date or social security number, according to the Department of Health and Human Services (DHS). For generations, obstetricians and midwives across America proudly posted photographs of newborn babies, but this pre-digital form of social media has gone the way of cigars given away in the waiting room. Pictures of smiling babies that once crowded a bulletin board in a doctor's office are now stored in a secured section of the doctor's office where no one can see them. While the display of photos is a minor part of the law, it has changed the way doctors treat healthcare information in all its forms and has made recordkeeping a time-consuming effort that doctors often are reluctant to adopt. People often misinterpret HIPAA guidelines, and the regulations have become, in many situations, a code of silence preventing hospitals and healthcare providers from providing information to loved ones. The law's flexibility in disclosing information is in the patient's interest. HIPAA does not oblige patients to give consent in writing before releasing health records to close family members, but facilities may legally demand a signature on a form before doing so.

Healthcare Services and Establishments

A long-term goal of HIPAA, enforced by the Department of Health and Human Services (DHHS), is to create a paperless standard in which patient information is digitally stored and shared electronically among authorized healthcare providers. There are penalties (both civil and criminal) associated with not following the HIPAA guidelines in storing and releasing patient information, but other government services tend to make the medical profession more involved in paperwork rather than in treating patients. A cross section of these services includes the following:

- *Protected Health Information (PHI)*: information that is electronically transferred and involves personal information that can be used to identify the patient – sometimes even inadvertently. PHI includes, but is not limited to, a patient's name, address, telephone number, age, diagnosis, surgery, date of procedure, and medications.
- *Department of Health and Human Services (DHHS)*: the U.S. government's principal agency for protecting the health of all Americans and providing essential services – especially for those least able to help themselves. DHHS administers more grant dollars than all other federal agencies combined. The DHHS Medicare program is the nation's largest health insurer, handling more than one billion claims per year. Medicare and Medicaid together provide healthcare insurance to around one in three Americans. The department has become more involved with hospital responsibilities since the enactment of HIPAA. Other important responsibilities are funneled through its Department of Substance Abuse and Mental Health Services Administration (SAMSHA) and the Center for Substance Abuse Treatment (CSAT), which developed a set of performance measures focused on assessing and treating tobacco, alcohol, and other drug use and dependency for all hospitalized patients.
- *National Institutes of Health (NIH)*: an agency within DHHS. It began recording how much radiation patients receive from CT scans and other

procedures in their medical records. The use of radiation procedures has grown dramatically in recent years, causing new cancers and hundreds of deaths a year. The increased exposure to radiation tests does not include the rare cases of machine malfunctions or mistakes caused by human error, accidentally giving hundreds of patients up to eight times the normal radiation dose during a stroke scan. A study in the Archives of Internal Medicine (now known as JAMA Internal Medicine) estimated that radiation exposure from medical tests over a lifetime might be dangerous and even fatal. Doctors at NIH began recording how much radiation patients receive from CT scans and other procedures into their medical records.

- *Centers for Medicaid and Medicare Services (CMS)*: governs all activities relating to the nation's Medicare and Medicaid programs. Healthcare institutions that accept Medicare and Medicaid payments are required to comply with federal standards called "Conditions of Participation" or COPs.
  - Since 1965, CMS has empowered The Joint Commission (TJC) to accredit and enforce COP compliance. TJC accredits nearly 4,000 community, academic, pediatric, long-term acute, psychiatric, rehabilitation, and specialty hospitals.
    - Accreditation is a condition of reimbursement and also reduces liability insurance and other premiums.
- *The Department of Homeland Security (DHS)*: was created following 9/11 and has now grown to approximately 200,000 employees within over twenty special agencies. Hospitals may not have been the focus of this department, but DHS has issued minimum requirements that relate to having medical centers prepared to meet the next catastrophe. Very few hospitals have initiated any efforts to meet the criteria listed in the requirements documents.
- *The Joint Commission – formerly JCAHO*: one of the most important organizations in the healthcare field. Their recommendations and regularly scheduled on-site visits to hospitals and other healthcare institutions can have a direct effect on the accreditation of a facility receiving federal funds (Medicare and so forth). TJC was founded in 1951 and seeks to continuously improve healthcare for the public by evaluating healthcare facilities and inspiring them to excel in providing safe and effective care of the highest quality and value. This commission evaluates and accredits more than 4,000 healthcare organizations and programs in the United States, including hospitals and home care

organizations – plus other healthcare organizations that provide long-term care, behavioral healthcare, laboratory, and ambulatory care services. As an independent, not-for-profit organization, TJC is the nation's oldest and largest standard-setting and accrediting body in healthcare. Failure to achieve accreditation can lead to fines or an accreditation suspension, which would place the hospital out of business.

- *Building Organization Construction Association* (*BOCA*): sets construction standards that most building developers and architects in the nation follow. The only exceptions are a few of the major cities that have the resources to develop their own Municipal Building Code – although these usually follow the construction guidelines, standards, and concepts that are issued by NFPA and BOCA. For example, the codes in Florida upgrade or modify BOCA requirements to stress construction standards for withstanding hurricanes, as contrasted with several Midwest communities that add specifications to resist tornado winds, etc.
- *National Fire Protection Association* (*NFPA*): an important national organization dealing with fire-alarm-system operation. Its many standards and regulations are passed by consensus vote of its almost 50,000 members and practically govern the methods used to install the hospital fire alarm and life safety systems (FAS). The organization issues standards and codes on every component for fire-alarm systems and includes the much-respected Life Safety Code 101, which covers the most important aspects for a building FAS. The NFPA attempted to expand their domain to include certain standards relating to security systems in 2008, but the practitioners within the security industry have largely ignored this intrusion.

  The fire-alarm industry and the security-protection industry have no history or intention of co-mingling or cooperating. *Agencies Having Jurisdiction* (*AHJ*) usually follows the national fire codes issued by the NFPA – but there is no equivalent code that defines security requirements.
- Congress created *OSHA* and *NIOSH* under the Occupational Safety and Health Act of 1970. *NIOSH,* the *National Institute for Occupational Safety and Health,* is part of the *Centers for Disease Control and Prevention* (*CDC*), which is under the U.S. Department of Health and Human Services. NIOSH is a federal agency with a staff of about 1,300 responsible for conducting research and making recommendations for the prevention of work-related injuries and illness. *OSHA,*

the Occupational Safety and Health Administration, falls under the Department of Labor. It ensures safe and healthy working conditions in the workplace by conducting periodic inspections of the workplace or after receiving complaints.

- *STATE DEPARTMENTS OF HEALTH* vary so greatly in their authority and oversight capabilities that there will probably never be a nationwide universal standard that applies to all fifty state health departments. A Northeastern state issued a special requirement concerning the storage of patient records in filing cabinets, a seemingly simple task. It was issued in response to reports that most cabinets were not locked or located in secured areas. Those that had installed the common cam locks were not always used properly, according to the regulation issued by this particular state. The problem arose after someone noted that when a cabinet was opened, the record clerk or medical staff member would close the file drawer but frequently neglected to manually re-lock it. It did not automatically latch, and cam locks do not have this relocking feature. The hospital had to design a special spring hasp to meet the state requirement. The hatch automatically latched when the cabinet drawer was closed – similar in operation to the spring lock on rear-exit doors. It was one of the many special devices developed specifically for the healthcare industry that had few applications for other categories of facilities.

EIS is the *Epidemic Intelligence Service.* EIS is an arm of the CDC. Due to its low profile, very few people recognize the important contributions carried out by this service. As of 2022, the agency boasts about 197 elite medical detectives in the EIS are mostly U.S. doctors who serve for two years in the field of public health. This agency was created in 1951, and its doctors travel all over the world on short notice to help identify illnesses such as Legionnaires' disease, Lyme disease, and Toxic Shock Syndrome (TSS). They work to stop outbreaks of diphtheria and other diseases before they can spread uncontrollably. They also attempt to discover the sources of deadly diseases like the Ebola virus and trace paralyzing cases of polio. Some investigations have led the Food and Drug Administration to remove potentially lethal products from the market.

EIS doctors are credited with discovering the link between a nerve disorder in children and lead poisoning in the early 1950s. They provided evidence that malaria had virtually disappeared from the United States, overturning the conventional wisdom that it was a leading cause of fever throughout the southern sections of the United States. Another prominent discovery involved the Salk polio vaccine after some recipients became paralyzed, apparently by a live virus. The EIS investigators found that the defective vaccine came from one of the six companies licensed to make and distribute it. The agency has conducted many successful studies, including one that pinpointed the source of a salmonellosis outbreak from salad bars in Oregon. The service also took a leading role in the investigation of the deliberate release of anthrax spores through the postal system soon after 9/11. This little-known agency has solved many medical mysteries, and its approximately 300 annual graduates have made significant contributions in the various disciplines that are defined as public health.

Notes

1. Earlene K.P. Dowell, Health Care Still Largest U.S. Employer, Census Bureau's 2018 County Business Patterns Provides Data on Over 1,200 Industries, *U.S. Census Bureau*, October, 2020.
2. U.S. Labor Statistics, Spotlight on Statistics, Website.
3. Center for Medicare & Medicaid Services, National Health Expenditure Data Website.
4. USA Facts Website, How does America care for the elderly?
5. AMA website, Medical cybersecurity: A patient safety issue.
6. CMS.gov, NHE Fact Sheet.
7. Cms.gov Website, NHE Fact Sheet.
8. Peterson KFF health System tracker, How does health spending in the U.S. compare to other countries, https://www.healthsystemtracker.org/

Chapter 2

The Need of Intensive Care

Choosing the Right Hospital Is a Life-or-Death Decision

Most people still pick a hospital based on convenience, a friend's recommendation, or where their doctor practices – even though that decision can be deadly. Patients treated at the worst hospitals are more likely to die than patients with the same health problem treated at the best hospitals. A personal doctor may not even be treating their patient because, once admitted to a healthcare facility, an in-house physician called a hospitalist (who has never met the patient) will take over. With these factors in mind, it is essential that every patient makes a serious effort to find out which hospital has a record of success.

According to research, this is especially important if the problem concerns a possible heart attack. Going to the wrong hospital can mean the likelihood of survival is substantially reduced. Patient safety is another risk that can be life-threatening. The possibility of contracting a bloodstream infection is higher at certain hospitals than others. The danger of infection and medical mistakes add to the stress of hospitalization, and it can get worse when the patients realize that their trusted personal doctor is not involved – and the on-site hospitalist doctor is a total stranger, who tends to spend less time at the bedside and discharge patients sooner.

Example: Two well-known hospitals in a major city. If a patient needs bypass surgery or a new heart valve, they can go to a highly ranked hospital for cardiology and heart surgery, according to U.S. News and World Report. U.S. News and World Report scores the other hospital as average for valve and heart surgery, but have the nation's highest rating for gallbladder

DOI: 10.4324/9781032630670-2

surgery. Choosing the right hospital is important because a patient's life could depend on it.

Deadly Infections

About one in twenty hospitalized patients will develop a new, hospital-borne infection during their stay. Malpractice errors are a great threat to patient survival, but an even greater threat is the spread of hospital-borne infections – which have reached epidemic proportions. Patients should be able to compare hospitals' infection rates, though relatively few hospitals even track them. The CDC healthcare-associated infection (HAI) prevalence survey found that there were an estimated 110,800 surgical site infections associated with inpatient surgeries in 2015. Based on the 2023 data, there was a 2% increase in the infection rate related to operative procedures compared to the previous year. In addition, 2023 data found a 3% increase in surgical site infections related to operative procedures compared to 2022.[1] Isolating patients and adding a focus on hygiene can significantly reduce the infection problem, which has finally attracted public attention.

Healthcare facilities that have tried to stop infections found (to their dismay) that as more bugs develop a resistance to antibiotics, containing the spread of disease has become an almost insurmountable struggle. Obtaining accurate statistics is almost impossible. Pennsylvania was the first state to provide infection data collected directly from its hospitals. The Agency for Healthcare Research and Quality indicated that 2% to 4% of all patients' surgeries develop surgical site infections. They are the leading cause of readmissions to the hospital following surgery, and approximately 3% of patients who contract an SSI will die as a consequence.[2]

At a large veterans' hospital in an eastern city, every arriving patient is tested for drug-resistant bacteria – and those found positive are housed in isolation rooms behind red-painted lines that warn people not to enter without wearing gowns and gloves. Every room and corridor are equipped with dispensers of foamy hand sanitizer, and each patient in these rooms is assigned his or her own stethoscope to prevent the transfer of microorganisms. Some states are passing laws requiring hospitals to report their infection rates and to screen all intensive care patients for bacterial infections. Paradoxically, hospitals are encouraged to screen for HIV – but not for bacterial infections – which are associated with seven times as many deaths. The guidelines relating to screening are lax, and this has given hospitals an excuse to do very little to contain the spread of infectious diseases. Preventable hospital infections have, for many years, been among the top ten causes of deaths in the United States.

One study found that even a doctor's necktie can be a carrier, after it was found that twenty out of forty-two ties tested contained bacteria and other infectious germs on them.[3] In 1987, scores of elderly and chronically ill patients at the Bird S. Coler Memorial Hospital in New York City began to fall violently sick with food poisoning from eggs tainted with Salmonella. By the time the outbreak ended (more than two weeks later), nine people had died, and about 500 patients had become sick.[4] That outbreak remains the deadliest incident in this country attributed to eggs infected with the Salmonella bacteria. In 2010, the same bacteria sickened thousands of people nationwide and led to the recall of half a billion eggs.[5] In spite of the decades between the outbreaks, there was a crucial link in both cases. The eggs came from the farms owned by the same company, which ranked among the country's biggest egg producers.

*Avoiding infections, according to the Committee to Reduce Infection Deaths.*www.hospitalinfection.org

- Patients should never be shy about reminding doctors, nurses, and aides to wash their hands.
- People who smoke or are overweight are more susceptible to infection – patients should try to quit or lose weight before surgery.
- Wash with 4% chlorhexidine antibiotic soap for several days before surgery.
- Don't allow the doctor to shave the surgical site – tiny cuts from a razor can get infected.
- Use hair clippers to remove hair.
- Have friends and relatives stay away if they are ill.
- If a patient is unable to speak for himself or herself, have a family member or a friend serve as an advocate.

To compare hospitals and doctors, check out www.HealthGrades.com *or the state health department's websites.*

The notion that infections in hospitals are similar to bad weather – unfortunate, but inevitable – is not the ideal attitude. However, the thought that when people are old or immunocompromised, they are likely to get infected may be a fable with some factual roots. Infections found in hospitals in a one-day survey of 183 hospitals in ten states turned up 504 infections likely caused by hospital care. The following were the most common:

- Pneumonia, 21.8%
- Surgical site infection, 21.8%
- Gastrointestinal infection, 17.1%
- Urinary tract infection, 12.9%
- Primary bloodstream infection, 9.9%[6]

Diff infection. In a growing number of hospitals, a relatively newly discovered bacterium exists. Some estimate it infects a half-million Americans every year, killing tens of thousands of hospital patients annually. The deadly germ ravages the intestines and preys on people in hospitals, nursing homes, and other medical facilities – the very places patients trust to protect their health. Federal data indicate those older than sixty-five account for about 90% of all deaths from C. Diff (Clostridium difficile) infection.[7] The bacterium is resistant to virtually all modern antibiotics. Appropriately, its scientific name is Clostridium difficile, commonly known as C. diff bacteria. Currently, it is found only in the hospital environment. Many highly contagious bacteria prevalent in hospitals are gram-positive and can be deadly, but are usually treated with available antibiotics – unlike the C. diff organism.

Medical Harm and Mistakes

Patients have died in America's hospitals and healthcare centers for reasons completely unrelated to the illnesses for which they were being treated. The leading cause of death for hospital patients is not a heart attack or stroke, but an infection caused by doctors, nurses, and others on the staff failing to wash their hands as they move from one patient's room to the next. A recent Johns Hopkins study claims more than 250,000 people in the U.S. die every year from medical errors. Other reports claim the numbers to be as high as 440,000.[8] This is due to doctors who fail to communicate effectively with their colleagues, nurses, and doctors who hand out the wrong medication, and doctors who are responsible for causing or spreading hospital infections.

Hospitals alone (not including clinics, surgery centers, doctor's offices, or nursing homes) are credited with preventable deaths far greater than fatalities resulting from car accidents, breast cancer, AIDS, or even gun violence. If a 747 jetliner crashed every day, killing all 500 people aboard, there would be a national uproar over aviation safety and an all-out mobilization by government agencies to attack the problem. The world of American medicine is far deadlier, and medical mistakes kill enough people each week to fill four jumbo jets – but these mistakes go largely unnoticed by the world at large. However, these issues have gained the attention of the federal government, which is trying to prevent hospitals from profiting from surgical mistakes as exposed by various surveys conducted by respected medical associations.

It seems that hospitals make money from their own mistakes, because insurers have traditionally paid them for the longer stays and the extra care patients needed to treat surgical complications that could have been avoided. Since 2011, insurers and Medicare have resisted reimbursing hospitals for their errors. Otherwise, hospitals have little incentive to improve healthcare in their facility. The entire healthcare system needs to move away from the "fee-for-service" system that emphasizes quantity more than quality to a method of payment that rewards better care – not longer care.

In the nation's hospitals, a shocking number of preventable deaths occur on a daily basis, with little or no public outrage. This is most likely due to the fact that patients die one at a time, rather than in a mass casualty event. This lack of attention to a medical crisis has gone on for decades, even after an analysis by the Institute of Medicine (funded by the Academy of Sciences) issued a report estimating that tens of thousands of avoidable deaths occur each year to patients under hospital care.

Medication Errors Another report by the Inspector General of the Department of Health and Human Services found that serious medical mishaps are not limited to surgical mistakes and could also be traced to the handling of prescription drugs.[9] Many wrongful deaths occur when a patient receives the wrong medication or is administered an incorrect dose of the right drug. Medication mistakes while in the hospital under the care of the medical staff are outrageously high when compared to the number of errors made by bank tellers, and tellers are not paid as well as an orderly in the hospital assigned to clean bedpans. Medication errors are a growing problem because, in any given week, four out of five adults in the nation take at least one medication with one-third taking at least five different medications. The drug errors caused by the hospital pharmacy are so widespread that a patient should expect at least one mistake every day they remain hospitalized.

The epidemic causing healthcare harm and medical errors affects as many people as the entire populations of North Dakota, Rhode Island, and Vermont combined – annually. It is a human-made calamity that is now one of the three leading causes of death in the United States. The government has not adequately addressed this avoidable situation at the same level it gives to lowering deaths from plane crashes, cancer, or drug addiction. Infections, surgical mistakes, and other medical errors contribute to the deaths of more than 100,000 patients a year, according to projections based on a study conducted by the Department of Health and Human Services, and their hospital care seriously hurt another 1.4 million. The medical mistakes in hospitals cost the healthcare community at least $4 billion annually, mostly paid by the government under Medicare and Medicaid and by private insurance plans. These organizations have started to use the "never list" of things they will not pay for.[10]

No-Reimbursement Pay Rules

The policy of not paying for hospital errors is meant to get the hospital to eliminate the errors in the first place. The Centers for Disease Control and Prevention estimates that patients develop 1.7 million infections in the hospital a year.[11] Urinary tract infections and hospital-acquired pneumonia can add more than $10,000 to a patient's hospital bill. The one drawback to this no-pay policy is that hospitals may find ways to turn away or divert patients who are at greatest risk of developing infections or bedsores. This should be a small price to pay if hospitals start to become more diligent in creating a safer and cleaner environment for patients. It is rare that a hospital screens incoming patients for bacterial colonies in any methodical way and, as a result, the public is becoming aware that a visit to a hospital can be a dangerous place for healthy people – simply because hospitals are full of sick people and contagious germs.

One element missing from the penalty placed for hospital errors is that it does not extend to the doctors who committed those errors. The hospital may now lose any extra payment for a second operation needed to retrieve an object left behind the first time – which is appropriate, given that nurses are supposed to keep track of all instruments and sponges. But an errant doctor, who is most likely culpable for the error, can get paid for both the initial surgery that left the object in the patient and then again for removing the device – even if a government insurance plan does not reimburse the hospital fee.

Medicare will no longer pay hospitals to retrieve surgical tools, sponges, or other objects left in a patient during surgery or to provide a patient with incompatible blood products. Treating bed sores and injuries caused by falls in the hospital are other expenses that the hospital must bear – not the government. Under a new policy, healthcare facilities learned that when a patient enters the hospital with pneumonia, they must die from that disease. If they were to leave the hospital with a broken arm, it would be non-reimbursable. The healthcare industry initially received this policy as a financial disaster, but the government believes it will force hospitals to take responsibility for their errors and unclean environments. Meanwhile, the government and private insurers will save more than $400 billion a year with a no-pay policy.

- About one in seven Medicare hospital patients (roughly 134,000 of the estimated one million) discharged in any one-month period were harmed by medical care.
- Another one in seven experienced temporary harm due to someone catching a problem in time and reversing the problem.
- About forty-seven million Americans enrolled in Medicare health insurance, a government health insurance program for people ages sixty-five and older and those of any age with kidney failure.
- Medicare patients still endure harmful consequences from improper medical care, with 44% of the reported errors being preventable.[12]

Private health insurance companies have started to follow the policy of Medicare and stopped paying for medical treatment caused by errors or conditions found within the hospital environment. Initially, these health plans stopped paying only for the gravest of mistakes, but they soon followed the lead of the government. Hospitals can no longer dun a patient to make up for the loss of insurance coverage. Traditionally, certain infections picked up while in hospital care were considered an inevitable part of the treatment and billed accordingly, with no oversight questioning the charges. This billing procedure will now come under more scrutiny, and hospitals will be forced to upgrade their level of care.

The drawback to the no-pay policy is that it may force hospitals to deny admission to patients requiring elective procedures or reject higher risk patients (particularly the elderly) out of fear of being denied payment if complications arise that could not have been predicted or prevented. Such a policy also leads to some unnecessary tests (perhaps not even pertinent) to protect the doctor from the accusation of not obtaining additional information.

Hospital Errors and Omissions

Most medical errors are the result of undiagnosed infections, surgical complications, medication errors, and sometimes due to operating on the wrong patient. Not all errors are preventable, as many Medicare patients are elderly and have complicated health problems when entering the hospital. It is strange how the public will not challenge doctors – yet before choosing a restaurant, they often look up its "performance ratings" before choosing to enter the premises for a meal. Therefore, it seems logical that there be some method to check on a doctor's performance. Nothing makes hospitals shape up more quickly than this type of public reporting. In 1989, the first year that New York hospitals were required to report heart-surgery death rates, those rates ranged from 1% to 18% – a huge gap.[13]

> With data available, patients could find out that the chance of dying from a coronary artery bypass graft in one hospital is one in six, compared to another hospital with a one in one hundred chance of dying.

With the nation focused on the high cost of healthcare, the general public has become understandably concerned about the rising number of deaths due to medical errors for patients of all ages. At the same time, these figures have to be balanced against the fact that hospitals are marvels of healing and continue to improve patient care systems, including effective use of electronic health records, to help staff avoid mistakes and alert them to problems. Vigilance saves lives, and it is important that family members educate themselves regarding medical treatment and expected outcomes and speak up when things go awry. Hospital staff should treat patients and their families as partners, welcoming family monitoring of patients as an additional safeguard against poor medical outcomes.

Readmission and Communication

Returning to the medical facility soon after being discharged is often a sign that something went wrong during the initial stay (such as an infection that worsens after the patient gets home). Research indicates that three in four readmissions may be preventable, and the hospital staff should prepare a written summary of what patients should do when they get home. This should include information on the drug regimen, how much activity is advisable, and when to take a shower, drive, return to work, and eat normally. Drug errors are common and sometimes serious, and poor discharge planning is the main cause of readmission. It is also important for patients to visit their primary care doctor within ten days after discharge.

Communication between the patient and the doctor before discharge has always been a problem. Someone should be present besides the patient when getting instructions for home care after discharge. Instructions should be made clear to prevent confusion about medication before the patient takes any, and directions should include a discussion of any potential side effects and what should be done if the patient has an adverse reaction.

Avoid Complications

Medical experts claim that certain events that occur in hospitals are inexcusable and should never be tolerated. Probably the worst offenders are doctors who operate on the wrong patient – or the wrong body part. But some of the less dramatic events are also inexcusable and include complications that occur in some hospitals far more often than others:

- *Bedsores*: Bedsores usually occur on ankles, buttocks, and hips, but they can occur in other areas of the body. Sores develop when a patient is left in one position for too long. If patches of skin have reddened, the nursing staff should be notified.
- *Collapsed lungs*: Less skillful doctors can puncture the lungs while inserting a catheter or needle into the chest. Physicians should use an ultrasound for guidance, especially if the patient is at high risk due to chronic lung disease.
- *Bloodstream Infection*: When using a central venous catheter, doctors and nurses should make sure the IVs used to deliver medicine and nutrients are kept clean and removed as soon as possible.
- *Hip fracture*: Post-operative care should prevent any falls that could break the hip again. Avoid taking more pain medication than needed or walking when groggy.
- *Blood clots*: Surgeries to replace hips or knees can cause clots in the legs that can break loose and travel to the lungs, causing a deadly complication called a pulmonary embolism. Moving around soon after surgery can prevent the clots, as can blood thinners and special stockings.

- *Opening a wound after surgery.* When a wound is opened after surgery, this creates a situation best described as "an infection waiting to happen". The patient should find out how to care for the wound, how long it should take to heal, and what to do if it does not.

Patient Responsibility

Finding solutions for persistent medical errors has become a priority for hospitals. Meanwhile, patients should initiate action to counter some of the more common types of preventable complications:

- Patients should request the surgeon to mark the surgical site on the body with a magic marker before the operation and while the patient is still awake.
- Patients need to be more forceful in speaking up when they sense something is wrong.
- Patients should understand that doctors and the nursing staff are not infallible.
- Patients should inform the medical staff about any drug allergies.
- After an operation, someone who is looking out for the patient should insist that the patient's position be changed every two hours to prevent bedsores, called pressure ulcers. Medicare received reports of a quarter of a million cases in recent years.
- If an IV is necessary, it should never stay in place for more than a week.

Hospitalized patients often have an array of clear plastic tubing sticking out of their bodies to deliver or extract medicine, nutrition, fluids, gases, or blood to veins, arteries, the stomach, skin, lungs, and bladder. After years of lax federal oversight of medical devices, hospital medical staff continue to mistakenly snake tubes intended for feeding food to the stomach into a vein. Putting food directly into the bloodstream is similar to pouring concrete down a drain. Patients die from this preventable medical error. Hundreds of such deaths or serious injuries are traced to tube mix-ups. The exact number of deaths is unknown because this type of mistake is rarely reported, as with medication errors.

Standards have been established to get the medical tubing industry to design different tubes for different bodily functions specifically. Some manufacturers have used color coding for this purpose – but with each manufacturer using a different color scheme, the colors have added to the confusion in some cases. Regulators have been waiting for manufacturers to develop a solution, while the manufacturers will not spend the money to design and produce something different until the regulators force them to do so. Getting a standard from an industry that has so many different organizations and too much self-interest to act in concert has proven to be an overwhelming task. This delay and lack of cooperation will allow patients to die for reasons that can be easily corrected. In the meantime, patients are self-diagnosing by using the internet and are often just as correct as a practicing physician.

Self-Diagnostic Health Aids

More young people are using their omnipresent mobile devices to keep track of their health, using the devices very differently than their parents' generation. They are seeking to use the wireless communication network for health information, according to the Pew Internet and American Life Project, which surveys technology trends. Nearly one hundred million Americans own a smartphone and are searching for health-related symptoms – with some of the top searches being for early pregnancy, herpes, and HIV.[14] These same mobile device owners frequently download apps to help manage their eating, drinking, and exercising, according to Everyday Health, an online company that has thirty-five million visitors a month to its health diet and exercise websites. Inquiries made on laptop or desktop computers are most likely done by older people.

The PC-user generation is more likely to search for gastroenteritis, heart attack, gout, shingles, muscle strain, and irritable bowel syndrome – and is prone to use the encyclopedic medical symptoms checker on WebMD. Older people are more often using their desktops to look up side effects of their medications and for more information about injections prescribed for their knees. Both the younger and older generations are entering the online viewing media in overwhelming numbers. By 2012, online viewing had reached parity with television, with around forty hours a week spent online and the same amount of time spent watching television. Advertisers are noticing the trend, and more medical-related ads are moving rapidly from TV to the online community. There is a downside to smartphone searches, since people now worry about the potential for privacy violations that can be traced to the inquiries made on mobile devices and PCs. Also, smartphones are more likely to be used in public places where they can be lost – but these fears have not abated the growing number of medical-based searches.

Dangers in Cancer Therapy

Patients with thyroid cancer are often cured by swallowing radioactive iodine that kills the malignant cells. The pills make patients radioactive and would activate any detection system used at airports throughout the world. Approximately 43,720 new cases of thyroid carcinoma are expected to be diagnosed in 2023 in the United States,[15] in effect, these people would light up any room they entered – not with their personality, but with their high level of radiation. The radiation levels emitted make patients potentially dangerous to people around them for up to a week. They are discouraged from staying in a hospital without isolation rooms and, in any event, most insurance plans would cover an extended stay in the hospital – only if a doctor said hospitalization was medically necessary. Many patients have conveniently found friendly doctors to write a proper excuse. Otherwise, the patients must become invisible to the general public as soon as possible. More than one outpatient following the treatment has boarded a bus and set off the radiation alarm at a tunnel entrance. Patients have put radiation-contaminated items in the trash, and garbage trucks that collected them have set off alarms.

In 1997, the Nuclear Regulatory Commission dropped a requirement that such patients be quarantined in the hospital. Instead, they are more often than not released right after their treatment – when they are at their most radioactive. They cannot recuperate with pregnant relatives or in a house with children who are highly vulnerable to radiation. Traveling to a distant location on an airplane is out of the question since a radioactive patient would give other passengers all types of illnesses. If a patient vomits, as many patients do, the radioactive contents of their stomach could pose a serious threat to everyone on the plane. There may not be a list of recommended actions that indicate what to do and what not to do, but there have been guidelines published that even advise against eating chicken wings or whole apples – because the bones or the core will be contaminated with radioactive saliva.

Scientists have estimated that the amount of radiation drugs given to a thyroid patient could exceed an average American's annual level from natural sources. It is three to four times the safe level recommended for pregnant women. The Nuclear Regulatory Commission strongly discouraged sending thyroid patients who received the radioactive iodine to a hotel, which often happens when the hospital where the treatment was administered cannot quarantine the patient until the radiation dies down. By remaining in the hospital after the treatment, the staff and doctors become at risk for radiation contamination. However, moving into a hotel (a common course of action) could result in vulnerable hotel personnel receiving significant doses unintentionally. It seems that the only alternative living accommodation that would reduce the risks of spreading the harmful radiation rays to others would be to simply become a recluse by staying away from others for a few days – but no one has suggested a safe location.

IBM Watson Computer Diagnoses Cancer

The public's first exposure to the Watson computer was in 2011, where it beat the best human champions on Jeopardy by answering complex questions in milliseconds. The machine was reprogramed to diagnose cancer treatments in 2017 – faster than a human doctor. Its initial release was an assignment at the Sloan-Kettering Cancer Center, but the computer was made available for rent to any hospital that wanted to get its digital-based opinion on subjects relating to diagnosing oncology. It took over a year to teach Watson how to understand complicated medical data about diagnosing lung, prostate, and breast cancer, and its knowledge has been expanded to treat other difficult-to-treat illnesses by 2020. The medical Watson is smaller than its Jeopardy predecessor, and its processing speed has increased by almost 250%.

The IBM computer can absorb and analyze vast quantities of data better than the typical medical staff, and its deployment through the cloud has also significantly reduced healthcare costs. Watson has learned the same amount of medical knowledge as an average second-year medical student, which means it can ingest more than 600,000 pieces of medical evidence and more than two million pages from medical journals. It can be programmed to instantly search through 1.5 million patent records for information, which gives it more knowledge than any human medical professional can ever hope to match. Watson's ability to collect this vast data faster than any human has allowed it to have a successful diagnosis rate for lung cancer that is 90% accurate, compared to 50% for its human counterparts.

Notes

1. Centers for Disease Control and Prevention, National Healthcare Safety Network, Surgical Site Infection Event (SSI), January 2025.
2. National Library of Medicine, Infection Drug Resistance, Healthcare-associated infections – an overview, Mainul Haque, Massimo Sartelli, Judy McKimm, Muhamad Abu Bakar, November 2018.
3. *CMAJ Open* 2018 January–March; 6(1): E26–E30. Published online 2018 January 12. doi: 10.9778/cmajo.20170126 PMCID: PMC5878945, PMID: 29339405, Health care professionals' neckties as a source of transmission of bacteria to patients: a systematic review, Pia Pace-Asciak, MD, Sanjiv K. Bhimrao, DM, Frederick K. Kozak, MD, and Brian D. Westerberg, MD.
4. The New York Times, METRO DATELINES; Food-Poisoning Toll Rises to 3 at Hospital, August 3, 1987.
5. The New York Times, An Iowa Egg Farmer and a History of Salmonella, September 21, 2010.
6. Multistate point-prevalence survey of healthcare-associated infections Shelley S. Magill, Jonathan R. Edwards, Wendy Bamberg, Zintars G. Beldavs, Ghinwa Dumyati, Marion A. Kainer, Ruth Lynfield, Meghan Maloney, Laura McAllister-Hollod, Joelle Nadle, Susan M. Ray, Deborah L. Thompson, Lucy E. Wilson, Scott K. Fridkin, Johns Hopkins University School of Medicine.
7. Clostridium difficile infection in older adults, Robin LP, Aging Health. 2013 August 1; 9(4): 403–414. doi: 10.2217/ahe.13.37
8. MODERN MEDICINE: The third-leading cause of death in the United States most doctors don't want you to know about PUBLISHED THU, FEBRUARY 22 2018 9:31 AM ESTUPDATED WED, FEBRUARY 28 2018 9:39 AM EST Ray Sipherd, special to CNBC.com
9. U.S. Department of Health and Human Services, Office of Inspector General, Hospital Incident Reporting Systems Do Not Capture Most Patient Harm, 01/05/2012. Report (OEI-06-09-00091).
10. Consumer Reports, How Safe Is Your Hospital?, *Consumer Reports Magazine*, August 2012.
11. Nurse staffing, burnout, and healthcare-associated infection Jeannie P. Cimiotti, DNSc, RN, a, b,* Linda H. Aiken, PhD, c Douglas M. Sloane, PhD, c and Evan S. Wu, BSc, American *Journal of Infection Control.*
12. U.S. Department of Health and Human Services Office of Inspector General, Op-Ed Column: Medical Mistakes Plague Medicare Patients, November 16, 2010.
13. New York State's Cardiac Surgery Reporting System: Four Years Later, Edward L. Hannan, PhD, Dinesh Kumar, MS, Michael Racz, MA, Albert L. Siu, MD, and Mark R. Chassin, MD, State University of New York, University at Albany, and New York State Department of Health, Albany, New York, *The Society of Thoracic Surgeons* 1994;58:1852–1857.

14. Smartphone usage and preferences among postpartum HIV-positive women in South Africa Phepo Mogoba, a, * Tamsin K. Phillips, Landon Myer, Linda Ndlovu, Martin C. Were, and Kate Clousec, *AIDS Care.* 2019 June; 31(6): 723–729. Published online 2018 December 31. doi: 10.1080/09540121.2018.1563283
15. Thyroid Cancer: A Review, Laura Boucai, Mark Zafereo, Maria E. Cabanillas, PMID: 38319329 DOI: 10.1001/jama.2023.26348.

Chapter 3

COVID-19, Influenza, or Cold Crisis

Misconceptions in Respiratory Virus Diseases

An epidemic is defined as the rapid spread of a disease among a significant local population in a short duration of time. When coronavirus began to develop in Wuhan province of China in late 2019, it was considered an epidemic isolated to that country only. When the virus spread to other countries and continents, and even worldwide in 2020, the epidemic became a pandemic. Pandemics are the spread of a disease, unlike seasonal flus – which are not considered pandemics, because they develop around the world simultaneously. There are many differences between influenza, the common cold, and COVID-19 even though all three diseases share similar symptoms. In addition, it is not always possible to determine the exact respiratory disease without a test. The situation becomes more conflicting if a person has two of the three diseases – known as a "twindemic".

There are approximately one hundred viruses that cause the common cold, but only four that cause the seasonal flu. The same number causes the novel coronavirus – which is, by far, the deadliest of the three. The public is aware of the symptoms of the flu and cold: fever, headaches, body aches, sore throat, runny nose, stuffed sinuses, coughing, and sneezing – which could lead to pneumonia. It is more complicated to determine whether a person has been infected with COVID-19, as there are many different symptoms, several of which could be mistaken for the flu.

DOI: 10.4324/9781032630670-3

Patients who contracted COVID-19 were at five times more risk of hospital death than patients with influenza, according to the CDC's Mortality and Morbidity report. The most common symptoms of COVID-19 are its flu-like high fever, often accompanied by chills, a dry cough, and fatigue. The main sign that distinguishes COVID-19 victims from other respiratory diseases is a sudden loss of a sense of smell and taste, being unable to register even strong odors like onions or coffee. Not all virus victims get "anosmia", the formal name for loss of smell, but most infected people do.[1]

During the height of the coronavirus attacks in 2020, the president at the time issued a misleading Tweet, which contained a scientifically incorrect comparison (that Americans should adapt to the presence of COVID-19 as they had with seasonal flu). The controversial message concluded that since over 100,000 die every year from the flu despite the vaccine, the country has learned to live with it and should do the same with COVID-19 since it is less lethal than the flu. Researchers estimated COVID-19 to have been about six times as deadly as the seasonal flu. In one month in 2020, nearly 40,000 daily cases of COVID-19 were recorded during the period when there was no vaccine for the COVID-19 disease.[2]

While the cold and the flu share a handful of symptoms (runny nose, stuffy head, or sore throat), there are also some similarities in the symptoms between COVID-19 and the flu. Many of the steps recommended to

Table 3.1 Sympton Comparisons Between COVID-19 and the Flu

	COVID-19	Influenza
Sneezing	Rare	Rare
Loss of smell and taste	Sometimes	Never
Shortness of Breath	Often	Rare
Congestion	Rare	Sometimes
Sore Throat	Sometimes	Sometimes
Diarrhea/nausea	Sometimes	Sometimes
Body ache	Sometimes	Often
Headache	Sometimes	Often
Fever/chills/shivers	Often (none to 100.4°F)	Often (100°F)
Cough	Often (usually dry)	Often
Fatigue	Often	Often

prevent the spread of COVID-19: mask wearing, handwashing, and physical distancing also helped to prevent the spread of seasonal flu. The Centers for Disease Control and Prevention reported that positive results for flu dropped from more than 20% to 2.3% during the pandemic. Overlapping common symptoms for the two most deadly respiratory diseases are noted in the following chart (Table 3.1):

The overall hospitalization rate in the United States for the 2019–2020 flu season was about sixty-nine hospitalizations per 100,000 people, according to the CDC. For COVID-19, it was 175 per 100,000 people. The mortality rate of COVID-19 is substantially higher – possibly one hundred times more than most strains of influenza.

Colds and the Flu – Chicken Soup Doesn't Cure Either Disease

The seven most common misconceptions about the flu and the common cold have been debunked and should be considered scientific myths:

- *People can get the flu from the flu shot*: The flu shot cannot cause transmission, as it is made up of inactive or weakened viruses that cannot cause any illnesses.
- *Chicken soup can cure a cold*: Many mothers of young children still insist this is true, even if it hasn't been proven. That being said, it can't hurt to use it as a warm homemade remedy.
- *A cold can turn into the flu*: According to the CDC, they are two distinct illnesses – with the flu being more severe than a cold. The common cold and the flu are caused by different viruses, and one cannot transform into the other.
- *Getting vaccinated a previous year protects an individual from catching the flu the following year*: False. The effectiveness of the flu shot dwindles over time – and each year, the vaccine is changed to fight against the virus that is the most common in the upcoming flu season.
- *You can treat a cold with antibiotics*: Because both the flu and the cold are caused by a virus, antibiotics are ineffective at combating their symptoms (since antibiotics fight against bacteria).
- *People can catch a cold or the flu from not bundling up properly*: Just because cold and flu season overlaps with winter does not mean

weather causes these illnesses. "Dry your hair before going outside" or "wear warmer clothes" are unproven adages, as the only way to catch a cold or the flu is to be exposed to the corresponding virus.

- *Feed a cold, starve a fever*: An old adage that goes back centuries states that fevers should be "cooled down" by fasting, but it should actually read "feed a cold, feed a fever" according to Scientific American. Fighting the symptoms of a cold and the flu causes the body to burn energy, which requires the need to eat. Drinking water also helps prevent dehydration.

Worldwide Pandemic (2020)

Coronavirus is a broader term that refers to a group of viruses that originated in animals and cause respiratory tract infections. SARS was first discovered in 2002 and caused CoV-2, which eventually became known as COVID-19. This disease killed over 250,000 people in the United States in 2020, which constitutes being called a pandemic. Scientific evidence indicates that the novel virus started in a bat, became rogue, and then jumped from animal to human. It spread from one person to another through respiratory droplets. Some theorists claimed (without substantial proof) that the virus was manufactured in a Chinese laboratory in the city of Wuhan, but there has never been any validation to this conspiracy theory. Regardless of its origin, it caused a health and economic disaster like no other in modern times.

COVID-19 was initially a confusing term used by the mass media, which was flooded by misinformation including speculation about the meaning. A Facebook post claimed that the word was an abbreviation of "Certificate of Identification of Vaccination with Artificial Intelligence", but that claim was totally without merit. When the outbreak first appeared, referred to as a "2019 novel coronavirus" or "2019-nCoV". Then the World Health Organization officially deemed it COVID-19. According to the Centers for Disease Control and Prevention, the CO stands for "corona", the VI stands for "virus", and the D stands for "disease" - the 19 is of course, the year it was discovered.

COVID-19 is not the same as the viruses that commonly circulate among humans and cause only mild illnesses. While available antiviral medications were useful in containing SARS, there is no known treatment or detection process for the much more deadly coronavirus rampage that killed over ten million people worldwide in 2020. This toll included over 225,000 Americans, with 30,000 living in New York City – a higher mortality rate than any city in the world, mainly due to its overcrowding with 28,000 residents per sq. mile. San Francisco has the next most crowded city with just 17,000 per sq. mile, according to data used by the Census Bureau. Roughly 60% of known infectious diseases and 75% of new or emerging infectious diseases are *zoonotic* in origin – meaning they're transmissible from animals to humans, according to the Centers for Disease Control and Prevention.

WHO Names the Virus

The public (including the President of the United States.) began, in 2020, to refer to the pandemic disease as the "Wuhan flu" or "Chinese coronavirus". These names can be interpreted as a form of racism against Chinese citizens. The World Health Organization (WHO) had issued a "best practices" recommendation in 2015 for naming new human infectious diseases. Under their new doctrine, a disease name should consist of a generic descriptive term based on symptoms (respiratory diseases, watery diarrhea, etc.), who it afflicts (infant, juvenile, maternal), season (summer, winter), and severity (mild, severe). Names of illnesses may also include other factual elements such as the environment (swamp, desert) and the year and month. However, it should avoid using geographic locations, people's names, species of animal, type of food, references to culture, population, industry, occupation, or "terms that incite undue fear". The name-change designation was due to the unintended stigmatization of certain communities or economic sectors, such as:

- Middle East Respiratory Syndrome (MERS), which may have originated in the Middle East, has spread to over two dozen other countries since it first appeared in Saudi Arabia in 2012.
- The 2009–2010 swine flu caused people to fear pigs falsely, as they were believed to be transmitting the disease. Egypt, in a misguided move, wiped out its entire pig population. After that pandemic, the disease is now known as pdmo9 – and even after this disease

dissipated, many people stopped eating pork (even though this influenza strain can infect poultry, bats, and other animals – and jump between them).[3]

- The city of Old Lyme, Connecticut still suffers the aftereffects of a tick-borne disease that first sickened children and adults in the 1970s. It became known as Lyme disease, despite the tick being subsequently found nationwide.

Herd Immunity: A False and Dangerous Remedy

Toward the end of the pandemic in 2020/2021, there was a growing number of self-anointed experts claiming that the spreading virus could be contained using "herd immunity". This optimistic assumption was not realized until right up to the discovery of the vaccine. At this point, there were 85–90% of Americans who were still susceptible to SARS-CoV – the virus that caused the deaths of over 250,000 Americans. Herd immunity (also known as community immunity) is defined by the Centers for Disease Control and Prevention (CDC) as "a situation in which a sufficient proportion of a population is immune to an infectious disease (through vaccination and/or prior illness) to make its spread from person to person unlikely". In other words, herd immunity occurs when lots of people in an area are vaccinated or have already been infected with a disease – fewer people get sick and fewer germs are able to spread from person to person.

The theory is that when someone gets vaccinated, it's not only that person who is protected from infection – but others too, because that person cannot transmit the disease in the community. In this way, herd immunity protects the people who cannot be vaccinated – people whose immune systems aren't strong enough and are therefore the most vulnerable to serious illness. A herd immunity situation that occurred in the 1980s measles outbreak among preschool-age children in the United States serves as an example of herd immunity via vaccination. Researchers who examined the association between incidences of measles and immunization among preschool-age children concluded that immunizing about 80% of the population may be enough to stop sustained measles outbreaks in an urban community.

The unproven claim of herd immunity was promoted by many in the mass media during the 2020 pandemic period. Conversely, this claim was false, and prominent public health officials considered the idea scientifically unfounded as well as dangerous. These same officials claimed the route to immunity without a vaccine would be through graveyards filled with hundreds of thousands of Americans who did not have to die.

The Controversial Face Mask

Many cities and states passed laws mandating the use of masks when in the public areas. This has caused violent confrontations between mask wearers and those who refused to cover their faces, regardless of the mandate. The non-wearing population seems to be more aggressive and believe that to wear a mask is to be submissive (a wrong assumption). Wearing a mask has been proven to be an effective method in reducing the suffering from the terrible coronavirus pathogen and has been extremely helpful in saving lives throughout the COVID-19 pandemic. The situation was also exacerbated by the president at the time who, at the beginning of the rampage, appeared in public rarely wearing a mask. Regardless of the conflicting attitudes, most disease control agencies and experts in the field believe that masks were effective in controlling the spread of the new coronavirus. Ironically, that same president caught the virus but survived using untested drug therapies.

Randomized trials usually are used in testing new drugs. In these trials, participants are randomly assigned to a group that gets the intervention material, and then there is a control group that receives nothing or a placebo. Attempting to find the value of a mask using this randomization test is all but impossible. Researchers would not be able to provide a precise understanding of how masks limit contagion, as the primary purpose of masks is to stop the transmission of the disease to others – regardless of how well it may or may not protect the wearer. At first, medical authorities recommended that only sick people wear masks, so that they wouldn't infect others. It soon became clear that people who were not yet showing symptoms, or had mild symptoms, were also infecting others. Preventing someone who wore a mask from becoming infected was considered a secondary benefit.

Scientifically proving which masks work better than others still remains a problem, as it's impossible for studies to confirm how effective they are. Lab studies found that aerosols and droplets can carry the virus when people talk, sing, shout, or do anything that expels air around others. In evaluating the effectiveness of a mask, it would be difficult to rely on clinical trials to prove how beneficial it is. At the end of the day, there are a few downsides to the simple act of respiratory etiquette. Not all masks are equally effective

– especially the questionable use of porous cloth masks as opposed to N95 and KN95 masks. However, cloth masks were acceptable when surgical masks were scarce, as something is better than nothing.

The gold standard for masks, especially the most effective N95, is that they typically have bands that strap over the back of the head for a tight fit. The next most effective mask is the KN95, which the Food and Drug Administration has approved for emergency use by healthcare workers. This has ear loops and is more comfortable than the N95. In a hospital setting, the N95 is the most suitable, as it is 95% efficient in filtering airborne particles, while only 70% of KN95 masks imported from China met the filtration standard.

Surgical Masks Outperform Cloth Material

The level of protection provided by a mask during the pandemic depended on the type of material used, along with its ability to prevent and reject the airborne virus. A great deal of the COVID-19 spread came from people who were asymptomatic and didn't know that they were infected. Studies done by government agencies indicated that many types of face coverings could reduce transmission. During the early stage of the coronavirus rampage, there was a suspected shortage of surgical masks, and the public was advised to use cloth masks as a stopgap substitute. Even the best cotton mask, made up of cotton-polyester blends, offers only 30% of the protection value of the superior surgical mask – but it is better than using a scarf. Many of the masks sold on Amazon claim to be effective against dust and allergens and closely resemble the blue masks worn by doctors and nurses, yet they aren't surgical masks.

A real medical procedure mask is approved by the Food and Drug Administration and designated as offering one of three levels of protection. A level two or level three medical mask is best, which is marketed as an N95 mask. If used properly, it will filter out at least 95% of infectious particles. In China, the equivalent mask is the KN95, and in Europe, the comparable designation is FFP2. Masks have also been evaluated by the National Institute for Occupational Safety and Health, a part of the Centers for Disease Control and Prevention.

Importing fake protection equipment during the pandemic extended to the supply of KN95 masks, which were mostly manufactured in China. The standard N95 mask is meant to filter out 95% of aerosol particles. Besides the filtration concerns, public health experts criticized KN95 masks for their inability to create a tight seal on someone's face – and many of the fakes had ear loop straps instead of the more secure head and neck straps. Until the vaccine became available in 2021, Americans were encouraged to wear higher-quality masks in order to try to contain the virus.

Counterfeit Fake Masks

Despite the deaths and long-term health problems experienced by millions of victims worldwide in 2020, there were enormous profits to be made by legitimate suppliers of materials and products used by the healthcare industry to attempt to control and eradicate the coronavirus. Sadly, unscrupulous manufacturers took advantage of the chaos and pandemonium that overwhelmed hospitals, long-term eldercare facilities, and first responders in 2020. The first of many products to see profits soar included breathing apparatus (respirators), gowns, masks, and even medical gloves. Some of these most sought-after items were poorly made and apparent fakes yet created many millionaires. Many of these fakes were even available on Amazon, which claims to eliminate knockoffs on its website, but clearly has not been successful in doing so.

While online companies sold face masks, there were several high reviews from supposedly independent users of the product. These cannot always be trusted, as some of the reviewers were given masks free of charge (the incentive for 4.5 stars). In visiting the website of some manufacturers, guidelines may be offered to determine the authenticity of the mask – this may involve scanning a bar code on a package with a phone camera, which is then used to perform a web search of the product for further verification that the mask is not counterfeit.

Fake medical gloves are another item that had a willing customer base in 2020. While there was a shortage of this critically needed commodity, the cost had tripled due to front-line workers working in harsh environments along with businesses, restaurants, and schools reopening. The sudden appearance of firms that had gloves to sell was often fake versions of "nitrile" or synthetic rubber gloves that were sold in boxes labeled "examination grade". This term is defined and regulated by the Food and Drug Administration as providing greater protection and durability than vinyl gloves, which break down and don't guard against certain chemicals. Most of the fake gloves were made in Malaysia and Vietnam, with the United

States importing over 70 billion annually for a market that exceeded $80 billion during the height of the pandemic.

The U.S. Customs and Border Protection seized disposable gloves arriving in the United States that were made by the world's largest glove maker, a Malaysian company, because it was using forced labor in its many factories.

Notes

1. Risk for In-Hospital Complications Associated with COVID-19 and Influenza — Veterans Health Administration, United States, October 1, 2018–May 31, 2020, Weekly / October 23, 2020 / 69(42); 1528–1534, CDC Morbidity and Mortality Weekly Report.
2. Centers for Disease Control and Prevention, 2020–2021 Flu Season Summary, October 25, 2021.
3. Is it a policy crisis or it is a health crisis? The Egyptian context – Analysis of the Egyptian health policy for the H1N1 flu pandemic control, Pan Afr Med J. 2013; 14: 59, Published online 2013 February 12. doi: 10.11604/pamj.2013.14.59.1631.

Chapter 4

Avoidable Medical Errors

Malpractice: A Well-kept Secret

A study conducted by the New England Journal of Medicine found that 75% of doctors who practice psychiatry, pediatrics, or family medicine will be sued at least once during their careers. Some medical specialties will be sued several times. Virtually 100% of neurosurgeons, orthopedic surgeons, and obstetricians will be sued before they finish practicing medicine – with some premiums exceeding $200,000 a year for malpractice insurance.[1] The malpractice debate is almost as old as the Hippocratic Oath, and physicians claim that they are forced to order seemingly unnecessary and expensive tests because of the ever-present possibility of a lawsuit. On the other hand, the legal profession believes they are protecting the public by making doctors accountable. Some hospitals are trying new approaches to prevent a growing number of lawsuits. One approach is to get the physicians to apologize for their errors.

In 2005, Congress attempted to sponsor a National Medical Act, which would have implemented apology laws throughout all fifty states. Although the proposed measure never became law, thirty-six states have passed legislation protecting doctor apologists from their apologies being used against them in court.

Transparency is the best solution for creating a more open, trusting, and healthy doctor-patient relationship. One attempt involved a mediating program that was started by a group of five privately operated New York City hospitals, in which each institution agreed to divulge medical mistakes early (before the lawyers got involved) and offer settlements quickly by using

DOI: 10.4324/9781032630670-4

special state "health courts", where judges help negotiate agreements before cases go to regular court. This unique agreement program did not satisfy the malpractice legal profession, but it did cut the billion or so spent annually in just New York on medical malpractice premiums by about a third. The three-million-dollar seed money to start this program was one of the several programs sponsored in part by the government in other sections of the country.

The program had a different focus for each area, such as reducing errors in obstetrics. Another facility directed a major emphasis on preventing surgical errors, and so forth. The arbitration process offered a forum before anyone went through the process of a jury trial. The major advantage of arbitration was the short time needed to settle the case. There was no legal fee, which otherwise amounted to about 33% of the settlement.

Cutting off malpractice insurance can be disastrous for a hospital, especially when it focuses on the maternity and newborn-infant wards. A large municipal hospital in Bronx, New York, was informed by its insurance company that the obstetricians would no longer be insured. The reason given was that doctors were predicted to claim far more than the cost of the policy. This made insuring them an unreasonable burden to other policyholders. A Bronx hospital delivers about 2,700 babies a year, mainly to women living in poverty whose pregnancies are at risk, because they are teenagers, have diabetes, have high blood pressure, or are experiencing other medical problems.

The doctors who would lose their insurance all deal with high-risk pregnancies. Losing their insurance coverage sent a shudder through surrounding hospitals, where officials claimed their facility could not possibly handle the influx of at-risk patients, if any nearby hospital lost malpractice insurance. This problem has confronted hospitals for more than a century. It is one that persists, even though there are laws in many states that place a cap on non-economic damage – such as pain and suffering for malpractice suits along with an indemnity fund for neurologically damaged infants. Both measures are usually vigorously opposed by trial lawyers, who argue that impoverished people would be most hurt by efforts to limit their ability to sue for damages. Many states do not have these laws.

Insurance fees for hospitals in the New York City metropolitan area are some of the highest in the nation, with a nearby county paying obstetrical premiums of about $190,000 a year. The Bronx averages about $180,000 a year. In Manhattan, the premiums average about $145,000 a year. Often, the awards from malpractice court decisions are distributed to trial lawyers through contingency fees under a New York State statute. Under a complicated formula, a lawyer who wins a one-million-dollar malpractice case can collect as much as $210,000.

Misdiagnoses are among the most common, costly, and harmful medical errors – and also some of the most preventable. Errors by doctors in determining the illness of a patient have led to permanent damage or death for as many as 160,000 patients each year, according to a report issued by researchers at Johns Hopkins Medical Center. The report also indicated that diagnostic problems are more common than other medical mistakes and are more likely to harm patients. These mistakes are the leading cause of malpractice claims, accounting for 35% of the nearly $39 billion in payouts in the United States from 1986 to 2014. Despite the frequency of avoidable errors by hospitals and attending physicians, very few wind up as medical malpractice lawsuits. A study conducted in 2015 concluded that about 1% of medical errors resulted in a claim. As an example, between 2011 and 2015, there were approximately 8,000 complaints against doctors filed each year with the New York State Office of Professional Medical Conduct. Most of the complaints alleged impairment, improper prescribing, sexual misconduct, and fraud. Only 290 of the complaints – less than 4% – resulted in serious sanctions or restriction of the physician's license.

The latter standard is the law in forty-four states, but when tried in New York State, the legislature defeated this legislation. The opposition to the proposed law came from the hospital and healthcare lobby, which expressed concern that the bill would result in more medical malpractice lawsuits. In reality, only a small handful of lawsuits are started outside the statute of limitations – but it is hard to convince victims that the legal system is not against them.

What is surprising about the number and outcomes of malpractice suits is that the public is unaware that most awards are generally modest. Thirty-three states restrict the amount of compensation for the pain and suffering victims endure. According to a report done by the Department of Justice, the average medical award in recent years by juries is $400,000. In bench trials, where the judge also serves as the jury, the median award is $630,000. These awards do not seem to make the hospitals and physicians more accountable, and hospitals should be forced to do a better job of policing themselves.

Never Events

The types of mistakes that should never happen in medicine include things such as operating on the wrong patient or sewing someone up with a sponge still inside their body. These are examples of never events, and they are happening with alarming frequency. A study published in the journal Surgery found that between 1990 and 2010, more than 6% of patients died in the operating room, 23% had a permanent injury, and 60% suffered temporary injury.[2] Based on the number of malpractice claims, a study estimated that only 12% of surgical adverse events result in indemnity payments. Researchers concluded that surgeons make serious mistakes more than a dozen times a day – a deadly, yet easily avoidable lapse.

The actual number of mistakes is much higher, but many patients never file claims after errors are found – and not all items left behind after surgery are discovered. Typically, they are found only when a patient experiences a complication after surgery, such as an infection – leading to further investigation. New technology, such as bar coding and wands or scanners waved over a patient may help track sponges and other products used in a procedure, but only a small percentage of hospitals that perform surgeries have purchased these scanning devices.

An estimated 6,000 "Never Events" or egregious errors occur every month among Medicare patients alone. Doctors have left surgical instruments inside the body during one in every 5,000 surgeries and then were paid (again) to remove the item they forgot to leave on the instrument table. According to a report from the U.S. Department of Health and Human Services (HHS), the total number of preventable errors is far higher than reported. Some studies suggest that up to a third of all hospital admissions result in harm to a patient. Far more common and preventable problems are stitches coming loose, blood clots forming during or after surgery, infections, and bedsores. A breakdown of the most grievous errors:

- Sponges – 67%
- Instrument – 3%
- Needles – 9%
- Other items – 21%

Never Events include:

- Letting patients wander or disappear.
- Administering the wrong blood type.

- Allowing the patient to fall.
- Operating on the wrong limb.
- Performing the wrong procedure.
- Using contaminated drugs or devices.
- Discharging an infant to the wrong person.
- Artificially inseminating a person with the wrong donor sperm or egg.
- Hospital-acquired bedsores.

Major studies about left-behind objects after surgery have concluded that sponges and other items are lost in anywhere from one in 5,500 to one in 7,000 surgeries. With federal data showing total invasive surgeries nationwide each year, this yields 5,400 to 6,000 cases a year as the actual incidence rate. The same data suggest that between one and 2% of these cases prove fatal. Hospitalization costs involving a lost sponge or instrument average more than $60,000, according to data compiled by Medicare – which denies payment for costs stemming from such errors. Related malpractice suits cost hospitals, on average, between $100,000 and $200,000 per case. While these avoidable mistakes and outrageous errors often make headlines, they should be balanced against the fact that more than fifty-three million surgeries occur every year in the United States. An overwhelming number of them are successful.[3]

Admitting Medical Errors

Most licensed professionals such as lawyers, dentists – and especially doctors – rarely admit they made a mistake, as it will affect their reputation and increase the possibility of malpractice lawsuits or result in a loss of their license. Doctors who admitted to a medical error or a wrong diagnosis were almost non-existent until about 2005, when a new trend began to evolve where doctors confessed to mistakes and apologized to the patient and concerned relatives. This new attitude may eventually change the normally estranged doctor-patient relationship. For decades, malpractice lawyers and insurers have counseled doctors and hospitals to "deny and defend their actions", because offering earnest apologies, an admission of fault, or even an expression of regret, is likely to invite litigation and imperil careers. Promptly disclosing medical errors was not an acceptable practice in the healthcare community in bygone years.

Despite some projections that disclosure would prompt a flood of lawsuits, hospitals are reporting decreases in caseloads and lower legal costs.

Interestingly, the disclosure of medical errors remains questionable; one study found that 50–96% of errors in the United States are underreported by physicians.[4] However, physicians still acknowledge the disclosure of medical errors as a fundamental part of patients' care. Currently, about thirty-four states enacted laws making apologies for medical errors inadmissible in court. Four states protect admissions of culpability, and seven states require that patients be notified of serious unanticipated outcomes.

Medical errors were once a very well-kept secret, but they are gradually being exposed by the new regulations followed by hospitals. The errors are becoming teaching opportunities rather than badges of shame. Fewer lawsuits could also lead to better medical treatment. A 2011 study from the American College of Surgeons found that doctors who had been sued were more prone to burnout, depression, and even suicide. As a result, these same doctors made significantly more mistakes than they did before the litigation.

Anesthetized patients who suffered harm were once another well-kept secret that remained within the confines of the operating room and were rarely disclosed to the public. Increasingly, anesthetized patients are immobilized on the operating table to prevent their movement during surgery. Yet, behind their taped-shut eyes is a mind that is still awake and can hear every word spoken by the doctors as they cut into their bodies. These patients cannot make a noise, as the partial anesthesia renders them unable to move and almost unconscious – but they can hear everything going on around their inert bodies. There have been several research studies on how often anesthesia awareness happens. On average, anesthesia awareness occurs in about 1 to 2 out of every 1,000 cases, less than 0.2% of the time.[5] There is a medical device, a Bispectral Index monitor, that can help doctors see when a patient is awake during surgery. However, only about half the operating rooms in the nation have spent the $5,000 to $10,000 to acquire this monitoring device. Even the facilities with the device do not always use it, since some medical personnel feel it is far from perfect. The vast majority of the twenty-one million people who are put to sleep in an operating room each year wake up after their procedures with no memory of it, but there is no excuse in allowing anyone to wake up in the middle of intrusive surgery. A registry sponsored by the American Society of Anesthesiologists captures stories and details of patients who were awake during surgery: http://depts.washington.edu/awaredb/

Hurrying the death of a terminally ill patient has caused some concern within the small select group of doctors who belong to the American Society of Transplant Surgeons. The first case in the nation occurred in 2008, when a doctor was accused of prescribing excessive and improper doses of drugs in an attempt to hasten death to retrieve organs sooner. This type of medical decision is not a case of malpractice in which a civil action results in a monetary penalty. Hastening the death of a patient is a criminal act and is prosecuted as a felony, with the penalty of a prison term. The action horrified the tight-knit field of transplant surgeons and will scare off future attempts to transplant organs. In an average year, about eighteen U.S. patients die each day waiting for a transplant. Hastening the death of a dying patient is not the only medical solution to the inevitable – there are alternatives such as palliative care.

Nurses are often too intimidated to report misconduct in medical procedures made by the doctors who they work alongside. Most hospitals seem to always side with the doctor over any other accusations made by other members of the hospital staff for obvious reasons. Two nurses were fired and criminally prosecuted for reporting allegations of improper medical treatment by a doctor at a Texas county hospital in 2010. https://www.nytimes.com/2010/08/11/us/11whistle.html

Experts on whistleblower protection claimed the prosecution of the nurses was unprecedented and sent a chilling effect on the reporting of medical misconduct in a hospital operating room. The nurses had a combined forty-seven years of employment at the hospital and wrote to the state medical board to report allegations of improper medical treatment by a doctor, who they claimed was harmful to patients and a cause for the doctor to be dismissed.

After the accused doctor was informed of the nurses' action, the doctor persuaded the county sheriff to investigate who originally filed the complaint. The sheriff promptly obtained a search warrant to seize the nurses' computers, found the draft of the accusation on the hard drive, and brought the case to the grand jury by asserting that the nurses had not acted in good faith by making out their complaint, as required by state law when reporting on the actions of the doctor. The jury took less than an hour to find the nurses innocent. The nurses then filed a lawsuit, asserting that they have been subjected to vindictive prosecution and denied their First Amendment rights. The hospital and other defendants agreed to a settlement of around $750,000 to settle the lawsuit.

The doctor continued to work at the hospital while awaiting the results of a hearing on the charges the nurses made. He was found to have performed poorly in certain medical practices, and his license in the state was revoked. He then started work at another hospital in a different state. The two nurses split the jury award but were never able to find work in the healthcare field after the hospital dismissed them, because of the sheriff's investigation. Hospitals do not like whistleblowers.

Snake Oil Peddlers

Unquestionably, the United States still has the best (and most expensive) healthcare available, possibly because medical treatment and drug therapy are closely regulated under strict guidelines monitored by different federal agencies. Still, each new medical discovery appears to give rise to miracle cures based on unproven scientific therapies and attracts twenty-first-century charlatans who rush into the marketplace before the discoveries are fully tested. Cosmeticians continue to claim that stem cells are a cure-all for everything from wrinkles to autism. While stem cell transplants offer great potential for patients with acute leukemia and for mending unhealable bone fractures, they are not the panacea promised by the many opportunists who claim that they have the secret for a longer and healthy life.

Some firms that offer questionable treatment – and are threatened with closure for false advertising by the Food and Drug Administration – move their operation to Mexico or another foreign country where medical procedures are far less regulated. This practice has created medical tourism, which attracts patients who cannot legally receive treatment in the United States to find a solution on the internet. Modern biotechnology in the medical field has outpaced regulators and laws, and people are seeking cures using drugs and practices not allowed in America. A study by the Harvard Gazette found websites that were offering cures for a dizzying array of serious conditions. A partial list offered includes cures for every possible ailment except headaches, the common cold, and bunions. These include Alzheimer's disease, autism, amyotrophic lateral sclerosis (ALS), brain damage, cancer, cerebellar ataxia, cerebral palsy, Crohn's disease, diabetes, diseases of the eye, lupus, genetic disorders, Huntington's, kidney disease, muscular sclerosis, muscular dystrophy, Parkinson's disease, pulmonary disease, rheumatoid arthritis, spinal cord injury, spinal muscular atrophy, stroke, and Tay-Sachs disease.

Safeguarding Radioactive Material

A subject of national security importance that is often neglected or overlooked is the method, or the technology, used to safeguard radioactive material in the hospital environment. A decade after Congress tried to make this dangerous material harder to obtain by terrorists, one hospital kept cesium in a padlocked room – with the combination to the lock written on the door frame. The people involved with the security of the radioactive material in this hospital testified before Congress that they were trained as physicists and radiation-health technicians, noting that they did not believe they were fully qualified to enforce security regulations.

About 1,500 hospitals and medical buildings nationwide store radioactive material. The radioactive material cannot be used to make a nuclear bomb. However, if incorporated into a device with conventional explosives, it could make a "dirty bomb" that would contaminate the air with significant amounts of radioactivity – which could prove to be disastrous, if not catastrophic. The Nuclear Regulatory Commission (NRC), which oversees regulating radioactive materials used for medical diagnoses and cancer treatment, had very flexible rules to protect this dangerous material while also avoiding adding to hospital costs. The result of this attitude was a mix of security controls and procedures that could leave radiological sources in some facilities more vulnerable than others to possible sabotage or outright theft.

After 9/11, security experts found poor controls used to protect radioactive materials. To overcome this deficiency, the National Nuclear Security Agency, which is part of the Department of Energy, offered grants to hospitals to purchase equipment to upgrade their protection of radioactive material. The same experts believed that poor controls over the material could allow terrorists to enter the country unarmed to later obtain the ingredients for attacks locally – which is not an isolated problem found only in hospitals. Metal fabrication plants, food processing, and other industries that also use radioactive materials are at risk. They all must follow the rules set out by the NRC, but the few inspections conducted each year to force compliance with the rules and regulations are sporadic and often receive little attention from the facility. At the hospital where the combination was written on a door frame in a busy hallway, the security administrator for the hospital admitted that he walks around the facility constantly erasing door combinations written next to the locks so as not to confuse people with short memories.

- In another hospital, the radiation-safety officer told auditors that he did not know how many people were allowed unescorted access to the radioactive sources, because the computer program that the hospital had purchased could not count beyond 500.
- The Government Accountability Office issued a report in 2012 that found four out of five high-risk hospitals across the country have failed to secure radiological material that could be used in a dirty bomb.

Hospitals store cesium-137, the most common radioactive form of the element, which was used in a medical device that was inadvertently discarded into the atmosphere in Brazil in 1987. That accident resulted in four deaths and thirty-five million dollars in cleanup costs. The accident made hospitals aware of the peril that could result from cesium leakage or theft, and many facilities upgraded their security controls. Those efforts gradually fell between the cracks – until 9/11, when the problem became serious once again. The NRC was forced to issue new rules in 2005, in response to the 2001 terrorist attacks, because the existing rules at that time were obsolete. Before 9/11, the rules were geared toward preventing inadvertent exposure in any of the 22,000 entities that held licenses to possess radioactive materials. In thirty-seven states, the rules are administered by the states, typically by the health department. The NRC directly regulates about 3,000 licenses.

Notes

1. Malpractice Risk According to Physician Specialty, Anupam B. Jena, M.D., Ph.D., Seth Seabury, Ph.D., Darius Lakdawalla, Ph.D., and Amitabh Chandra, Ph.D., *New England Journal of Medicine,* 2011 Aug 8;365(7):629–636.
2. Surgical never events in the United States, Winta T Mehtsun, Massachusetts General Hospital, Andrew M Ibrahim, Marie Diener-West, Johns Hopkins Bloomberg School of Public Health, Peter J Pronovost, Johns Hopkins Medicine, Surgery, December 2012;153(4), DOI:10.1016/j.surg.2012.10.005, PubMed.
3. Peter Eisler, What Surgeons Leave Behind Costs Some Patients Dearly, *USA Today*, March 8, 2013.
4. LL Leape, Error in Medicine. *JAMA* 1994;272(23):1851–1857. [PubMed] [Google Scholar].
5. Anesthesia Awareness (Waking Up During Surgery), Cleveland Clinic, https://my.clevelandclinic.org/health/articles/anesthesia-awareness

Chapter 5

Wide Range in Medical Education

Healthcare Practices and Compensation

Some of the highest-paid administrative officers in organizations that receive most of their funding from federal, state, and insurance programs are in the healthcare field. The public, along with all politicians running for an elected office, constantly complain about the inefficiency of medical care. These same people then express outrage when state officials attempt to close medical centers that are losing money. This shortage of funds does not seem to have a ripple effect at the biggest hospitals in metropolitan areas. For example, officials at one municipality owned twenty-five hospitals and collected a salary of more than one million annually, plus an equal amount in bonuses. Private hospital administrators in the same city collected double that amount, which is comparable to the outrageously high salaries usually associated with Wall Street firms.

A 2021 report from the Economic Research Institute (ERI) found that the average annual hospital CEO pay was $600,000. In 2018, Bernard Tyson, then-CEO of nonprofit health care giant Kaiser Permanente, made nearly $18 million, making him the highest-paid nonprofit CEO in the nation. The previous year, the top 10 highest paid nonprofit health system executives each made $7 million or more. Even the bottom 25% of nonprofit hospital CEOs enjoyed annual compensation of about $185,000 according to ERI – more than the highest-paid quartile for CEOs in nonprofit arts and culture, environmental, human services, and religion-related organizations.[1] The former

DOI: 10.4324/9781032630670-5

was listed as working twenty-two hours a week. These exorbitant executive salaries are far higher than those of the most experienced heart surgeons and almost as high as the salary given to Alex Rodriguez, the baseball player who has driven in more home runs than the number of "patients' lives saved" by any of these hospital executives.

Doctors are traditionally assumed to be the highest paid of all the professions, but their salaries should be balanced against the fact that doctors do not start to make significant salaries until they are at least thirty years old. Even at that age, they are probably still burdened with medical school debts that often exceed $150,000— sometimes reaching the $250,000 range. Before doctors start a practice or are full-time staff physicians at a hospital, they are already ten years behind their undergraduate age group. Some former classmates are lawyers who have had seven to ten years of experience by the time a doctor starts a practice. Other classmates may receive more than one million dollars in salary by the age of thirty and have no college loan debt still outstanding, as most doctors do.

Anyone attempting to get into an accredited medical schools in the United States needs to make great sacrifices, as well as have a strong dedication. The medical system forces many students to attend the growing number of foreign medical schools. No new medical schools opened in the United States from 1985 to 2000, amid fears of a doctor glut. Predictions of a shortfall of 90,000 physicians by 2020 have encouraged a building boom, with seventeen new schools accredited in 2002, and nine more applying for accreditation since 2015. In comparison, the American Bar Association has approved 201 law schools.

According to applicant data released by the Association of American Medical Colleges, 55,188 people applied to medical school in 2022, sending out an average of 18 applications each. A total of 990,790 applications were sent out across the United States. A total of 22,712 applicants were accepted, meaning 41% of applicants earned a medical school acceptance in 2022.[2] M.D.s graduated from U.S. medical schools in 2023 were 28,811.[3]

Not every doctor becomes a millionaire by the age of fifty, mainly because government regulations and insurance guidelines limit payment. Medicaid and Medicare fees, along with the costs health insurance companies pay for their services, are on a strict fee schedule. Additionally, mandatory malpractice insurance premiums can be as high as $200,000 per year or even higher in obstetrics, for instance. The average cost of four years of private medical education in the United States is well over $200,000, followed by four to seven years of postdoctoral training reimbursed at wages below the minimum wage— established by law when factoring in the long hours most doctors put in during their residency. There is one physician for every 416 Americans, with severe shortages in many specialties and geographic areas. In comparison, there is one lawyer for every 180 and one Starbucks barista for every 650 Americans.

The federal government has attained the legal authority to regulate the medical profession totally and completely in almost every aspect, with no consideration given to the actual time and cost of their many years of training. This situation has reached a level that is forcing many medical professionals to shutter their practices and work as full-time staff members at a hospital or other healthcare facility.

While the average physician in private practice has regularly earned as much as $350,000 a year (an income that places most doctors in the top of

Table 5.1 Specialty Doctors Pay

Specialty	Average Annual Income
Neurosurgery	$788,313
Thoracic Surgery	$706,775
Orthopedic Surgery	$624,023
Plastic Surgery	$571,373
Vascular Surgery	$557,632
Oral and Maxillofacial Surgery	$556,642
Radiation Oncology	$547,026
Cardiology	$544,201
Urology	$505,745
Radiology	$503,564
Gastroenterology	$496,667
Otolaryngology (ENT)	$488,536
Dermatology	$468,509
Anesthesiology	$462,506
General Surgery	$451,489
Ophthalmology	$449,315
Oncology	$447,312[4]

wage earners), this statistic does not consider the approximate $300,000 in education costs and the ten years of training – at a minimum wage that was a prerequisite for that income. However, some specialists in private practices earn more than a million a year. Yet, these salaries are still less than the bonuses given to hedge-fund managers whose unique skills are obtaining inside information about stock transactions.

The following list is the highest-paid doctors by specialty in 2023, which includes a base salary and not bonuses. Bonuses almost always exceed the salary.

Some find it a little bewildering that so much emphasis is placed on where newly hired attorneys attended law school before offering them a position with a law firm – or the emphasis placed on the reputation of a firm before potential clients hire that firm to be their legal representative. Strangely, there is no such elitist attitude when people select their family physician, nor is there much attention to where the attending doctor attended medical school. In contrast to the medical profession, no leading law firm would ever consider hiring a staff associate who attended a law school in the Philippines or Granada. However, hospitals sometimes find themselves with 40% to 50% of their medical staff from there or from countries outside the United States. The more prestigious the law firm, the more likely they would be to recruit their associates from either Yale or Harvard Law School (all nine Supreme Court justices have attended an Ivy League law school). However, when it comes to life-and-death medical decisions, patients and hospitals do not seem to be concerned about whether their medical staff came from a small Caribbean Island medical school or was a graduate of Harvard Medical School.

With high educational and required intern training costs, doctors are forced to seek better-paying jobs in inner-city hospitals and specialties that pay the most – resulting in severe shortages in many specialties and geographic areas.

The Highest-Ranked Medical Schools in the United States

1. Harvard University
2. Johns Hopkins University
3. University of Pennsylvania
4. Columbia University
5. Duke University
5. Stanford University

5. University of California– San Francisco
5. Vanderbilt University
10. Cornell University
10. New York University
10. Yale University
13. Mayo Clinic School of Medicine
13. Northwestern University
13. University of Michigan – Ann Arbor
13. University of Pittsburgh
13. University of Washington
18. Icahn School of Medicine at Mount Sinai
18. University of California – Los Angeles
18. University of Chicago
21. University of California – San Diego
22. Baylor College of Medicine[5]

B. MCAT – Revised

Aspiring doctors who took the 2015 MCAT (Medical College Admissions Test) found it to be different from the exam that their predecessors had been taking since 1991. According to the Association of American Medical Colleges, which develops and administers the test, it was three hours longer than before, and the students had to demonstrate not just what they knew – but how well they could apply it. A large new section (one-quarter of the test) covers psychology, sociology, and the biological foundations of behavior. It also includes (for the first time) questions on social inequality, class consciousness, and racial and ethnic identity. The test is given at different sites on fourteen test dates.

There is a writing section that requires students to prepare two essays. Responding to given statements was eliminated. Instead, there are more questions (a total of 230), but more time is given to spend on each one than on previous exams. The test is more than seven hours long. Scores have changed – instead of the old range of three to forty-five, the new range is 472 to 528. The scores for each of the four sections are reported separately, so medical schools can emphasize or de-emphasize some parts if they choose. Competition for medical school admission has remained as fierce as in previous years. Of the 82,000 test takers, more than 50,000 usually apply for approximately 20,300 first-year places in U.S. medical schools. Another

18,000 will apply for the 6,700 places in thirty schools of osteopathic medicine, which also require the MCAT.

New York University (NYU) Medical School has instituted a free-tuition policy for newly admitted students. The purpose is to produce doctors who are not encumbered by severe student loan debt, so that they might be able to choose general medicine instead of the higher-paying medical specialties. The need to make the highest possible pay upon graduation has caused the number of general practitioners to dwindle in recent decades. New York University's policy is a brave and costly move aimed at reversing the trend. Score profiles that show applicants' strengths and weaknesses on the new exam are accurate enough to provide information across the four sections. The final score report brings together MCAT scores, percentile ranks, confidence bands, and score profiles in a way that highlights those strengths and weaknesses.

Offshore Medical Schools

Students enrolled in offshore medical schools spend the first two years of basic science study in these mostly Caribbean for-profit institutions. There are other medical schools, all over the world, that have less stringent entrance requirements than the 300+ medical schools in the United States. All medical students spend the third and fourth years (regardless of where their school is located) in clinical training and shadowing doctors in teaching hospitals or clinics in the United States. Once the students complete the four years, they graduate as "doctors" with diplomas from a U.S. teaching hospital – with little distinction as to where they started their medical education. Of course, they all must undergo several years of residency training – practicing medicine under a doctor's supervision – before they can treat patients or open a private practice.

Offshore and other foreign medical schools are obligated to get their students into U.S. teaching hospitals for their third and fourth-year training to complete the clinical portion of their education to stay in business. Since New York State has one of the nation's largest concentrations of teaching hospitals, it has become a popular destination for offshore students, with New York City's eleven municipally owned hospitals employing most of these students. The city has a very liberal policy toward accepting foreign-educated students. In 2012, the number of students performing third and fourth-year hospital rotations from offshore programs almost equaled the number of students from New York State's own medical schools. Many of the third-year offshore students come from one of the fourteen dual-campus medical schools accepted for training in the state, with half of the schools located in the Caribbean.

Some hospital officials claim that New York State medical school students are crowded out of opportunities because of the influx of foreign-trained students for the third-year rotation program. They claim that offshore students have been poorly supervised and are inadequately prepared to practice medicine. As a result, they argue that there should be higher standards for offshore students to be accepted by an American teaching hospital. The Caribbean and other offshore schools contend that there are plenty of slots in New York hospitals and that medical deans use the training issue as an excuse to limit the third-year class size. Doing so would deny New York students from seeking a medical education. Meanwhile, international medical school graduates make up 36% of New York State's physician workforce, compared to 25% nationwide. A little-known fact is that New York hospitals have a financial incentive to accept as many students as possible from offshore schools.[6]

In the 2019 application cycle, 1,890 foreign applicants applied to M.D. granting programs in the United States, and 325 of those applicants were accepted. Of those accepted, 272 matriculated into medical school.[7]

The average graduating class size in medical schools can vary greatly:

- New York State medical schools can average about 120 a year.
- St. George's in Grenada graduates about 650 a year.
- Ross University in Dominica graduates about 750 a year.

Regardless of the school attended in the first two years, some 50% of those who complete their residency in an American hospital receive one hundred or more job offers from healthcare facilities.

Foreign medical schools can pay as much as $400 to $450 per week for clinical training at training hospitals. These costs are covered by the medical student's tuition – a cost comparable to that of American-based medical schools. Since American schools pay little or nothing to the hospitals for clinical placements, it is hard for a U.S.-trained student to compete for third and fourth-year clinical study positions. In 2010, the eleven municipal hospitals (owned and managed by the City of New York under their Health and Hospitals Corporation) signed a ten-year agreement for $100 million to provide clinical training at its hospitals for students from one school, located in Granada.[8]

The American Association of American Colleges and Universities forecasts a physician shortage of between 50,000 and 100,000 by 2030. U.S. medical schools have increased first-year enrollment by more than one-quarter over the last fifteen years, with 21,000 students in 2017. Nonetheless, the demand for a medical education far exceeds the supply of seats on U.S. campuses, creating a boom in enrollment in foreign medical schools. In 2016, there were almost 3,500 U.S. citizens from international medical schools certified to enter American residency programs, up from 1,800 in 2006.

A nonprofit school in Australia achieved a residency match rate of 95%. Graduates from the for-profit Ross University Medical School in Dominica, American University of the Caribbean School of Medicine in St. Maarten, and St. George's University School in Grenada (plus a few others) regularly post-match rates exceeding 85%.[9]

Many students graduating from highly ranked or Ivy League colleges with a 3.5 GPA are rejected by U.S.-based medical schools and are forced to seek their medical education in a foreign school. Many international medical schools have long been described as pricey and often too close to beaches for proper dedication to studying – resulting in a reputation for lax admission standards and poor training. This reputation attached to offshore and other international institutions has been challenged in recent years, and foreign-trained doctors from the United States are finding success in gaining positions in American hospitals. A few schools outperform others when it comes to gaining acceptance into residency programs at U.S. teaching hospitals.

Good medical schools exist in other countries – and in many instances, it is easier to gain admission into foreign medical schools than into one of the U.S. medical schools that graduate about 20,000 physicians each year. Students who are driven to enter any medical school right out of college should recall that it is advisable to consider working to address weaknesses in their applications for as long as two years before applying to a U.S. school. For students with a strong interest in primary care, the preferred option is osteopathic medicine – particularly if planning to practice in the

United States. Students applying to a medical school abroad will still have to take the United States Medical Licensing Examination (USMLE) step exams to return to and practice in the United States. The Educational Commission for Foreign Medical School Graduates http://www.ecfmg.org/ explains this in more depth.

A report by the U.S. Government Accountability Office, "Foreign Medical Schools: Education Monitors Medical Schools that Participate in the Federal Student Loan Program" states that the Department of Education administers the federal student loan program and monitors domestic and foreign schools that participate in the loan program on specific statutory requirements. Some of the more well-known offshore schools include:

Caribbean Medical Schools

Offshore medical schools in the Caribbean afford many unsuccessful applicants to U.S. medical schools the opportunity to pursue a medical education and then return to the United States to fulfill their dream of practicing as a physician. However, the person contemplating this should recognize the challenges of studying in a foreign environment, which include being immersed in a different language and culture, trying to secure residencies in the United States, passing the boards, and so forth. The Ross Medical School in Grenada is one of the largest in the Caribbean. It has an agreement with the New York City Health and Hospital Corporation (which controls eleven major facilities) to use their students for the two-year internship period, guaranteeing hundreds of positions. Some opposition to this agreement came from American medical schools, which cannot get accepted into the program – as future doctors from the Caribbean almost always fill them.

Medical Schools in Israel

University medical schools in Israel: Technion in Haifa, Gurion University in Beer Sheva, Tel Aviv University, and the Hebrew University in Jerusalem all follow the European six-year model of medical education. However, since 2009, Tel Aviv University has a four-year program (like the U.S. system) for students with a bachelor's degree in certain biological sciences. Currently, the Technion Medical School, Ben-Gurion University, and Tel Aviv University Sackler Faculty of Medicine offer four-year M.D. programs for American students who have American college degrees, have taken the MCAT, and are interested in completing rigorous medical education in Israel before returning to the United States or Canada.

Medical School for International Health (MSIH)

The Medical School for International Health (MSIH) is a collaboration of Ben-Gurion University of the Negev Faculty of Health Sciences and Columbia University Medical Center.

Atlantic Bridge Program in Ireland

There is a cultural diversity program that allows a small number of Canadian and U.S. students to study medicine or veterinary medicine at an Irish university called the Atlantic Bridge Program. Since its inception more than twenty years ago, more than 3,000 students have undertaken medical, dental, or veterinary studies in Ireland. Students can apply to all six Irish medical schools – using just one common application and submitting only one set of documents (transcripts, letters of reference, etc.). Students who graduate from Irish medical schools through the Atlantic Bridge Program have the choice of entering postgraduate residency training in the United States, Canada, or abroad.

University of Queensland School of Medicine

This University Medical Degree Program accepts applications for January entry – the start of the Australian academic year, which is not considered a mid-year entry. This program is designed for U.S. students or permanent residents and provides students with two years of rotations in the United States at the Ochsner Clinical School. Students complete their first two years studying the basic medical sciences at The University of Queensland's School of Medicine and then complete their third and fourth years of clinical rotations at the UQ Ochsner Clinical School in New Orleans. The University of Queensland has six internationally significant, interdisciplinary research institutes offering a variety of research/study opportunities to students in the School of Medicine, including the Australian Institute for Bioengineering and Nanotechnology, the Brain Institute, and the Diamantina Institute for Cancer, Immunology, and the Metabolic Medicine Research Center. Ochsner Health System is a nonprofit, academic, multi-specialty healthcare delivery system dedicated to patient care, research, and education. The system includes seven hospitals and more than thirty-five health centers located throughout Southeast Louisiana. Medical students from UQ work alongside students from Tulane University and the University of Louisiana School of Medicine who also pursue clinical studies through the Ochsner Health System.

France

Thirty-four medical schools in this country offer a medical degree that takes place in three cycles. The following website explains this: http://scopeblog.stanford.edu/archives/2009/11/the-french-and.html.

Italy

This country has a quite different structure from U.S. medical schools, but its medical school diplomas are recognized in the United States.

England

Students enter medical school directly after finishing the equivalent of high school.

Doctorate of Osteopathy (D.O.) – Not a Doctor of Medicine (M.D.)

DOs and M.D.s are both considered physicians who can practice in any area of medicine, including the familiar "primary care doctors". DOs and M.D.s can also specialize in dermatology, cardiology, psychiatry, or any other medical or surgical field. Both types of doctors can also prescribe medication and train to do surgery. They have similar training that includes four years of medical school and experience in a hospital setting (either as interns, residents – and for some, as fellows in their chosen field for three to eight more years). A good percentage of medical students are studying to become DOs and have to pass state exams to receive a license to practice medicine in all fifty states. However, the main differentiator is that they have a different viewpoint on the body's health and healing capacities than traditional physicians.

Someone holding a Doctorate of Osteopathy will likely check on your whole body – not just specific symptoms – using a "holistic" approach. Some Medical Doctors also use this approach to medicine, but osteopathic doctors get extra training in the musculoskeletal system (muscles, bones, and joints). This knowledge helps them understand how illness or injury can affect other parts of the body. DOs also learn something that M.D.s don't: osteopathic manipulative treatment in which they use their hands to help diagnose, treat, and prevent illness and injury – a key part of their medical training. Not all DOs use osteopathic manipulative treatment routinely, but when they do, they apply techniques such as gentle pressure, stretching, and resistance to help restore range of motion and encourage good health.

There used to be separate osteopathic residency programs, but now M.D. graduates and the DO graduates train alongside each other in common programs that accept both doctors. Applications to the thirty-seven colleges of osteopathic medicine hit record levels in the 2020–2021 application cycle, with a record increase over the previous year. Across the United States, they are treating patients at all levels and specialties that are defined within the medical profession.

Chiropractic Medicine

Like DOs, chiropractors focus on the entire body and how different bodily systems work with each other. Chiropractors also use their hands to diagnose and treat people. They do "adjustments" to correct alignment, improve how the body works, and restore health – but they can't prescribe medicine or operate on a patient. Chiropractic medicine is a healthcare profession that focuses on disorders of the musculoskeletal and nervous systems along with the effects of these disorders on general health. Their treatment is most often used to treat neuromuscular-skeletal complaints, including but not limited to back pain, neck pain, joint pain in the arms or legs, and headaches.

Doctor of Chiropractic, often referred to as chiropractors or chiropractic physicians, practice a drug-free, hands-on approach to healthcare that includes a patient examination, diagnosis, and treatment. They have broad diagnostic skills and are also trained to recommend therapeutic and rehabilitative exercises, as well as provide nutritional, dietary, and lifestyle counseling. Doctor of Chiropractic may assess patients through clinical examination, laboratory testing, diagnostic imaging, and other diagnostic interventions to determine when chiropractic treatment is appropriate or when it is not recommended.

Chiropractors will readily refer patients to the appropriate healthcare provider when chiropractic care is not suitable for the patient's condition, or the condition warrants co-management in conjunction with other members of the healthcare team. The founding theory of the chiropractic profession dates to 1895, when it was first believed that everything is connected – and that harm to the nervous system caused by a skeletal misalignment can lead to a gamut of health problems. The medical profession discredited that unproven theory over the next century.

Almost all M.D.s criticized the practice of chiropractic medicine, and the American Medical Association waged an all-out and well-publicized war late into the 1960s with its formation of the Committee on Quackery, which labeled chiropractors as an "unscientific cult". The committee was disbanded following a 1987 federal judge's ruling that the medical association had tried, unjustly, to destroy the chiropractic profession. The U.S. chiropractic market size is expected to reach USD 28.71 billion by 2030, according to a new report by Grand View Research, Inc. The market is projected to witness a 26.3% increase from 2023 to 2030.[10] Chiropractic colleges graduate about 3,000 new practitioners each year since 2010, with more than ten million Americans visiting a chiropractor each year – and many insurance plans now reimbursing patients for basic chiropractic treatment.

The standard procedure to obtain a license to practice as a chiropractor involves four to five years of postgraduate study at a chiropractic college and one year of supervised patient care. Before chiropractors can practice, they must also pass a national exam and be licensed by their state.

The most common therapeutic procedure performed by chiropractors is known as spinal manipulation (also known as chiropractic adjustment). The purpose of manipulation is to restore joint mobility by manually applying a controlled force onto joints that have become hypomobile or restricted in their movement because of a tissue injury. Tissue injury can be caused by a single traumatic event (such as improper lifting of a heavy object) or through repetitive stresses (such as sitting in an awkward position with poor spinal posture for an extended period). In either case, injured tissues undergo physical and chemical changes that can cause inflammation, pain, and diminished function for the sufferer. Manipulation, or adjustment of the affected joints and tissues restores mobility — thereby alleviating pain and muscle tightness.

Notes

1. Nonprofit Hospital CEO Compensation: How Much Is Enough? Vikas Saini, Judith Garber, Shannon Brownlee, February 10, 2022, Health Affairs.
2. Medical School Acceptance Rates: How Many Applicants Get In, BY MED SCHOOL INSIDERS, MAY 3, 2023, PRE-MED ADMISSIONS COMMITTEE, MEDICAL SCHOOL APPLICATION.
3. KFF, the independent source for health policy research, polling, and news, total number of medical school graduates – 2023.
4. Highest-Paid Doctors in the U.S. (2023), April 25, 2024, Luke Hartstein, Inspira Advantage.
5. U.S. News and World Report, 2023–2024 Best Medical Schools – Research.
6. Katherine Mangan, Students from Caribbean Med Schools Head for New York, Angering Some Local Programs, *The Chronicles of Higher Education*, December 12, 2010.
7. AAMC Students & Residents, Applying to Medical School as an International Applicant, website: https://students-residents.aamc.org/applying-medical-school/applying-medical-school-international-applicant#:~:text=In%20the%202019%20application%20cycle,applied%20via%20AMCAS%20and%20TMDSAS).
8. The Chronicle of Higher Education, New York City Hospital Corporation Signs $100 Million Deal With Caribbean Medical School, August 5, 2008.
9. MedSchoolCoach, Is a Caribbean Medical School Right for You? 6 Best Schools + FAQs, Website: https://www.medschoolcoach.com/caribbean-medical-schools/.
10. Grand View Research, U.S. Chiropractic Market Size to Reach $28.71 Billion by 2030, December 2023.

Chapter 6

Conflicting and Unreliable

Medical Care Varies

A new and controversial phenomenon began when publications and organizations ranked the selective specialties of our nation's major healthcare facilities to identify the very best – and the very worst – mortality rates for patients suffering from different ailments. The ratings were so broad that consumers may not find them useful in deciding which institution they should select to entrust their life. However, the ranking was part of a growing movement to provide more information to consumers and to hold hospitals accountable for the quality of care they deliver. For example, an estimated 290,000 in-hospital cardiac arrests occur each year in the United States. However, there is limited evidence to support clinical decision-making. An increased awareness with regard to optimizing clinical care and new research might improve outcomes.[1]

While these ratings may prove to be more useful in future studies, they do not consider the health of the individual admitted for treatment. One hospital will not admit someone more than ninety years of age for a heart procedure, while another hospital will – resulting in a higher fatality rate than the hospital with the more selective policy. This rating system provides an example of how many levels of scrutiny, investigations, and regulations are specifically developed for hospitals. While the United States has undoubtedly the best healthcare in the world, hospitals cannot overcome certain limitations. Through reports on different areas of concern, the public can become aware that certain hospitals are safer for one procedure rather than another – and patients can expect better treatment in some facilities than in others.

DOI: 10.4324/9781032630670-6

Rankings Involve Some Skepticism in Healthcare

When the U.S. News and World Report annual ranking is released, hospitals at the top of the list react instantly. They quickly tout their rankings in hopes of attracting new patients who will pay top dollar for treatment at their top-ranked facilities. Many Americans use the ranking pecking order when selecting their next elective procedure – as it makes no sense to go to the third-best cancer center in the nearby area when the best is not very far away. The problem with using only the magazine ranking to determine the hospital with the best medical care is that the data is flawed, rendering the ranking order almost useless. While the U.S. News survey may be the most well-known of the four major services that publish ratings for consumers on hospitals, it is not any more objective or reliable than the other three.

Hospital rankings are, in many ways, similar to the scoring system used for colleges and universities. The criteria used in both college and hospital ranking are generally unrelated to quality, easily manipulated, and minimize some of the more important categories that encourage perverse incentives to achieve a higher ranking. The hospitals are broken up into sixteen specialties. In twelve of these fields, about two-thirds of the score is based on reputation. In the other four categories, the ranking is based solely on reputation. A third of the score is supposedly based on a more objective data-based survival rate for patients who enter a given hospital. U.S. News measures thirty-day survival for risk – meaning the severity of the patient's particular illness. This important measure uses only Medicare data, so it comes only from patients older than sixty-five, which is not a representative group of people. Furthermore, this thirty-day measurement has no relevance to cancer care, which would favor a five-year survival over thirty days.

U.S. News sent out surveys to randomly selected specialists and then averaged the responses over the last three years. The result is a seriously flawed statistic:

- The sample of the number of specialists is too small to have any meaningful value. The survey report is sent to 200 physicians per specialty, who list the hospitals they consider to be the best in their specialty for difficult and complex cases. The response rate is a low 30% – meaning the responses over a three-year period are only from 200 physicians. With response rates that low, such results would not qualify for publication in any reputable medical journal.

- Another problem in the survey process is that most physicians have little or no direct knowledge of the quality of care delivered at neighborhood hospitals, much less at ones clear across the county. Physicians rarely treat patients who have been treated at a hospital in another state, which results in an echo chamber effect that amplifies the reputation score of previous rankings. This is not a quality measure.

In 2015, no single hospital received high marks from all four companies (U.S. News and World Report, Consumer Reports, the Leapfrog Group, and Healthgrades). The confusion about the rankings is that some institutions can appear on both ends of these "report cards", indicating a lack of clarity, consistency, and understanding among the various methodologies that render the results highly questionable. With all the criticism of the ranking system, demand for such data is surging. Consumers increasingly comparison shop – using the existing ranking systems for medical services, and efforts to choose a hospital for its quality of care are almost impossible.

> It is highly likely that a patient can go into most towns in America and the local hospital is on somebody's list of top something.

All four services use different rating methodologies, eligibility criteria, and data sources. They even describe their results differently:

- Consumer Reports calculates a safety score for hospitals from one to one hundred, based on rates of infection, readmissions, and other measures.
- Leapfrog's Hospital Safety Score assigns hospitals letter grades from A to F, reflecting how well they keep patients from preventable harm and medical errors.
- Healthgrades calculates an annual list of the country's fifty and one hundred best hospitals, based on mortality and complication rates for different conditions.
- U.S. News focuses on care for serious conditions and scores hospitals from one to one hundred in sixteen specialties, also ranking them nationally and regionally.

Only 10% of the hospitals that were rated highly by one service received top marks from one of the other services. The measures were so divergent that

Table 6.1 How Hospitals Are Ranked

Ranking Service	High Performance Hospitals	Low Performers
Consumer Reports	Score of sixty-five or higher	Score of thirty or lower
Leapfrog	An A rating	D or F rating
Healthgrades	Top one hundred	N/A – not listed
U.S. News	Honor Roll – high scores	Ten or lower in a specialty

US News Health, How and Why We Rank and Rate Hospitals: What's behind our specialty rankings and ratings of procedures and conditions for Best Hospitals, Ben Harder and Kaylan Ware, MPH, July, 2025.

twenty-seven hospitals were simultaneously rated among the nation's best by one service and among the worst by another.

The Best and the Worst Hospitals (Supposedly)

In the March 2014 Consumer Reports, the safety score for more than 1,150 hospitals throughout the nation was based on basic procedures evaluated on a scale of zero to one hundred (the lower the score, the better the ranking). It included categories such as fatal errors, communication, CT screening, complications, the frequency of treatment for infections from catheters, and how many patients treated for heart attacks, heart failure, or pneumonia were readmitted within thirty days, and so forth. No hospital in the nation got anywhere close to a perfect score of "zero". A small hospital in Montana received the highest-ranking score of sixteen, with the worst hospital having a score of seventy-two in Chicago.

Wrong-Side Surgery

While it may not be considered a common error, estimates are that 15% of the population, due to a quirk of the mind, confuse left and right responses. The mistake is hardly noticeable in everyday life but could be disastrous when the so-called wrong-side surgery occurs in the operating room. Reports reveal hundreds of these types of cases every year – in which doctors operate on the wrong body part or perform a perfect hip replacement on the wrong patient. The frequent errors are termed "never" events and are

Table 6.2 Consumer Reports Ten Best Hospitals in 2014

Ten Best	Score	Ten Worst	Score
Billings Clinic – Montana	16	Sacred Heart – Chicago	72
St. Clair's Weston – Wisconsin	71	Harlem Hospital – New York City	20
Alton Memorial – Illinois	71	Lake Regional – Montana	22
Central Vermont – Berlin	71	Kings County – New York City	23
Kadlec Medical – Washington	71	Our Lady of the Resurrection – Chicago	24
St. John's Hospital – Montana	70	Kimball Medical – New Jersey	24
Mayo Clinic – Phoenix	70	St. Rose Dominican – Las Vegas	25
Northern Michigan – Petoskey	69	Clinch Valley – Virginia	25
Bon Secours St. Francis – S. Carolina	69	Westchester Medical Center – New York	25
Memorial of Union Ct. – Ohio	68	Hanford Medical Center – California	26

Consumer Reports, Consumer Reports Scores More Than 2,500 U.S. Hospitals on Safety, March, 2014.

the basis for many malpractice suits. Hospital administrators suggest that all applicants to medical school be asked if they "know their right from their left".

The principal reason for wrong-side events is due to communication errors and the fact that patients in operation rooms may lie face-up or face-down or even on one side. Drapes conceal the patient's body, and the operating table may rotate – adding more confusion to the surgical staff. Other human defects could complicate medical treatment, such as color blindness – which may be a trivial shortcoming, but it can complicate the way a pathologist distinguishes colors under a microscope. No perfect protocol can be used to prevent mistakes when operating on a sleeping patient. It is best if the patient prepares for the worst and uses a magic marker to write "correct hip" and "wrong hip" on the appropriate limbs.

Avoid Hospital Visits during Certain Hours and Days

A doctor shortage may not be present, but it does not change the fact that there is always going to be a problem in properly staffing a healthcare facility – leading to certain caveats. It is best to avoid entering a hospital or clinic at night unless for emergency reasons. The graveyard shift is the worst time to be in a hospital when requiring life-or-death medical treatment. Many of the nation's full-service healthcare institutions use a "code blue" signal over the public address system or intercom when a patient's heart has stopped. If the code blue response works well, a team speeds to the bedside and revives the patient. If a patient goes into cardiac arrest, they are more likely to die if it happens after 11:00 P.M. (or on weekends) – when staffing may be lower, or patients are watched less closely.

It is also not advisable to check out of the hospital on a Friday, which is the most common discharge day. Doctors try to send patients home for the weekend, and studies involving millions of patients over a decade found that individuals released on those days show an "increased independent risk of death" or readmission to the hospital within thirty days. Another caveat is to never get sick in July, since the summer months are the time that medical residents enter the hospital community and learn how to become doctors. They learn by taking care of patients – and learning means making mistakes. The so-called "July effect" is when the medical error rates increase. Medical experts in the deployment of new residents and interns explain the change as like having rookies replace seasoned football players during an important game in the middle of the final drive for a touchdown during the playoffs.

Whether the July effect is statistically validated as a cause of fatal hospital errors, it is regarding the adequacy and quality of care delivery. July is an especially difficult month in a teaching hospital, as first-year residents are taking on life-or-death responsibilities, with little real knowledge of healthcare treatments and diagnoses. Care is becoming more specialized, and nurses with years of experience often know more than the greenest of physicians – but they cannot counteract obvious misdiagnoses made by a would-be doctor. The problem can be limited by better supervision from senior residents and attending physicians. In any event, it would be wise for all concerned if a patient could avoid a hospital stay until September, when seasoned doctors return from their vacation villas on St. Bart or their mansions in the Hamptons.

Security staff can provide a valuable function during emergency situations and have to be trained in these areas. Performing in this way is far different than following the duties assigned to security staff working in less hectic environments. This special training requirement is the main reason that the use of contract guard services has been met with some reluctance from some of the larger healthcare centers. Only the cost difference justifies the use of the contract guard services – not the quality of their service. In hospitals that operate large emergency rooms, it is always better to have a proprietary guard service who is trained for medical facility activity over an outside and usually less-trained contract guard service.

While security staff should be trained for medical emergencies, they are not to interfere with the medical staff when handling patients. Security personnel should be aware of certain basic response practices in case they are called upon to assist. As an example, the nation's leading medical groups have endorsed practicing certain measures for every heart attack and heart failure patient. Medicare fines hospitals that do not report performance on these measures.

Medical Procedures for Heart Attack

- Give an aspirin upon arrival and prescribe aspirin upon discharge.
- Give beta blockers upon arrival and discharge to reduce blood pressure.
- Provide drugs (inhibitors) upon arrival to reduce heart workload.
- Clear the artery, if possible, with balloon angioplasty. If not, use clot busters.
- Give anti-smoking counseling.

Medical Procedures for Heart Failure

- Test the heart's pumping power.
- Provide drugs that reduce the heart's workload.
- Supply information on salt intake, diet, drug regimen, weight control, and smoking to enable patients to care for themselves.

Security systems in hospitals have never been properly evaluated or rated. However, statistics – if properly analyzed – would result in a "security rating" after considering factors such as the number of malpractice suits, emergency room attacks, number of thefts, infants kidnapped, etc.

Hospital CEO Falls Off Pedestal. The chief executive officer of one of the nation's most prestigious hospitals (New York City Hospital for Special Surgery) was caught taking kickbacks from both staffers and outside consultants, amounting to $1.4 million in three separate schemes. The CEO had a salary of more than one million and was facing $720,000 in fines and up to twenty-five years in prison. Under a plea deal in 2013, the CEO was sentenced to two years in jail, received a fine of $60,000, and had to forfeit $720,000.[2]

Biologic Drug Therapy and Biosimilar Copies

BIOLOGIC DRUGS. In 2014, with an estimated three million people affected by hepatitis C in the United States, the Food and Drug Administration (FDA) approved two wonder drugs as a cure – both requiring only twelve weeks of drug therapy and having few side effects. The newer and less-expensive drug, Sovaldi, had a bargain price of $84,000 for a typical course of therapy, or about $1,000 for the daily pill. The older drug, Harvoni, cost $95,400 for the same twelve-week treatment with a regimen of four pills a day. This drug, approved in 2013, became the fastest-growing drug launch in history with revenue of $10 billion in 2013.[3]

The FDA encourages pharmaceutical companies to invest in developing new drugs to treat diseases rarer than hepatitis C through its orphan-drug development program. In return for these investments by the drug industry, the FDA grants priority approvals for drug sponsors willing to tackle long-neglected conditions that most people have never heard of. The FDA program has contributed to the development of more than 400 drugs and biologic products for rare diseases, even though it represents a small market and a costly venture. The five most expensive biologic drugs prescribed for patients include:

- *Lenmeldy*: is an autologous hematopoietic stem cell (HSC) gene therapy for the treatment of children with metachromatic leukodystrophy (MLD).
  - Generic Name: atidarsagene autotemcel
  - Cost – $4.25 million per one-time treatment
- *Hemgenix*: is approved to treat hemophilia B, a rare, lifelong bleeding disorder.
  - Generic Name: etranacogene dezaparvovec-drlb
  - Cost – $3.5 million per one-time dose

- *Elevidys*: approved for the treatment of children aged four through five years with Duchenne Muscular Dystrophy (DMD) with a confirmed mutation in the DMD gene.
  - Generic Name – delandistrogene moxeparvovec-rokl
  - Cost – $3.2 million per one-time dose
- *Skysona*: is a lentiviral vector (LVV) gene therapy approved for the treatment of adult or pediatric patients with beta-thalassemia who require regular red blood cell (RBC) transfusions.
  - Generic Name – elivaldogene autotemcel or eli-cel
  - Cost – $3 million per one-time dose
- *Zynteglo*: requires only six weeks of treatment and is prescribed for a rare form of cancer.
  - Generic Name – betibeglogene autotemcel or beti-cel
  - Cost – $2.8 million per one-time dose[4]

BIOSIMILAR DRUGS. Most brand-name drugs eventually lose their patent protection, opening the market to lower-priced generic products. One class of drugs, known as biologics, includes some of the most expensive medications. It has been insulated from the competition of cheaper copies for years. That insulation was breached in 2015, when members of a panel (convened by the FDA) agreed to recommend approval of a drug that represents a new concept in medicine. The particular drug is known as EP2006, which is a copy of an existing medication called Neupogen. The FDA followed the recommendations of the panel and approved generic copies of biologic drugs, in addition to EP2006, that fell into a class of biosimilar drugs. Samples of these drugs are Remicade, Humira, and Ethbrel for autoimmune disease and Herceptin, Rituxan, and Avastin for some forms of cancer. They became available in the United States in 2015.

Bogus Hospital Bills

Hospital visits are becoming a way of life (and death), due mainly to people living longer and the increased number of elderly patients who need medical care. Since most visits are paid for directly by the insurance company, the public is probably unaware that billing errors appear on 80% of the invoices – unless they are billed for treatment and medical services that require the patient to pay, which is called co-insurance. The healthcare community recognizes the problem but has done little to address the issue. Not only can billing errors lead to undeserved higher costs for consumers, but they can also sabotage otherwise well-heeled borrower's ability to get mortgages or other types of loans. Medical billing errors mar the credit reports of roughly fourteen million Americans, according to a study conducted by the Commonwealth Fund – a nonprofit focused on healthcare research. Medical bills sent to collection in error have become the single greatest threat to credit scores. More than half of all accounts in collection are medical accounts.

Despite the labyrinth of unreadable changes and mysterious codes that appear on medical bills, the process itself is relatively simple. As a result of electronic billing snafus, the bills are often inaccurate or outright fraudulent. Among the most common problems, researchers say, assumptions for types of care that never were given. Other errors often are a result of simple clerical errors, including anything from the mischaracterization of care provided to double billing for the same procedure. Many of these errors arise when overburdened staff are deluged with bills from patients who cannot or will not pay, forcing hospitals to become debt-collection agencies.

Borrowers typically need a 730 score to get the best loan rates. Otherwise, they must come up with a larger down payment and/or pay a higher interest rate. Any unpaid debt, whether for $100 or $10,000, can shave up to one hundred points off a person's credit score. Because of address mix-ups, some patients do not realize they have outstanding medical bills until they try to get a new mortgage with credit scores of less than 700. Unpaid medical bills can go undetected for years – and by the time the debt is uncovered, it may have torpedoed a credit rating that can take many months to correct. A crop of medical billing advocates has emerged to help patients negotiate their bills, find errors, and correct any mistakes – for a fee, of course. They are especially advisable if the patient is very sick or for those who do not have the time or energy to haggle with the hospital over bills. Most advocates can charge between 20% and 30% of what they save the client, and some even tack on an hourly fee as well.

Patients who want to challenge a hospital bill without any outside assistance should check the price of each item involved in the care they received against the Medicare rates for the same care, which can be found online at the Medicare site hosted by the U.S. Department of Health and Human Services (www.cms.gov). If there is a wide discrepancy, the challenge should be successful. The errors can be enormous, and there are documented cases in which a hospital charged forty-one times for a single intravenous drip, resulting in billing for thousands of dollars that was lowered when it was corrected. That type of overcharge is not the exception, and compounding of the problem can occur if patients fail to notify the three credit bureaus that an error was made, before their credit is destroyed.

Outrageous Hospital Charges

A hospital bill has always been a very confounding document, because the price tag of a medical procedure depends on the rate that hospitals negotiate with individual insurers. The actual amount for each treatment is kept confidential and is substantially marked up from how much the procedure costs the hospital. Under a federal rule that was issued on the first day of 2021, hospitals are required to disclose the rates they negotiated with their insurers. The penalty is only around $300 a day, which is extremely low compared to what hospitals charge both the insurers and patients, but it is a first step toward making the previously mysterious changes more transparent.

A study released in 2015 by the Bloomberg School of Public Health found that some hospitals are making up prices by as much as 1,000%. These hospitals were not located in Beverly Hills, by the luxury townhouses of New York's Upper East Side, or in the Hamptons. Most of the named institutions were not known for their research or any specialty and were not among the most sought-after healthcare providers in the nation. The top five were:

- North Okaloosa Medical Center (FL)
- Carepoint Health-Bayonne Hospital (NJ)
- Bayfront Health Brooksville (FL)
- Paul B Hall Regional Medical Center (KY)
- Chestnut Hill Hospital (PA)[5]

The Bayonne Hospital went bankrupt in 2007. A group of investors purchased the hospital, and the profits soared after the new owners increased its service charges for every treatment and medical procedure. An insurance provider sued the hospital for overcharging, claiming that Bayonne Medical's emergency room charges jumped each year since 2010 and that it was six to twelve times as high as those of surrounding hospitals – however, the suit was dismissed. The investors then went on a buying spree and purchased several of the surrounding hospitals, and those hospital charges increased tenfold.[6]

These small, privately owned for-profit medical facilities were not the only institutions that had strange billing standards. One prestigious Manhattan hospital charged twice as much as an equally high-end hospital to implant a cardiac pacemaker. Medicare considered the two institutions so similar that it paid both about $20,000 for the procedure. While discrepancies in charges for the same medical service may seem unjustified, the hospital claimed the charges were irrelevant because virtually no one – private insurers, Medicare, or even the uninsured – pays anywhere near those amounts billed to patients. Medicare sets standard rates for treatment, and insurers negotiate with hospitals. The hospital deliberately overcharges, and when it gets less (as anticipated), it declares that the difference was a payment to the under-insured and takes it as a tax deduction.

Surgery costs can vary drastically depending upon the procedure, hospital, location, and even type of insurance, since insurers negotiate with providers over rates. For instance, a 2022 study of several U.S. healthcare systems found that the average allowed in-network charges by private insurance for hip and knee replacements ranged from $25,000 to $70,000.

Some typical average costs for common surgeries are:

- Heart valve replacement: $170,000
- Heart bypass: $123,000
- Spinal fusion: $110,000
- Hip replacement: $40,364
- Knee replacement: $35,000
- Angioplasty: $28,200
- Hip resurfacing: $28,000
- Gastric bypass: $25,000
- Cornea: $17,500
- Gastric sleeve: $16,000[7]

Generally, an arthroscopy costs for hip or knee surgery anywhere in the United States is outlandishly higher than in the rest of the free world. Even within this country, the cost and the frequency of the operation vary significantly. The cost of having a knee or hip replaced can be up to four times more in one place than in another – even in the same geographic area. A total knee replacement averages about $31,000 in sixty-four markets throughout the United States, while in Dallas it ranges from $16,000 to $61,000. Some of the price differences are expected, due to the cost of living and overhead in cities such as New York when compared to Alabama.

Nonetheless, the reasons hip replacements in Colorado cost tens of thousands more than in Pittsburgh may have more to do with whatever the market will bear than any other factor. Another hard-to-explain statistic is that Medicare patients in Lincoln, Nebraska, were nearly four times more likely to have their knee replaced than those in Honolulu – where the rate for this surgery was almost half that of the national average.[8]

Having a Less-Expensive Procedure in Foreign Countries

Within developing countries, such as India or Thailand, is where so-called medical tourists often end up. Some hip and knee replacement patients choose hospitals in countries such as Belgium that use the same device as American hospitals do, but for much less of a cost. The total cost of about $14,000 for an operation in a Belgian hospital includes not only the hip joint, but also all doctor's fees, operating room charges, crutches, medicine, a hospital room for five days, a week in rehab, and even the round-trip airfare from America. The markup for the hip replacement device is often two to three times the cost of an artificial hip, which is somewhere around $350 to manufacture in the United States. It seems that the cost of the implant and Belgian prices for surgery are based on a different logic. The Belgian government oversees major medical purchases, approving dozens of different types of implants from a selection of manufacturers.

Accordingly, the average price a Belgian hospital pays for each implant is about $3,000 and can be marked up by about $180 per device – the same model sold to American hospitals is about $8,000. While most Belgian physicians and hospitals are in business for themselves, the government sets pricing and limits profits. Hospitals have a fixed daily rate, and surgeons receive a fee for each surgery – which they negotiate each year. Belgium pays for healthcare through a mandatory national insurance plan, which requires contributions from employers and pays for 80% of each treatment. Patients are responsible for the remaining 20%, and many have private insurance to cover that amount.

As many as 700,000 people in the United States spend an estimated $4 billion in annual medical costs for knee surgery each year to treat tears in a crescent-shaped piece of cartilage known as the meniscus, which acts as a shock absorber between the upper and lower portions of the knee joints. The tears are thought to create loose pieces of cartilage that interfere with the motion of the joints, causing pain and suffering.

A study published in the New England Journal of Medicine involved two sets of patients – one set received knee surgery, and the other was a control group, which was led to believe that it had undergone surgery but had not. Doctors, who treated the control group of patients, physically simulated the procedure by pressing instruments firmly against the skin that felt like an incision. It was very similar to giving some patients sugar pills or placebos in drug studies. The researchers observed no significant difference in improvement between the groups after one year.

In addition to the hundreds of thousands of knee replacements each year, doctors perform around 300,000 hip replacements in the United States. Nearly all the implants for both the knee and hip involve sterilized pieces of tooled metal, plastic, or ceramic – and only five companies make them. The basic design of the artificial joints has not changed for decades. Foreign-made joint implants are kept out of the United States by trade policy, patents, and an expensive Food and Drug Administration approval process that deters start-ups from entering the market. Hospitals typically pay between $5,400 and $7,500 for an artificial hip, a cost that balloons up to $35,000 or $50,000 when billed to patients. The final hospital bill for all the services and the implant averages about $70,000 to $100,000 before the insurance carrier and Medicare negotiate it down.

Orthopedists tend to make about half the income of their American counterparts, whose annual income averaged $500,000 in 2024.[9] In the following example, a patient with an arthritic hip who cannot walk or work for extended periods because of the pain seeks a joint replacement. However, his health insurance will not cover the cost of the operation because the degenerative disease is related to an old injury – therefore, the injury is considered a pre-existing condition. A medical-device manufacturer is willing to supply the implant for about $13,000, the local hospital charges as much as $65,000 to perform the surgery, and then the surgeon's fee of about $17,000 is added to the overall cost.

Avoiding Hospital High "List Prices"

A popular, low-cost "indemnity" type of health insurance policy has no provider network requirements or preferred hospital requirements – patients can go anywhere. It is the type of insurance designed for healthy, young people – mostly self-employed. The policy has certain drawbacks, one of which is that the policy pays up to a fixed amount for doctors and hospital bills, based upon the diagnosis. There are no negotiations on fixed prices, as with most health insurance policies. Medicare is one of those policies. Someone with an indemnity insurance policy can be exposed to the unpredictable and outrageously high costs charged by hospitals and doctors who normally expect to have their fees automatically lowered by the insurance company.

A typical case reported in a national newspaper involved a holder of an indemnity policy who arrived at a hospital for routine hernia surgery. The admitting clerk reviewed the terms of the policy and estimated the amount of the bill that would be paid by insurance. The patient was asked to pay his estimated portion of the total bill in advance, which is a practice adopted by a growing number of hospitals – as patients commonly do not pay their portion of the bills after the insurance has paid. The insurance policy would cover up to $2,000 for the surgeon – more than enough – and up to $2,500 for the hospital's charges that covered the operating room, nursing, recovery room, and so forth. The hospital's portion was $23,000, and the patient was asked to pay the rest ($20,000) to cover the estimated balance.

The doctor who was to operate for less than the allotted $2,000 was informed that the patient canceled the surgery due to the high cost of the hospital services. This situation made everyone realize that having an insurance policy does not mean the patient has to use it in every medical situation. The prior situation is like what happens after people experience a fender-bender – they will often settle the damage privately rather than file an insurance claim. In the surgery situation, had the doctor been bound by a preferred-provider contract or by Medicare, the doctor would have been forced to use the hospital for the surgery at their cost estimates. It seems that hospitals and most providers make list prices deliberately high knowing full well that, when negotiating with health plans and Medicare regulators, the costs eventually paid will be significantly lowered. No one is ever expected to pay the list price.

When patients receive the "Explanation of Benefits" statement from a health plan, they will note a very high charge from the provider (hospital) and an "adjusted charge" based upon the contracted fee schedule – which usually leaves patients with little or nothing in out-of-pocket expenses. People with policies that do not include a pre-negotiated fee schedule with contracted providers are out of luck, essentially having no insurance at all. Most people in this situation are unaware that if they do not use the insurance, they can negotiate an upfront cash price with hospitals and providers substantially below the "list price". Doctors are happy to have patients pay promptly without having to pay office staff to wade through insurance payment forms.

In the hernia example, the patient declared as being self-pay (or uninsured) and received quotes from both the doctor and another hospital that was willing to accept a reasonable upfront cash price for the same services as the $23,000 hospital offered. The total bill was about $3,000, instead of the $24,000 list price. Another example is Lasik eye surgery or cosmetic surgery – neither of which is covered by insurance. Providers compete on quality, outcomes, and cost.

America: Medical Costs High – Level of Treatment Low

U.S. citizens do not get better healthcare, but the cost for healthcare is more than in any other developed nations – regardless of whether other nations operate a private or national health system. A list of drug costs, scans, and other medical procedures compiled by the International Federation of Health Plans found that the United States came out as the costliest in all twenty-one categories studied – often by a huge margin. Americans pay, on average, about four times as much for a hip replacement as patients in Switzerland or France and more than three times as much for a cesarean section as those in New Zealand or Britain. Numerous studies have repeatedly shown that Americans are, far and away, the world leader in medical spending.

In most of the other developed countries, a basic colonoscopy costs just a few hundred dollars or well under $1,000. Gastroenterologists in Austria perform the thirty-minute procedure in a doctor's office for an approved rate of between $200 and $300. In Italy and most other European countries, the cost is between $400 and $800 to perform one – including biopsies and sedation. The U.S. costs for a colonoscopy can vary significantly in different sectors of the country, but they are always four to five times higher than those found in any other country.

The high cost of healthcare is not only caused by the high rates paid for relatively simple medical procedures, but researchers also trace it to the pressures that encourage doctors to perform far too many unjustified medical procedures and operations. In many situations (especially when doctors are full-time members of the hospital staff), there is an understanding that the medical staff should perform as many operations as possible. The public does not know what portion of the unnecessary surgeries are related to these subtle pressures, as opposed to poor training or even fraud. In the real world of medical care, doctors get paid for the operation – essentially rewarding those who put patients under the knife. Medical treatment and procedures are carefully defined, and there should be no disparity in the number of operations for a particular illness. The percentages should be approximately the same in all hospitals throughout the United States, but they are not.

A very busy dermatologist in Florida treated hundreds of mostly elderly skin cancer patients for more than a decade, taking in millions of dollars from private insurers and Medicare. This doctor would deliberately misdiagnose patients, claiming they had skin cancer, then perform unnecessary surgeries – often multiple times on a single patient – to remove lesions he knew were benign. When federal agents caught the doctor in the fraud, they found he treated victims who never had any form of cancer. In 2006, he was sentenced to twenty-two years in prison for the scam and was ordered to pay $7 million for intentionally misdiagnosing more than 800 patients.[10]

The National Average for One Day in a Hospital Room

According to the International Federation of Health Plans, a global network of health insurance industries, the most expensive hospitals among all the developed nations in the world are in the United States. Some American hospitals charge, on average, $4,000 a day for an overnight stay in one of their rooms – and charges can be as high as $12,500 in the more expensive inner-city medical care facilities. Hospitals also make most of their profits in the emergency room (ER), where one of the simplest and oldest medical procedures — closing a wound with a needle and thread – costs at least $1,500 and often much more (as shown below). Insurers and patients negotiate lower prices.

Hospital charges represent about a third of the $2.7 trillion annual U.S. health bill – the biggest percentage of any segment of the total cost. The charges are completely unregulated and arbitrary, not connected to underlying costs or market prices. Since there are no market restraints, hospitals can charge any level they want. Prices are set for any item or service, move up and down annually, and vary greatly even in hospitals in the same city. One San Francisco hospital charges about $20 for codeine and about $137 for a bag of IV fluid, while a hospital across town charges only about $1 and about $16, respectively. But the first hospital charges only about $685 for an amniocentesis, while the second hospital charges about $1,600. There is no real pattern in the way the hospitals set up charges billed to patients.

Price lists typically can have more than a thousand entries, listing everything from aspirin, IV fluid bags, a visit from a physical therapist, or help for a patient to get out of bed. In all other countries, the price of a day's stay in the hospital usually includes almost every item listed above. A great number of American hospitals use a 400-page charge master list that clearly shows how expensive some medical procedures can be before negotiating the final price with the insurer. There is little science to show how hospitals determine the prices eventually printed on those long hospital bills. This list is of little practical value to patients because insurance companies negotiate down the prices to get better deals than others. After each hospital stay or visit, computer programs and trained billers use the charge master price list to translate the services rendered into a final, shockingly high bill.

Hospitals can bill for emergency room care with relative impunity since injured patients generally rush to the nearest treatment facility without the opportunity to shop around for the lowest cost for the same service. The uninsured are particularly vulnerable to high prices, since they have no one to argue on their behalf. Sometimes a hospital will grant a "charity care discount" – but even that price is extremely high. Hospitals are relentless in their collection process – without these enormous charges, hospitals could not afford to pay their executives their enormous salaries.

Hospitals were required under the Affordable Care Act (ACA) to make their prices transparent by publishing their "chargemasters," or list prices, for all the services they provide. Congress passed the amendment to the ACA in 2021, with a provision that hospitals must publish this information on their website in a machine-readable, or computer-friendly, format – as required by the government regulation, which makes health care more affordable and prices more transparent.

The rule has required hospitals to publicly disclose the prices they negotiated privately with insurers or face fines. The rule is intended to improve transparency in a system that some officials say had been as clear as mud. It has also increased competition, better enabling consumers to shop for hundreds of medical items and services – including procedures like X-rays and lab tests, doctor care, and facility fees.

The government had already forced hospitals to publish list prices, but the new rule goes further by requiring hospitals to post prices paid by various insurers, prices for out-of-network care, and charges for patients paying in cash. Furthermore, the rule requires insurers to allow patients to get estimates for their out-of-pocket costs before they receive care.

Ambulance Chasing Hospitals and Doctors

A growing number of wealthy hospitals, nationwide, have quietly increased their income by challenging the legal profession and becoming "ambulance chasing hospitals" – using a century-old hospital lien law to increase revenue. The lien law allows for claims on assets such as a home or a settlement payment to ensure someone repays a debt. Hospitals can collect money that otherwise would have gone to the patient to compensate for pain and suffering. This approach allows hospitals to ignore the steep discounts they are contractually required to offer to health insurers and instead pursue their full charges. The difference between the two prices is staggering, with certain treatments getting compensated at a lower price when using insurance versus a price about ten times higher when a hospital pursues a lien.

Some people insist that it is unfair to think Medicaid patients would be charged the full-billed price if they were involved in an accident. Lien is most lucrative when used against low-income patients with Medicaid, which tend to pay lower reimbursement rates than private health plans. One litigation, by a hospital in Washington State, estimated that this practice generated $10 million annually.

A hospital in Oklahoma offers some accident victims a waiver to sign, stating they did not want their health plan billed for care. One patient received the waiver shortly after a car accident in which her head hit the windshield. The patient claimed she had no recollection of signing the document but faced a $34,106 lien as a result.[11]

Hospitals have come under scrutiny in recent years for increasingly turning to the courts to recover patients' unpaid bills, even in the midst of the coronavirus pandemic. Hospitals – many of which received significant bailouts in 2020 – have used court rulings to garnish patients' wages and take their homes. Less attention has been paid to hospital lien laws, which many states passed in the early 20th century (when fewer than 10% of Americans had health coverage). The lien laws were meant to protect hospitals from the burden of caring for uninsured patients and to give them an incentive to treat those who could not pay upfront.

A century later, hospital liens are mostly used to pursue debts from car accident victims. This method has become so lucrative, documents and interviews show that some hospitals use outside debt-collection companies to scour police records for recent accidents to make sure they identify which of their patients might have been in a wreck – so that they can pursue them with liens. Some laws limit what share of a patient settlement a hospital can lay claim to, and others allow only nonprofit hospitals to collect debts this way. Certain states require hospitals to bill accident victims' health plans rather than using a lien. This approach is seen as more consumer-friendly because patients benefit from the discounts that health plans have negotiated on their behalf.

A growing number of hospitals defend the practice of using liens, claiming that it is only used when privately insured patients don't provide coverage. When a lien is issued, it can torpedo patients' credit scores and leave them unable to pay for needed follow-up care. Hospitals argue that patients should be held accountable for their medical bills rather than relying on the government to pay under Medicare and Medicaid policies.

COVID-19 Tests – A Lucrative Niche amid the Pandemic

Many hospital workers performed extraordinary tasks during the 2020 pandemic, sometimes dying because of their selfless efforts. The entire medical profession deserved accolades for working under almost unbearable conditions. Yet, there were other people who took advantage of the crisis – the biggest abusers being the gouging laboratories that conducted millions of tests and charged whatever they wanted – without government regulations or intervention.

Billing for the testing service abused not only the public but especially the insurers who paid the cost for a standard nasal swab. A typical procedure reported in the mass media described that the hospital charged $199 to take the nasal sample and sent it off to a lab, which billed the insurer $6,408 for the same test. More than eight times what the federal Centers for Medicare and Medicaid Services reimburses for the COVID-19 standard test.[12]

A congressional committee conducted a study and found that charges varied from $300 to $6,000, which they found to be unconscionable and excessive. One doctor testified that he went to a Texas lab to get the COVID-19 antibody test, and his insurance plan was charged the entire amount of $10,984. Another survey, conducted by America's Health Insurance Plans, found hospitals and independent labs that were not in contract with insurance plans charged the most. About one in ten of these out-of-network providers charged an average of $390 for a test. By comparison, Medicare pays labs $100 for each test processed.[13]

The cost of coronavirus-related medical supplies was also questionable. While there was little concrete data on the cost of medical items during the pandemic, most distributors and manufacturers of medical supplies claimed that prices across the board in 2020 had surged amid the continuing waves of COVID-19 infections around the United States. For example, medical-grade gloves jumped from about $3 for a box of one hundred gloves pre-pandemic to as much as $32 during the pandemic. This price surge also occurred in the price of regulators, masks, gloves, and nurses' gowns.[14]

Another example of the inflated prices for critically needed coronavirus supplies was the scandal surrounding the peddling of counterfeit medical gloves, as the shortage of this item had tripled in price. Compounding the problem of price gouging was the fact that the gloves were often fakes.

Notes

1. National Library of Medicine, In-Hospital Cardiac Arrest, Lars W. Andersen, MD, MPH, PhD, DMSc, Mathias J. Holmberg, MD, MPH, Katherine M. Berg, MD, Michael W. Donnino, MD, and Asger Granfeldt, MD, PhD, DMSc, March 26, 2019.
2. U.S. Department of Health and Human Services, Office of Inspector General, Former Chief Executive Officer of Hospital for Special Surgery Sentenced in Manhattan Federal Court to 18 Months in Prison for Participating in Fraudulent Kickback Scheme, November 7, 2013.
3. Scientific American, We Now Have the Cure for Hepatitis C, but Can We Afford It?, September 1, 2014, BY JESSICA WAPNER.
4. Leigh Ann Anderson, 10 of the Most Expensive Drugs in the U.S., Medically reviewed, *Drugs.com*, PharmD. Last updated on April 1, 2024.
5. Chris Sipsma, Study uncovers 50 Most Expensive Hospitals in America, *Website: News Channel 3*, June 8, 2015.
6. Julie Creswell, Barry Meier, Jo Craven McGinty, New Jersey Hospital Has Highest Billing Rates in the Nation, *The New York Times*, May 16, 2013.
7. Maureen Milliken, Hospital and Surgery Costs, *Debt.org*, November 30, 2023.
8. Blue Cross Blue Shield website, A study of cost variations for knee and hip replacement surgeries in the U.S., January 21, 2015.

9. Salary.com, Orthopedic Doctor Salary, https://www.salary.com/research/salary/recruiting/orthopedic-doctor-salary#:~:text=The%20average%20Orthopedic%20Doctor%20salary,have%20spent%20in%20your%20profession.
10. Tampa Bay Times, Dermatologist guilty of fraud, Rebecca Catalanello, Published March 4, 2006|Updated March 4, 2006.
11. Sarah Kliff, Jessica Silver-Greenberg, How Rich Hospitals Profit from Patients in Car Crashes, *The New York Times*, Published February 1, 2021, Updated February 12, 2021.
12. Sarah Kliff, Two Friends in Texas Were Tested for Coronavirus. One Bill Was $199. The Other? $6,408, *The New York Times*, Published June 29, 2020, Updated July 15, 2020.
13. Marshall Allen, A Doctor Went to His Own Employer for a COVID-19 Antibody Test. It Cost $10,984, *ProPublica*, September 5, 2020, 5 a.m. CDT.
14. Giacomo Tognini, Billionaires Making "Boatloads Of Money" From Once-Cheap Medical Gloves, *Forbes*, April 30, 2022, 05:00pm EDT.

Chapter 7

Highest-Earning Hospital Executives

Salary of $1 Million Is at the Bottom of Scale

Healthcare institutions constitute one of the largest employers in the private sector in the United States, second only in size to restaurant workers. Eight of the twenty-five largest private corporations located in New York City are health care institutions, with Northwell Health as the largest non-municipal employer in the city (with 10,000+ employees).[1] The list of salaried executives in the forty-three hospitals that have a birthing unit does not include any New York State nursing homes, which control facilities, have 20,000 beds, and involve a $10 billion annual budget. The chief operating officers and presidents at the major U.S. hospital systems receive high compensation packages. There does not seem to be any correlation between the size of the facility and the salary of the Chief Operating Officer. The table listed below shows the annual expenditures and the salary of the highest-paid hospital administrative officials in 2021. The average salary is substantially greater than many corporate executives:

Tenet Healthcare – $21.2 million
HCA Healthcare – $20.6 million
Universal Health Services – $14 million
Community Health Systems – $9.5 million[2]

DOI: 10.4324/9781032630670-7

These high-salaried officials contend that their pay package is fair compensation compared to Wall Street bankers, who lack their enormous responsibilities and skills. Critics of these administrative-level salaries believe the compensation is almost "scandalous," since both the private and municipal hospitals are tax-exempt and rely on state and federal money from Medicaid, Medicare, and other government subsidies. Saint Vincent's Catholic Medical Center filed for bankruptcy in 2005 and 2010 and went out of business in 2010. Its president received an annual salary of about $2 million during the two-year bankruptcy proceedings, when he oversaw the gradual elimination of the hospital. The CEO of New York City's $6.3 billion Health and Hospital Corporation – with 39,000 employees, eleven hospitals, four nursing homes, and many neighborhood treatment centers, and the nation's largest public system – is paid a salary of about $300,000.

The twenty-one top-earning hospital executives received millions collectively at their nonprofit posts, while hospitals throughout the nation are under financial pressure to cut costs and lay off thousands of healthcare workers. Nonprofit salaries for hospital executives on average are way beyond the norm for work in a charitable organization. Nonprofit hospitals have tax-exempt statuses in exchange for serving charity missions. The state pays them largely through Medicaid (the federal and state healthcare program for the poor). When the state designates a hospital as "financially distressed", it is eligible for even more state aid.

Insider Deal – Lavish Pay and Bankruptcy

Hospitals throughout the nation have filed for bankruptcy protection or have been forced to close far more often in the last two years than in the previous two decades. Poor management and the tight economy are blamed for some of the closings, but this trend has not seemed to affect the salaries of the hospital administrators overseeing the bankruptcies. One of the more flagrant abuses in the salary structure at a nonprofit hospital occurred in one of New York City's poorest neighborhoods. While fighting off the bankruptcy by seeking city and state aid and lamenting cuts in government assistance, it was rumored that the chief executive drove around in a Bentley Continental (a $160,000 automobile), and the hospital paid for the vehicle's insurance. When the executive lost his license due to a car accident, hospital security guards chauffeured both the executive and his wife around the clock, in a Cadillac Escalade or a Lincoln Town Car.

The Joint Commission, which accredits hospitals, rated this hospital well below average, and the number of complaints received by the state health department set a record. To sum up the situation, Consumer Reports rated the facility as the sixth worst hospital (out of eighty-one) in the New York area for patient safety. Under heavy criticism and scrutiny by the district attorney, the chief executive finally resigned and received a fifteen-month severance package worth around $875,000. Hospital executives are making more money than insider traders, without the threat of being indicted and sentenced to jail.

Self-Insurance Can Be Expensive

With malpractice insurance rates becoming too expensive to purchase for many healthcare facilities, along with the fact that hospitals are sued all the time for malpractice and other medical errors, many hospitals take a gamble to cover court-mandated awards by self-insuring and setting aside funds to cover lawsuit awards. Some lose that gamble and go bankrupt when a judgment against the hospital is much larger than the monies set aside for such contingencies. Other medical facilities will close a specific department (such as maternity, if the award was based on an infant injury or death) if budget strains had depleted the reserves the hospital had built up to cover malpractice settlements.

While there is no central record of which hospitals have insurance or those that self-insure their staff, it is well-known that the number of self-insured hospitals is significant and growing every year. When a hospital must decide on either paying for nurses or malpractice insurance, the hospital is going to choose the former. In most of the large inner-city networks of hospitals, such as New York, Cook County in Chicago, and Florida's Dade County, it is not effective for a hospital to buy coverage due to the high cost. Other hospitals in the same city were partially self-insured and had bought insurance to cover lower-dollar or "primary" claims, but not "excess" judgments. The other nine had excess coverage, not primary — and this ratio may hold true across the nation's inner cities.

Hospitals generally try to subsidize or reimburse their staff physicians, especially in areas such as the emergency room and in obstetrics and gynecology, but the funds for this purpose are often insufficient (or the hospital has completely exhausted its reserves). When there are no self-insured funds available, claimants who win awards will never get paid. Insurance companies that offer malpractice policies are not very enthusiastic about covering inner-city hospitals, particularly in municipalities known for being extremely litigious and having awards that are unreasonably high. The lack of funds that are court-ordered has had a serious effect on lawyers who consider medical malpractice insurance a lawsuit magnet. The so-called ambulance chasers must inform the plaintiffs they represent that they may well end up with nothing by pushing the hospital into bankruptcy, if they do not take the little bit that is offered to them by an almost insolvent hospital.

Personal injury lawyers are no longer collecting their huge contingency fees and have been forced to change their demands. They will take payments on an installment plan, if that is the only alternative – with some plans that can stretch out to eight or more years. Plaintiffs are made to fully understand that trying to collect a substantial settlement could bankrupt the hospital – and by reducing their demands, they can collect some money. A law firm will sometimes change its tactics and try to pin more blame on physicians, who may have malpractice insurance that could cover million-dollar settlements. Each time the insurance company pays out settlement funds under a physician's malpractice policy, the premium goes up – sometimes forcing a physician to give up his or her medical practice. Annual premiums of a quarter of a million are no longer a rarity.

Hospital Excesses Underreported

Hospitals are by far the biggest cost in the nation's $3.5 trillion healthcare system, with spending now growing faster than the gross domestic product, inflation, and wage growth. According to researchers at several elite universities, hospital prices increased 42% from 2007 to 2017 for inpatient care and 25% for outpatient care. This increase cannot be justified when compared to the 18% and 6% for physicians. The cost for a hospital stay in the U.S. averaged $5,220 a day in 2015, and by 2020, the average cost was $17,000 a day. In more realistic terms, the cost in Australia is $775 a day.[3]

Since about 2015, hospitals and healthcare facilities have consolidated and have become the biggest employers in major cities and in half the states. They have replaced manufacturing and retail outlets – and in many dust-belt cities, they are the hometown industry. Yet, hospitals continue to claim that they operate on the thinnest of margins – partly a choice they made due to extravagances that include equipment they don't need and salaries for executives that can often exceed $2 million a year.

Notes

1. Glassdoor, Top Healthcare Companies in New York City, website: https://www.glassdoor.com/Explore/top-healthcare-companies-new-york-city_IS.4,14_ISEC10012_IL.25,38_IM615.htm#:~:text=Northwell%20Health%20is%20New%20York,the%20standard%20of%20health%20care.
2. Dave Muoio, Here's What CEOs at the US' Top for-Profit Health Systems Earned in 2021, *Fierce Health*, April 26, 2022.
3. Elisabeth Rosenthal, Analysis: How Your Beloved Hospital Helps to Drive Up Health Care Costs, *KFF Health News*, September 5, 2019.

Chapter 8

Nonprofit Hospitals Are Highly Profitable

Tax Exemptions That Don't Exist

The general public are understandably confused when they enter a healthcare facility that resembles a luxury hotel and then read headlines from publications like Health Affairs that found seven of the ten most profitable hospitals in America are nonprofit hospitals.[1] That is a conflicting and odd statement, but it is relatively easy to understand by separating hospitals into three financial categories:

- Fully private hospitals that mostly function like any other business, responsible for shareholders and investors.
- Public hospitals, which are owned by state or local governments and have obligations to care for underserved populations.
- "Private nonprofit" hospitals, a category that represents more than half of the nation's hospitals.

Nearly all of the nation's most prestigious hospitals are considered nonprofits, which define the more famous medical meccas like the Mayo Clinic, Cleveland Clinic, Johns Hopkins, Mass General, and more. The nonprofit label comes from the fact that they are exempt from federal and local taxes, in exchange for providing a certain amount of "community benefit". Nonprofit hospitals have their origins in charity hospitals founded in the early 1900s. However, over the last century, they have gradually shifted from

 DOI: 10.4324/9781032630670-8

that model. Now, explosive growth within these institutions has changed the definition of "nonprofit" and which sort of responsibility these hospitals have to the communities in order to obtain this financial dispensation. Tax exemption is a gift provided by the community and should be treated as such, requiring proof that they provide tangible medical benefits for local residents.

Nonprofit hospitals are often more profitable than for-profit hospitals. If a private business doesn't have to pay taxes, its expenses will be lower. Nonprofit hospitals are defined as charitable institutions, and they can benefit from tax-free contributions from donors and bonds for capital projects – things that for-profit hospitals cannot take advantage of. The real question surrounding nonprofit hospitals is whether the benefits to the community equal what taxpayers donate to these hospitals in the form of tax-exempt status.

On paper, the average value of community benefits for all nonprofits equals the value of the tax exemption. However, there is tremendous variation among individual hospitals, with many falling short. There is also intense disagreement about how those community benefits are calculated and whether they actually serve the community in question. Charity medical care is what most people think of when it comes to a community benefit – and before 1969, that was the legal requirement for hospitals to qualify for tax-exempt status. In that year, the tax code was changed to allow for a wide range of expenses to qualify as community benefits. Charitable care became optional, and it was left up to the hospitals to decide how to pay back that debt. Hospitals could even declare that accepting Medicaid insurance was a community benefit and write off the difference between the Medicaid payment and their own calculations of cost.

Charitable Care

An analysis by Politico found that since the full Affordable Care Act coverage expansion, which brought millions more paying customers into the field, revenue in the top seven nonprofit hospitals (as ranked by U.S. News & World Report) increased by 15%, while charity care, the most tangible aspect of community benefit, decreased by 35%. Communities are often conflicted about the nonprofit hospitals in their midst.[2] Many of these institutions are enormous employers (sometimes the largest employer in town), but the economic benefits do not always trickle down to the immediate neighborhoods.

It is not unusual to see a stark contrast between these gleaming campuses and the disadvantaged neighborhoods that surround them.

In some communities, nonprofit hospitals are beloved institutions, with a history of caring for generations of families. In other communities, the sums of money devoted to lavish expansions, aggressive advertising, and eye-popping executive compensation are a source of irritation. The average chief executive's packages at nonprofit hospitals is worth $3.5 million annually. According to IRS regulations, "No part of their net earnings is allowed to inure to the benefit of any private shareholder or individual".

From 2005 to 2015, average chief executive compensation in nonprofit hospitals increased by 93%. Over that same period, pediatricians saw a 15% salary increase, while nurses got 3%.[3]

A significant number of communities believe nonprofit hospitals take more than they give back and have started to sue. The University of Pittsburgh Medical Center fought off one lawsuit from the city's mayor to revoke its tax-exempt status. In 2020, it faced another from the Pennsylvania attorney general, alleging that the medical center – valued at $20 billion – did not fulfill "its obligation as a public charity". The lawsuit was eventually dismissed. A large hospital in New Jersey lost most of its property-tax exemption, because it was found to be behaving as a for-profit institution. The judge in the case wrote that if all nonprofit hospitals operated like this, then "modern nonprofit hospitals are essentially legal fictions". Many nonprofit hospitals, especially in rural areas, struggle mightily. Scores of rural hospitals have closed, and hundreds more are teetering—leading to spikes in local death rates. At the other end are hospitals that earn several thousand dollars in profit *per patient*.[4]

Exceptions

The most profitable nonprofit hospitals tend to be part of huge health care systems, since consolidations are one of the driving forces behind the towering profits. Monopoly hospitals are known to charge more than non-monopoly hospitals. These highly profitable institutions are exempt from the taxes that pay for local roads, police services, fire protection, and 911 services. If residents should have to pay for the garbage collection for institutions that can afford multimillion-dollar salaries for top executives, is a question that is rarely answered.

Experts in the healthcare field believe that tax exemption needs to be redefined, and low-impact projects (such as community health fairs that function more like marketing) shouldn't be allowed as part of the calculation nor should things that primarily benefit the institution, like staff training. Additionally, hospitals should not be allowed to declare Medicaid "losses" as a community benefit. While Medicaid typically pays less than private insurance companies, it plays a crucial role for private insurance markets by acting as a high-risk pool for patients with severe illness and disability. Large medical centers also enthusiastically accept taxpayer money for research, something that burnishes their image and bolsters their rankings. This enthusiasm needs to be mandated to extend toward Medicaid patients and the face value of their insurance.

The IRS states that charitable hospitals "must be organized and operated exclusively for specific tax-exempt purposes". Charitable care should be treated as a priority – and spending on social determinants of health can also be a legitimate community benefit. The community that is footing the tax break needs to have a forceful say in how this money is spent, rather than leaving it solely up to the hospital. Many policy scholars have noted that tax exemption is a blunt instrument for struggling hospitals, particularly in communities with a shortage of health care resources. In medically saturated areas, where profits and executive compensation approach Wall Street levels, tax exemption should raise eyebrows.

Notes

1. Johns Hopkins, Nonprofit Hospitals Earn Substantial Profits, *Bloomberg School of Public Health*, May 2, 2016, https://publichealth.jhu.edu/2016/nonprofit-hospitals-earn-substantial-profits
2. Dan Diamond, How Hospitals Got Richer off Obamacare, *Politico*, July 17, 2017.
3. Meg Bryant, CEO Salaries at Nonprofit Hospitals up 93% since 2005, *HealthcareDive*, August 17, 2018.
4. Danielle Ofri, Why Are Nonprofit Hospitals So Highly Profitable?, *The New York Times*, February 20, 2020.

Chapter 9

Overpaid Physicians

Rating Doctors

Many states keep medical statistics publicly available regarding the mortality of patients and the names of the hospitals and doctors caring for them. However, little information is available on patient opinions relating to doctor care or their treatment by the hospital staff. Ratings of doctors' skills were almost nonexistent or very elusive until recent years, when the ubiquitous Zagat guides (known for their assortment of mostly leisure-related topics including hotels, spas, golf courses, movies, and nightlife) started to ask a selected group of patients (served by the country's largest commercial insurers) to post reviews of their doctors. They were to rate them on a thirty-point scale, as they had done for restaurants for almost forty years. The rating categories (death rates were ignored) focused on personality characteristics such as trust and communication – plus availability, office environment, and personal comments supported by patient experience.

In 2012, the University of Utah Healthcare was the first hospital in the country to begin posting its ratings. Other medical facilities that closely followed included the Cleveland Clinic, University of Pittsburgh Medical Center, Wake Forest Baptist Health, Stanford Healthcare, and Piedmont Healthcare. North Shore-LIJ Health System became the first organization to do so in the New York City metropolitan area in 2015. The North Shore site encouraged patients to rate 783 doctors on a scale of one to five stars and (as with other hospitals) only included physicians rated thirty times – the minimum to be considered as statistically significant. In general, doctors retain the right to

DOI: 10.4324/9781032630670-9

challenge comments that they consider invalid or unfair. The hospitals will not publish comments that are vulgar or include personal attacks.

Among the growing lists of websites that rank doctors is the annual publication of America's Top Doctors (fourteenth edition in 2015). Other sites include Healthgrades and RateMDs (with 1,370,000 doctors in the United States and Canada) along with the older, more versatile sites such as Yelp and Angie's List.

Doctors have considered any rating service a poor guide in comparing levels of healthcare, since they treat medical care provided by dedicated and caring physicians as if they were chefs preparing a meal. The healthcare survey is available to the millions of subscribers of Zagat's restaurant guide (also available on the internet). Rating services that focus on restaurants and hotels have practically revolutionized how the public selects their next dining experience or vacation room and may have the same effect (if enough people participated in rating their medical care experience with an objective and honest appraisal). The rankings published thus far are not very reliable, have too small a database, and are not based on objective research. Besides the Zagat review, magazines such as U.S. News and World Report publish annual rankings of both hospitals and doctors in different specialties. Nevertheless, the subject pool is limited, and the public does not seem to place as much importance on doctors' ratings as they do for restaurants. The Web is awash in reviews for hundreds of categories, but it is puzzling that there is still no authoritative collection of reviews for physicians – the choice of service with the highest stakes.

Patients commonly rate doctors. Doctors rating their patients is rare. However, an instance of this may have occurred when, right after the federal government passed universal healthcare legislation in 2010, a staunch Republican urologist in Florida placed a sign on his office door strongly suggesting that patients consider going to another doctor's office if they had voted Democratic in 2008. Civil rights law prevents discrimination based on sex or religion, but legal experts claim that political differences are not specifically protected and can legally be used for patient filtering. The actions of the doctor who sanctioned the sign refusing to see a patient for political reasons may not be ethical, but they were not illegal. The doctor then added that if a Democrat sought care with another doctor, it would be best for all concerned. The sign read: "If you voted for Obama, seek urologic care elsewhere. Changes to your healthcare begin right now—not in five years".[1]

Selecting a reliable website for a professional service rating of any kind must factor in certain characteristics for each profession or occupation. Are the reviews to be paid or unpaid, anonymous, or real time? A few sites, such as Healthgrades and RateMDs, have tried to establish a model doctor-rating system but have had little success. The RateMDs site may include many doctors in its list – but they have been sparse in substance, with few reliable and objective contributors. Several other companies have tried to collect reviews of doctors since the early days of the Web. The founder of RateMDs .com tried to use the same technique as it did with a site that included a popular "hotness" description for the successful RateMyProfessor.com, a site used by college students to rate their teachers. However, there is a big difference between a tough teacher and a competent doctor. With all these caveats, there will never be a Michelin Guide for the medical profession.

Another problem: past attempts to gather information for the previously untouchable medical professional have inevitably led to legal threats and subpoenas for the identity of negative reviewers who had posted what they thought were anonymous comments. The reviewers end up being sued. Furthermore, the ratings are too obtuse and not directly related to the actual level of healthcare provided. Instead, the ratings seem to relate to the doctors' communication skills – not his or her competence and success rate with patients. The reviewers also place too much attention on availability, office environment, and trust – but very little is directed toward medical outcomes. While it is nice to know how long different obstetricians make you wait, it would also be helpful to know how many babies they end up delivering by cesarean section and how much time they spend during a patient visit. The controversial healthcare law passed in 2011 requires Medicare to share all sorts of data about doctors, but that has led to many legal challenges. As a result, listings for doctor skills may be far off into the future.

The problem when asking friends and relatives for a reference when finding a general practitioner or specialist is that each patient is different, and the person asking for a reference may not have any idea whether the doctor is a good clinician or if he or she is board certified in the specialty for which a patient seeks treatment. Carefully selecting the best doctor and hospital by relying only on personal recommendations could add up to a useful measure of a doctor's skill or non-skill – but the patient may not know anything about whether the reviewers are people like themselves. Getting a review of the doctor's skills is too subjective to be useful, and a better method would be to use the internet to find the medical records listed by the state health department, which collects data on the success rates of both the doctor and the hospital. Of course, the best environment for a rating system is in major cities where many doctors would have few repercussions against the reviewer. In a small community, any criticism of a doctor that includes the name of the reviewer could have dire consequences. Doctors in a small town probably know the patient reviewer, and that could be a problem.

No one is as smart as all of us, and if most of the people decline to contribute to the collected knowledge about the medical community and continue to place all doctors on a pedestal, the public will eventually lose out. Not all doctors are miracle workers who are untouchable, and many of them should be exposed for their shortcomings – especially if any medical treatment has had deadly consequences.

Rating both doctors and hospitals can often provide statistics that are misleading and faulty. When a patient seeks treatment for diabetes, one hospital can show a success rate of 99% and another 80% – yet the comparison numbers lack the fact that the higher-rated hospital does not admit those over the age of eighty-five, while the lower-rated facility will take patients of any age and with other disabilities. Thus, these ratings can be used as a guide but should not be treated as the last word in selecting the best hospital and the most competent doctor. Many other factors should be considered during the selection process, including the day of admittance and the time of day for an operation. Nonetheless, the schedules are rarely noted – even though they are very important. Another useful way to research is to find out which doctor has the most malpractice suits and how they were eventually settled.

Job Requirements

Prospective brain surgeons are required to complete an undergraduate degree, earn a medical degree, complete a residency, and earn a license. They must also be board certified to become a brain surgeon:

Step 1: Earn a Bachelor's Degree

Brain surgeons are not required to earn a particular undergraduate degree. However, medical school admissions boards look for individuals with strong science coursework in biology, chemistry, math, and physics. Additionally, aspiring doctors are expected to round out their undergraduate coursework

Table 9.1 Common Requirements for a Brain Surgeon

	Common Requirements
Degree Level	Bachelor's degree with science coursework; medical graduate degree*
Degree Field	Any undergraduate degree; medical degree required*
Experience	Typically, seven years of residency***
Licensure and Certification	Must pass a national exam and obtain a state license; certification offered by the American Board of Medical Specialties*
Key Skills	Manual dexterity, physical stamina, strong verbal and written communication, problem-solving skills, empathy, attention to detail*
Computer Skills	Knowledge of medical software required to manage patients' charts**

Sources:
**U.S. Bureau of Labor Statistics*
***New England Journal of Medicine*
****American Board of Neurological Surgery*

with courses in English and social sciences. Coursework should prepare students for the Medical College Admissions Test (MCAT), which measures a person's knowledge of physical and biological science, verbal reasoning, and cognitive skills.

Step 2: Earn a Medical Degree

In the first two years of medical school, students learn the fundamentals of medicine through science courses on topics such as psychiatry, pharmacology, and gastroenterology. Students take courses in problem-solving and patient care. In the latter two years of the program, students typically work in clinical settings – completing rotations in areas of medicine, including surgery and neurology. Students may also have the choice of completing a neurosurgical clerkship.

Step 3: Complete a Residency

A neurosurgical residency usually lasts seven years. During this time, residents gain experience working in emergency medicine, elective surgery, and pediatric and adult surgery. They also can work in other areas of the neurological system, such as the spinal column and the extremities. Residents learn more about neuroradiology and neuropathology and may be required to complete a research project. They also might gain experience in working with special populations, including children and senior citizens.

Bonus: Complete a fellowship. Brain surgery is a specialty area of neurosurgery, and participating in a fellowship can help brain surgeons gain valuable experience specifically with maladies of the brain. Fellowships may focus on strokes, epilepsy, brain tumors, and pediatrics.

Step 4: Obtain a Medical License

For engaging in the practice of medicine, all doctors must have a license from a state board. The details of licensing requirements vary by state, but they all require that doctors submit proof of training and pass all three parts of the United States Medical Licensing Examination (USMLE). Students generally take part three of the exam during the first or second year of residency.

Step 5: Become Board Certified

Doctors who work as brain surgeons can become voluntarily certified by the American Board of Neurological Surgery. To be eligible for certification, they must complete an application, submit proof of residency verified by the program director, and successfully pass a written and oral exam. Certifications must be renewed every ten years.

Step 6: Earn Continuing Education Credits

To maintain certification status, brain surgeons must participate in the Maintenance of Certification (MOC) program implemented by the American Board of Medical Specialties. This four-step process integrates patient care, communication skills, professionalism, medical knowledge, and practice-based and systems-based learning skills. The ten-year process consists of three mini-cycles and culminates in an exam during the tenth year.

Website Rates Top Surgeons

A nonprofit group developed a free surgeon-rating service, www.surgeon-rating.org, allowing consumers to type in a ZIP code and search for the top-performing surgeons in fourteen areas of major surgery. Some of the medical categories include heart valve and bypass surgery, total knee and hip replacement, gastric (stomach), hernia, and spinal fusion surgery. Ratings are based on an analysis of federal government records and more than four million surgeries performed by more than 50,000 doctors. By using star ratings (five stars being the best), the service identifies surgeons who have better-than-average performances based on three criteria:

- Death rates
- Other bad outcomes, such as infections, falls, and complications resulting in longer hospital stays or readmission
- Recommendations by other doctors

The website allows consumers to select a type of surgery after typing in a ZIP code and then search for the performing physicians as far away as 500 miles. Once a physician is listed, consumers can also select which doctors they want to compare. The profile on the site will also show the doctors' board certification, education, and any special training. The information will include the performance at the hospital where the surgeries are done. Some surgeons may not be listed because the website only includes doctors who have performed enough surgeries to provide statistically meaningful comparisons. To ensure a good track record is not the result of luck alone, any surgeon who receives a five-star rating means the rating service provider is 97.5% sure that the surgeon is better than the average U.S. surgeon.

The ratings included top doctor specialists in more than fifty metropolitan regions and another rating for more than 5,400 acute care hospitals. Surgeons' results are adjusted to consider how frail or sick their patients were. For heart valve and heart bypass surgery, the patients of the best-performing one-tenth of surgeons had death rates of less than 3% in the hospital or within thirty days of discharge – compared to death rates of more than 11% for patients of the worst-performing one-tenth of surgeons. The rating does not always consider the fact that some hospitals and surgeons will not operate on patients older than a certain age or with a debilitating illness – which would give these institutions a higher rating than hospitals that perform surgery on high-risk patients.

Board-Certified Physician Specialists

In order to practice medicine, a physician must have graduated from medical school, fulfilled applicable residency requirements, and been approved by the state's official medical board. With board certification, these same general eligibility requirements apply – but the physician must also meet additional training requirements, complete a thorough application process, and pass standardized examinations. In short, board certification is intended to be a rigorous process, signifying the physician has obtained expertise in the same field of medicine.

It is important to note that not all physicians are board certified in the specialties they practice. Therefore, it is always important for patients to research the credentials of a physician in all specialty areas:

While board certification is not required to practice medicine, it is a valuable qualification for determining the expertise and experience of a physician in a particular field of medicine. Every physician is required to be licensed to practice medicine in the state they work. Board certification is an extra step a physician may take to assure a patient of their specialty training. There are specific benefits to board certification that extend beyond the credential. At the American Board of Physician Specialties® (ABPS), for example, the members have the necessary resources to stay up-to-date within their specialties to continue their competency in the medical field. Furthermore, the learning doesn't stop when a physician becomes board

Table 9.2 Training Requirements for Physician Specialties

Allergy and Immunology	*Anesthesiology*	*Family Medicine*
Dermatology	Emergency Medicine	Family Medicine
Internal Medicine	Medical Genetics	Genomics
Neurological Surgery	Neurology	Pathology
Obstetrics and Gynecology	Nuclear Medicine	Pediatrics
Ophthalmology	Orthopedic Surgery	Preventive Medicine
Otolaryngology–Neck Surgery	Colon and Rectal Surgery	General Surgery
Physical Medicine/Rehabilitation	Plastic Surgery	
Psychiatry	Radiology Surgery	
Thoracic Surgery	Urology	

certified – no matter their qualifications. ABPS board certified physicians are required to recertify after a set number of years. During each recertification process, ABPS reviews the physicians' credentials and administers tests to assure that the physician still demonstrates exemplary knowledge and mastery within their field of certification.

While specialists have completed advanced education and clinical training in one of the specific areas that require certification, it is not always easy for a specialist in one field to treat patients with an illness that falls into another area of medical specialty. Panels of professionals who make up individual boards that grant certification are very protective that specialists maintain a high degree of integrity and are fully aware of advancements in their particular field of expertise. In 2013, a controversy arose within the American Board of Obstetricians and Gynecologists when they withdrew the certification of a member because the doctor had treated a male patient for a sexually transmitted infection and screened other men for anal cancer. The policy of the board was that gynecologists would lose their board certification if they treated men, regardless of the circumstances. The board defended its decision by claiming its action was to protect the profession as a female specialty and limit the non-gynecological work performed by its members.

Screening men who were at high risk for anal cancer was not permitted, and the threat of losing their certification forced some gynecologists to find colleagues in other specialties who were willing to track those who were enrolled in studies of HIV-infected patients. Similar to cervical cancer, anal cancer is caused by a virus that is sexually transmitted and is closely associated with patients who have a form of HIV. Patient advocacy groups felt the prohibition would interfere with research and make it harder for male patients to accumulate screening data so that they might receive proper treatment for the anal cavity.[2]

The board finally reversed its original decision and agreed that the gynecologist had a long tradition of treating sexually transmitted infections in both men and women and that the disease of anal cancer involved techniques adapted from those used to screen women for cervical cancer. They were, therefore, well-qualified to treat precancerous lesions in the anus since it fell into that category.

The American Board of Obstetricians and Gynecologists is not the only organization that oversees the work of a gynecologist – and recently, the U.S. Food and Drug Administration warned that a popular surgical device used to remove common benign uterine growths, known as fibroids, could spread cancerous cells. The device is a laparoscopic power morcellator that is used an estimated 50,000 times a year – but many hospitals and doctors stopped using it, and some regional insurers stopped covering its use. Many gynecologists resisted the FDA warning by claiming that the risks are unknown, and the warning was overblown. Lastly, the doctors contended that the government should not interfere with patient treatment.

This is a typical instance of the long dispute between the medical profession, the government, and insurance companies that have interfered in medical treatment without knowing all the facts. Insurance agents often force doctors to use generic drugs instead of the prescribed drug. Even though the federal government has the authority to regulate pharmaceuticals and medical devices, it does not have the authority to oversee the practice of medicine – where doctors should retain their wide latitude.

Patient Costs Soar – Specialists' Incomes Skyrocket

In a country where the top hospital executives typically make more than a million a year, American physicians may feel entitled to high fees. They face costs that their European counterparts do not. For example, medical schools in the United States or Caribbean Islands are expensive, and new doctors graduate with an average debt of $150,000. After, they have to spend years training in a low-salary environment. Additionally, many specialists pay malpractice premiums of more than $100,000 a year, in addition to society dues to cover the more than 750 lobbyists who represent groups of health professionals in Washington. Such lobbyists make sure that any effort by Congress to limit the specialists' income is discouraged. As expected, specialists who perform delicate medical procedures, such as the gynecologist's controversy noted above, command the highest income among doctors. Their income goes from about $200,000 for pediatrics and internal medicine to more than a million for orthopedic surgery. Very few specialists in America make less than half a million dollars a year in income, even those who work full time for a hospital.

The incomes of dermatologists, gastroenterologists, and oncologists rose 50% or more between 1995 and 2012, while those for doctors in primary care rose 10% – mainly because insurers pay far less for traditional doctoring tasks (such as listening to a heart murmur or prescribing an antibiotic).[3] Primary care doctors make up only 25% of practicing physicians, and that percentage is decreasing since newly ordained physicians realize that specialists earn an average of two to four times as much as primary care physicians – a differential that far surpasses that in other countries.[4] There are many cases in which a hospital charged $500 for the five-minute removal of a wart that was done by the specialist rather than the emergency room doctor. In contrast, in Germany, where the government sets private doctors' allowable charges, dermatologists are paid $30 for a whole-body skin check, $40 for a standard biopsy, and $20 for a pathology exam.

Often, little correlation exists between compensation and the investment of time in treating a patient. Some specialists fall into a category called the "lifestyle specialties" because their training is more compatible with home life than what occurs in other disciplines. They also encounter fewer emergencies. About 80% of dermatologists see patients for forty hours or fewer each week, which is not true for many other specialty areas of healthcare. For example, urologists generally make about 50% of their income from dealing with patients and the rest from investing in the machines that deliver radiation for prostate cancer or to treat kidney stones. In 2014, a urologist's average income can be about $420,000 before investment income.

Brain surgeons operate on the brain to treat problems such as bleeding and hemorrhaging, tumors, infections, or tissue and nerve damage. They also treat symptoms of brain diseases. Brain surgeons are trained in neurosurgery and likely will have the necessary training to operate on the spinal column as well. These surgeons work in hospitals and are on their feet a good deal – especially when they are performing surgery. The U.S. Bureau of Labor Statistics reported that these medical professionals earned a substantial median annual salary of $239,200 in 2023.[5] However, they are expected to work long hours and be on call for medical emergencies. They also must deal with the stress of having someone's life in their hands when they operate.

Some Doctors Collected $10 Million (Medicare)

In recent years, according to federal data, an average of ten doctors received more than $10 million in reimbursements for services billed to Medicare. These millionaire physicians range from ophthalmologists (who routinely submit claims for specialized high-cost drug treatments) to pathologists (who bill the government's public insurance program for seniors for thousands of clinical tests performed in their laboratories). Among the 880,644 physicians in the United States, most of these healthcare practitioners billed Medicare and collected an average annual reimbursement of $87,883, with more than 2,000 of these providers receiving more than $2 million in Medicare receipts. Among doctors who bill Medicare, the highest-paid 2% accounted for almost one-quarter of total Medicare payments.

Medicare Payments to Physicians by Top Specialty

Doctors Cure People – Even Those Who Are Not Sick

A report recently found that over one in five coronary stents placed between 2019 and 2021 were unnecessary, costing Medicare $800 million a year and putting patients at risk of complications like stroke, heart attack, and death. An unnecessary coronary stent is inserted into a U.S. patient every seven minutes, costing Medicare upwards of $2.44 billion in unnecessary stent procedures, according to a report by the Lown Institute, an independent research firm. The report looked at over 1,700 general hospitals nationwide and found more than 229,000 procedures were nonessential, estimating over 20% of stents were placed unnecessarily across the three-year period.[6]

A prominent Baltimore hospital notified hundreds of former patients that a cardiologist on its staff might have given them unnecessary coronary stents.[7] Many of these patients then sued the hospital because they claimed the implants may have threatened their health. The same cardiologist sued the hospital for damaging his reputation by making false claims about his care. While litigation over these suits proceeded through the courts, the hospital agreed to a $22 million fine to settle a federal investigation overpaying

Table 9.3 Medicare Reimbursement by Physician Specialty

1. Internal Medicine	$7.8 Million	6. Cardiology	$3.9 Million
2. Ophthalmology	$7.3 Million	7. Orthopedic Surgery	$3.1 Million
3. Hematology/Oncology	$6.4 Million	8. Physical Rehabilitation	$3.0 Million
4. Family Practice	$5.0 Million	9. Dermatology	$2.8 Million
5. Diagnostic Radiology	$4.1 Million	10. Rheumatology	$2.5 Million

Statista, Medicare payments to physicians in 2021, by top specialties, https://www.statista.com/statistics/298467/physicians-medicare-collections/

illegal kickbacks to the busy cardiologist's medical practice. The hospital did not admit liability but paid the fine to avoid the expense and uncertainty of litigation. The future survival of the hospital remains uncertain.[8]

The same Baltimore cardiologist first attracted the attention of Senate investigators when it was discovered that he had inserted stents in thirty patients in a single day. In addition to the record-breaking day, that same doctor had implanted 585 stents between 2007 and 2009 that were considered medically unnecessary, based on an analysis made by the hospital. Medicare had paid $3.8 million of the $6.6 million charged for those questionable procedures. Stent insertions probably represent the biggest profit center for many hospitals, which would explain why hospital executives throughout the nation rarely question the unusually high number of stent operations performed by staff physicians. They generally celebrate doctors who can insert a large number of stents in a day, because the revenue they bring in can easily exceed $10,000 per procedure – or $300,000 from a single cardiologist on the record-setting day.[9]

The Baltimore situation is far from unique – and prosecutors, malpractice lawyers, and state medical boards have started to recognize the serious problem of stents prescribed far too often. More than one in five coronary stents doctors placed in Medicare patients from 2019 through 2022 weren't needed; and they cost the federal health program and beneficiaries about $2.4 billion, according to the analysis by the Lown Institute, a nonprofit think tank.[10] In many cases, patients would be better off either with major bypass heart surgery or with drugs alone. Cardiology is a lucrative business for hospitals, and the profits from testing and performing heart surgeries can play a critical role in a hospital's bottom line. Many of the nation's 40,000+ hospitals that use stent procedures thousands of times a year will collect about $10,000 for a cardiac stent and about $3,000 for a diagnostic catheterization. It is not that unusual for some patients to have been given up to ten stents within a few years. In many cases, those fees can account for 35% of the hospital's net profit.

Greed History #1: The U.S. Justice Department regulators announced in early 2013 that a community hospital in Ohio agreed to a settlement of $4 million for allowing a group of doctors to perform unnecessary angioplasties that were medically unnecessary. The group of cardiologists in a private practice agreed to pay an additional $540,000.[11] Medicare patients had been receiving angioplasties at a rate of four times the national average, a figure that prompted questions from insurers and raised concerns about overtreatment. The investigation began after receiving a whistleblower's complaint that alerted the government about how doctors urged nurses at the Ohio hospital to falsify the unnecessary stent procedures and then forced patients to come back for multiple treatments – the whistleblower received $660,000 from the settlement.

Greed History #2: Other physician groups (besides cardiologists) are also known to have regularly steered patients to the most lucrative treatment, depriving patients of the full range of treatment choices – including potentially no treatment at all. Patients are often unaware that their doctors stood to profit from a particular test or medical procedure, and the same pattern was found when doctors owned the imaging centers that billed Medicare for unnecessary CT scans and magnetic resonance imaging. A report issued by the Government Accountability Office, using information provided by congressional investigators, found that doctors who have a financial interest in radiation treatment centers are much more likely to prescribe this type of treatment for patients with prostate cancer.[12]

Because of actions such as those described above, doctors are facing a high level of scrutiny due to billing, unwanted tests, and new health laws concerning the acceptance of expensive gifts they receive from pharmaceutical and medical-device manufacturers. Starting in mid-2013, companies in the healthcare field must record every transaction with doctors – from sales reps bearing pizza to compensation for expert advice on research – to comply with the Sunshine Act provision of the U.S. healthcare overhaul. Doctors fear that the public will misinterpret the information and view the payments as tainting medical decisions.

Pharmaceutical companies collectively pay hundreds of millions of dollars in fees and gifts to doctors every year. The payments can be for participating as a consultant member of the company research and development team for tests on new drugs or designing new medical procedures. Some doctors earn more than $50,000 a year for speaking at conferences sponsored by manufacturers. However, under the added scrutiny, doctors will be reluctant to continue in this gray area that has grown to be a major income provider that supplements their normal outrageous fees charged to a patient in their general practice.

Doctors Fall Off Their Pedestal

As found in every occupation and profession, there is a strict and traditional adherence to a specific chain of command. Generals order captains around, captains are above lieutenants, and so forth. Executives dictate to the office staff, and managers have more authority than their working staff. However, the MD designation holds a unique place in the pecking order – ever since the medical profession used leeches to cure illnesses many centuries ago. That special position affords a physician a distinct place within the hospital chain of command – which has turned them into an almost untouchable, God-like figure. Doctors are revenue-producing staff members, and they represent the very reason that a healthcare facility even exists. Sometimes these amazing men and women of medical science make mistakes, causing serious injuries to patients. Nonetheless, the hospital administration rarely initiates any action against these self-anointed "untouchables", regardless of the infraction or the dire consequences of their actions – even if the whistle-blower is a respected staff member, such as the Director of Nursing.

Studies today have compiled some surprising statistics on physician abuse and distrust. Distrust of physicians is believed to be the number one cause of this violent attitude. Few physicians are killed by patients, although thousands are attacked and injured – not always in the emergency room or psychiatric wards. One well-publicized event took place in 2010 at Johns Hopkins Hospital, where the son of an elderly mother, who was in a bed in a regular hospital room, was told that his mother could no longer be saved. He then took out a gun and shot his mother, the doctor, and finally himself. That event caused many of the nation's hospitals to re-evaluate how they treat weapons and how to get a response from law enforcement officials when such a weapon threat is discovered. There are few ways to prevent a gun from being brought into the hospital facility, but there should be procedures in place to get the police involved. The two main causes of patients attacking the physician include:

- Blaming the physician for prescribing inadequate care to a close relative.
- Angry visitors who feel the physician did not support their compensation claim.

Violent confrontations against doctors by patients occur frequently in medical facility – and after each incident, the nation's medical facilities react by instituting new security procedures that are more to satisfy the accreditation authorities than for any practical reasons. After that doctor was killed in Baltimore in 2010, it caused procedures to be revised, and special training programs were established to teach the medical and security staffs how to react to a violent individual and how to report such situations to police authorities.

Violence against medical staff is only a minor infraction in the United States, but it is a major source of contention in a Mexican city only a few miles from El Paso, Texas – where doctors are routinely kidnapped and killed on an almost daily basis. In the Mexican town of Juarez, doctors have become prime targets for violent gangs, as their middle-class status has made them vulnerable to kidnappers and extortion demands. Between 2006 and 2010, approximately half of the 2,000 physicians practicing medicine have fled the city, while medical-assistance missions have drastically scaled back in the city of 1.3 million. A growing number of doctors live across the border in El Paso and commute to Mexico to practice medicine, since they do not have a U.S. license. Violence in the city claimed 3,000 lives in 2009 and has hit physicians especially hard (with four doctors killed and at least fifteen kidnapped that same year). Hospitals and clinics have been declared "high-risk zones" since criminal gangs raid the facilities on a regular basis to finish off their wounded rivals. They will blame doctors if patients do not recover and then kidnap the doctors for ransoms – potentially killing them if the ransom is not paid.[13]

Prior to the onset of the violence usually caused by drug traffickers, doctors were collecting huge fees – due to the large number of obese patients from the United States who would visit the clinics in Juarez for inexpensive gastric bypass surgeries and other medical procedures that cost patients about one-tenth the cost if performed in an American facility. The Mexican doctors' incomes have all but disappeared, since no one will cross the border with all the gang warfare. The medical staff are now treating people with gunshot wounds who refuse to pay – and there is little the doctors can do to enforce payment. There are now collection agencies in Juarez, but they have been mostly ineffective.

Relatives of the patients often carry guns into medical facilities, since the hospital security staff is almost nonexistent. The guard force is limited to asking for credentials and will not confront the armed gangs. Doctors no longer wear name tags and have formed their own associations to train the medical staff on topics dealing with kidnapping survival techniques. While Mexican doctors have a problem with potential violence, their American counterparts have their own problems with Mexican patients.

American Doctors under Attack – Online

Patients who post comments on the internet are scrutinizing the medical profession, much in the way customers have done by reviewing restaurants, movies, and resorts since the early 90s. A survey conducted in 2014 by a state medical society showed that nearly one in five physicians had a negative review, while only 5% said that their society had a policy to respond to such reviews. Several websites exist, such as Yelp.com, where people can make comments – and this has spawned an entire cottage industry.[14] Medical journals now carry numerous ads promising to build up a physician's online image, and some consultants offer media advice on methods to counteract the poor reviews. Dentists and medical doctors are now polling patients and then posting the results, since there is no practical way to make every patient happy. The way to overcome a negative review is to get a positive one. One starkly critical comment can be harmful, but one negative review out of one hundred is harmless.

The emergence of online comments has also created a new front for litigators, and physicians file a growing number of lawsuits against patients over negative online comments. Most patients back down when threatened by a suit – but in the few cases that go to trial, the court always rules for the patients and their argument of protected free speech. One of the more publicized cases involved a dentist who had insisted patients sign an agreement promising not to make disparaging online comments. When a patient puts critical remarks online anyway, both the dentist and patient end up filing suits against each other – resulting in the dentist losing money to attorney fees, while the patient gets new cavities. The use of online comments does not benefit either the patient or the medical professional, and the negative opinion would serve a better purpose if the patients voiced their comments while still in the dentist or doctors' office.

Some Doctors Are Not Overpaid

With skyrocketing medical costs and stories about doctors' salaries and how some are ripping off Medicare and other medical insurance firms, the public may believe that much of the health costs in America can be traced to the exorbitantly high fees collected by physicians and the medical profession in general. A 2014 survey by the Medical Group Management Association found that internal medicine doctors had a starting salary of $190,000, while an anesthesiologist's salary approached $300,000. The numbers substantiate the fact that U.S. physician salaries were twice as much as those in countries such as France, and that the high pay was a significant reason the United States spends more per person on healthcare than any other developed country.

U.S. doctors defend their salary structure by claiming that a more useful comparison than foreign physicians' salaries is to compare their compensation to other U.S. occupations in the top 5% income bracket. The talent pool that supplies doctors also produces other high earners: business executives and lawyers. This guidepost found that U.S. physicians were less well-paid than non-U.S. doctors, relative to their high-earning peers who are less educated than the average physician. Besides the undergraduate degree, there is the four-year tuition to a private U.S. medical school (about $300,000), and physicians must complete a three to seven-year residency before they can practice independently.

Economists who specialize in the healthcare field found that physicians' salaries constitute only 10% of healthcare costs, and slashing physicians' salaries by as much as half would result in a 5% saving. Another factor to be considered when analyzing medical costs is that administrators and executives in the hospital and insurance sectors take 20–30% of healthcare's overall cost. The average CEO health insurer's base pay was $590,000, and for a hospital administrator, it was $240,000.[15]

Those attempting to bring the earnings of U.S. doctors in line with those of Europe must also offer government-subsidized medical education and malpractice systems that many European nations enjoy. The best way to lower healthcare costs is to eliminate wasteful spending, have better oversight by the government in handling Medicare billing, and control the outrageously high administrative overhead.

Future Doctor Shortage

According to the doctor-friendly Association of American Medical Colleges, there will be an imminent shortage of 130,000 physicians (in all specialties) by 2030 or even sooner. This dire prediction also cautions that the shortage will drive up wait times, shorten office visits, and make it harder for Americans to access the proper care for their illnesses. The warning was based on two major factors: (1) the aging population, since the proportion of Americans who are sixty-five and older will increase to 19% in 2030 from the current 13% and (2) Obamacare, which will be insuring thirty million more Americans by 2024, even factoring in Republican efforts to repeal and defund it, during the Trump presidency.

A more realistic assessment seems to indicate that a potential shortage is overblown, and warnings of waiting lines and improper treatment are more a scare tactic rather than a scientifically based conclusion. While the population is aging fast, the methods of treating illnesses in old age are also changing quickly – and more patients can be cared for in sub-acute settings rather than in hospitals. Furthermore, new technologies mean treatment of many medical conditions require fewer medical-related resources, so fewer doctors are needed to prescribe remedies and perform operations. Drugs and devices can also obviate the need for costly treatments – many of which would normally require a hospital stay.

Another trend that shortens treatment is the minimizing of more invasive procedures. The average patient staying in a hospital in 2017 was about two days or less following a stent or even a more serious heart bypass operation, compared to around seven days in 2012 following a bypass. Research on radiation treatments for breast cancer care indicates that fifteen treatments can be just as effective as the traditional thirty treatments. Also, one larger dose of radiation can be as good at relieving pain from bone metastases as five to ten separate, smaller sessions with an attending physician.

Other medical personnel can have their roles expanded to alleviate the burden on a doctor's time – such as nurse practitioners, health aids, pharmacists, dietitians, psychologists, and others already providing care for patients in numerous ways. Skilled health aides can monitor patients at home and alert a doctor if certain medical signs decline. Pharmacists can provide more counseling and urgent care. All these healthcare aides will not eliminate the need for a proper diagnosis by a physician, but they will back up the decision by a team who will help manage the more routine features of chronic illnesses. Instead of building more medical schools and expanding the nation's doctor pool, it would be more effective if the productivity of a physician was increased, while incorporating new technologies and practices that make care more accessible and less expensive than it is today.

The Association of American Medical Colleges issued a report in 2024, which projected that by 2036 there would be a shortfall of up to 86,000 physicians in the United States.[16] Obamacare alone is projected to require 16,000 more doctors than would have been required without it. This dire prediction is based on the fact that the United States has fewer practicing physicians per 1,000 people than twenty-three out of the twenty-eight countries that report data on the ratio of doctors to population:

Lowest Ratio of Doctors per 1,000 People	Highest Ratio of Doctors per 1,000 People
America: 2.56	Austria: 4.99
Canada: 2.46	Norway: 4.31
Poland: 2.24	Sweden: 4.12
South Korea: 2.17	Germany: 4.04
Mexico: 2.17	Switzerland: 4.04

Chinese Doctors under Physical Attack

American doctors are criticized for high fees and malpractice and are often attacked in court during a lawsuit initiated by a patient, but they are rarely physically attacked as doctors are in other countries (such as China). Chinese hospitals have become dangerous places for a doctor to practice medicine. In 2022, the country's China Judgment Online System provided statistics on hospital violence that included attacks by patients or their relatives. The number of cases of hospital violence gradually increased from 2013 to a peak in 2016 before gradually decreasing in the following years. The most common perpetrators were patients' relatives (58.2%), followed by patients themselves (38.2%).[17] Pediatricians are injured after leaping out of upper stories of hospitals, attempting to escape angry relatives of a newborn who had died under their care. In 2007, 2,000 people rioted at a hospital in one of China's major cities after reports that a three-year-old was refused treatment – because the grandfather could not pay the $82 upfront fee. As a result, the child died.[18] Such episodes are, to some extent, a standard operating procedure in the world's most populous nation. Protests covering a wide range of issues have continued to rise and could threaten the power structure of the communist nation in the future if the trend continues.

Three out of every four Chinese have health insurance, although the coverage is for very basic healthcare – considered the bare minimum by the World Health Organization, which ranked China's health system as one of the world's most inequitable (188th among the 191 nations surveyed).

Almost half the nation's doctors have no more than a high school degree, according to the Organization for Economic Cooperation and Development. Many doctors in remote rural villages did not make it past junior high school – and this lack of medical education may explain why so many of that nation's doctors appear as unhappy as their patients and often complain that they are underpaid, undervalued, and mistrusted. One in four suffers from depression, and fewer than two out of every three believe that their patients respect them. Their public image is far removed from the "pedestal position" that most American doctors still enjoy.[19]

The Chinese Ministry of Public Security issued guidelines in 2013 recommending that the number of security guards in each hospital be at least one per twenty patient beds, or no less than 3% of the medical staff. The guidelines also called for alarm buttons, security doors, scanning equipment to detect weapons, camera surveillance, and foot patrols. Besides the increased hardware, authorities requested better mediation of medical disputes and more patient education. Anger is often compounded by the need to pay bribes to guarantee good service and to supplement doctors' usually low wages. If the patient dies after the doctor accepts a bribe, a good possibility exists that the patient's relatives will attack or even kill the doctor.[20]

In 2012, more than one hundred doctors and nurses in a major Chinese province staged a sit-in after the hospital paid $31,000 to the family of a patient who died. The doctors were upset because after the patient died, relatives took a doctor hostage – setting off a bottle-throwing melee that injured five of the medical staff. Many of China's medical centers have placed police officers at their entrances alongside the regular security staff, specifically to protect the doctors from the patients. The situation facing doctors in China may be dangerous, but it is not as deadly as what doctors face in northern Mexican border towns since the drug wars started in 2005.[21]

Notes

1. Stephen Hudak, Doctor Advises Obama Voters to '"Seek Care Elsewhere," *Los Angeles Times*, April 4, 2010.
2. Denise Grady, Gynecologists Run Afoul of Panel When Patient Is Male, *The New York Times*, November 22, 2013.
3. National Library of Medicine, Training physicians for the future US Health Care System, June 2014.
4. Association of American Medical Colleges, New AAMC Report Shows Continuing Projected Physician Shortage, March 21, 2024.

5. U.S. Bureau of Labor Statistics, Healthcare Occupations, https://www.bls.gov/ooh/healthcare/home.htm.
6. Arianna Johnson, Taxpayers Spent Over $800 Million For Unnecessary Coronary Stents a Year, Report Finds, *Forbes*, November 2023.
7. CBS News, $37 Million Settlement Reached in Unnecessary Heart Stent Case, April 7, 2014.
8. US Department of Justice, Office of Public Affairs, St. Joseph Medical Center in Maryland to Pay U.S. $22 Million to Resolve False Claims Act Allegations, November 9, 2010.
9. Gardiner Harris, Doctor Faces Suits Over Cardiac Stents, *The New York Times*, December 2010.
10. USA Today, Once every seven minutes, a Medicare patient gets a coronary stent they don't need, report says. Portrait of Ken Alltucker, October 31, 2023.
11. The Federal Bureau of Investigation website, EMH Regional Medical Center and North Ohio Heart Center to Pay U.S. $4.4 Million to Resolve False Claims Act Allegations, U.S. Department of Justice, January 07, 2013.
12. Robert Pear, Doctors Who Profit From Radiation Prescribe It More Often, Study Finds, *The New York Times*, August 18, 2013.
13. Steven Fisher, We Need More Protection: Violence in Rural Mexico Ensnares Doctors, *The New York Times*, June 2022.
14. Charles Ornstein, Doctors Fire Back at Bad Yelp Reviews and Reveal Patient's Information Online, *The Washington Post*, June 2026.
15. Timothy B. Norbeck, Drivers of Health Care Costs: A Physicians Foundation White Paper - First of a Three-Part Series, *Missouri Medicine*, 2013 January–February; 110(1): 30–34.
16. Association of American Medical Colleges, New AAMC Report Shows Continuing Projected Physician Shortage, March 21, 2024.
17. Yu Xiao, Ting-ting Chen, Shao-yi Zhu, Ling Zong, Na Du, Chun-ya Li, Hao-fei Cheng, 1 Qi Zhou, Li-shi Luo, and Juan Jia, Workplace Violence Against Chinese Health Professionals 2013–2021: A Study of National Criminal Judgment Documents, *Front Public Health*, October 2022, PMID: 36339236.
18. NBC News, What Chinese hospitals need most: Police?, Sharon LaFraniere, August 2010.
19. Sharon LaFraniere, Chinese Hospitals Are Battlegrounds for Discontent, *The New York Times*, August 2010.
20. Calum MacLeod, China Trying to Stop Patients from Killing Doctors, *USA Today*, October 2013.
21. Laura Zhou, Doctors and Nurses Stage Protest in Northern China, Demanding Justice after Grieving Family Beats Up Colleagues, *South China Morning Post*, December 2015.

Chapter 10

Safe Healthcare – Unattainable Goal

Mandatory and Voluntary Standards

Certain states have enacted laws – California being the first – requiring healthcare facilities to annually review existing security and safety assessment plans to ensure patients and staff do not become victims of acts of aggression and violence. These events are usually found in the emergency room but can take place anywhere in a facility. The current plans far exceed those of the Joint Commission of Healthcare Organizations' (JCAHO) set of basic standards, since they are mandatory under state law – not suggested under JCAHO regulations. Not adhering to JCAHO rules can affect accreditation, and ignoring state laws can get hospital personnel indicted.

An important aspect of the state rules is the training of security personnel, with a strong emphasis on the emergency room – as it is often a high-profile entry point for people with mental and physical problems. As part of the training, hospitals will have to collaborate with local lawenforcement agencies and determine the crime index that lists the number of murders, burglaries, and other neighborhood criminal activities surrounding the hospital.

The guidelines in the plan review will require security directors to carefully evaluate the credentials of the individual making the security assessment, since that person will not always be assigned or selected by the director. Typically, the plan will be assigned in-house, though it may be assigned to an outside security consultant. The security consultant should

DOI: 10.4324/9781032630670-10

possess one of three certifications, plus a degree in engineering or one of the disciplines in a criminal justice program. Having been employed in law enforcement (police, FBI, etc.) is valuable, but without any additional certification, the background of having worked in the criminal justice system is not adequate in itself. The certifications are an important indicator that the consultant has been involved in other hospital studies and understands the value of the certification.

- CPP – Certified Protection Professional, from ASIS International.
- CHPA – Certified Healthcare Protection Administrator, from the International Association for Healthcare Safety and Security.

In compliance with the state laws for security assessment and planning, certain steps have to be met to fulfill the requirements:

- Request funding for the outside consultant every three years and have the in-house security director develop the plans in the interim two years.
- Establish a safety committee and upgrade the membership continually.
- Get senior management approval of the plan and make periodic reports during the preparation process.

- Update training and offer classes frequently.
- Emphasize the operation of the physical security system and have a report prepared on the need to expand and upgrade the system(s) in the following areas:
  - Access Control (Are the card readers becoming obsolete, or has the system reached saturation?)
  - CCTV Surveillance–describe the upgrade to digital communication from analog systems.
- Upgrade emergency room security controls.
- Expand the existing exit-door locking system and the infant protection system.

Medical Response Plans

If a hospital has the foresight to develop emergency plans, they better follow the plans when the occasion arises – or they will be exposed to possible lawsuits for any injuries that may occur after an emergency situation arises and the hospital fails to provide a proper response. Ignoring a plan (ill-conceived or not) would be a costly error since ignoring the suggestions and recommendations of an outside security consultant can be used in an eventual court action after a tragedy occurs that was described in the plan.

Sometimes a hospital would be better served if they had not sought out the services and the recommendations of a consultant, as illustrated in the controversy surrounding a 2005 court decision on the lawsuits started after the 1993 garage bombing of the World Trade Center. In that situation, the Port Authority of New York and New Jersey was fined for damages to tenant property, because they admitted to having ignored recommendations made by a consultant they had hired to mitigate damages from any outside attacks. The costly litigation took more than twelve years, and the legal fees during that period were more than $5 million to cover the cost of depositions and testimonies.

Many hospitals have a radioactive machine called a cesium-137 blood irradiator, which uses a radioactive isotope to sterilize blood. The machine is mounted in conformance with safeguard regulations monitored by the National Nuclear Security Administration (NNSA). The big concern is keeping the radioactive material from falling into the wrong hands and potentially being used to make a "radiological-dispersal device", also known as a dirty bomb. There are dangers when the device is left in a place where many people could be exposed to its radiation. Exposure to cesium-137 could be lethal in a matter of minutes – depending on proximity and the extent of exposure.

Few outside of the medical community have heard of the radiological-dispersal device, since it is hidden in the dark recesses of the hospital building. It becomes a serious problem when a medical facility closes – as the NNSA must remove the unit by unbolting the 4,000-pound, lead-lined piece of equipment, placing the machine inside an eight-foot-tall hazardous-materials cylinder, and then load it onto a tractor trailer. Before setting off on the journey, the trailer is flanked by federal escort vehicles with armed guards to ensure that the material does not fall into terrorists' hands before it reaches the storage area in a secret location, somewhere in the southwestern part of the country.

Setting Stricter Standards

Installing a security system acceptable to all concerned parties in a hospital environment should be considered a fantasy – regardless of the many well-intentioned regulations, codes, and other oversight conditions mandated by various governmental and healthcare sanctioning agencies. Hospital requirements frequently change due to "cookie-cutter" type solutions and often become obsolete or cannot be expanded to incorporate building expansion, while meeting the ever-present threat of terrorism and facility violence. There are no acceptable standards that will meet the test of time, and hospitals continue to operate under unusual conditions that encourage them to follow their own set of rules—setting them apart from all other major facilities that are open to the public.

After the 1999 report issued by the Institute of Medicine, "To Err Is Human", the entire subject of patient safety was brought to public attention. Medical errors are of great concern to the healthcare community. Conversely, the report pointed out that many of the patients' deaths while under hospital care were caused by factors unrelated to the illness that the patient was admitted for, and many fatalities were preventable. The number of accidental deaths due to medical staff errors is higher than those from highway accidents and breast cancer combined.

As strange as it seems, medical providers do better, financially, when they make mistakes – because they get paid again to fix the problem. As a result, hospitals now account for the largest slice of the nation's medical spending. Despite this enormous expenditure, hospital care is uneven and often deadly. This policy fails to account for whether that particular service did any good. In other words, doctors get paid for the quantity of care they deliver, not the quality. Insurance companies pay healthcare providers on a "fee-for-service" basis, and doctors have traditionally billed for their services—even if the patient became more disabled, or died, due to the wrong treatment (similar to getting a bonus for failure); The same doctor who caused the injury is reimbursed (under the former healthcare policy) to correct the mistake. Now, double billing has ceased, and hospitals are now responsible for any recovery treatment. According to StatPearls, medical errors have increased every year, prompting government agencies to try to stop the policy of automatically reimbursing a hospital for medical mistakes by the medical staff.[1]

Insurance companies have traditionally reimbursed caregivers twice, once for the original treatment and a second time for treating the complications they created.

Drug control is a common problem within the hospital environment and presents challenges not covered by code and regulation. For example, one nurse was sentenced to a long prison term when it was discovered that she used drugs she stole from the operating room and injected into her body while on the premises and then used the same needle on patients undergoing surgery. Dozens of patients were infected with Hepatitis C. In other incidents, deranged members of the medical staff would easily obtain a deadly drug and inject it into the IV, causing a death recorded as "natural causes". Some of these drugs that are usually undetected in an autopsy include:

- Succinylcholine, which can kill and never shows up on a routine toxicology test. This chemical compound breaks up in the bloodstream immediately, causing respiratory failure within thirty seconds. Brain death occurs within six minutes.
- Epinephrine (adrenaline) is a wonder drug to treat severe allergic reactions – but when administered in large doses, it can cause a heart attack or a stroke.

Imaging-machine technologies are advancing so rapidly that hospital staff members are not always adequately trained to properly use the newest and the most complex devices – particularly radiation-based systems. One of the more serious abuses publicized had to do with patients given dangerously large doses of radiation that caused death and debilitating injury. The misuse of medical radiation equipment (both diagnostic and therapeutic) is mostly the result of the staff that operates the radiological devices. In many states, they do not need to be licensed, and the requirement to report errors and the penalties for making errors have been nonexistent or not enforced. While the entire medical profession realizes the value of the newest technology, there remain many flaws as to how the equipment is administered and how to establish some oversight monitoring of the systems.

A device that produces 3D images of the inside of a body has virtually eliminated exploratory surgery. Similar advances in radiation therapy have saved many lives – a feat that could not have occurred a few years ago. This increase in technological sophistication of new life-saving technology has created its own set of problems, due to inadequate training and a realization that even some of the older CT scans can deliver approximately the same radiation as getting 1,500 dental X-rays. Over-radiation occurs much too often in hospital examination rooms, and manufacturers of medical imaging machines are incorporating alerts and warnings when doses exceed recommended levels.

Some patients have had to call 911 since they could not get any response from the hospital medical staff assigned to monitor the patients while in the hospital room. This lack of response is not so unusual. Other problems include failure to administer the proper antibiotic, which is compounded by the fact that more than 10,000 drugs are being distributed in the marketplace – with many sharing similar sounding names. Poor penmanship by a doctor could result in prescription errors and overworked and inexperienced interns handle many emergency procedures.

Mistakes in hospital rooms tend to multiply during the night shift, a fact known to the medical world – but less widely circulated to the general public. Errors in the injection of drugs or bad arithmetic can cause patients to get dosages ten or fifty times the properly prescribed amount.[2]

Fewer Blood Transfusions

Patients getting procedures, such as coronary bypasses, once required a lot of blood. Fortunately, radical changes in modern medicine have eliminated the need for millions of blood transfusions every year, forcing blood banks to close and a wave of mergers for those banks that still survive. Transfusions were down almost one-third between 2008 and 2015 to about eleven million units from fifteen million units, according to the American Red Cross (which has 40% of the market). In 2008, blood bank revenue approached five billion, but by 2015 it was less than $1.5 billion. The number of employees at the banks has decreased by almost a third. The Red Cross currently has 26,500 employees, with 17,000 working in the blood bank program until cutbacks in 2015.[3]

An analysis published in 2023 examined the median amounts charged to consumers in 2021 for blood transfusions at 200 hospitals across the U.S. While the average cost for the hospitals to purchase one unit of red blood cells was about $200, the hospitals charged consumers a median price of $634 per unit. And the median price for a blood transfusion procedure was $2,388.

Every surgeon who's ever lived has seen somebody whose life was saved by a blood transfusion.

What individual locations charged varied significantly based on the type of hospital and payer (insurance company or self-pay).[4] Around a million units a year are discarded, mostly because the units were not used soon enough. Blood is not something that can sit on a shelf for twelve or eighteen months, according to the American Association of Blood Banks. Red cells have a life of forty-two days and platelets last five days. With all those limitations, hospitals must stock a variety of blood types and try very hard not to run out of any category.

New guidelines by the Society of Thoracic Surgeons changed the rules governing transfusions after coronary artery bypass grafts led to the oversupply of blood stored by blood banks. A normal hemoglobin count is twelve to sixteen grams per deciliter of blood, and some doctors automatically order a transfusion after surgery. Others do so only if the patient's hemoglobin level falls to ten. Under the new guidelines, transfusion is not recommended until the level falls to seven. Without a full understanding of the grams per deciliter ratio, it is obvious that American physicians are requesting fewer blood transfusions than ever before.

Overwhelming evidence suggests that blood transfusion is a dual-edged sword, as it saves some lives but harms others. This was reflected in guidelines that, among many recommendations, emphasize treating patients for anemia in the weeks before surgery to minimize the need for transfusion. Cancer therapies have also changed in a way that reduces transfusion needs and so have other surgical procedures. In a total hip replacement, loss of 750 milliliters of blood, about 1.5 pints, was considered standard – now, it is just 200 milliliters. Some insurance plans discourage transfusions, including Medicare, which pays doctors a flat fee for a procedure – whether it involves the transfusion of one unit, two, three, or more. Another factor that has encouraged doctors to adopt the new guideline faster is the recent computerization of medical records, which allows a physician to order transfusions from a computer screen. The computer has been programed to follow the guidelines, and it will alert the doctor if the order falls outside the norm.

Medical Checklists

"Preventable Complications" could easily be lowered without much effort. Healthcare workers who do not wash their hands between treating patients may infect a patient needlessly – one of the main causes of so many fatalities. To eliminate correctable errors, a growing number of hospitals are instituting the practices used by the aviation industry, which follow checklists before taking a plane into the air and reporting all errors or malfunctions to authorities. Doing so would eliminate errors due to miscommunication and may also inspire practices such as pre- and post-operative briefings, annual competency reviews, and better accident reporting systems. All these practices have been used in the aviation industry for more than half a century, and many pilots have become part-time healthcare consultants for fees ranging up to $40,000. One problem in devising aviation-protocol measures is that when pilots conduct the checklist protocol, they understand that their lives depend on it. Doctors are not in personal danger if they foul up a medical procedure and are hesitant when reporting errors for fear of malpractice litigation and/or losing their medical licenses. Aviators (licensed pilots) are protected against punishment, if they promptly report a violation to aviation authorities before the Federal Aviation Authority notes the mistake.

Using a modified "Checklist" procedure in an operating room could not only save time, but it could also save lives. Most medical errors occur in the emergency room simply because a staff member forgot a step in the process that could prove to be fatal. The checklist could improve the recovery rate in every medical procedure. When hospitals used a checklist, they experienced a large reduction in deaths from surgery due to eliminating errors caused by a skipped procedure. With more sophisticated equipment becoming available, more opportunities are available for medical errors. Many of these errors can be traced to improper training in the use of the advanced technology now found in the average healthcare facility. Medicine has become so complex that even the sharpest doctors can no longer be expected to retain everything they need to know in their heads. Only about half of heart attack patients get the best care within the recommended time frame. Even after discoveries, research shows it takes an average of seventeen years for that treatment to reach even half of the public who could benefit from it. The public has been led to believe that having the best doctors and the newest drugs can cure all ailments. This is like having the most skilled pilots in the most advanced aircraft crash, because someone thought another person had checked the gas level in the empty gas tanks.

There will always be things that fall through the cracks unless a detailed list of procedures is followed – even if the medical team is all as brilliant as Dr. House (from the television program with the same name). Medical checklists are used by only a small number of the nation's healthcare facilities, but a growing number of hospitals are gradually adopting it.

A life-saving basic list:

- Require surgical teams to pause at crucial points before and after surgery.
- Ensure that enough blood is on hand in case of severe bleeding.
- If antibiotics are administered, ensure everyone is informed.
- Determine the anesthesiologist's and nurses' main tasks.

Going over any checklist takes just two minutes and gets the "dumb stuff" out of the way, allowing the medical team to focus on the most demanding tasks. A simple checklist is effective in transforming half a dozen specialists who have never worked together before into a well-informed team – similar to the pilots in the plane's cockpit cabin, who have been required to strictly follow a checklist since commercial flights started in the early 1930s. Regardless of the size of the plane, a checklist is mandatory.

Pilot Checklist

No airline or private pilot would dream of taking off without using a checklist and increasingly, medical personnel are encouraged to use a checklist. A typical checklist that all pilots follow requires about fifteen minutes of time for the smallest plane and more time if the plane is a 747. No pilot, especially a private pilot, would ever skip the procedure and jump onto the plane as though it were a car. Customers renting a car are expected to walk around a vehicle to check for dents and scratches. When checking a plane, missing one of the procedures could prove fatal. About eighty items are on the pilot's checklist and can be checked quickly by visual inspection and some hands-on movement of parts of the fuselage. The pilot-in-command follows a sequence before entering the plane and then gets permission to move a plane to the runway before being allowed to take off. Hospitals are copying similar "checklist" procedures to avoid errors and hazards in the operating room that occur due to inadvertently skipping procedures. All private pilots go through a detailed checklist before every flight—without exception and regardless of the size of the aircraft or type of engine.

Patient Checklist

While there may be no similarity between starting a plane and entering a hospital, both activities should require a basic checklist – for the safety of the pilot, as well as the patient. Doctors cannot be expected to create miracle cures without correctly diagnosing the patient's illness. The medical profession is often overwhelmed, drowning in patients and the paperwork that has changed the profession. Patients need to closely and tenaciously monitor their care to ensure that they are treated by the most experienced surgeons or, after a biopsy, the most expert pathologist.

Unless there is an emergency, it is important for patients and doctors to think things through before undergoing what may be the wrong treatment. Some physicians believe that they should apply smart care, not more care. Serious complications can arise from unnecessary testing and gratuitous procedures, which can be as dangerous as under-treatment. More than thirty-five million Americans are admitted to the hospital each year, and patients have few resources.

Notes

1. Thomas L. Rodziewicz, Benjamin Houseman, Sarosh Vaqar, John E. Hipskind, Medical Error Reduction and Prevention, *StatPearls*, February 12, 2024.
2. Sandra G. Boodman, Shifting the Risks at Night, *The Washington Post*, June 2011.
3. Jefferson M Jones, Mathew R P Sapiano, Sanjida Mowla, Dorothy Bota, James J Berger, Sridhar V Basavaraju, Has the Trend of Declining Blood Transfusions in the United States Ended? Findings of the 2019 National Blood Collection and Utilization Survey, *Transfusion*, 2021 September;61(Suppl 2):S1–S10. doi: 10.1111/trf.16449. Epub 2021 June 24.
4. Michael Schroeder, Does Medicare Cover Blood Transfusions? *GoodRx Health*, February 14, 2024.

Chapter 11

Patient Treatment and Other Common Abuses

Doctor Care – Sharing Responsibility

Under the chain of command in large teaching hospitals, common practice is to have several doctors involved in patient care. That being said, it is not always clear which attending physician is in charge.

Department Chair	*Oversees the Unit and May Handle High-Risk Cases.*
Attending Physician.	Board certified, oversees residents, and is ultimately responsible for patients' care.
House Physician.	Defined as fellows, residents, and interns – all have finished medical school and are in training. They are directly involved in a patient's care.
Fellow.	Board certified in one specialty and participating in additional training in a subspecialty.
Resident.	The doctor has undergone three to seven years of training to be board certified in a specialty, such as pediatrics or cardiology.
Intern.	New MD in the first year of residency.

Not all doctors are equal in ability (which is true for any profession or occupation), nor did they all receive an "A" grade in the specialty they

DOI: 10.4324/9781032630670-11

chose while attending a Caribbean medical school for their first two years of training. Conversely, not all hospitals disperse the same level of care; a fact substantiated by the death rates reported at each medical facility to the departments of health in their respective states. The actual death rates are among the best-kept secrets in American medicine, along with the formulas for sauce used at Kentucky Fried Chicken and the ingredients for Coca-Cola. To educate the public and bring awareness to the number of patient fatalities for a particular treatment, the Centers for Medicare and Medicaid Services (CMS) established a broad comparison of the death rates for heart attack and heart disease by providing a transparency program offering the death-to-discharge ratio, found at https://www.cms.gov/.../HospitalQualityInits/OutcomeMeasures.html.

Hospital Report Cards give higher grades to hospitals in richer urban environments, which usually pay higher salaries to attract better medical staff. They give lower grades to so-called high-risk hospitals, where certain diseases prove more fatal than in other hospitals in the same metropolitan area. When the public has access to the success-to-failure rates for a hospital, a patient will choose the hospital rather than leaving that decision to their HMO-approved physician – who is generally affiliated with one institution. Under the CMS "transparency" program, hospitals are required to provide information to allow a patient to choose the facility where they are treated for a particular disease. For many years, a majority of states made these records available to the public.

Choosing a doctor is not always left to the patient. This type of choice is usually made by the hospital, not the patient. There are, of course, many exceptions to that rule, and it is not always desirable to have a patient select the physician – since this can result in choosing a doctor based on bedside manners rather than on competence. One factor never discussed in the selection of the surgeon is the age of the physician. Surgeons in their first five years of practice had higher-than-average incidences of complications, but so did surgeons older than fifty years of age. The best performances came from the doctors from older age groups indicating that the accumulation of experience alone is not enough to keep surgeons in top form.

Medical Interpreters

To avoid deadly misunderstandings, as the nation becomes more diverse, trained and skilled interpreters who help doctors and patients communicate are in great demand. Healthcare regulations require medical providers who receive federal funding to supply professional interpreters, and there are not enough medical interpreters to support the increased demand for their important services. Speaking two languages is not useful in situations in which the patient has little or no familiarity with the English language – particularly in areas relating to medical diagnostic tests and treatment.

A great difference exists between interpreters and translators, especially when dealing with non-English-speaking hospital patients. Interpreters convert spoken words from one language to another, while translators convert written documents. Bilingual employees or a patient's family members are sometimes tapped to interpret what a doctor is saying, but experts say doctors should avoid this practice. Hospitals are realizing the need for trained interpreters, as some hospitals have had to settle lawsuits from errors attributed to language barriers. Instead of hiring interpreters for special situations, they have one or two on the in-house staff – supplemented by other staff members who are proficient in certain languages.

The best and most popular programs use the guidelines set by the National Council on Interpreting in Healthcare to train and certify interpreters in medical terminology, ethics, and cultural differences. The forty-hour training includes an emphasis on medical treatments and includes observations of surgeries. The National Board of Certification for Medical Interpreters has more than 500 certified interpreters trained in Spanish, Russian, and many African languages. Interpreters earn salaries that vary depending on whether they work on their own, for a hospital, or for an agency, as well as which language they speak.

The U.S. Bureau of Labor Statistics reports that interpreters and translators in hospitals earn a national average of twenty-two dollars an hour and $45,000 a year.

Gallows Humor – Doctor Talk

Medicine is a serious business. Some physicians who practice it are not serious. Getting life-or-death treatment is not a laughing matter. However, according to an issue of the Mayo Clinic Proceedings Journal, someone has accused about 75% of doctors of "humorously promoting death". The study suggests that euthanasia remains too sensitive to be the subject of a joke. Another study on the same topic found that in murder and euthanasia investigations, most accusers are healthcare professionals who are likely to object on moral grounds. On the other hand, some studies argue that "gallows humor" can be helpful to medical workers – and it is acceptable, if patients are respected. After traumatic episodes, doctors need to laugh before they can eat, and they need to eat to be at their best.

Humor is a self-protective mechanism that has a positive impact by reducing tension and helping to prevent burnout – but a fine line exists between humor and truth. Sometimes doctors use humor to depersonalize the patient. All too frequently, this leads them to stop seeing patients as people. The medical language doctors use verges on humor, but it is used to keep outsiders from learning more about the treatment than doctors may think is proper:

- Donorcycle: refers to a motorcycle and the injuries associated with accidents that affect the head but leave the organs in good condition for organ donation.
- Handbag positive: this is a confused patient – usually old – lying on a hospital bed and clutching a handbag.
- LOBNH: Lights On But Nobody Home is a nonresponsive patient.
- Bury the hatchet: this means accidentally leaving a surgical instrument inside a patient.
- Ash cash: this describes money received for signing cremation forms.

Some of the more visionary doctors noted that many prescription drugs have a brand name and a generic name – examples being Tylenol and Acetaminophen, Aleve and Naproxen, and/or Anvil and Ibuprofen. None of the generic names describe the product. With that thought in mind, doctors have been suspected of submitting generic names for the FDA to consider for generic drugs that duplicate the wondrous effects of Viagra. The suggested names have included Mycoxafloppin, Mycoxafalin, and Mydixarism. The FDA rejected all the names as being far too descriptive.

Nursing Ratios

A misconception was enhanced by many popular TV medical shows, starting in the early 1950s with Dr Kildare and Dr Casey, and continuously used in newer versions of medical cures practiced by grouchy Dr House and other fictional characters. These miracle workers seemed to be constantly running to a patient's bedside to save a life whenever the monitoring device sounded an alarm at the nurse's station. None of the TV patients would even dream of criticizing Dr House on any website. While doctors are depicted as the people who can do no wrong, it is often the nurses who are the first to respond – since they are assigned to watch over the patient. The nurse's responsibility is to react immediately in the event of an in-hospital emergency. TV doctors and nurses always arrive in time to help a struggling patient – but in real life, when the medical staff is overworked, they may overlook a patient in distress. This results in nurses and doctors making thousands of deadly errors. Almost 100,000 patients die every year from an ailment or disease that they did not have when they were admitted to the hospital for treatment.

Cost-cutting measures in medical facilities became routine during the business downturn, and this often resulted in fewer nurses. Because of this, the remaining nurses must care for an increased patient load – leading to countless unnecessary deaths. To prevent this overload, some states passed minimum-ratio laws often using the one to five ratio for surgical patients and one to two ratio in intensive care. While this low ratio has proven effective in lessening fatalities, hospitals have resisted mandated ratios by arguing that hospitals that already have good ratios have no justification to change their current ratios. The benefits of mandating nurse-to-patient ratios are so compelling that Congress has, since 2010, become involved and may eventually make low ratios a federal law. Meanwhile, many nurses are providing treatment and prescribing drugs that were usually restricted to the domain of "doctors" with MD degrees.

Expanding Healthcare Fields

More than fifty healthcare-related occupations offer options in a wide variety of jobs, from a phlebotomy technician to someone who cuts nails. Since almost all these healthcare occupations involve people's health or appearance, a license, possibly an examination, and a specified level of training are usually required. A sample list of jobs that do not require an MD license includes:

- Athletic Trainer
- Audiologist
- Barber
- Cardiovascular Technologist

- Chiropractor
- Dental Hygienist
- Dietetic Technician
- Dietitian and Nutritionist
- Medical Coder
- Nurse Practitioner
- Pharmacy Technician
- Physical Therapist
- Physician Assistant
- Psychiatric Technician
- Recreation Therapist
- Social Worker
- Sonographer

There is a need to expand the role of non-physician health providers in medical care with doctors in short supply and Americans gaining health insurance. Physician assistants, nurse practitioners, and other physician extenders are increasingly taking on duties once performed solely by doctors.

Compassion Fatigue

A little-understood mental condition that nurses frequently experience when treating terminally ill patients is compassion fatigue. Nurses are constantly witnessing the suffering of others and burn out, which can lead to feelings of sadness and despair. These feelings can negatively affect their health and well-being, causing a reduction in nurses' empathy (sometimes leading them to avoid certain patients). Compassion fatigue is linked to decreased productivity, more sick days, and higher turnover than among other providers. Nurses who avoid patients will not form the relationships necessary to truly understand the patients, identify their problems early, and adapt therapies to their patients' needs.

A growing number of hospitals recognize the emotional aspects of caregiving – which often result in traumatic stress syndrome or fatigue. These hospitals have started training sessions that include a checklist of symptoms that nurses may unconsciously exhibit, and they offer antidotes by creating support groups that deal specifically with compassion fatigue. Participants are taught the importance of focusing on the caring instincts that brought the nurses to the healthcare field in the first place. The course also teaches known physical, stress-relieving exercises to overcome and control anxieties found in many stressful environments – often causing bodies to clench tightly in anticipation of danger. The exercises are directed toward releasing tension and depression and have proven to be so successful that they may become a mandatory program in hospitals with high-risk patients.

Male Nurses Earn More

Women still dominate the nursing profession, but not in earnings – which is partially because men are more likely than women to work full time. According to the Census Report, men made up nearly 10% of all registered nurses in 2012, up from less than 3% in 1970. The average female nurse earned $51,000, which was 16% less than the $60,000 earned by the average male nurse. Part of the reason can be explained by the phenomenon known as the "glass escalator", in which men earn higher wages and faster promotions in female-dominated professions.

Male nurses tend to be over-concentrated in the highest-earning segments of the field. For example, male nurses make up 41% of nurse anesthetists, who earn nearly $148,000 on average. Males make up only 8% of licensed practical nurses, who make an average of $35,000. Male nurses are more likely than female nurses to have a doctorate and are more likely to work evenings and on the night shift. The Census Report noted that the gap is smaller in nursing than in the economy as a whole, with women earning 77 cents to the dollar collected by their male counterparts (on average).[1]

Less-Educated Healthcare Practitioners

In recent years, the number of workers in the major healthcare occupations who lacked a bachelor's degree surged to more than 60% of the industry's 12.1 million employees.[2] This growth could help bridge the divide between low and high-paying jobs nationwide, as it provides less-educated people with a career ladder and a path toward upward mobility. Diverse metropolitan areas with the highest share of healthcare jobs filled by less-educated workers (60%–70%) include Lakeland in Florida, Dayton in Ohio, and El Paso in Texas.[3] These areas typically have fewer medical schools and teaching hospitals and require a less-educated and specialized workforce.

About half of the diagnostic technicians and registered nurses may possess either an associate's degree or some college, but not a bachelor's degree. They still command median annual salaries of about $86,000 per year. Licensed practical nurses earn about $59,000 a year while emergency medical technicians typically have some college and earn about $44,000 a year.[4] At the lower end of the scale are the personal care aides and home health aides, generally only having high school diplomas – earn between $25,000 and $30,000. The bulk of the job gains in the field of healthcare for the less educated have been in positions such as nursing aides and medical assistants.

Paid Faux Patients

Very few medical schools offer courses to improve doctor-to-patient communication. Some schools have added mandatory classroom sessions to teach doctors to be more compassionate and to understand the importance of connecting on a personal level with the patient – in contrast to the traditional method that has long neglected personal touch in patient care. Another shortcoming in the education of new doctors is trying to expose them to the treatment of rare illnesses and injuries, while there are no patients available with these diseases. Many healthcare facilities address the need to find sick patients with various types of rare illnesses by simply hiring out-of-work professional actors to portray sick patients for fees ranging from $12/hour in rural hospitals to $25/hour in one of the many hospitals along a stretch of the New York City East Side hospitals called "Bedpan Alley".

Aspiring actors audition before medical staff supervisors to be paid to wear the hospital gowns, pretending to be newspaper editors with severe chest pains, someone who has dementia, or someone in an advanced state of Parkinson's disease – all to help aspiring doctors learn their craft. The going rate in New York City for a professional actor/patient is about $30/hour for an eight-hour day, which is better than waiting on tables while hoping to be discovered. Along with dozens of exam rooms stocked with medical equipment, hospitals have set aside rooms where actors perform in front of hidden cameras that record every interaction between students and actors. Two-way mirrors allow faculty to observe. In these simulated encounters, students can practice and make mistakes – no one gets hurt, and the actors get a chance to perform.

Some areas of the country have a shortage of both patients with strange diseases, along with actors, and are forced to hire regular people to play these roles at $15/hour (most are college-age students, retired, or out-of-work individuals between job interviews). These so-called ordinary people make better patients than some of the actors who cannot help but overact at the slightest provocation. The medical staff is acting too, since they know the patient is performing, but they must relate to them as they would to a real sick person. The actors have makeup applied (fake blood) or are instructed to limp and look as though they are in extreme pain. Medical students are judged on how empathetic they are, how well they communicate, and on their diagnostic skills. Awkward moments occur when nervous first-year medical students ask men or women more than the age of eighty if they are pregnant – and when reminded that the "patient" is male or very old, the intern will often repeat the question.

Fingers, Wrists, and Baldness Indicators

Some illnesses can be self-diagnosed, simply by studying the body's skeleton or the size of an appendage. One of the more unusual studies on cancer risks involved finger length as a simple indicator for prostate cancer risk. Previous studies had shown that having too much testosterone also raises the risk of prostate cancer, just as prenatal exposure to estrogen increases a woman's breast cancer risk. The finger-pattern study was more specific, since it found that men whose index finger is longer than their ring finger are at a lower risk of developing prostate cancer. Researchers published their findings in the British Journal of Cancer, which studied the ratio between the second and the fourth fingers on the right hand of 1,500 prostate cancer patients and 3,000 healthy people for more than fifteen years before releasing the results of their unusual findings.

Men with longer index fingers were less likely to develop prostate cancer, and men under sixty years of age had a 90% lower risk. In the prostate cancer group, index fingers were longer in about 25% of the participants and shorter in 60%. In the control group, index fingers were longer in 30% and shorter in 52%. Other similar studies had involved a much smaller test group and found a significant association between the digit ratio and prostate cancer risk. Finger length is determined before birth and is believed to be the result of hormonal influences.[5]

A lesser-known study conducted by a French research group and published in the Annals of Oncology claimed that men who showed signs of balding at age twenty are twice as likely to develop prostate cancer in their lifetimes as those who keep their manes or lose them later in life. With these two very unscientific studies in mind, a bald man with short index fingers may never live long enough to collect a Social Security check.

A study conducted by a research group at a university in Italy in 2011 found that the measurements of a child's wrist size were somehow tied to the person's future heart health. The study found that overweight children with a large wrist bone measurement had higher insulin resistance, a risk factor for developing heart disease. Such resistance occurs when the body makes insulin but cannot use it efficiently to break down blood sugar. While researchers knew that excess body fat is linked to heart disease risk, this study offered evidence (for the first time) that a larger wrist circumference can make the same prediction. The concept of being big-boned may very well offer a correlation between wrist size and insulin resistance.[6]

Not all appendages can be associated with other bodily characteristics – some of which are based more on unsupported mythology than on scientific research. Bald people are not smarter than hairy people, left-handed individuals are not better at math, and people with large bellies are not necessarily big drinkers of beer. There are still those who firmly believe that males with extra-large shoe sizes have larger and longer penises than those with a size seven shoe. This is not true – as shown by the results of a 2009 survey taken at a house of prostitution in Nevada that claimed that there is no such correlation. Besides, as the old saying goes, "size does not matter".[7]

Breath Reveals Health Issues

Exhaled breath contains thousands of chemical compounds that can signal health issues and, as more reliable data become available, doctors will be able to use a unique breath fingerprint to diagnose several serious illnesses. Generally, anything that shows up in a blood test will also show up in a painless breath test – which is less expensive and can be repeated as often as needed. The breath could conceivably become the ultimate noninvasive medical test; however, this may be years away. The concept is not new and goes back to Hippocrates, who wrote about breath aroma and disease around 400 B.C. For centuries afterward, doctors noticed that patients with liver or kidney disorders had distinctive smells to their breath. Researchers have successfully developed tests to diagnose and monitor not just liver and kidney disorders, but a dozen other physical ailments:

- Asthma: nitric acid levels rise when airways are inflamed.
- Ulcers: certain bacteria, when mixed with a tracer, emit a carbon isotope in breath.
- Diabetes: levels of acetone in breath indicate insufficient glucose.
- Kidney Disease: "nose test" recognizes the ammonia-like odor
- Liver Disease: shows changes in carbon dioxide levels.
- Irritable Bowel Syndrome: hydrogen can indicate bacterial overgrowth in the small intestines.
- Heart-Transplant Rejection: produces methyl alkanes in breath.

Millions of people worldwide suffer from chronic halitosis that has nothing to do with serious illnesses. Bad breath is often caused by bacteria buildup, often on the back of the tongue, where postnasal drip collects – according to reports from the International Society for Breath Odor Research. Bacteria also thrives between teeth and gums, where it produces sulfides and other malodorous compounds that are usually found in decaying meat and certain acids that smell like sweaty feet.[8]

About a quarter of the people who seek help from dentists or clinics for bad breath have halitophobia, the fear of bad breath every time they experience a bad taste in their mouth. It is useless to try to detect bad breath by licking a wrist, blowing into a cupped hand, or blowing out under a blanket. An easier way is to ask a trusted friend or family member if that person can smell bad breath. Some dentists have "Halimeters" that can measure sulfur compounds in breath, but patients rarely request a dentist to use it. Breath sprays and mints only mask the problem temporarily. Gargling with mouthwash can help, although those containing alcohol can dry the mouth and make the problem worse. Drinking plenty of water and eating breakfast regularly – preferably with rough foods such as whole wheat toast – can help mobilize bacteria that accumulate overnight, reducing the volatile sulfur.

Flatulence

Little formal research is available in the medical profession to discover a link between the stink of a fart and the cause of embarrassing anal discharge. Without much scientific data on the subject, many old wives' tales have evolved that are more humorous than factual. In simple nonmedical terms, a fart comes from two sources: most originate from the breakdown of food by the digestive system, and some come from swallowed air. Foodstuffs are broken down by enzymes, stomach acids, and intestinal bacteria for the energy in them to be made available to the body.

Through the processes of digestion and fermentation, gases can be liberated from food. Air is swallowed when eating, drinking, breathing, chewing gum, or just being stressed (among other entryways) – and when not expelled during a burp, travels through the intestine into a fart-ready mode. The gases flow down through the rest of the digestive tract and eventually exit the body – expelled as a single fart or a series of rapid-fire small eruptions. This silent or noisy expulsion of air can help bring about some relief and comfort from a buildup within the lower part of the body.

Olfactory Body Odor

The proper term for the unpleasant smell that usually indicates a lack of cleanliness is bromhidrosis or osmidrosis. It can be caused by eating spicy food and can also be indicative of certain medical conditions, such as diabetes. Each person's unique body odor can be influenced by diet, gender, health, and even the effects of certain medications. People may never suspect that something they take to make them better could cause body odor. Sweat itself is virtually odorless in humans. Nevertheless, the rapid multiplication of bacteria in the presence of sweat breaks it down into acids that cause the unpleasant smell. Most cases of body odor are not serious enough to seek the advice of a doctor. The individual may be aware of the annoying smell, or a good friend may tell them about the condition (tactfully, as it is a sensitive topic).

Taking a shower or bath once a day can eliminate 99% of body odor. Changing underwear daily – particularly in warm weather – is also important. Keeping armpits clean and wearing clothing made of natural fibers such as wool, silk, or cotton is also key. Certain spicy foods, such as curry or garlic, have the potential to make people sweat. Some experts believe that a diet high in red meat may also raise the risk of developing more rapid body odor. Individuals may also have the problem of bromodosis (which differs from bromhidrosis), which refers to smelly feet. To mitigate the odor, keep socks and shoes on when in the vicinity of other people, walk around barefoot if no one is around, and use foot deodorants and antiperspirants.

Notes

1. Ben Casselman, Male Nurses Make More Money, *The Wall Street Journal*, February 25, 2013.
2. Federal Reserve Bank of Kansas City, Decline in Number of Workers with "Some College" Is Boosting Healthcare Wage Inflation, Emily Pollard, December 20, 2023.
3. KSDK.com, Health Care Jobs Lift Less-educated Workers, July 24, 2014.
4. US Bureau of Labor Statistics, Registered Nurses, https://www.bls.gov/ooh/healthcare/Print/registered-nurses.htm
5. British Journal of Cancer, Hand Pattern Indicates Prostate Cancer Risk, 2011 January 4; 104(1): 175–177, PMCID: PMC3039824.
6. American Heart Association, Wrist Circumference Is a Clinical Marker of Insulin Resistance in Overweight and Obese Children and Adolescents, Volume 123, Number 16.
7. J. Shah, N. Christopher, Can Shoe Size Predict Penile Length? *National Institutes of Health*, October 2002, PMID: 12230622.
8. Journal of Breath Research, ISBOR'07: Annual Meeting of the International Society for Breath Odor Research 2007, John Greenman and Daniel van Steenberghe, Volume 2, Number 1.

Chapter 12

Medical Insurance – Controversy

Exorbitant Charges for All Procedures

The bill for a hospital room and doctor's visit fee, along with the always-present prescription costs (that may include $6 for each aspirin), is becoming outlandish. Healthcare costs have risen at double the rate of inflation. A three-day stay for treating a gallstone can easily surpass $60,000 – a cost that is usually discounted to the insurance company to about $9,000. These huge bills and the associated low settlements have confused the public for generations. The exorbitant charges for non-emergency treatments vary from lab to lab and hospital to hospital.

The cost for an exercise echo stress test can vary from $2,500 to $5,000. However, if the patient is willing to pay cash up front, the charge can be as low as $1,000. The charge for a CT scan of the abdomen may be as much as $4,000 – meanwhile, the negotiated cost to the insurance company can be about $2,000, and the cash price can be as low as $250. The discounted cash approach is becoming more commonplace, but the cash option is only intended to be more affordable for the uninsured (not to provide an option to those who are insured). Hospitals claim they are forced to charge private insurers more because of the care the hospital provides to the uninsured and Medicaid patients.

Clearly, far too many healthcare dollars are spent paying for overpriced tests, overpriced drugs, and high fees for many surgical procedures. The inflated costs have resulted in skyrocketing increases in health coverage

DOI: 10.4324/9781032630670-12

that force workers to pay higher deductibles while excluding some tests and procedures altogether. Hospitals should not be allowed to inflate healthcare prices to compensate for the bills they have to write off. Patients and insurers across the country, whether public or private, cash customers or third-party payers, should pay the same price for a procedure. Unless there is a level playing field, healthcare costs will continue to rise, along with the absurdly inconsistent prices that have no relationship to the actual cost.

Obamacare aka Patient Protection and Affordable Care Act (ACA)

The Patient Protection and Affordable Care Act – commonly referred to as the Affordable Care Act (and best known as Obamacare) – is a sweeping piece of legislation that was passed by Congress and signed into law by President Barack Obama in 2010. The law was intended to improve the affordability and quality of health insurance in the United States. This law included major provisions intended to make health coverage on the individual market more affordable, with subsidies and expanded Medicaid eligibility. The ACA prevented insurers from discriminating against applicants based on an individual's pre-existing medical condition(s) or gender. Health reform advocates hailed Obamacare for its many provisions designed to expand coverage and to prohibit discrimination. The law includes numerous provisions designed to reduce Medicare spending, drive down costs, and improve coverage for Medicare beneficiaries.

The law included more than 1,000 pages of provisions intended to make coverage affordable for and accessible to millions of Americans who struggled to pay for individual coverage – many of whom could not buy individual coverage at any price due to pre-existing medical conditions. The law sharply reduced the number of uninsured Americans, although the uninsured rate has crept upwards under the Trump administration's watch. In early 2019, nearly 9.3 million Americans were receiving Obamacare's premium subsidies. The subsidies (or premium assistance tax credits) offset some of the cost of premiums.

Generally, Americans eligible for the subsidies have incomes between 100% and 400% of the Federal Poverty Level (FPL). That being said, there are a handful of other factors including immigration status, age, and access to government-sponsored or employer-sponsored coverage. Americans not eligible for premium subsidies include individuals whose employer offers comprehensive "affordable" coverage, those who are eligible for Medicaid/Medicare/another government program, and individuals who are incarcerated.

Millions of Americans have been able to enroll in Medicaid, since 2014, through the ACA's expansion of Medicaid eligibility. The Supreme Court made the expansion optional for states – but as of 2019, thirty-four states and the District of Columbia have accepted federal funding to expand Medicaid, providing coverage for more than twelve million Americans. Two more states, Idaho and Nebraska, are implementing Medicaid expansion that is expected to continue well past 2024.

The Affordable Care Act added a new alternative to COBRA that will give employees the option of continuing their group coverage after leaving a job or otherwise losing access to their employer-sponsored coverage. Since the mid-1980s, COBRA provided a realistic way for people to maintain coverage while between jobs if they had pre-existing conditions and were unable to qualify for medically underwritten individual health coverage. COBRA allowed these individuals to keep the same coverage they had at their job. However, the coverage was expensive, as the employee assumed the full price of the plan – including the portion the employer had been paying.

Under Obamacare, small businesses that provide employees with health insurance could be eligible for an ACA-created tax credit to make offering coverage more affordable. The ACA put coverage standards in place to prevent insurers from discriminating against applicants – or charging them higher plan premiums – based on an individual's pre-existing medical conditions or their gender. Before implementation of the ACA, Americans with pre-existing conditions could find it expensive – or impossible – to buy health coverage on the individual market. The law also eliminated waiting periods that employer-sponsored plans would impose before starting coverage of pre-existing conditions.

Obamacare also mandated minimum value standards for employer-sponsored plans offered by large employers (in most states, that means over fifty employees). Large employers are required to offer affordable coverage that provides minimum value, which means it can't be a "mini-med" or similar type of plan, with gaping holes in the coverage. Employers that don't comply face potential penalties under the employer mandate. The standards also rescued ACA-compliant plan buyers from lifetime and annual benefit limits. Before Obamacare took effect, plan buyers who needed expensive care could exhaust their health insurance benefits and have nowhere else to turn.

These rules apply to student health insurance as well, and those plans commonly had very low lifetime limits pre-ACA.

Some Private Insurers Are Charged Twice the Medicare Fee

Many administrators in the hospital community had considered that by 2021, medical prices had become so high that they were uncontrollable. In some states (according to a RAND) like West Virginia and Florida, private insurers paid three times what Medicare did for overnight inpatient stays and outpatient care. Employers provide healthcare coverage for more than 153 million Americans. The companies and their insurers in the same RAND study paid nearly twenty billion more than Medicare would have for the same care from 2016 to 2018. The widening gap cast doubt on the ability of private insurers to competitively purchase healthcare for workers and their families compared to the federal government.[1]

Hospitals have warned that they might not function if they are paid for all services at the Medicare rate. Some hospitals would lose billions of dollars in revenue, forcing many to be shuttered if forced to operate at the lower Medicare rate. The pandemic in 2020 made the situation worse, as big hospitals scooped up struggling physician practices or their smaller competitors. Other hospitals argued that they charge more due to delivering better care – and there does seem to be validity to that claim. Attempts by large buyers of health care insurance have been made to try and negotiate for lower prices – with little or no success. Many employees have traditionally opposed government action, but others are growing more open to the idea of some level of government intervention – ranging from more regulation to a public option.

Note

1. Reed Abelson, Many Hospitals Charge More Than Twice What Medicare Pays for the Same Care, *The New York Times*, August 22, 2021.

Chapter 13

Nursing Titles

Nursing Doctors

The term "Dr. Nurse" is a new title for a medical profession falling somewhere between a medical doctor and a registered nurse. The first doctorate in nursing was awarded in 2004 by four schools to 170 nurses. By 2023, more than 420 nursing schools granted a Doctorate of Nursing degree, providing graduates of the nursing practice programs with an education equivalent to a primary care physician. From 2022 to 2023, the number of students enrolled in Doctor of Nursing Practice (DNP) programs increased from 41,021 to 41,831. During that same period, the number of DNP graduates increased from 11,149 to 11,718. This two-year doctorate program includes one year of residency and creates a hybrid practitioner with more skills, knowledge, and training than a nurse practitioner with a master's degree. In the nineteen years since the position statement was endorsed, more than 73,000 nurses have graduated with a DNP.[1]

Having a PhD degree in any field has traditionally entitled the holder to be called "doctor". It is an essential credential in the higher education field, but in the medical and healthcare profession, "Nurse-Doctor" is not as easily accepted by physicians for obvious reasons.

Some of the hospital staff may wear the familiar white lab coats and a symbolic stethoscope in one pocket and introduce themselves to a patient as, "Hi, I'm Dr. Anita Lang, and I'm your nurse." before prescribing an allergy medication. Doctorates are popping up in more than just the health

DOI: 10.4324/9781032630670-13

professions. The result is a quiet battle not only with the title "doctor," but also the money, power, and prestige that come with it – both in the academic and medical communities. The American Academy of Physicians claims that having thousands of nurses calling themselves "doctors", a word that has defined professions for centuries, will be followed by the loss of control more than the profession itself. Patients will be confused about the roles of various health professionals who all call themselves "doctors". A proposed law in Congress would bar people from misrepresenting their education or license to practice. Existing laws in Arizona, Delaware, and several other states forbid nurses, pharmacists, and others to use the title "doctor", unless they immediately identify their profession.

The demand for healthcare services keeps growing, and many physicians have stopped serving as the sole medical advisors for their patients' entry into the healthcare system. Physicians have increasingly allowed the sharing of their patients – not only with one another but also throughout other professions. Nurse practitioners and physician assistants have become important members of a team of providers in healthcare – particularly in rural areas. This expanding support network has produced many benefits in healthcare. However, not all physicians are willing to surrender the traditional understanding that they should be leading the team, as they feel that their education is so extensive that they alone should diagnose illnesses. They base their argument on the fact that six to eight years of collegiate and graduate education generally earn pharmacists, physical therapists, and nurses the right to call themselves "doctors", compared to nearly twice that many years of training for most physicians.

For decades, a bachelor's degree was all that was required to become a pharmacist – which changed in 2004, when a doctorate replaced the bachelor's degree as the minimum needed to practice. Physical therapists once needed only a bachelor's degree too, but as of 2015 (the same year that nursing leaders set forth a standard to require doctorates of all those becoming nurse practitioners), the profession began to require doctorates from all students. Nurse practitioners must generally graduate from college and take an additional twelve to sixteen months of classes, which include months of treating patients for both mild and serious illnesses in clinics and hospitals under the watchful eyes of instructors. Those earning doctorates generally take a further four semesters of twelve to sixteen months of additional classes.

An analysis of Medicare billing records in recent years reveals a steady increase in the number of nurse practitioners (NPs) and physician assistants

(PAs) who receive payment for all types of care, while the number of general practice physicians paid by government insurance programs has dropped significantly. NPs are replacing chest tubes, interpreting EKGs, and caring for trauma patients with severe problems (such as aortic aneurysms). Lumbar punctures of the lower back and cystoscopies to check on the urinary tract are now commonly handled by physician assistants, who also assist doctors in complicated operations.

The salary and job outlook for both professions are also very similar. According to the U.S. Bureau of Labor Statistics, the PA profession is expected to grow 31.3% through 2029, and the median annual salary is $112,260. The NP profession sees equally strong numbers with an expected growth of 52.4% through 2029 and a median annual salary of $109,820.[2] By contrast, a study conducted in 2015 by the Association of American Medical Colleges indicated that a doctor shortage is expected to reach 37,000 to 120,000 by 2034.[3] NPs and PAs generally receive payment of about 85% of what doctors get for office visits. After a periodic crackdown on incorrect, fraudulent, or careless billing, regulators found that some doctors inappropriately bill for a PA's service under their name to collect a higher fee.[4]

Nurse Practitioners

About twenty states allow NPs to do their work independently – unlike physician assistants, who are licensed to practice only under a doctor's supervision. Typical NPs have more education and training than registered nurses and PAs. A nurse practitioner can serve as a patient's primary health provider, as they are trained to examine, diagnose, and treat patients and manage acute and chronic illnesses. Plus, they can prescribe medications in all fifty states. An NP can specialize in certain healthcare areas, such as a specialist in the medical field. States vary widely on how much physician oversight NPs must have. In seventeen states, NPs can set up practices and treat patients autonomously. Twelve states require them to be supervised to varying degrees by a physician or other healthcare professional. In the remaining thirty-two states, NPs must have a collaborative agreement with a physician. The period of collaboration can be as low as two years or as high as eleven years.

Nurse Practitioner (NP) refers to a sector of the healthcare field – a category of nurses who can prescribe a certain medication, such as antibiotics and blood pressure drugs – with some states adding controlled substances to the list. These nurses can also perform other (mostly routine) tasks, such as signing a child's immunization certificate or certifying the need for employee sick leave. There is, of course, a great deal of resistance from medical associations representing doctors that contend that nurse practitioners are trying to act as physicians without the proper medical school training – and restrictions are needed on how much authority the nurse practitioners should be granted.

Even with this opposition from within the medical profession, there are strong indications that an increasing number of states see how cost-effective these nurses can be, especially given the shortage of primary care physicians. In many situations, a nurse practitioner can be a replacement for a doctor, without compromising the health of the patient. The general attitude is that people will often seek basic medical care from a nurse practitioner rather than from a doctor for the most common ailments. Nurses are often the ones who take care of patients in hospital environments – and if the patient requires the opinion of a medical specialist, the practitioner will send the patient to a doctor.

Studies show that both MDs and NPs deliver safe and high-quality care, and the states that require greater doctor supervision of NPs do not have better patient safety records. A survey of several thousand patients in 2013 published in the Journal of Health Affairs found that about half of those surveyed would rather have a physician as their primary healthcare provider, but nearly 60% claimed that they would prefer to see a nurse practitioner or physician assistant today rather than wait a day to see a doctor. Each state sets up regulations for nurse practitioners. According to the American Nurses Association, twelve states allow nurse practitioners to prescribe even controlled substances independently. In another twenty-nine states, laws require physician collaboration for prescribing controlled substances. In states such as Florida and Alabama, nurse practitioners are prohibited from prescribing any controlled substance. The Department of Labor issued the expected salaries (2023) for a typical nurse practitioner at $128,000, while the salary for a typical family practice physician averages $339,000.[5] Private practice physicians can make twice that amount, but have twice the overhead (insurance, invoicing, collections, and so forth).

The benefits for patients of nurses receiving doctorates are unclear, as there is no evidence that shows that nurses with doctoral degrees provide better care than those with master's degrees do. Other studies show that nurses with a master's level of training offer care in many primary care settings that is as good as (and sometimes better) than physicians' care, despite the physicians generally having more extensive training. In defending their profession, physicians with MD degrees contend that they have the training and education to treat rare problems and recognize certain illnesses – claiming that nurses cannot duplicate properly and effectively, even at all levels of training, with all degrees and certifications. Studies have trouble measuring this contention from physicians against their effectiveness. Conversely, little evidence shows that moving to doctorates in pharmacy, physical therapy, and nursing achieves many positive effects in overall patient care.

Nurses with doctorates generally receive the same salaries as those with master's degrees, due to insurers paying the same rates for both. Physician groups fear that the real reason behind the creation of the controversial Doctor of Nursing degree is to persuade more state legislatures to grant nurses the right to treat patients without supervision. Twenty-three states allow nurses to practice without a physician's supervision or collaboration, as most are in the mountainous areas in the West and northern New England – geographic areas that have trouble attracting enough physicians. Advocates of allowing NPs to practice medicine without a doctor's supervision point to the predicted U.S. shortage of primary care physicians by 2030. The NPs would mainly set up practice in sections of the nation with insufficient primary care doctors – especially in rural areas.

Opponents of allowing NPs to practice unsupervised medicine include medical associations representing physicians, who have expressed concern about giving NPs full autonomy. They contend that NPs receive, on average, only five to seven years of education compared to eleven years for most doctors. They argue that giving more medical independence to NPs would ultimately harm patients and decrease the quality of care. Critics also claim that a new phrase will be used in the waiting room for an appointment with the NP when patients will be told that the "The Nurse Will See You Now". Nurse practitioners are registered nurses who have earned an advanced degree, but they have never been to medical school. They have half the years of training a doctor gets – generally six years beyond high school (instead of twelve), and they do not take the same licensing exam as a doctor.

With a serious lack of availability of medical staffs in rural sections of some states, nurse practitioners have greater roles, almost identical to licensed MDs. Nebraska is one of many states with laws that require nurses – including nurse practitioners – to get a doctor to sign off before they perform the tasks for which they were nationally certified. Some of the most remote areas in that state are several or more hours away by car from a medical doctor, which discourages any qualified nurse to provide a much-needed medical service. In 2015, Nebraska became the twentieth state to adopt a law that makes it possible for nurses in a variety of medical fields with advanced degrees to practice without a doctor's oversight.[6] Nurse practitioners with a master's degree or higher no longer need to get a signed agreement to do what their state license allows. They can order and interpret diagnostic tests, prescribe medication, and administer treatment. Maryland passed a similar law, and eight more states were expected to follow suit by 2025.

Opposition to all new nursing titles may be somewhat neutralized in the future with the increasing use of programmable Robo-nurse machines that roll on wheels throughout hospital halls, enter elevators, and get off at the desired floor to deliver prescribed medicines and perform other tasks that used to be done by nurses. These robotic cabinets have taken away some of the routines formerly performed by the medical staff. There are rumors that these robots may take online degree courses and eventually go by Dr Robot.

Physician Assistants

Better known as PAs, physician assistants are licensed to practice medicine as a member of a physician-led team. The scope of responsibility varies from state to state, but PAs generally do whatever tasks doctors delegate to them within those responsibilities. That could include examining patients, prescribing medications, conducting rounds in hospitals, and even closing surgical incisions. About 80% have master's degrees, with an average of twenty-seven months of classroom and clinical work after college. They must pass the Physician Assistant National Certifying Examination, sponsored by the American Academy of Physician Assistants, and apply for a license in the state in which they wish to practice. The PAs duties are determined by and under the supervision of physicians, surgeons, and state law. They are trained to provide diagnostic, therapeutic, and preventive healthcare services – as delegated by a physician.

Demand has grown for the services provided by PAs – particularly in primary care. In general, they work under the supervision of an MD. However, they may be the principal care provider in rural or inner-city clinics (in which a physician is present for only one or two days a week). When insurance expanded to cover thirty million more Americans under the Affordable Care Act, doctors could not provide all the services required. As a result, the demand for PAs will continue to increase over the next two decades. A PA may make house calls or go to healthcare facilities to check on patients. PAs can also work in specialties, such as general internal medicine, thoracic surgery, emergency medicine, orthopedics – and very often, in the geriatric field. Those specializing in surgery provide preoperative care and work as first or second assistants during major surgery.

Some medical doctors have voiced serious concerns about giving PAs too much authority since they are not licensed physicians and do not go through the same intensive training as a physician. The same concerns are also directed against nurse anesthetists, nurse midwives, psychologists, and podiatrists. As these professionals seek more autonomy, and authority, they meet more opposition from physician groups. Now, all fifty states allow PAs to write prescriptions – though, two states do not allow them to prescribe controlled substances. In 2010, the number of PAs in primary care was estimated at 23,830. This number could increase to 127,821 by 2025.[7]

Special Physician Assistants

Special physician assistants are a relatively new category that started in 2014, when the state of Missouri passed a law allowing medical school graduates to treat patients on their own after working under the supervision of a physician for thirty days. Such a brief residency is a departure from the one-year residency required to practice medicine independently in the United States. Most young doctors spend at least three years in these types of programs, which include intense on-the-job training and supervision. This law considers recent graduates to be PAs. Their patients can be as far away as fifty miles from a medical facility, and they are allowed to prescribe most medications. The American Medical Association opposed special licensing for doctors who have not completed at least one year of a residency.

Nurse Anesthetists

Nurse anesthetists are a more specialized category of nursing that requires advanced training. The Veterans Health Administration (VHA) was the first to allow them to practice medicine without physician supervision throughout the system. This is the nation's largest healthcare system, providing care at more than 1,321 healthcare facilities, including 172 VA Medical Centers and

1,138 outpatient sites of care of varying complexity (VHA outpatient clinics) to over nine million Veterans enrolled in the VA healthcare program.[8]

More than thirty-five states and national physician groups – led by the American Society of Anesthesiologists, expressed opposition to this policy. Meanwhile, forty nursing organizations – including the American Academy of Physician Assistants – supported the policy by claiming that it would facilitate the timely delivery of high-quality healthcare to the nation's servicemen and women. Training differs between Physician Anesthesiologists and Nurse Anesthetists, among other differences in compensation and in the amount of medical education and training.

Mental Health Practitioners

This category consists of professionals such as therapists, psychologists, counselors, psychiatrists, and social workers. These specialized medical positions require a focused higher education degree, intensive training, and state licensing exams. All are generally covered under most healthcare insurance providers. A brief description of each profession:

Title	Can Prescribe Medicine
PSYCHIATRIST:	YES
PSYCHOLOGIST:	NO
LICENSED PROFESSIONAL COUNSELOR	NO
LICENSED MARRIAGE FAMILY THERAPY (LMFT)	NO
PSYCH RN	YES
LICENSED CLINICAL SOCIAL WORKER	NO

All the above professions require advanced degrees along with a lengthy period of training. Marriage and family therapists help enhance communication and understanding among family members in anywhere from twelve to fifty sessions and combine individual and family therapy. Marriage and family therapists work at mental health centers, hospitals, treatment centers, government departments, and postsecondary institutions. They deal with clients who suffer from severe familial conflicts, which pose a stressful and

Table 13.1 Requirements to Become a Marriage or Family Therapist

Degree Level	*Master's Degree*
Degree Fields	Marriage and family therapy, psychiatry, clinical social work, psychology, or related field
Licensure	All states require licensure
Experience	Two years of supervised clinical experience required for licensure
Key Skills	Good listening, critical thinking, problem-solving, and people skills; compassion; proficiency with medical software such as SOS Case Manager and Software Client Data System
Salary	$50,090 (2018 median for marriage and family therapists)

Sources: U.S. Bureau of Labor Statistics, American Association for Marriage and Family Therapy, Occupational Information Network

demanding profession. Some therapists travel to patients' homes to administer treatment.

Aspiring marriage and family therapists will need to be licensed in their state of residence. According to the U.S. Bureau of Labor Statistics (BLS) (see Table 13.1), the American Association for Marriage and Family Therapy, and the Occupational Information Network, typical requirements include a master's degree in a field related to marriage and family therapy – like psychiatry, psychology, clinical social work, or other fields. Two years of supervised clinical field experience are also required, as are passing scores on a state-approved written exam.

A Licensed Clinical Social Worker must undergo 5,000 hours of supervised experience and an examination before being licensed by the state where they intend to practice. Licenses limit which states one can practice in. Sessions to be conducted in virtual meetings between therapists and their clients must take place in the state the license was received. The other listed positions require similar extensive training in an appropriate medical environment.

Physical Therapists

Cardiologists, brain surgeons, and plastic surgeons are not the only specialists in the healthcare profession who take millions every year from Medicare and private insurers. Physical therapy has become a Medicare gold mine, with physical therapists collecting more than $1.8 billion in recent years and becoming the tenth highest-paid field among seventy-four medical specialties. One therapist collected $4.1 million by treating an astounding number of 1,850 patients in a twelve-month period. This amount works out to an average of ninety-four separate procedures for each patient – or 183,000 treatments a year, 500 a day, and twenty-one an hour. The number of separate procedures is more than three times the nation's average. Nationwide, of the ten physical therapists Medicare paid the most, half listed Brooklyn as their office address. On average, physical therapists collected about $48,000 in Medicare payments in 2013. Experts are openly skeptical of the high number of treatments a typical patient receives during an office visit.

Billings for physical therapy services have come under scrutiny by regulators and law enforcement. As a result, there are numerous crackdowns on physical therapy clinics around the country, which have produced many penalties. In 2011, a physical therapist pleaded guilty to submitting nearly $12 million in false and fraudulent claims to Medicare over a five-year period.[9] Another therapist was sentenced to fifteen years in prison for a $77 million fraud, in which patients were paid kickbacks to induce them to remain silent about services – including treatments that were never performed but were billed to Medicare.[10]

Architects That Mis-design Hospitals

The architect and consultant engineering community traditionally have placed security considerations very low on the priority list for hospitals – just ahead of bathroom doors and locking hardware. Over the last half century, the security features of new or renovated facilities have slowly taken on a level of importance that architects and engineers can no longer ignore. Furthermore, they are starting to recognize what a security specialist can offer during the early stages of the building design.

Since 9/11, a revolutionary advancement has occurred in security technology, along with changes in codes issued by local municipalities and in the safety and security features mandated by the major accreditation organizations. This new emphasis on security for a hospital facility and for protecting its occupants (patients, staff, and visitors) has made the healthcare community one of the largest purchasers of security systems in the nation. The only drawbacks to this sudden attention are that (a) many of the design plans specify obsolete systems, and (b) very little thought is being given to where to place the different departments that are indigenous to a healthcare facility.

Locating the essential medical service specialties is a factor that is often given little attention by healthcare administrators and the professionals who design the building infrastructure. Leaving all decisions to the architect or engineering consultant can, and often has, proven to be the main cause of the security problems that affect the operation of the occupied building.

Design-related steps to be taken by hospital officials should include:

- Examining basic design features indigenous to a healthcare facility.
- Eliminating common design mistakes.
- Avoiding the growing tendency to create obsolete security systems.
- Not limiting knowledge to the claims of the ever-present alarm salespeople.
- Understanding the many advantages of IP addressable over analog cameras.
- Avoiding ward locations that are often poorly planned and in the wrong area of the building.
- Establishing a relationship with the IT department ASAP.
- Placing the nursery above the first floor to discourage wandering visitors.

Notes

1. American Association of Colleges of Nursing. Fat Sheet: The Doctor of Nursing Practice (DNP).
2. Massachusetts College of Pharmacy and Health Sciences, Physician Assistant vs Nurse Practitioner, 6/11/2024.
3. Association of American Medical Colleges, AAMC Report Reinforces Mounting Physician Shortage, June 11, 2021.
4. American Academy of Professional Coders, Billing a PA's Services Incident to a Physician's, May 2023.
5. Panacea Financial, What Is The Average Family Medicine Physician Salary? Michael Jerkins, MD Med, January 2023.
6. The New York Times, Doctoring, Without the Doctor, Sabrina Tavernise, May 25, 2015.

7. Public Health Reports, Predictive Modeling the Physician Assistant Supply: 2010–2025. Roderick S. Hooker, PhD, PA, James F. Cawley, MPH, PA-C, Christine M. Everett, MPH, PA-Cc, 2011 Sep-Oct; 126(5): 708–716, PMCID: PMC3151188.
8. US Department of Veterans Affairs website, About VHA, https://www.va.gov/health/aboutvha.asp
9. The New York Times, One Therapist, $4 Million in 2012 Medicare Billing, Julie Creswell and Robert Gebeloff, April 27, 2014.
10. US Department of Justice, Office of Public Affairs, Brooklyn Clinic Owner Sentenced for Role in $77 Million Medicare Fraud Scheme, November 12, 2013.

Chapter 14

Pharmacists

Requirements for PharmD License

Obtaining the License: Following high school graduation, it usually takes six to eight years of schooling to become a pharmacist – which doesn't include the mandatory license examination. A pharmacist has to earn a Doctor of Pharmacy degree (PharmD) from a college of pharmacy accredited by the Accreditation Council for Pharmacy Education. The PharmD programs typically take four years to complete unless the school offers an accelerated two to three-year option. Some pharmacy schools accept students directly from high school and then require them to complete their education in six or seven years.

- Most pharmacy schools prefer students to possess a bachelor's degree before applying for the PharmD program. The Pharmacy College Application Source maintains a list of PharmD schools and their required classes.
- There are a limited number of programs that offer a degree in pharmacy in which students start directly out of high school and then can gain admission to an accredited pharmacy school after completing at least two years of undergraduate coursework.
- Many PharmD programs require applicants to take the PCAT, a pharmacy school entrance exam.
- Most programs require applicants to use PharmCAS, an online application accepted by most PharmD programs.

DOI: 10.4324/9781032630670-14

- All states require pharmacists to be licensed – and the license can be transferable from state-to-state, but sometimes requires additional exams.

Small, independent pharmacies have slowly been taken over by drug store chains and pharmacy food store chains. CVS employees about 34,000 pharmacists and 65,000 technicians. Pharmacists in big and small stores had been laying off their staff right up to mid-2020 – at the height of the pandemic – and the job outlook for recent graduates at pharmacy schools was very disappointing. After the vaccines were discovered and distributed in early 2021, the situation changed abruptly and stores like CVS and Walgreens had agreed to work with the government to serve as COVID-19 vaccination sites.

Stealing Medication from Hospital Pharmacy – Drug Diversion

Pharmacists not only disperse medications prescribed by healthcare professionals, but they also answer questions about drugs and over-the-counter products. They also keep track of what drugs individuals are taking. Pharmacists advise doctors about drug selections, dosages, and interactions. According to Loss Prevention magazine they also steal highly sought-after, addictive, and illegal drugs – especially during the decade-long opioid epidemic and the COVID-19 pandemic.[1] This contrasts with the public's image of the white coated close-cropped haircut and square glasses that inspire confidence and sobriety. However, in many hospitals, this image is an elaborate front to the fact that taking drugs from the pharmacy is an expected perk of their position. Some pharmacists believe that such behavior was supported – or even encouraged by their supervisors.

Pharmacy workers purloin pills and do so in small amounts – which can go undetected until they're caught. It's not just a few bad apples – as the study noted above, there are reports of workers opening a seam in their shirtsleeves and tucking pills in, shoving pills in their socks, and forging scripts and keeping the drugs. Additionally, the study said, there is a "code of silence", wherein pharmacists cover for each other. It's another collateral consequence of the War on Drugs – these substances are hard to get on the street, making it highly profitable for hospital and drugstore pharmacists.

Sometimes pharmacy workers do get caught for filching in bulk – like the case of the pharmacists in Georgia stealing $20 million worth of drugs: 420,000 doses of Xanax, 1.2 million doses of Vicodin, and 110 gallons of codeine syrup to make a popular drink called "Purple Drank." These hourly employees were getting half the pay of licensed pharmacists but were driving Mercedes Benzes and BMWs, which brought the attention of law enforcement agents.[2]

Over-Prescribed Opioid: Physician Fraud

The largest "healthcare fraud" enforcement operation involved the arrest of 412 medical professionals in 2017. Included among that group were fifty-six physicians, as well as dozens of nurses and pharmacists. They were charged with more than $1.3 billion in fraudulent transactions across twenty states – with one of the doctors accused of writing 12,000 prescriptions for opioids (enough for more than two million illegal doses in a city with a population of 32,000).

Some Doctors Were Writing More Prescriptions Than Full Hospitals

In that same year, an estimated 60,000 people in the United States died from drug overdoses – many linked to opioid abuse, according to the Drug Enforcement Agency. Enforcement operations were conducted by thirty FBI field offices around the country and more than 300 agents. Investigators found opioid addicts "packed in standing room only" waiting areas at doctors' offices, waiting for their prescription painkillers. Following, The Associated Press issued a report that the 2020 pandemic left people stressed and isolated, disrupting treatment and recovery programs – which resulted in over 95,000 drug-related fatalities.[3]

South Florida produced the largest number of fraudsters in a case of seventy-seven conspirators charged with $140 million in false billing – with nearly half near a Florida addiction-treatment center that recruited addicts to relocate to Florida so the operator could bill insurance companies for treatment that was never rendered. In return for their cooperation, the addicts were offered gift cards, airline travel, trips to casinos, trips to strip clubs, and free drugs. Many cases of drug theft involved a licensed hospital pharmacist who stole various addictive drugs (mainly opioids).[4]

Before COVID-19, the nation experienced the deadliest drug overdose epidemic in history with a record of 71,000 overdose deaths in 2019.

Opioids are a class of drugs, naturally found in the opium poppy plant, that work in the brain to produce a variety of effects – including pain relief. Opioids are sometimes referred to as narcotics. Although they do relieve pain, they do not fall into the same category as over-the-counter painkillers such as aspirin and Tylenol. These drugs can also be prescription medications (often referred to as painkillers), or they can be so-called "street drugs". The most popular being:

- Prescription opioids, primarily OxyContin and Vicodin
- Fentanyl, a synthetic opioid – fifty to one hundred times more potent than morphine
- Heroin
- Cocaine
- Morphine

The nationwide opioid addiction rampaged throughout the nation in 2020 and caused a record number of deaths. However, this received little publicity, because most headlines focused on the more deadly coronavirus pandemic occurring simultaneously. Many prescription opioids are used to block pain signals between the brain and the body and are typically prescribed to treat moderate to severe pain. In addition to controlling pain, opioids can make some people feel relaxed, happy, or "high" – and can be addictive. Additional side effects can include slowed breathing, constipation, nausea, confusion, and drowsiness.

Opioid use obviously does not come without risks. Regular use of these prescribed medications can increase your tolerance and dependence, requiring higher and more frequent doses. In some cases, longer-term use can lead to addiction (or what doctors will call "opioid use disorder"). In addition, opioids can restrict your ability to breathe when taken at a higher dose – and when misused, can lead to a fatal overdose. The risk of respiratory depression (slowed or even stopped breathing) increases if you have never taken an opioid before or if you are taking other medications/drugs that interact with the opioid. Opioids, which can interact with diseases, too, should only be used if needed for pain – including if alternatives for pain control are not effective.

Deadly Opioid – Manufacturer Fined $8.3 Billion

Hydrocodone and oxycodone are drugs that are normally used to relieve pain. Certain prescription pain relievers contain high amounts of both, including Percocet, Vicodin, and OxyContin. By far, the most addictive drug is OxyContin (made by Purdue Pharma), which spent millions on advertisements and bribed hundreds of doctors to prescribe the drug beginning in 1999 – until a government lawsuit shut the company down, with a $3.8 billion penalty in 2020.[5]

According to the American Society of Addiction Medicine, addiction is a chronic disease. It is reflected in individuals who pursue relief from pain and for recreational purposes that often lead to addiction. Hydrocodone and oxycodone are powerful drugs that doctors only prescribe as a last resort. The ingredients in these drugs are habit-forming, and some people may become addicted to them. People who become addicted often build up a tolerance to the drug. This means they will need to take larger amounts to feel its effects. This type of behavior can often lead to an overdose. Others may use these types of drugs without a prescription to get "high". This is an extremely dangerous practice that is growing among young adults. According to the National Institute on Drug Abuse, 6.1% of high school seniors reported abusing these drugs from 2010 to 2020.

In 2020, the federal government sued the makers of OxyContin for pushing the sales of this opioid. The manufacturers pleaded guilty to criminal charges related to the marketing of this addictive painkiller, which killed about 450,000 Americans between 1999 and 2020. The financial penalty for the distribution of the OxyContin drug was the highest ever given to a drug company, coming in at $8.3 billion. This fine did not even preclude the filing of criminal charges against the bankrupt manufacturer (Purdue Pharma) and its owners. Additionally, the company agreed to plead guilty to three federal criminal charges for its alleged role in fueling America's opioid epidemic.

Drug Abuse Is Soaring

Opioids are drugs that stimulate the brain's opiate receptors. Some are made from opium and some are completely synthetic. In the United States, the most prescribed opioids are hydrocodone and oxycodone – which are classified as semi-synthetic because they are synthesized from opium. Heroin is also a semi-synthetic opioid. The effects of hydrocodone and oxycodone on the brain are indistinguishable from the effects produced by heroin.

Drug overdose deaths (once rare) have become the leading cause of accidental death in the United States, surpassing peak annual deaths caused by motor vehicle accidents, guns, and HIV infection – since 2010. Until opioids are prescribed more cautiously and effective opioid addiction treatment becomes easier to access, overdose deaths will likely remain at record high levels. Opioids are essential medicines for palliative care and are helpful when used after major surgery or a serious accident (with limited use). That being said, the bulk of the opioid prescriptions in the United States are for common conditions like back pain.

Opioids are more likely to harm patients than help them – as the risk of addiction outweighs potential benefit. Opioids have not been proven effective for daily, long-term use. Evidence suggests that chronic use of opioids can even make pain worse – a phenomenon called hyperalgesia. The increase in opioid prescriptions was fueled by a multifaceted campaign underwritten by pharmaceutical companies. Doctors heard from their professional societies, their hospitals, and even from state medical boards that patients were suffering needlessly due to an overblown fear of addiction.

Until 2011, most opioid overdose deaths involved prescription opioids. Then, prescription opioid overdose deaths leveled off, as deadly overdoses involving heroin began to soar. A common misconception is that so-called "drug abusers" suddenly switched from prescription opioids to heroin due to a federal government "crackdown" on painkillers. Most people who started using heroin after 1995 switched from prescription opioids, because heroin was easier to obtain. From the beginning of the opioid crisis, young adults who became addicted to prescription opioids would switch to heroin, a less expensive option.

Consultant Fined $573 Million for Promoting Drug

The global business consulting firm McKinsey & Company agreed to a $573 million settlement over its consulting role in advising companies (mainly Purdue Pharma) on how to "supercharge" opioid sales amid an overdose crisis. In 2021, McKinsey (considered one of the world's most prestigious consulting firms) acknowledged its role in advising companies on how to "supercharge" opioid sales amid an overdose crisis.[6] The record-setting settlement came just months after the Justice Department announced that it had reached an $8 billion settlement with McKinsey's former client, Purdue Pharma – the company that makes most of the OxyContin on the market. The main reason for the McKinsey fine was the recommendation made to Purdue in 2013 that encouraged the manufacturer to boost annual sales by targeting prescribers and take other steps to "Turbocharge" Purdue's Sales Engine.

Switzerland Lowers Threshold for Medical Added Treatment

Switzerland has found an unorthodox method (at least by U.S. standards) of solving its opioid crisis. They have decriminalized substance use and offer twenty-four-hour access to methadone programs. For treatment in serious addiction cases, pharmaceutical - grade heroin is provided in clinics. This program has resulted in the country's overdose deaths decreasing by one-third since instituting the program. In contrast to this company's openness to this type of activity, the United States considers it criminal. As a result, this country locks up more people per capita than any other nation. More than 860 adults are incarcerated for every 100,000, according to the Bureau of Justice Statistics. This is more than ten times Switzerland's incarceration rate (eighty-three per 100,000) and more than seven times that of Europe (117 per 100,000), according to Council of Europe data. U.S. citizens are not more violent and don't engage in more criminal behavior than those in Europe. The difference is the radically different approach to illicit drugs.[7]

Half of all federal prison inmates in the United States are drug offenders, according to the United States Sentencing Commission. Many of those convicted of a drug crime must serve a mandatory minimum sentence – and more than double the average nonmandatory sentences. Nearly half of those convicted of a drug offense carrying a mandatory minimum have had little to no prior criminal history (46%).[8]

By the 1980s in Switzerland, communes of impoverished addicts had taken over several large public parks, with up to 3,000 people openly injecting heroin in just one of these "needle parks" daily. Most were homeless and jobless. In 1991, paramedics were called in 3,600 times to one needle park alone to resuscitate people who had overdosed on heroin. HIV/AIDS and hepatitis C were rampant among these heroin users, and the country was often referred to as a "drug swamp" in popular media. Starting in 1991, the country began a major paradigm shift based on the concept of harm reduction to try and stop overdose deaths along with the spread of HIV/AIDS. It decriminalized drug consumption and opened clean, supervised consumption rooms where users can inject themselves with substances they bring in. Additionally, they can exchange used needles for clean ones.

Twenty-four hours a day, Swiss heroin users can now call a hotline staffed by psychiatrists and other mental health professionals and begin immediate methadone treatment. Patients in the program do not have to visit every day (which would hinder employment opportunities), and they are given a two or three-week supply of methadone to use at home and then head to their jobs. Methadone patients who continue to use illegal heroin are offered heroin-assisted treatment (HAT), which provides pharmaceutical-grade heroin during daily visits to a clinic staffed by medical professionals. HAT is even being piloted in one men's jail.

Other positive results include a huge drop in overdose deaths, crime, and the spread of HIV and hepatitis. Participants have improved social functioning and increased employment.

The cost savings for these opioid abuse treatment programs have been great. The six-month cost to the Swiss government for treating a person in its outpatient methadone treatment was $1,750, compared to $20,000 for six months of incarceration – or $21,500 for not providing any treatment.[9]

Notes

1. Joseph Muha, Drug Diversion: Preventing Retail Pharmacy Theft, *Loss Prevention Magazine*, October 2017.

2. Sun Herald, How theft ring stole millions of drugs from hospital pharmacy, WILLOUGHBY MARIANO, March 2016, https://www.sunherald.com/news/local/crime/article66010822.html#storylink=cpy
3. U.S. Department of Justice, Office of Public Affairs, National Health Care Fraud Takedown Results in Charges Against Over 412 Individuals Responsible for $1.3 Billion in Fraud Losses, July 13, 2017.
4. U.S. Attorney's Office, Seventy-Seven Charged in Southern District of Florida as Part of Largest Health Care Fraud Action in Department of Justice History, July 13, 2017.
5. U.S. Department of Justice, Office of Public Affairs, Justice Department Announces Global Resolution of Criminal and Civil Investigations with Opioid Manufacturer Purdue Pharma and Civil Settlement with Members of the Sackler Family, October 21, 2020.
6. Siladitya Ray, McKinsey Has Reached A $573 Million Settlement With States For Its Role In Marketing Opioid Drugs, *Forbes*, February 2021.
7. Emily Widro, States of Incarceration: The Global Context 2024, *Prison Policy Initiative*, June 2024.
8. U.S. Sentencing Commission, Mandatory Minimum Penalties for Drug Offenses in the Federal Criminal Justice System, October 2017.
9. Psychiatric News, Switzerland Halts War on Drugs, Cuts Deaths, Volume 53, Number 12, June 2018.

Chapter 15

Emergency Unpreparedness

Katrina – New Orleans (2005)

One of the worst storms in U.S. history was Katrina, costing the economy more than $125 billion in damages and killing almost 1,900 people – many of whom were in medical centers and nursing homes. Most of the damage resulted from flooding, as New Orleans is below sea level. However, the flooding was not as widespread as the Sandy superstorm that came ashore along the heavily populated Eastern Seaboard in 2012. Medical facilities suffered badly in both storms due to the failure of mechanical and electrical equipment that is essential in keeping a hospital complex operating during a blackout. Standby generators are not highly visible, and their location is generally in basements or below ground locations, usually placed in locations that could be vulnerable to natural disasters. As a result, this could possibly be the cause of the complete evacuation of the hospital facility – as they have failed to generate the power they were designed to provide. Only starting in 2005 did the HVAC, air circulators, and power-generation equipment receive more attention due to the lawsuits that have resulted from the negligence of the hospital authorities (who had not anticipated the breakdown of the buildings' power-generating systems, which made headlines after the Katrina and Sandy storms).

Several years before the destructive storm that inundated New Orleans, practically no hospital in the nation had assessed the vulnerability of the building's infrastructure to the type of flooding that occurred due to Hurricane Katrina. One of the major hospitals in New Orleans had two main generators – one located on a high floor or the roof (typical) and the

 DOI: 10.4324/9781032630670-15

second unit on a lower level that would become non-functional when two feet of floodwater surrounded the unit (also typical). When this vulnerability became known to the hospital administration (several years before the hurricane), the hospital estimated that relocating the emergency generator and the fuel supply would cost about $7.5 million. As a result, the power plant remained in place. When the floodwaters in 2005 reached six feet, the power went out – and the hospital's life-support machines stopped working.

The disaster made the nation's 4,300 hospitals and more than 15,000 nursing homes realize that they have a responsibility – both ethically and financially – to prepare for possible catastrophic circumstances. More than one hundred deaths occurred in New Orleans area hospitals and nursing homes after Katrina – when emergency backup power systems failed, and patients languished for days awaiting transport. People filed more than 200 lawsuits in Louisiana, alleging that the healthcare facilities were liable for the deaths plus the suffering of the patients who survived. They alleged that the lack of emergency preparedness and corporate failure to plan adequately for flooding and implement evacuation constituted negligence or medical malpractice. The New Orleans lawsuits were precedent-setting after the Louisiana Supreme Court decided the allegations were based on general negligence claims, as opposed to medical malpractice (in which damages would be capped at $500,000). That decision markedly increased the hospital owners' potential liability.[1]

The high-salaried hospital administrators' response to the court's decision was that Hurricane Katrina was an "act of God" that they could not foresee, that the hospital was not negligent, and that it would be unreasonable to expect a hospital to be impervious to all of the unlikely catastrophes its emergency plans contemplate – including tornadoes and even "terrorist-inspired events". The argument that guidelines issued by any authority (public or private) may not always be sufficient in the event of a catastrophic event is not compromised by the fact that hospitals in New Orleans had not fallen short of applicable electrical codes and standards and met the guidelines followed by the Joint Commission. National electrical standards for hospitals were traditionally oriented toward maintaining electricity during common, brief local power outages – not prolonged emergencies that result from devastating natural disasters.

All the nation's municipalities follow the National Fire Protection Association (NFPA) standards. They call for careful considerations in protecting electrical components from "natural forces common to the area", such as storms, floods, and earthquakes. The guidance is not specific, and emergency systems do not have to be designed to power air conditioning or heating systems. Following the filing of the New Orleans lawsuits, there was the realization that the flooding problem was recognized years before Katrina when Tropical Storm Allison flooded Houston in 2001 – compounding the problem. Some of the largest hospital complexes in the nation lost power in that city because emergency generators and other electrical components were located below flood level. Officials at New Orleans' hospitals were well aware of the problem faced in Houston after the New Orleans Health Director brought the flooding subject to hospital officials. However, since the cost of raising the generators would be millions of dollars, they dropped the subject and decided that the money would better serve the community by being spent on purchasing critical machines for the intensive care unit or the operating room versus moving the emergency electrical system. Raising generators is not mandatory for hospital accreditation, and government agencies have rarely provided funding for this expensive work leading up to a disaster.

Sandy – Eastern Seaboard (2012)

Sandy, a destructive hurricane, caused more damage (though fewer deaths) than most hurricanes. Sandy may have been the most widespread storm ever – sending water surges over eight states (from Virginia to the Canadian border), with more than ten million people losing power to their homes for several weeks. The area affected was equal to the size of Western Europe. Hurricane Sandy caused the complete destruction of many Jersey Shore towns and cities and stopped all public transportation facilities in the New York City metropolitan area for more than a week. The flood surge reached the highest levels in New York City history, causing three hospitals on its East Side to lose regular power – forcing the activation of standby power generators located on high floors or the roof. The fuel to feed the generators was in the basement, and the water shorted out the pumps needed to get the fuel up to the generators.

One of the three hospitals that lost all power was Bellevue Hospital, the country's oldest public hospital in continuous operation. The other two were New York University Hospital and one of its satellite facilities in lower Manhattan. After losing power supplied by the local utility, the standby power generators located on the higher floors and roof area were automatically activated as they were designed to be. Eventually, the fuel tanks in the basement that fed the generators lost their pumping power due to the floodwaters. The staff and first responders carried the fuel up to the generators using a daisy chain maneuver. When the lights and elevators stopped operating, all 350 patients had to be carried out by the staff to ambulances and then transported to other flood-free area hospitals.

The problem of the failed fuel pumps created a huge controversy. The public outcry that hospitals should have stored fuel on the higher floors did not account for the fact that fuel tanks must be in basements due to municipal building codes. Furthermore, many older buildings in the city have sump pumps to expunge the water intrusion from the streams beneath Manhattan Island. These pumps are designed to handle 100 to 200 gallons per minute – but not a tidal surge of tens of thousands of gallons that burned out the pumps. In the immediacy of a disaster of a Sandy scale, the public demands better emergency power and bold solutions. These demands withered over time without continuous public support behind them. Everyone agrees that power failures, especially in medical facilities, should never happen again – but memory recedes. The next day, the sun is shining, the refrigerator cools, and the trains are running. No one wants to pay the enormous bills to change the infrastructure or waterproof underground power lines. It would take billions of dollars to make any permanent and meaningful change, and utility bills are already too high.

Little mention was made about the inefficiencies and confusion that result from any patient relocation, as these emergency-evacuation procedures never go smoothly and are never rehearsed. When the three hospitals were flooded, they dispersed patients and staff to nine other citywide medical facilities. Some of the receiving hospitals set up conference rooms just for the people from the flooded hospitals with water coolers and microwaves. Sometimes, patients were sent to different hospitals than their doctors. Medical records were not found, and the new doctors could not find X-ray rooms or the point person for the pharmacy, and so forth. It was, in every sense, a foreign system to most of the transferred medical staff.

For all the disquieting feelings the doctors experienced, the patients suffered the brunt of the dislocation. Sometimes, it took a week before patients were placed with their doctors. By that time, they had the exhausted look of refugees. Patients had missed days of medication during the storm and its aftermath, resulting in patients worried about scheduled colonoscopies, CT scans, cataract surgeries, or physical therapy sessions. Even after the storm passed, it took weeks to restore the abandoned facilities to their former operating condition, and the displaced doctors had to stay several weeks in the unfamiliar wards of the host hospitals.

Note

1. Sheri Fink, The New Katrina Flood: Hospital Liability, *ProPublica*, January 2010.

Chapter 16

Surveyors, Advisors, and The Joint Commission

The Joint Commission

The Joint Commission (TJC) is the abbreviation for the very important, private, and not-for-profit organization whose staff of inspectors/surveyors put fear into the hearts of every hospital administrator. The organization, which changed its name to The Joint Commission in 2009, has a history that goes back to 1973 – when the American College of Surgeons set up standards to improve hospital surgery and other hospital safety procedures. The organization took its present form in 1951, when four medical associations' societies sponsored the Joint Commission on Accreditation of Hospitals (JCAHO). Their mission was to continuously improve the safety and quality of care provided to the public through the provision of healthcare accreditation and related services that support performance improvement in healthcare facilities. The commission lacks the authority and enforcement powers of a federal agency, yet it is the organization that 17,000 hospitals, nursing homes, and assisted living providers fear most.

While the Joint Commission does not concentrate on any single procedure, it often will discover errors in the way a hospital processes patients, including the safety of each patient. The long list of requirements is intended to ensure a safe and secure environment and is independent of other local, state, and federal requirements that may also cover safety and security conditions – such as the Uniform Building Code. Many hospitals have prepared for more than a year in anticipation of the unannounced TJC visit to ensure

DOI: 10.4324/9781032630670-16

that their facility meets all the regulations, especially those that relate to certain life-safety and security safeguards. Visits now happen every three years (unannounced) or if a catastrophic event occurs within the medical facility.

Unlike some European nations, including France, the United States has no federal agency charged with hospital oversight. Instead, it relies on a patchwork of state health departments and The Joint Commission – which lacks legal authority and enters the hospital premises only upon request for accreditation. This organization conducts a self-policing program, based on the fact that the work of the survey team is paid for by the hospital that is surveyed. TJC is a very powerful influence in the way the nation's healthcare institutions treat their patients and how each department functions. A poor evaluation by the survey team rarely results in closing a hospital, as every hospital is a major employer – and communities generally rally behind them when there is the slightest threat of closure.

Still, without the "accreditation" and approval, the very survival of a hospital may be jeopardized as government subsidies. Recognition from other healthcare providers could be irreparably damaged. The triennial scheduled visits to hospitals with a minimum of 200 beds are treated with such importance that most hospitals prepare for a year before the visits. Up until 2004, the approval was provided on a percentage scale – obtaining a 98% rating instead of 90% could actually affect careers – even though these ratings were far from a scientific evaluation. Due to some complaints, the rating was changed to "pass-fail" in 2005.

The specialists who conduct the evaluation are known as "surveyors" and usually spend between three to five days at each facility. A typical survey/inspection team represents various backgrounds that include administration, registered nurse, medical practitioner (doctor), and facilities professional. Recently, the team was expanded to include a life-safety code specialist. Part of the survey is a review of policy and procedures, and it is important for the hospital to demonstrate that it has carefully followed the guidelines that relate to establishing a safe and secure environment.

The Joint Commission (TJC) started a program in 1996 to improve patient care through gaining and sharing knowledge and statistics on the adverse events occurring in every organization that the Joint Commission accredits. This descriptive phrase was changed to "Sentinel Event" because the word "sentinel" sends a signal or sounds a warning that the incident requires immediate attention. Each organization is voluntarily requested to report certain tragedies and unexpected occurrences (such as accidental deaths, serious physical or psychological injuries, and infant abductions) and complete an in-depth investigation to determine what caused the event and how they can prevent it in the future. The Sentinel Event most frequently reported in the twenty-four-hour care facilities are suicides; Almost 90% of these reported suicides have resulted from deficiencies in the environment of care – such as the presence of non-breakaway bars, rods, or safety rails, lack of testing breakaway hardware, and inadequate security. More than 34,000 individuals die each year from suicide. Males are four times as likely to die from suicide than females. However, females attempt suicide more often than men.[1]

Sentinel Event: A sentinel event is an unexpected occurrence involving death or serious physical or psychological injury – or the risk thereof. Serious injury specifically includes loss of a limb or function. The phrase "or the risk thereof" includes any process variation that, if it recurred, would carry a significant chance of a serious adverse outcome. The healthcare industry is often involved in life-or-death situations with its clientele. When these organizations discover the reasons behind an adverse event, they are obligated to establish procedures to prevent its recurrence. The information remains in-house. No policy encouraged the dissemination of the findings in a way that could help other organizations avoid the same adverse event.

- Adverse or Undesirable Events: these include patient falls, medication errors, procedural errors/complications, completed suicidal behavior, and missing patient events. An adverse event can also be categorized as either a sentinel event or a near miss.
- Near Misses: these are situations that could result in an accident, injury, or illness – but did not. An example of a near miss would be a surgical or other procedure almost performed on the wrong patient due to lapses in verification of the patient's identification but caught at the last minute by chance.

Even if a hospital elects not to report a sentinel event, TJC still expects organizations to conduct a full investigation into why the event occurred and what could be done to prevent it from recurring. These investigations are called "Root-Cause" analyses and are instrumental in making changes. For example, hospitals included in one study group experienced an attempted or actual abduction of an infant. As a result, these institutions made the following changes in infant security procedures:

- Issued badges to all staff members and trained mothers in hospital policy.
- Strictly enforced visiting hours and alarmed doors leading to nursery.
- Removed all signs directing people to obstetrics.
- Added numerous video cameras, with monitors at nurses' station and in the security office.
- Installed mirrors to allow viewing around corners.
- Posted a list of mothers' names and room numbers only in staff areas.
- Stopped providing information on patients' rooms to telephone callers.
- Locked stairwell doors with fail-safe delay magnetic locks – approved by AHJ.
- Always placed infants in bassinets when they were moved (rather than carrying).

Root-cause analysis is a process for identifying the basic or contributing factors that underlie variations in performance – including the occurrence of an adverse sentinel event. This analysis focuses primarily on systems and processes, not individual performances. Root-cause analysis is not about blame or negligence – it is about finding methods to improve the situation and learn how to prevent the recurrence of the sentinel event. For example, death can result from a hospital's total loss of electric power while a patient is undergoing surgery. This adverse outcome is the result of a special cause in the operating room, but it can also be the result of a common cause in the organization's system for preparing for a utility failure. While the operating room staff may be unable to prevent a future power outage and more deaths, the hospital can redesign its system to provide emergency electric power in the operating room in the future.

Human error from a physician prescribing a drug or a nurse administering it may be the immediate special cause of a patient's death. However, even the best -intentioned and most competent human beings always have and will make errors. A hospital will try to institute procedures to prevent an error in prescribing or administering a drug in the future that may lead to actions from the pharmacy and the information management staff to establish a computer-based ordering system with online reminders to assist the physician and a drug distribution system for the unit to assist the nurses. The actions taken as a result of the root-cause analysis did not mean that the pharmacy and information services were to blame or were in any way negligent – it just means that they are in a position to change the design of the organizational systems that will reduce these special cause variations in the future.

Joint Commission Resources

The Joint Commission Resources (JCR) was formed in 1987, as an affiliate of TJC, to support many of its goals by providing educational services and publications to assist in improving the quality, safety, and efficiency of healthcare services. Most importantly, it assists in meeting the accreditation standards of TJC. One of its publications, Essentials for Healthcare, includes a series of guidelines on topics related to patient care and safety. They avoid any reference to a particular infant protection system. The publication does suggest one electronic-tag system technique – a system that is more or less obsolete. None of the literature published by JCAHO and its affiliates indicates an understanding of the life-safety codes and standards that affect the locking hardware on nursery doors or the value of incorporating a sophisticated electronic-sensor tag for the newborn.

The 2005 issue of the Essentials booklet includes the statement that the information and examples were provided with the understanding that "the publisher is not engaged in providing medical legal or other professional advice. If any such assistance is desired, the services of a competent professional person should be sought". The mystery that had caused some confusion within healthcare began in 1983, when security first called upon the attention of hospital administrators, forcing them to seek more qualified individuals for the position of security director. The main question: how does a hospital find this elusiv "competent professional"?

The qualifications for a security director are very vague, and some hospital executives still do not accept this position as a "senior administrative position". Until the last few years, salaries did not attract so-called professionals. However, since 9/11, security personnel have experienced significant raises in their pay scale, greater respect for the director's position, and qualifications have become much more stringent – replacing the traditional twenty years of police experience. Many hospital administrations took advantage of the fact that a retired police officer had a pension – so the position of security director was a second income, and salary demands were usually a non-factor. The reason the turnover rate for new security directors was so high during the first two years was that the human resource officials preparing the job description were not familiar with the duties of a security director. They were unable to separate competency from complacency.

The Joint Commission Resources Consultative Technical Assistance is a service provided by the JCR that offers trained personnel to visit a healthcare facility (for a substantial fee) to assist in the preparation for a TJC accreditation visit. They make recommendations to improve patient care and enhance medical staff procedures and other relationships. This service was considered a conflict of interest with the main goal of TJC, but it is no longer considered unacceptable. The service comes with the disclaimer that the services are independently conducted, and they will not disclose any information about the client facility to TJC or others. These independent surveyors do not participate as members of the TJC team that provides a follow-up visit to the healthcare facilities.

Deficiencies in the environment of care are frequently among the root causes of sentinel events such as patient suicides, infant abductions, and restraint-related deaths. Although environmental care-related root causes can be just one of many factors contributing to a sentinel event, organizations should take proactive steps to address these causes to enhance patient safety. Adequate security equipment along with a well-designed and monitored physical environment is likely to prevent abductions. Security equipment that is not available, operational, or not used as intended might not prevent infant abduction – as can factors such as having no line of sight to entry points and unmonitored elevators or stairwells. To discourage opportunities that expose infants to abduction possibilities, the hospital should:

- Develop and implement a proactive infant abduction-prevention plan.
- Control access to nursery/postpartum units using equipment such as swipe card locks, keypad locks, entry-point alarms, or video surveillance – however, a locking system must comply with fire codes.
  - A high-tech approach to prevention may not be financially feasible. Nevertheless, many facilities find the most helpful electronic aid to be video surveillance cameras strategically placed at entrances to the obstetrics unit, in stairwells, and at unmonitored exits.
- Designate a public entry point and restrict access to other entry points. Large facilities might have secondary entry points that are locked or under twenty-four-hour surveillance.
- Restrict access to all staff changing rooms and lounges.
- Attach secure, identically numbered bands to an infant (wrist and ankle bands), mother, and father or significant other immediately after birth.

Check the ID of the baby and parents whenever the baby is passed to a parent or returned to the nursery from a parent. Match the bands when the mother and infant are discharged.

- Ensure that infants are transported only by authorized staff. Never leave the hallway without direct supervision. Take babies to mothers one at a time, and always have staff push them in bassinets, rather than carry them.
- Require staff to wear up-to-date, conspicuous, color photo-identification badges and educate mothers and families about infant security – including the design of the unit. Mothers also need to be educated on how to recognize staff members, such as by special badges or uniforms of a specific color.
- All staff members should know the organization's policies and procedures that pertain to infant/child abduction-prevention strategies, what constitutes suspicious behavior, and when to call a "Code Pink" (or other code to signal an infant abduction).
- Conduct quarterly Code Pink drills on all shifts.
- Attach a security tag system to the infant (perhaps the strangest suggested measure).

TJC surveys are very vague about recommending a particular system because they do not want to be responsible for the selection of a system. This is understandable, since the barcode-type of detectors have not been available to the healthcare community; it was abandoned in 1996.

Mock Survey and Independent Consultants

Independent security consultants, a relatively new profession, are not associated with any accreditation organization. In many ways, they compete directly with the JCR experts. They deal exclusively with hospitals and are a growing influence within the healthcare industry. They seem to be former hospital administrators and do not appear to have any particular certification, licensing, or any special credential other than a working knowledge of the Joint Commission site-survey ritual. These "consultants" provide an independent "Pre-Survey Report" and examine critical areas throughout the hospital and recommend corrective measures before the official visit by experts (exactly like the JCR). A significant number of the recommendations relate to safety and security, which includes infant safety. The survey effort is similar to the tutoring courses given in preparation for the SAT exam – only the mock survey costs a lot more.

Defining Medical Mistakes

Healthcare facilities are responsible for providing reasonable care when selecting, supervising, retaining, and training employees. Like the medical staff, non-professional staff members also come into daily contact with patients and members of the public – when patients are the most vulnerable. The courts hold hospitals and other healthcare facilities to a higher standard of conduct than other organizations that deal with the public. This attitude places a great deal of pressure on the entire hospital staff. Unless the staff is well-trained in the complicated and ever-changing laws that affect their duties and responsibilities, they are at risk for lawsuits for negligence. These suits are the result of lack of proper supervision, violation of HIPAA, a lack of staff training, and medical errors that have become unacceptably high. Wrong-side surgery accounts for an estimated one in 1,500 operations, and a recent judgment against a surgeon for removing the wrong lung cost the hospital/insurance company close to $7 million.

Each year more than thirty-three million Americans walk into the forbidding and unfamiliar world of a hospital and place their lives in the hands of doctors, nurses, technicians, and paramedical orderlies only to fall sick from an illness caused or contracted during their hospital stay. More than 100,000 patients become ill due to medical mistakes while under hospital surveillance and care, most of which are proven to have been preventable.[2]

Sooner or later, most people will encounter a lawyer – whether it is for preparing a Will, incorporating a business, closing on a house, or making a divorce settlement. The nation has become a litigious society in which every mishap (real or imaginary) ends up in court. This mentality has resulted in people suing hospitals for so many frivolous violations that an entire legal community exists that deals only in malpractice or other medical infractions. Other litigated issues include privacy under HIPAA, medical fraud, and the unauthorized release of medical records. A growing number of negligence lawyers are emerging, specializing in any mishap related to healthcare activity including falling down the stairs – a specialty of "trip-and-fall" lawyers.

Malpractice cases against doctors and hospitals have become a cash cow for the legal profession due to the huge jury verdicts in court cases against hospitals and their medical staff. This growth of what are often considered frivolous lawsuits has forced many medical professionals to leave the field because of the cost of malpractice insurance. For economic survival, a growing number of hospitals have begun to self-insure with impressive results. There seems to be a correlation between the amount of the award and a higher-priced lawyer from a prestigious law firm, the defense lawyers from the in-house staff of a hospital – the former wins significantly more lucrative cases. Certain legal firms seem to win all the time – regardless of whether the merits substantiate the verdict. Jury awards appear to be based more on the skills of the lawyer (and the name of the law firm) rather than the facts of the case. It appears that the likelihood of winning a case increases when an expensive lawyer (for example, $500/hour) is hired to represent it, as opposed to the $40/hour organization's in-house staff attorney.

Lawsuits initiated due to the actions of a security guard or a lack of proper procedures taken in monitoring security controls will make it likely that security officers will need to testify in court at least once in their careers. Several lawyers who specialize in security-related legal conflicts are usually of the opinion that security officers are woefully unprepared to testify. Many lack adequate communication skills and are easily intimidated when speaking in an open court before a judge and jury. Security officers do not make the same impression as the trained police officers who are called to testify weekly on a "Law and Order" type-TV programs (who seem to be more qualified than the attorneys assigned to the case). In the real world, many cases are lost because of the poor impression made by members of the security staff during testimony. No accurate statistics could be used to predict the decisions of a jury of peers, and many of those decisions are often overthrown on appeal. In complicated lawsuits involving security violations, there is little reason to believe that an untrained jury listening to an inept security guard will testify being questioned by an inexperienced lawyer before a politically appointed judge – resulting in an appropriate decision.

Suits against military hospitals or Veteran Affairs (VA) healthcare facilities are not allowed under the federal law. Physicians employed in a VA or an army/navy/air force medical facility cannot be sued, and neither can any physician employed by the federal government (which also applies to nurses). Furthermore, if there is a malpractice claim, the patient cannot sue an individual doctor for medical negligence. Instead, the suit must be against the federal government. A doctor working in a federal facility may be making 50% less than a civilian doctor, but as a government employee, the government-employed doctor does not have to pay for any malpractice insurance (a valued perk).

Notes

1. Los Angeles County Department of Mental Health, PSP-Facts and Research Findings About Suicide FACTS AND RESEARCH FINDINGS ABOUT SUICIDE.
2. Charles-Hervé Vacheron, MD, Amélie Acker, MD, Melanie Autran, MD, Frederic Fuz, MD, Vincent Piriou, MD, PhD, Arnaud Friggeri, MD, PhD, Alexandre Theissen, MD, PhD, Insurance Claims for Wrong-Side, Wrong-Organ, Wrong-Procedure, or Wrong-Person Surgical Errors: A Retrospective Study for 10 Years, *Journal of Patient Safety*, 2023 January; 19(1): e13–e17, Published online November 22, 2022. PMCID: PMC9788930, PMID: 36538340.

Chapter 17

Conventional Security, Unconventional Environment

Security Safeguards

Security safeguards have grown in importance, paralleling the rapid expansion of the entire healthcare industry. Most hospital administrators involved in the selection of security systems were unfamiliar with the features and limitations of the new changing technologies and the special requirements found only in the hospital environment. Selecting a security system for a healthcare facility is becoming an overwhelming and complex undertaking, often requiring an outside expert – someone with knowledge of internet protocol and bandwidth. There is a scarcity of information on subjects relating to hospital security in general, but the biggest mystery remains in protecting the nursery areas, emergency rooms, and the (sometimes dangerous) behavioral health units.

Hospital security is a very expensive necessity that is often difficult to justify, since it is not a revenue-producing feature for a healthcare facility. Security must be visible without being intrusive and cost-effective without compromising the safety of patients, visitors, and hospital personnel. Security must now include plans and procedures in preparation for catastrophic events, while still complying with Federal, State, and Municipal codes – plus HIPAA regulations and the requirements of regulatory agencies, such as The Joint Commission. Healthcare facilities must maintain a haven for millions of visitors and patients in the nation's 5,400 hospitals, almost 16,000 nursing homes, and a growing number of clinics and physician

DOI: 10.4324/9781032630670-17

offices. While there are no accurate statistics, some estimate that more than two million people seek some care each day involving medical-related situations. Besides the millions of patients and visitors who move through the nation's healthcare centers, in 2022, 14.7 million people age 16 and older were employed in healthcare occupations, accounting for 9.3% of total employment.[1]

In the era since September 11, 2001, hospitals throughout the nation have been forced to increase their security budget tenfold, with very little improvement in the overall security environment. The technology is available, funds are being appropriated, and needs exist – but there is still a complete lack of any educational credentials or minimum level of experience required for the position of security director. Nevertheless, the security director is a position that requires more than supervising a group of uniformed guards. There is a growing need to understand IT networks and systems, software, and digital imaging – all essential responsibilities for this complex position. The material covered in this book may not make an expert out of the reader, but it will prepare the reader to defend themselves against the average alarm salespeople (while also removing much of the mystery surrounding the subject of physical security).

It is important to understand that the healthcare community represents a major influence on the nation's quality of life and is one of the largest employers in the country. In fact, hospitals and health systems are economic anchors that support one of every nine jobs in the United States and provide more than $1 trillion annually to the nation's gross domestic product (GDP) in goods and services.[2] A growing portion of that money is spent on security systems, surveillance equipment, and safety control. Not all the security funds are spent wisely or effectively.

Stolen Blank Prescription Forms

Hard-to-read handwritten prescription forms are a tradition practiced by physicians since the Hippocratic Oath was instituted (in fact, very few people in the fifth century could understand the writings in the oath). Written prescription forms can be dangerous to patients' health if misunderstood by pharmacists. That being said, there is also just as great a problem with blank prescription forms. Controlling the distribution of these official forms is important – whether in a doctor's private office or a hospital environment. Once stolen, drug addicts or others could forge prescriptions using these stolen forms. The security of the forms extends to keeping unauthorized hospital personnel from stealing the documents and selling them. Medical schools should be forced to offer penmanship courses to medical students. At the same time, they can provide some information on improving bedside manners and communication skills when talking to patients and their immediate families.

Back in the 1990s, the States passed statutes that require more protection for these highly sought-after forms by mandating that blank forms in a hospital must be housed in a locked cabinet or drawer. New statutes issued by health departments in several states mandate that each form has to be accounted for at all times. When a prescription is written in the doctor's office inside a medical center, it is transmitted over the hospital's network to dozens of printers scattered throughout the hospital complex. Each printer has a secure (lockable) paper tray housing these valuable forms. The regulations concerning blank forms intend to keep them from falling into the wrong hands. More importantly, medical staff are forced to use a keyboard to write a prescription. This procedure ensures that the names of the drugs are electronically printed, rather than having the prescription written in longhand (using a language known only to the doctors and a few pharmacists). Rumors since Hippocrates are that doctors had to prove that their handwriting was indecipherable before getting a medical license. Handwritten medication prescriptions still represent a common practice in hospitals worldwide. Prescriptions may be illegible as well as incomplete in terms of missing prescriber initials, missing or wrong dosage, missing or wrong frequency, and missing or wrong route of administration.[3] Today, in the advent of computer technology, there is no need for paper prescription forms or lockable printers. Prescriptions are now sent electronically over the internet directly to pharmacies. This has reduced the ability to steal or forge a prescription making the desire for illegal drugs more prominent.

Medical Equipment Theft

Crime in hospitals has remained at the same level over the last three decades, even with a fivefold increase in the purchase of alarms and the expansion in the number of personnel in the security department. Several surveys conducted by national organizations dealing with subjects related to the security system industry indicate that certain violent crimes, theft of hospital property, and theft of patient valuables have decreased – but, they have been replaced with other criminal activity. Property theft by patients and visitors – very often by family members – seems to have remained at the same level for the last four decades.

Thousands of devices and equipment found in any hospital are usable in the home – from toilet paper, pillowcases, and food supplies to items such as defibrillators and anesthesia machines. In the last decade, a lot of endoscopes and dialysis machines have left a medical facility unlawfully (usually carried out in three trips in a doctor's medical bag) and then appeared the next day on eBay. Endoscopes can cost upwards of $20,000.

During the 1990s, the most popular item removed from hospital property was the scrub gown worn by the medical staff. The public started wearing this "uniform", and hospitals had to abandon issuing scrubs like they did towels and disposable gloves. Staff received a clean green, long coat, only if they returned a dirty one. The number of scrubs leaving hospitals has declined significantly – not because of the added scrutiny, but simply because the public seems to have lost interest in the out-of-style scrub uniform.

Security checkpoints are often set up at large, inner-city hospital exits to search outgoing packages carried by personnel, patients, and visitors. This standard procedure can become a confrontation when doctors are requested to open a package or medical bag they are carrying for a search. All too often, a physician will refuse to comply and rush past the security desk and out of the building – along with half of the parts of a $50,000 diathermy machine (intending to remove the rest of the components at later dates). Hospital theft represents an enormous loss, and not all the stealing is done by non-professional staff members and/or visitors.

Property Losses ***involve five (5) categories***

1. Larceny Theft
2. Burglary
3. Motor Vehicle Theft
4. Arson
5. Vandalism

As newer and very expensive medical-testing devices are perfected and purchased by hospitals, the amount of thievery by employees (particularly doctors) has increased appreciably. Teaching hospitals have been forced to add security patrols during graduation week, when the number of stolen medical supplies and devices goes up fivefold. Interns and residents seem to feel a sense of entitlement for their long hours and low pay, so they steal anything that fits in a briefcase – or that can be removed a piece at a time for future re-assembly (similar to a dialysis machine). The theft of laptops and other computer-related devices does not reach a peak during graduation week. Computers may no longer be considered an expensive item – but because of the information stored in a hard drive, they can become very desirable items for database thieves seeking identifying information for billing fraud.

Other major losses include both small and large equipment from stethoscopes, surgical tools, microscopes, and endoscopes. While these are the butt of many jokes, they are also very expensive and easy to sell (on eBay, Craigslist, etc.). Endoscopy's booming popularity has made these flexible endoscopes a golden goose for thieves (both employees and visitors), since they cost between $23,000 and $39,000 and can easily be carried under a coat or arm. Many endoscopes find their way onto eBay, and their serial numbers and email addresses are easily traced back to medical staff.

Property-theft problems are shared by every hospital – regardless of its location, the surrounding neighborhood, or the income of the patient base. These problems are particularly rampant in larger cities such as Chicago, Los Angeles, and New York – where facilities may be in low-income neighborhoods and in some of the richest sections of the richest cities in the nation. Here, 350-square-foot studios sell for $900,000. While these observations may be slightly exaggerated, they serve to illustrate that all hospitals share a similar set of security problems – with a slight variation in the types of items stolen by patients. For example, property theft in hospitals in the poorer sections of a city consists of stolen toilet paper, towels, and diapers, while teaching hospitals located in the wealthy Upper East Side of Manhattan experience huge thefts of wheelchairs and medical office test devices (stethoscopes, endoscopes, and so forth).

Stealing Ink and Toner

In the open environment of a typical healthcare facility, trying to prevent thievery by the large staffs, the changing patient population, and the constant arrival of unsupervised visitors is an almost impossible challenge for hospitals. The value of material and medical equipment left indiscreetly in all areas of the hospital premises offers a great temptation to thousands of people who pass through the corridors of the nearly 5,400 U.S. medical facilities each year. Nurses have been caught removing drugs and common household items, and doctors – especially interns – "borrow" enough medical equipment to furnish their new office, and patients and visitors take their share of the valuable loot. Stealing a $100,000 diathermy machine or $20,000 proctoscopes are done in stages to ensure a later resell on eBay. On occasion, equipment is found in the trunk of a doctor's car (as it is about to leave the hospital parking lot). This act of recovering stolen property often results in disciplinary action from the hospital administration – not to the doctor who claims he was taking the machine home for reprogramming. The thief, in this incident, is a valuable revenue-producing asset.

The amount of equipment and material stolen each year from medical facilities is an unknown statistic. Some estimates indicate that it is a hundred times greater than theft from retail department stores and far greater than losses due to armed bank robberies in any given year. The problem of goods being stolen faces any business employing thousands of people, while leaving millions of dollars of equipment exposed to the public. One of the strangest and most innovative thefts occurred at New York City hospital, where a receiving clerk ordered boatloads of unnecessary printer cartridges and resold them before they were placed in the hospital storeroom. The rewards from the scheme funded a lavish lifestyle that allowed the $37,000-a-year clerk to move from a housing project to a luxurious Trump high-rise and install expensive furniture.

The unsupervised clerk would order, almost daily, ink cartridges for various models of printers from Office Depot to be delivered to the shipping dock at the hospital (many of the ink cartridges were unusable for any of the machines in the hospital). Delivery drivers were instructed to call when they were close to the shipping dock so he could personally receive the packages. The clerk would then move the boxes of toners to a garage area. Each load was small enough to fit into a car while avoiding any attention from the receiving department. These almost daily deliveries went on for more than five years before an outside auditor discovered old TV surveillance tapes that recorded the daily transfer of boxes. The ruse eventually involved more than $3,500,000 of toners and ink cartridges stolen – which were easily resold by the clerk on the internet using a third-party distributor. Each time some lowly employee gets away with criminal activity for many years (completely unnoticed), it raises justifiable concern among authorities who can only wonder what is being stolen by someone on the hospital staff who is even more well-versed than a shipping clerk.

Resistance to E-prescribing

Drugstore pharmacies are incorrectly deciphering illegible handwriting on prescription forms or compounding the problem by simply handing the task of filling the prescription to their technicians. Either of these actions has caused fatalities and resulted in huge settlements awarded by the courts for these inexcusable errors. Walgreens, the nation's largest drugstore chain by sales and profits, employs about 39,000 technicians and 24,000 pharmacists. In most situations, the technician fills the prescription, and the pharmacists supposedly check to see that the proper drug was prepared.

CVS is the largest retail chain regarding store count and employs about 41,000 technicians and 20,000 pharmacists. Technicians do most of the administrative work formerly performed by pharmacists – such as prescription data entry, counting pills, filling vials, and ringing registers. The advantage of this arrangement is that it frees the pharmacist to do more important work, such as making sure the technician did not make a mistake. However, the busy pharmacists have little time to catch every error – and sometimes, they lack the patience to properly train technicians on how to tell the difference between drugs with similar names:

Product	Has Been Mistaken for
Lipitor – Lowers cholesterol	Labetalol – Blood pressure
Lopid – Lowers cholesterol	Zocor – Lowers cholesterol
Zoloft – Anti-depressant	Zofran – Nausea medication
Zomig – Pain medication	Zyrtec – Antihistamine
Amoxicillin – Antibiotic	Amoxapine – Anti-depressant
Ampicillin – Antibiotic	Amoxapine – Anti-depressant
Augmentin – Antibiotic	Amoxapine – Anti-depressant

As email and texting become the preferred means of written communication, handwriting has almost disappeared. However, doctors are probably the last people to give up this form of communication. Penmanship is becoming a modern form of hieroglyphics and remains meaningful only to literary scholars. Sloppy writing or inappropriate directions on a prescription form can lead to what doctors delicately refer to as preventable adverse drug events (PADEs). The results can be minor, such as rashes or diarrhea, or can cause much more serious events – including death. Studies show that errors are much less likely if a doctor clicks to select medications from a screen list and sends the prescription data through a computer to the pharmacy.

Medication errors are the most common and preventable cause of patient injury. These errors typically involve administering the wrong drug or dose, using the wrong route, administering it incorrectly, or giving medication to the wrong patient. The reported incidence of medication errors in acute hospitals is approximately 6.5 per 100 admissions. These events are estimated to cost between 37.6 and 50 billion dollars of added health care costs, disability, and lost productivity.[4] Now, most prescribers have e-prescribing capability integrated into EHRs. Virtually all pharmacies can accept e-prescriptions, and 92% of prescribers e-prescribe, an 85% increase from 2008 when only 7% of prescribers were sending e-prescriptions.[5]

The stimulus package passed in 2009 included a provision to pay doctors and medical facilities for most of the cost to change from a paper-file system to the e-prescription-based filing. The provision was to theoretically ease the financial burden for doctors, but the payments are tied to Medicare and Medicaid reimbursements spread out over five years. This leaves substantial upfront costs – causing private practitioners to go slowly before committing to entering the new age of e-medical record storage and transfer. Additionally, this adds more hours to the workday to enter data, because the available systems are far from plug and play.

Doctors had the option of joining the e-prescription crowd or refraining from joining the movement. Today, it has been completely embraced eliminating prescription errors usually associated with misreading the written prescription. Since the 1990s, using computers to store medical data and electronically circulate easy-to-read, keyboard-generated prescriptions has been available. One day the prescription pad will take its place next to the jar of leeches in the Museum of Medical Curiosities.

Ambulance Alert System for Lawyers

The century-old image of professionals with law degrees chasing ambulances into the emergency room to get clients for a malpractice suit is an unfair stereotype that has tarnished the reputation of some lawyers. Over-aggressive and sometimes unethical attorneys solicit clients at the scene of an accident, in the hospital emergency room, or in any situation in which the medical profession may have caused medical harm to a patient. The origin of the derogatory term "ambulance chasers" dates from 1897, when newspaper articles described how attorneys sought out clients through targeted mail solicitation. For the most part, the phrase is no longer in popular use and is replaced by the more accurate description, "Trip and Sue Lawyers". In recent years, this phrase has evolved into "negligence lawyers", describing lawyers who are not ambulance chasers or trip-and-sue lawyers. This group of lawyers advertises in every media with claims of no charge for their services unless they win the lawsuit – then they take only a 33% cut.

Much of the criticism of the law profession is undeserved, since only a small proportion of lawyers become ambulance chasers. Shakespeare was wrong when he wrote, "Let's kill all the lawyers", as most lawyers serve the public well and perform a valued service in all areas of public concern – even in medical malpractice cases. Without lawyers, this nation would probably resemble a third-world country.

Employees in a hospital emergency-room facility are particularly vulnerable to the more aggressive and unethical members of the legal profession, once they discover that being the first to chase the ambulance into the emergency receiving areas can result in large lawsuit judgments. As a result, any referrals from an emergency-room staff member result in a flat fee or a percentage of the recovery amount. These comments are not meant to be an attack against the entire legal profession, but the public has witnessed a growing number of lawsuits against hospital medical staff. The enormous monetary awards against the hospital center have forced some state governments to place a cap on the penalties – and some hospitals have had to adjust to these courtroom judgments by closing some of their facilities, notably, the birthing wards and psychiatry sections.

The New York State Bar Association, like a few other state bar associations, specifically forbids attorneys ambushing victims and relatives to solicit legal services in the wake of a tragedy. In 2013, a commuter train traveling to New York City at too high a speed to make a turn ended up derailing all the cars, killing four and injuring 63. This presented the perfect situation for attracting the so-called ghoulish lawyers to make a quick buck – a clear violation of the state code. Similar situations have occurred after public transportation disasters – such as a bus crash in 2011 that killed fifteen people and the 2009 plane crash in Buffalo that killed all forty-five on board.

After each incident, lawyers practicing in the state were reminded that they had to recognize the importance of respecting the privacy of the victims and their families before they tried to initiate personal injury and wrongful death lawsuits. The State court's conduct rule says that lawyers cannot approach disaster victims or their families for thirty days after an incident – except when the law requires a case to be filed within that time frame. Of course, this cooling-off period does not apply to victims if they want to sue and voluntarily seek legal representation any time after an incident.

Flying-Ambulance Chasers

Among the most lucrative booms in healthcare since 2008 are helicopter-ambulance services. These indisputably save lives, often in dramatic circumstances. Nevertheless, they have the potential to cause heart attacks after a patient receives the bill. The air-ambulance industry has aggressively expanded its fleet of expensive helicopters, because health insurance has covered a large share of the cost. The air-ambulance industry can place an unplanned burden on a patient, if an insurance company that offers air-ambulance coverage no longer covers the full cost of the emergency service – leaving patients to pay the difference. Medicare has typically covered a smaller portion of the bills than private insurance – with Medicaid covering even less.

Over 550,000 patients use air-ambulance services annually in the United States, but often these trips represent a significant economic burden with a per-trip median cost of $36,000.[6] These high charges typically catch patients by surprise. In emergencies, they are transported, and a helicopter will pick people up – regardless of their ability to pay. Patients generally object to the high cost, with some going into voluntary bankruptcy to avoid payment.

Other complaints include:

- Questioning why the relatively short rides could cost so much, the bills only contribute to more stress during their recovery period, and the patients' injuries often prevent them from returning to work.
- Wondering whether a regular ambulance (a much cheaper option) would have been a more appropriate response for the injuries sustained.
- Patients contend that they could have reached the hospital more quickly by road than by air.

The median price for an air-ambulance trip is $36,000. For context, the average cost of operating an air-ambulance flight (according to air-ambulance providers) is between $6,000 and $13,000. In recent years, several pieces of legislation have been enacted at the federal level to address this issue. Section 418 of the 2018 Federal Aviation Administration (FAA) Reauthorization Act requires the Secretary of Transportation and the Secretary of Health and Human Services to establish a committee that will "make recommendations with respect to [the] disclosure of charges and fees for air-ambulance services and insurance coverage, consumer protection and enforcement authorities of both the Department of Transportation and State authorities, and the prevention of balance billing to consumers". The Consolidated Appropriations Act of 2021 addresses the high cost of air ambulances by establishing in-network cost-sharing. A resolution process for resolving conflicts between service providers and insurance plans and issuers, and mandates the increase of data collection pertaining to the number and location of air bases, the reasons for denied claims, the number and type of aircraft used as air ambulances, and the costs of flights.

Notes

1. U.S. Bureau of Labor Statistics, Spotlight on Statistics, Healthcare Occupations: Characteristics of the Employed, Sean Smith and Andrew Blank
2. Mary Scott Nabers, The Rise of Hospital Infrastructure & Modernization Updates, *Construction Business Owner*, April 8, 2024.
3. Journal of Clinical Nursing, A new approach of assessing patient safety aspects in routine practice using the example of "doctors handwritten prescriptions", 2019 April; 28(7–8): 1242–1250.
4. National Library of Medicine, Medication Dispensing Errors and Prevention, Rayhan A. Tariq; Rishik Vashisht; Ankur Sinha; Yevgeniya Scherbak, February 12, 2024.
5. HealthcIT buzz, A Decade of Data Examined: The Evolution of Electronic Prescribing, Meghan Gabriel; Tricia Lee Rolle and Chelsea Richwine, July 15, 2024
6. American Action Forum, Addressing the High Costs of Air Ambulance Services, Dan Goldbeck, Malcolm Mahoney, August 2023.

Chapter 18

Electronic Recordkeeping

Improving Healthcare by Sharing Medical Treatment

Americans overwhelmingly agree that creating a medical record storage center that would be shared by healthcare facilities throughout the nation would significantly improve medical treatment and save the lives of many of its millions of citizens. The government issued a regulation in 1994, proclaiming that all physicians and healthcare providers would have to computerize medical records for their patients (including doctor's notes) by 2008. In the intervening fourteen years since that decree was issued and the compliance date expired, the medical community (as expected) made little effort to comply. In 2009, the federal government provided cash incentives to doctors and hospitals to adopt electronic health records, and this impetus accelerated the program to replace the office-stored paper trail of medical records that had been placed in eight-foot-high file racks that took up entire storage rooms in both hospitals and doctors' offices.

According to available data, every other industrialized country is doing a better job of medical recordkeeping than its American counterpart. The slow acceptance in the United States for electronic recordkeeping can be blamed on the massive bureaucratic healthcare system and the lack of easy-to-use software that would be compatible among the different programs offered by competitive services that specialize in digitalizing healthcare records. The slow adoption of worthwhile programs could be due to a lack of a centralized care structure along with the enormous effort and cost to implement the computerized recordkeeping technology. It will take years for a "return on the investment" for hospitals and independent doctors, even though

DOI: 10.4324/9781032630670-18

much of the initial cost may be covered under incentive grants from the federal government.

Federal incentives were instituted in 2009 under the Health Information Technology (HIT) program to expedite electronic recordkeeping. Hospitals still resisted adopting electronic health recordkeeping procedures, since it can cost $20 to $100 million for a medical facility to purchase and maintain such a system (and thousands for individual doctor's offices). As an example of the costs, the healthcare company Kaiser Permanente installed an electronic recordkeeping system for its thirty-six hospitals and more than eight million members. The estimated cost for the software and related costs, including equipment and training employees, totals around $4 billion for that company alone. Further complicating the decision to convert from paper to digital storage is the chance that, when hospitals become more efficient, they could potentially lose money. Insurance companies might offer lower reimbursements based on the cost savings.

It took much longer for the healthcare industry than it took for banks and airlines to accept electronic data storage and programming. In banking, the types of data are much more limited and known, while healthcare data (based on information from doctors, nurses, patients, and others) is constantly changing. Making a plane reservation on a digitalized, fixed schedule is a relatively simple programming operation – unlike analyzing new medical discoveries, protocols, and government requirements that all add more complexity to any health-record program. Furthermore, unlike other industries, healthcare data can be a matter of life or death. Using computerized record systems is the best way to search for and evaluate information in ways that paper files can never duplicate.

With the average American visiting up to nineteen different doctors in their lifetime, it is vital that records of patients be shared and available in all situations. Paper records are still used by some doctors for billing and patient orientation – which means nineteen different physicians could be asking patients about the same allergies, medications, and test results. Getting one fact wrong can result in disaster. Once medical records are digitally stored and made available to healthcare providers, doctors will be able to follow decades of data on diabetes patients and will be able to determine which medicines are absolutely the best and then personalize the doses. Even after all the funding and encouragement by the government and the obvious value of having digital records available, nearly 80% of hospitals and 86% of ambulatory clinics in the United States have implemented an EHR as of 2015 and 2017.[1] Experts expect that this percentage will grow to qualify with the 2009 federal stimulus package, and they hope that 100% of all patient records will be online by 2025.

Some practitioners in the medical service field claim that the shared record-storage procedure means that doctors see fewer patients while providing worse care.

Another dilemma that arose during the period when hospitals were supposedly trying to implement the digitization of healthcare records involved "outsourcing" – the task of sorting electronic medical records to other countries, such as India. It caused a great deal of concern among American hospitals that had become sensitive about privacy issues relating to HIPAA regulations. Furthermore, companies in India that have experience in performing software outsourcing work for pharmaceutical companies and insurers have not been as successful in attracting business from U.S. hospitals that were expected to spend a total of $19.9 billion in 2024, which estimated hospital EHR spending to be more like $9.9 billion.[2] Hospitals have practical reasons for being reluctant to work with offshore vendors on digital medical records. It is more efficient to do the work on-site, and there are potential legal complications that can result from shipping sensitive health information to foreign countries. Designing and installing new medical record software is hard to do off-site, let alone offshore.

Even with the criticism and reluctance coming from many doctors to install medical records electronically, doctors' offices and hospitals that provide Medicare or Medicaid have complied with the government's request. Records now allow a patient's doctor to see what tests have been performed and which medications have been administered. This could stop duplicated prescriptions and bad drug interactions. Providers understand that these electronic records are a step away from fee-for-service payment programs and a step toward team-based healthcare. Doctors need to be able to share information easily. Before electronic records, doctors did not always know when their patients were released – or even that they were in the hospital.

Hospitals and private physician practices must continue to show a concerted effort to adopt electronic records completely or risk losing federal reimbursements for medical care. This could be the stimulus that could get the nation's doctors to make electronic recordkeeping a high priority. A typical 500-bed hospital could be eligible to receive $5 million from the government for implementing digital health records. However, a hospital that had not acted by 2017 lost as much as $3.2 million a year in Medicare funding. Many U.S. software firms were trying to get into the business before it was outsourced to India. One firm that seems to have satisfied all parties in the outsourcing debate has its headquarters in New Jersey, but most of its staff are in India. The current leaders in the digital health record industry are Epic Systems, IBM, and Cerner.

Three out of four physicians who responded to several surveys claimed that electronic health records do not save them time, and doctors reported spending an average of forty-eight minutes each day dealing with the record system. Another criticism, according to the Agency for Healthcare Research and Quality, was that the average five-physician primary care practice would spend $162,000 to implement the system, followed by $85,000 in first-year maintenance costs. Small private practices often find it difficult to pay such large sums without passing the costs onto their patients.

Opposition to Digitalized Medical Records

In the decade since the federal government mandated the sharing of medical records more than $29 billion has been appropriated and spent in establishing information technology for recordkeeping in doctors' offices and hospitals. This task has not been met with a lot of enthusiasm. Some hospital administrations claim that tech companies, hospitals, and laboratories have been intentionally blocking the electronic exchange of health information – because they fear that they will lose business if they share information on patients with competing providers. Also, some of the largest providers of health information technology try to "lock in" customers by making it difficult for them to switch to competing vendors.

Information Blocking

Information blocking is when users are prevented or discouraged from obtaining electronic health information:

- A doctor may have to pay exorbitant fees to transfer information regarding patients from the medical record system of one vendor to that of another.

- A network of doctors and hospitals often refuses to share information on patients with providers outside the network – even when the information is needed to treat patients, and sharing the data is allowed by federal rules.
- Doctors obtain laboratory services and health records technology from one company, which will not let them connect to a competing laboratory – even though the connection is technically feasible, and the doctors are willing to pay for it.

Under a typical arrangement, a vendor can charge millions to build a connection to another system and as much as $500,000 a year to maintain that connection. Then, they charge another two dollars each time the patient's record is sent to a facility that uses a different system. Very few hospitals are willing to meet this financial burden. Congress has tried to stop the information blocking arrangement by making it a federal offense – resulting in doctors, hospitals, and technology vendors potentially being punished with civil fines up to $10,000 for each violation. Even with this threat, conversion to the universal acceptance of digitalized records is many years away from implementation.

Doctors Can Become Robots

Not too long ago, the medical profession based its treatment on using a physician's presence and touch. Doctors treated entire families (often in their homes) and wrote expansive notes that captured not only the vicissitudes of illness but also the lives of patients. By the middle of the second decade of the twentieth century, thousands of "service robots" entered the healthcare field to perform many of the functions once left to medical staffs. These changes are not solely the result of advances in technology but are also a result of this country's healthcare system facing cost pressures and a shortage of doctors and nurses that will worsen as baby boomers' Medicare health benefits explode. Many administrators are starting to rely on robots by reassigning some of the less glamorous work on robotic mobile machines. By doing so, they have inadvertently created a new industry for software and application developers to write programs for these uncomplaining devices.

A medical robot will duplicate many of the features increasingly found in smartphones, gaming consoles, and other consumer electronics – such as advanced sensors, motion detectors, powerful microprocessors, and voice-activation devices. Robots have been proven to respond with artificial intelligence and can navigate through changing environments – even in chaotic hospital settings. They have already staked out a place in the healthcare world, with surgical droids that can suture a wound better than the human hand. In the military, specialized robots can defuse bombs and help navigate hostile environments in Iraq and Afghanistan.

Doctors can use the robots to obtain essential clinical information from monitors and other gadgets remotely, in real time. They connect doctors to far-flung patients with videoconferencing, which enables a doctor to make his or her rounds virtually and check on patients even though they may be miles away. These roving machines earn their keep by responding to commands to track goods, as well as haul food trays, linens, trash, medical records, medication, and other items from one area of the facility to another. Using sophisticated GPS programs, robots can stay out of the way of rushing doctors and nurses and stop on a dime when someone is directly in front of the unit. While a robot can operate efficiently at half the cost of hiring staff, many lament the replacement of human workers with machines – especially union delegates. They argue that robots take away the community spirit that is important in treating patients and that the machines hog the elevators. Robots were controversial when they were first introduced into the hospital environment, but they will proliferate in spite of some resistance shown – mostly by some of the workers they will replace.

Verbal Charting Data

Many physicians use tape recorders to collect their observations following a consultation with a patient. A transcriber types the notes into a paper form to be filed in the medical record. Doctors used the dictation process for many years when compiling patient care history – mainly for post-care summaries, orders, and prescriptions. With the growing use of new voice-recognition technology introduced by the iPhone and its all-knowing Siri, doctors can now use software that allows them to talk directly to the record file, without the need for a translator or a tape recorder. The developers of voice-recognition systems for the medical field are interested in getting doctors to document patient information more immediately and more thoroughly.

Some of the early systems can highlight and validate medical facts and spot inconsistencies that the physician did not notice, such as an allergy to a certain medication. The system asks follow-up questions, similar to Siri's response to iPhone voice inquiries. The federal government's call for hospitals to install electronic medical records systems has encouraged the development of more sophisticated voice-recognition systems for medical record storage and the sharing of information between treatment facilities through the internet. It will eventually replace the paper trails and thick files found in the "doctors' offices' cluttered storeroom shelves".

Online Access to Patients' Records

In the past, patients could legally get their records. Yet, many patients either did not know this or found the process expensive and tedious to even try. Since the passage of the recordkeeping regulation act, physicians are concerned that patients would not understand the information that appears on a medical record. Another fear was that patients unfamiliar with medical diagnostic terminology might incorrectly second-guess their doctors' findings. A study involving 38,000 patients around the country and hundreds of doctors appeared in the Annals of Internal Medicine in 2011 and indicated that, in direct contrast to the doctors' fear, a vast majority believe the information will empower patients to take charge of their health:

- 94% believe the records should be available.
- 90% said the information would give them more control.
- 80% said they would take better care of themselves because of the information.
- Half believed the information would help them take their medication properly.

A long history exists of doctors telling patients what to do without anticipating patients' questioning their advice – a traditional patriarchal relationship that assumes the doctor knows best. Doctors still firmly believe in this philosophy and worry that giving patients access to their notes (albeit mostly illegible – like the scribbles on prescription forms) would only confuse patients. More than 80% of the doctors in that same annual survey expressed great concerns, also indicating that notes placed online serve no practical medical purpose. They also believed that in the future, doctors would be discouraged from adding these notes to the medical digitalized permanent records.[3]

Adding to the arguments surrounding electronic medical records are studies that raise doubts about saving money for office-based physicians. Experts have long contended that computerized patient records will save the healthcare system money by helping doctors reduce the number of redundant or inappropriate tests they order. An article in a noted publication in 2012, based on a survey of thousands of doctors and patients, strongly suggested that office-based physicians (who have access to the electronic record of patient care) are more likely to order additional imaging and laboratory tests than doctors who rely on paper records. While there are also studies that support the value of computerization, there are now cautionary statistics that may make the federal government re-evaluate spending billions of dollars to encourage the adoption of digitalized medical records.

The study challenging the effectiveness of computer record storage was based on a federal survey that collected data from 28,000 patient visits to 1,100 doctors. It found that doctors who could call up electronic images of a patient's previous imaging tests – such as X-rays and CT scans – ordered new imaging tests in 18% of visits. Physicians without such access ordered imaging on only 13% of visits. The rate was 70% higher for the most advanced and expensive tests. The study points out that the leading medical centers have sophisticated technology, while most doctor's offices buy off-the-shelf systems (primarily for billing purposes) that may not be able to track down redundancies – or they lack the software to help doctors decide if a test is appropriate.[4]

There may be no question that healthcare will be improved and that costs will be reduced by the widespread adoption of electronic medical records. It is also clear that many office-based physicians will need to take advantage of the federal program aimed at encouraging physician practices to make the switch and that the program has helped in making the transition. No matter how adept doctors become with computerized records, they need to be pushed to rein in excessive use of unnecessary tests – even after they receive the transferred electronic medical records.

Data Storage and Other Catastrophes

Healthcare facilities with electronic records are proving more resilient in the face of not only natural disasters – but other unexpected dangers, such as fires. Because they are stored in large databases that are not on-site, they can be quickly reconstructed. Concerns about the costs associated with the adoption of electronic records and taking adequate measures to ensure patient confidentiality are outweighed by improvements in access to care and patient safety. Although the United States has been slower than many other wealthy countries in adopting computerized records on a broad scale, the nation is catching up. As electronic records have become more widespread, it is clear they are not only the key to improving twenty-first century healthcare, but they also have proven to be of critical importance in emergency preparedness and can foster community resilience. Electronic medical records are designed first and foremost to make healthcare delivery safer and more efficient – but are also proving valuable when a natural disaster strikes.

After recent natural disasters, like the deadly tornado that tore through the city of Joplin, Missouri and killed 161 people in 2011, we can see the importance of having easy access to medical records. The twister heavily damaged the region's main medical facility, sucking up patient files and X-rays and depositing them up to seventy miles away. Three weeks earlier, the hospital had the foresight to switch from paper to electronic health records, without having predicted the destruction ahead or the benefits the electronic records would quickly provide. Even as the hospital's patients were evacuated, the staff was busily accessing and printing out patient records from a remote site, sending copies with the patients to the hospitals where they were transferred. Days later, patient care resumed in a makeshift field hospital erected in a parking lot. The availability of the computerized records also allowed doctors affiliated with the hospital, whose own clinics were destroyed, to resume care at new sites.

The potential tragic consequences of not having a computerized record system were sadly evident in 2005, after Hurricane Katrina, when thousands of patient records were destroyed in all the New Orleans medical centers and at other healthcare facilities along the Gulf Coast. Physicians receiving evacuees at makeshift facilities were forced to provide treatment without a clear record of patients' medical histories, allergies, medications, or test results. The lack of records for civilians contrasted with the military veterans who were also evacuated. Their records were maintained through the Veterans Health Administration's groundbreaking electronic recordkeeping system, and doctors were able to provide uninterrupted care at other VA medical centers throughout the country where the evacuated veterans were taken.

Scribes – Medical Office Temps

Without much fanfare or planning, a new medical profession has evolved: Medical Scribe Specialists. They have been employed since 2011, to enter existing medical records and data from hundreds of clinics and emergency rooms into computers. Doctors and hospitals had gotten serious about meeting the government's mandate to digitalize medical records by 2016, and their current staff did not have the time to complete the conversion. Modern electronic health record systems (once in a network) will eliminate the constant note-taking by a physician that takes too much attention from a patient during an examination and follow-up treatment. The scribe is a modern-day stenographer who translates a patient's illness into a computer language that can be read and circulated to other doctors online or can be shared between medical centers anywhere in the nation – as long as they use the same software.

Scribes improve a physician's predictability and allow them to focus on a patient without interruption during an examination. The growing army of trained scribes not only digitalize medical records – but they also include observations, treatment, prescription data, and the patient's past medical history. They are usually provided by a rent-a-scribe service, since most of the work is getting the paper files onto the network so that doctors or emergency room staff can add to the process without increasing their staff. The rates for an entry-level scribe can range from $12 per hour to $20 an hour. For an experienced scribe, the rate can be from $18 to $22 an hour. Each scribe takes an online course and passes an examination from the American College of Medical Scribe Specialists (ACMSS) to obtain a nationally recognized certification. The course costs about $2,000.[5]

New Frontier for Identity Thieves

A detailed spreadsheet from a medical billing contractor working for a hospital to manage the digitization of medical records somehow found its way onto a website called Student of Fortune. This 2011 medical security breach took place at one of California's largest hospitals, Stanford Hospital in Palo Alto. The breach in security was notable – not only for the information that became public but also for the length of time that the data remained publicly available without detection (one year). The confidential medical records posted on the commercial website contained the personal data of 20,000 emergency room patients – including names, diagnosis codes, account numbers, admission and discharge dates, and billing charges for patients during a six-month period. The California Department of Public Health fined Stanford Hospital $250,000 (the maximum allowed) for failing to report the breach within five days of discovery – as is required under state law. This was not an isolated case.[6]

In 2023, 725 data breaches were reported to OCR and across those breaches, more than 133 million records were exposed or impermissibly disclosed.[7] Over half of the reported breaches resulted from stolen laptops, but a great number of information leaks could also be traced to hacked networks, unencrypted records, misdirected mailings, missing files, and wayward emails. The Stanford violation exposed the fact that even the most prestigious medical centers in the country are not immune to risk. This raises fears that less sophisticated institutions may be even more vulnerable to security breaches. Hospitals are also having difficulty teaching doctors and other staff members how to use the PC record platforms, let alone protect the data. The lack of training is not as much a concern as the growing incidents of data being stolen, creating a gold mine for identity thieves.

- Massachusetts General Hospital, a facility that trains Harvard medical students, agreed to pay $1 million in settlement fees after an employee left paper medical records for 192 patients on a subway while commuting to work. The pages included the names of hundreds of patients and diagnoses for about one-third of them, including information on their HIV/AIDS status. They were never recovered. All these breaches violate the Health Insurance Portability and Accountability Act (HIPAA), the 1996 law that requires protection of medical records.[8]
- The Luxottica Group PIVA-owned vision insurance company, EyeMed Vision Care, experienced a data breach in June 2020 involving the protected health information (PHI) of 230,572 individuals. An FTC server had been left exposed over the internet. OCR's investigators identified a risk analysis failure, a lack of a business associate agreement with a subcontractor, and an impermissible disclosure of the PHI of 230,572 individuals. The case was settled for $350,000.[9]

An unintended consequence of digitalizing medical records is that the number of breaches has surged. Data breaches increased once again in 2022, with OCR receiving reports of 720 data breaches of 500 or more records. There was no letup in cyberattacks on healthcare organizations in 2023, which set two new records – The most reported data breaches and the most breached records. In 2023, 725 data breaches were reported to OCR and across those breaches, more than 133 million records were exposed or impermissibly disclosed.[10] The healthcare community has begun to realize that this new security threat focuses on data rather than equipment. Far too much emphasis relating to hospital security has traditionally been focused on designing physical protection systems, such as CCTV surveillance cameras and access control systems. In this age of digital communication, the real security problems are no longer solved by selecting detection and surveillance hardware. The problem is in protecting the integrity of hospital software, medical records, and the internal computer networks.

Medicare Scams

Compared to the growing number of Medicare cheats, stealing a few endoscopes is petty cash for a hospital's balance sheet. Healthcare fraud has become so prevalent that the old-fashioned bank robbers have given up their previous dangerous occupation and started billing Medicare for items never delivered, services never performed, and unnecessary tests – for millions of federal dollars. Medicare has become the biggest drain of the federal budget, and epidemic fraud is the biggest drain of Medicare. CBS News reported recently that scammers have taken more than $100 million meant for senior citizens' Medicare bills, which comes from taxpayer money. The swindlers were only caught after making $3 billion worth of fake Medicare claims.[11]

Major problems for containing fraud is that Medicare pays first, then asks questions later – a sequence of events that leaves criminals with a time gap, allowing them time to bank the funds, shut down their empty storefronts, and abruptly leave the state well before an investigation begins. In a recent year, the federal government handed down more than ninety-four indictments nationwide in one day. However, the chances of getting nabbed for Medicare fraud remain relatively small. The potential profits from Medicare crimes remain large. Recently, a Florida man and woman were sentenced for their roles in a wide-ranging conspiracy to defraud Medicare by billing over $93 million for home health therapy services that were never rendered.[12] When the federal government grew suspicious of the scam, they placed a cap on claims for homebound patients receiving insulin injections, forcing the scam artists toward other exploitable areas – in particular, mental health and physical therapy treatments. Medicare is the biggest drain on the federal budget, and epidemic fraud is the biggest drain on Medicare. Most older Americans depend on the program to cover many healthcare expenses, but the system is sagging and bloated. For example, experts say Medicare fraud in South Florida costs U.S. taxpayers between $3 billion and $4 billion annually. It's predictable that Miami-Dade, Broward, and Palm Beach counties would be the hotbed, and also the venue for one of every three federal healthcare fraud prosecutions.[13]

Healthcare fraud has become an appealing career for former bank robbers and other out-of-work felons who no longer need a gun to steal money. Money can be made by using a pencil when filling out the government Medicare reimbursement forms – without arousing the suspicions of local law enforcement authorities.

Doctors in southern areas of the country that attract older, retired seniors prescribe so many tests that patients often contact their physicians from their old residences up north for advice. Unnecessary tests for retired seniors are a trend that has prompted doctors to warn their older patients before they depart for Florida and other winter getaways to check with them before agreeing to undergo exams and procedures. Medical testing is a huge industry in the United States – with prices that are highly variable in different parts of the country. Medicare is the government insurance program for those older than sixty-five or with disabilities. While the costs for the tests are strictly regulated, doctors who treat seniors can increase revenues by simply expanding the volume of such services and ordering tests of questionable value. It is very easy for doctors and dentists to take advantage of this retired population – and they do.

Florida has emerged in recent years as the epicenter of Medicare abuse. High-volume testing is also a good way for physicians to supplement their income when insurers are cutting back on payments for individual services for younger people. Doctors now often own the testing equipment as they move more equipment and technology into their offices. This once-limited category has grown to include a wide range of tests – from X-rays to expensive cardiac testing to suites where they can perform biopsies.

For the year 2022–2023, the State of Florida closed 335 fraud cases. Of those, 218 involved Medicaid fraud investigations. Highlights from those cases include:

- Advanced Bionics Corporation (ABC), a manufacturer and distributor of cochlear implants. ABC allegedly violated the federal and various state False Claims Acts by submitting false or fraudulent claims for reimbursement to federal healthcare programs, including Medicaid.
- Southeast Florida Hematology and Oncology Group (SEFHOG), a now-defunct specialty medical practice in Fort Lauderdale, Fla., has agreed to pay $100,000 to resolve allegations that it violated the False Claims Act with respect to the Florida Medicaid program by receiving "upfront discounts" from its specialty pharmaceutical distributor, Cardinal Health, in violation of the Anti-Kickback Statute.
- Florida Cardiology, P.A., Sandeep Bajaj, Karan Reddy, and eight other physicians have agreed to pay the United States.
- Agreed to pay the United States and the State of Florida $199,497.62 to resolve allegations that it violated the False Claims Act by submitting inflated claims to Medicaid and for billing while the physicians were outside the United States.[14]

Ransomware Target Healthcare Facilities – With Success

Since around mid-2015, hackers have increasingly targeted healthcare institutions and threatened people's well-being as their software attacks become more sophisticated and brazen. With 386 health care cyberattacks reported through October 2024, data-theft crimes and ransomware attacks against health care and our mission-critical third-party providers appear to be unfolding at the same elevated rate as in 2023, which was the worst year ever for breaches in health care. The scope and impact of this year's breaches, however, have been much more profound.[15] Payment of the ransomware bounty demands are often paid. These instances are rarely revealed, as certain governmental spokesmen have publicly claimed that payment only encourages more digitally based threats. It is very much like condemning a family that pays a ransom to get their child back from kidnappers.

Attacks on hospitals have mostly involved ransomware that focuses on holding the hospital data hostage by encrypting it – and then only releasing it upon payment (if the inexperienced hackers remember how to undo the program). Experts in cyberattack technology claim that in the coming years, attacks could control the hospital's online systems to overtake the facility's online systems and manipulate machines – with instances like increasing the dosage of intravenous drops, swapping blood types in patients, or even sending an ambulance on a fake call.

These cyberattack demands against large organizations can range between ten and thirty million – and some of the more brazen hackers follow up their monetary demands with threats to publish the stolen and sensitive data. Targeted companies (including hospitals) effectively face a tough choice: either pay the attackers or hire others to help recover systems, which can take weeks or longer. In the long run, victim organizations, institutions, and municipalities find it cheaper to pay the ransom.

Notes

1. National Library of Medicine, Burnout Related to Electronic Health Record Use in Primary Care, Jeffrey Budd PMCID: PMC10134123 PMID: 37073905, April 2023.
2. Kat Jercich, Hospital EHR Spending Projected to Reach $9.9B by 2024, *Health IT News*, May 21, 2020.
3. Leila Gray, Doctors Cautious, Patients Enthusiastic about Sharing Medical Notes, *University of Washington News*, December 19, 2011.
4. Steve Lohr, Digital Records May Not Cut Health Costs, Study Finds, *The New York Times*, March 2012.
5. Aya De La Cruz-Pandy, How Much Does a Medical Scribe Make? Our In-Depth Guide, *Wing*, February 2023.
6. Kevin Sack, Patient Data Posted Online in Major Breach of Privacy, *The New York Times*, September 2011.
7. Steve Alder, Healthcare Data Breach Statistics, *The HIPAA Journal*, October 2024.
8. Carey Goldberg, MGH Settles for $1 M After HIV Patient Records Lost on Subway, *WBUR*, February 2011, https://www.wbur.org/news/2011/02/24/mass-general-privacy
9. The HIPAA Journal, HIPAA Violation Cases, https://www.hipaajournal.com/hipaa-violation-cases/#:~:text=Green%20Ridge%20Behavioral%20Health%20was%20determined%20to,the%20PHI%20of%20more%20than%2014%2C000%20patients.
10. The HIPAA Journal, Healthcare Breach Statistics, Steve Adler, October, 2024.
11. Lauren Victory, Nationwide Medicare Scams Have Taken $100M+ Meant for Senior's Medical Bills, Investigation Reveals, *CBS News Chicago*, September, 2024.
12. Office of Public Affairs, US Department of Justice, Two Florida Residents Sentenced for $93M Health Care Fraud and Money Laundering Scheme, January 2024.

13. The Olympian, Florida is a center for Medicare corruption in the United States July, 2010, https://www.theolympian.com/opinion/op-ed/article25259422.html#storylink=cpy
14. FLORIDA'S EFFORTS TO CONTROL MEDICAID FRAUD & ABUSE: FISCAL YEAR 2022–2023, Maureen Barker, Bureau of Medicaid Program Integrity, Agency for Health Care Administration, 2727 Mahan Drive, MS#6, Tallahassee, FL 32308, email Maureen.Barker@ahca.myflorida.com.
15. American Hospital Association, A Look at 2024's Health Care Cybersecurity Challenges, October 07, 2024, John Rigg.

Chapter 19

Crisis Intervention

Emergency Rooms

—In most hospitals, emergency treatment rooms face a common challenge that involves maintaining a haven for both the patients and the medical staff. The emergency room areas, as well as the nursery floor, are the two main locations in a hospital facility that pose the biggest concerns for the security department staff and the hospital administration. These two critical areas require completely different security controls, as an emergency room patient can be violent whereas nursery infants can be kidnapped. The emergency room may not be as profitable as a birthing center, but it seems to offer more adventures for TV programs dealing with hospitals and their staff. The emergency room requires special attention from its security department personnel, simply due to the number of people seeking treatment and the type of illnesses or injuries that can sometimes overwhelm the specially trained emergency room medical staff (in real life — never presented on TV).

At least two dozen television shows are centered around medical miracles performed in the emergency room and the sexual tension between the skinny nursing staff willing to sleep with the handsome physicians who never seem to want to leave the emergency room to open a private practice. Many of the storylines show the medical staff frantically trying to save the lives of patients, who never seem to have to wait more than fifteen minutes for their diagnosis and treatment. Regardless of the romances, emergency rooms have created a challenge for security professionals, as this is where the first responders are sent after manmade or national disasters (like 9/11 or Hurricane Katrina). The often chaotic and overcrowded emergency room

 DOI: 10.4324/9781032630670-19

with scant data available about new patients is among the top areas in a hospital responsible for malpractice suits and diagnostic errors. Potential overuse or inappropriate use of emergency departments (EDs) for non-emergent care has been a concern for many years. EDs are a large and important component of the healthcare system in the United States, both in terms of number of patients served and spending. Overall, there were over 143 million ED visits in 2018, and of these, more than 20 million ended in admission to the same hospital while over 123 million ended in a release (HCUP NEDS 2018). In 2017, over 18% of adults reported having visited an ED at least once in the past year (NCHS 2018). One analysis suggests ED visits accounted for approximately 12.5% ($328.1 billion) of overall national health expenditures in 2010.[1]

Some of the more affluent hospitals have (in recent years) spun off the operation and ownership of the emergency room to privately owned enterprises (usually a group of investors made up primarily of doctors). This transfer of financial supervision takes the bookkeeping and collection efforts away from the hospital and the resulting savings on insurance and the salaries and benefits paid to the emergency room staff. The private service firm assumes these obligations. The hospital still receives a percentage of the emergency room income, along with all the funds paid by patients for a hospital room and follow-up treatment.

Hospitals serving poorer, inner-city populations cannot always franchise out the emergency room to the private sector and are forced to establish procedures that identify all waiting patients so that those who are uninsured can have their treatment costs billed to Medicaid or some other government-sponsored program. This identification process is not always easily accomplished, and it is important to discourage patients from leaving the emergency room because of the usually long wait time for treatment. Some facilities have issued RF wristband tags to all patients so that if they attempt to leave the room, an alarm alerts the staff to the movement – and the patient is returned to the treatment area to be properly registered and treated.

Nearly 124 million people are treated in the nation's emergency rooms in an average year. A vast number of people are often wrongly diagnosed because a doctor who was handling ten cases at once misjudged symptoms – which in almost all cases are the result of missed or delayed essential pieces of information that were not available at the time of treatment. The situation is exacerbated by an ER becoming more crowded — which prevents doctors from giving optimal care. With emergency rooms closing, the situation will not improve in the near future. There is an alarming trend of a decreasing number of ERs and an increasing number of ER visits. Between 1990 and 2009, the number of hospital-based ERs in non-rural areas decreased by 27% (from 2,446 to 1,779). During that same time frame, the number of ER visits increased 44% (from 88 million to 127 million visits). This increase is not merely due to population increases during that time, the utilization rate actually increased 18%, from 351 visits per 1,000 population in 1990 to 415 visits per 1,000 population in 2009.[2] Researchers examined the factors that led to closings and found certain hospitals at higher risk of closing than others. The emergency rooms that shut down share several similar factors, including:

- Low or no profit margins.
- Treating patients who are below the poverty level.
- Serving those with poor forms of insurance, including Medicaid.
- Being part of a for-profit hospital.
- Existing in more competitive markets.

Since the terrorist attack in the downtown area of New York City on 9/11, many laws and procedures have been adopted and enforced to make emergency rooms more adept at handling a surge expected after the next attack by terrorists. This new responsibility meant a far different approach than hospitals had operated under for decades, when processing the patients admitted to their emergency rooms. Until the 1960s, hospitals simply were not designed to treat real emergencies – regardless of their nomenclature. When a patient was brought into a hospital at night, the doors would be locked – with admittance allowed only after ringing the doorbell. A nurse would then come down to see what the medical problem was. A doctor would be called at home who could come in at their discretion. More often than not, the patient was directed to another hospital that accepted uninsured patients. A local mortician often drove ambulances. This was a mismatched combination, since the funeral director was being placed in charge of helping a patient live — rather than getting paid to bury the patient.

The aftermath of 9/11 changed everything by exposing the lack of expertise found in the average emergency room. The next terrorist attack could produce a thousand injury cases. Those injured could not be admitted on a timely basis – since almost all hospitals design their emergency room entrances to handle only a few ambulances at a time (not dozens, as expected after a major disaster). The openings at docking station platforms are usually built high enough to accommodate a delivery truck but are often too high for an ambulance. With many emergency rooms operating at 90% capacity today, it will be unrealistic to expect them to handle a surge during the next terrorist attack.

In the immediate aftermath of the World Trade Center tragedy, city officials placed more than sixteen hospitals on emergency alert. Each emergency room in these institutions became fully staffed by medically trained trauma professionals waiting for the imminent inflow of victims. Surprising to all concerned, only the one hospital nearest the World Trade Center treated survivors from the horrendous event – and all the injuries treated at that one hospital required the removal of glass from their eyes. There were almost 3,000 deaths at the site but few injuries.

While never depicted in TV shows, one of the most prevalent reasons that patients seek treatment at the emergency room is not a massive injury or near-death from a mysterious disease — but rather for a headache. Headache disorders are among the most common neurological disorders, with a worldwide prevalence of 46% in the adult population. Severe and sudden headaches often lead patients to seek emergency medical attention, accounting for 3.5 million emergency department (ED) visits per year in the United States. Migraines are the most common complaint among patients – and for some, they can be disabling. Patients who think they are going to die from one are often admitted to the hospital. People also seek treatment for a non-migraine headache, the most common type being a tension headache — of which 80% of people will experience at some point. This illness is short-lived and can be relieved with an over-the-counter analgesic.

Patients with primary headache disorders often receive unnecessary neuroimaging or medications with low-quality evidence during ED visits due to the difficulty in differentiating primary headaches from secondary headaches, incomplete relevant medical histories, and a lack of consensus on the best treatment strategies in ED settings. The priority in headache management in the ED is to identify potentially life-threatening conditions, and thus neuroimaging can be ordered for patients with red flags for secondary headaches. Due to multiple reasons that lead to overuse of imaging in ED settings (i.e., fear of missing a serious diagnosis, preventing potential medical malpractice, patient demands, financial incentives), patients with primary headache disorders may undergo unnecessary neuroimaging despite guidelines discouraging routine neuroimaging.[3]

For some unexplained and unpredictable reason, hospital emergency rooms – while functioning at the intersection of mayhem and medicine

– tend to be fire-free zones for the criminal class. One reason may lie in the tradition of the medical arena as non-combatant territory – a custom borrowed from past wartime battlefields, where medics with white and red crosses emblazoned on their backs were not targeted. Hospital officials believe that most violent episodes are caused by patients with a behavioral or mental health problem. If they are armed, it is usually not with a firearm, but with some odd object they managed to grab (such as a piece of furniture).

Code compliance dictates that carrying the gunfire into the brightly lit, densely populated spaces of public hospitals has an unacceptable risk-to-reward ratio: the likelihood of being caught outweighs the chances of success. Furthermore, the public views hospitals, generally, as a sanctuary. Similar to a church, the street violence found around a hospital facility does not enter the premises. A well-trained hospital security staff is adept at quelling combustible situations and defusing threats. In general, hospital police officers are not armed. While they do not carry pepper spray, they often do carry batons.

Centers of Mayhem and Long Lines

With about 25 million Americans uninsured, the rules of most municipal governments insist that no one should be refused treatment in an emergency room center – regardless of their circumstances. This policy has caused long lines waiting for treatment in emergency rooms – especially in poorer neighborhoods of larger cities, such as Los Angeles and New York City. Some enterprising individuals have discovered a way to almost eliminate the long waiting period in crowded emergency room centers by wearing gray clothing purchased in a uniform store and sewing on the arm patch easily obtained through the internet. When the other patients become aware of the uniform, more than 90% of the foreign-born patients immediately leave.

The dangers of patient attacks against the emergency room staff have probably been the most challenging area confronting the hospital staff and are difficult to control. More than half of the nurses who work in emergency departments report instances of physical assault while on the job. These incidents involve patients scratching, kicking, shoving, and punching them while on duty. The attacks can be partly a result of the job and the fact that emergency rooms accept all types of patients who cannot get help anywhere else – especially those who have no means to pay for the service. These patients include those under the influence of drugs and alcohol and a large percentage of psychiatric patients. Laws protecting emergency department nurses vary widely by state, and some states have no laws. Every hospital must have a plan to handle violence-prone patients, and that task is usually assigned to the security department. These responsibilities include:

- Creating a safe emergency room environment
- Ensuring that emergency department staff know that senior administrators are aware of the problems and support efforts to prevent and mitigate outbreaks or acts of violence.
- Encouraging senior nursing staff members to upgrade the safety features periodically.
- Establishing a culture of acceptance for reporting incidents of violence.
- Developing clear and consistent procedures for reporting violent incidents.
- Providing access to medical care and follow-up counseling for emergency department staff who are victims of workplace violence.
- Instructing both the emergency room staff and security officers in the legal liabilities involved.
- Training all involved that a patient cannot be ignored if exhibiting serious injury or illness.

On 9/11, every one out of forty hospitals was put on alert right away, but only two hospitals in the city used their emergency room facilities to treat people after the World Trade Center disaster: St. Vincent (a private hospital in Greenwich Village) and Bellevue Hospital (municipally owned). St. Vincent treated 1,500 survivors for glass in their eyes. Bellevue set up a morgue on the sidewalks around the building identification of the remains of almost 3,000 who died at the site.

Of the more than 475,000 units of blood donated in the aftermath of the 9/11 attacks, medical staff used only 258.

Urgent Care Clinics

Since their beginning in the 1970s, storefront urgent care centers have been expanding rapidly. Today, it is estimated that there are over 1,400 locations in the U.S. – staffed with some of the best doctors. Founded by emergency medical physicians to fill the need for walk-in clinics without sacrificing the qualifications of doctors, they started out only providing very basic care for colds, flus, aches, and other small issues. The most common diagnosis was an upper respiratory condition, and the most common procedure was wound repair. Gradually, they have increased their available treatments – and since around 2015, they can provide physicals, testing for COVID-19, and digital x-rays. The majority of centers (85%) provide care seven days a week, with expanded hours – so it's likely that when the traditional doctor's office is closed, they're open.

Urgent care centers have been the unsung heroes of recent years. In an era where we're seeing emergency rooms and even doctors' offices drowning in patient congestion, urgent care doctors have been a much-needed saving grace. With their ability to do a quick checkup, treat various strains and sprains, or even provide STD testing, they have the ability to do most of the things patients need right on-site. With the various treatment options now available, combined with their cost-effectiveness and timely care, these convenient centers may be the one thing to help end congestion in other health sectors like the ER. By 2022, there were an estimated 71 million patients who saw doctors at urgent care centers – and that number is expected to continue to rise.[4]

The Behavioral Health Unit – Sedation Treatment Clinics

Ever since Sigmund Freud defined the treatment of people with mental ailments, the psychiatric clinics in the hospital for many generations were the scene of physical attacks against doctors – a situation the security department has never addressed adequately. Some patients are prone to violence, and placing a disturbed patient in a room alone with the psychiatrist is not the best situation for all concerned. Doctors in these private rooms often receive handheld panic buttons, CCTV, and a security officer standing at the nurse's desk. The shortcomings of all these practices are that they do not prevent the attack – and the staff is not adequately trained to control the attacker.

The first-generation behavioral health unit security system was a simple series of panic buttons mounted under all office desks, along the corridors, and hardwired to the nurse's station. These devices provided some level of security, albeit a false sense of security. By the time a security officer (if there was even an officer assigned to the ward) arrived at the scene, the attack had already occurred – and the doctor was found injured or unconscious. The other problem was that the doctors had to be at their desks, within easy reach of the button – and it assumed that the security officer was trained to control a violent patient. These two assumptions eventually rendered the approach practically useless.

The second generation of personal alarms was to equip each doctor with a wireless variation of a garage-door opener, with all doctors having their own coded RF transmitter frequency. When the panel at the nurse's station lit up with the coded signal 1235, it identified Dr. Jones as needing assistance in his office. Coded signal 4536 was assigned to Dr. Sherman in her office, and so forth. It was initially considered a slight improvement but soon fell out of use – since it proved ineffective when a doctor was attacked in the corridor area or if they were in another doctor's office. Doctors could not wander away from their assigned offices.

The third generation for wireless signaling of an impending or ongoing attack was a pen-shaped wireless coded device with an RF transmitter (such as the garage-door opener) with the doctor's code – but it also had a second code that received an ultrasonic signal with a location code. Ultrasonic transmitters were installed on the ceiling of each office and every ten feet along the corridor. As the doctor moved about the ward, the nearest ultrasonic coded transmitter would change the location code but retain the doctor's basic ID code. The pen-shaped device always had to be exposed. When the doctor triggered it, the transmitter sent out the basic code 1234 (Dr Jones) along with the second series of numbers, indicating the exact location of the attack. The latest version of this technology is to install RFID receivers throughout the hospital to track movement, which had an automatic alert button programmed into the unit. The doctor had to always carry the phone – otherwise, the patient could steal the phone and compromise the entire system.

Stationing a uniformed security officer at the entrance to a behavioral health unit or in any section of the hospital is a knee-jerk response to an increasing number of attacks on the general staff. That approach is a Band-Aid solution to the problem that confronts many healthcare institutions, and it has not stopped the attacks – just as placing a guard in a bank lobby rarely stops bank robberies.

Sedation – Not Confrontation

All the devices and procedures to protect doctors in the behavioral health unit have had little effect in solving the potentially dangerous atmosphere associated with the psychiatric units. What made working in these patient rooms safer was not any complex electronic-based security system but the fact that patients rarely attacked their psychiatrists – because the visits were too short or they were sedated. In years past, the psychiatrist knew the patients' inner lives better than they knew their family's thoughts. Now, they often cannot remember a patient's name. Doctors used to see patients ten or more times before arriving at a diagnosis. Now, under the present insurance rules, the same doctors have to make a suggested treatment protocol or prescribe medication within the first forty-five minutes in order to get paid. This change has resulted in a loss of intimacy between doctors and patients. While the insurance cost factor has influenced every medical specialty, it has been more profound in psychiatry.

Talk therapy sessions, followed by most of the nation's 25,000 psychiatrists, dominated the profession for decades.[5] This changed to conform to the rules that discourage talk therapy by granting a psychiatrist visit somewhere in the vicinity of $150 for three fifteen-minute medication visits, compared to ninety dollars for a forty-five-minute therapy session. Also, there is not a great deal of competition from psychologists and social workers – who (unlike psychiatrists) do not attend medical schools, so they charge less. Surprisingly, there is no evidence that psychiatrists provide higher quality talk therapy than psychologists or social workers. Still, thousands of psychiatrists offer talk therapy to all their patients – but their expensive care is mostly limited to the worried wealthy who pay in cash. In some of the major cities, a select group of the most sought-after psychiatrists can charge as much as $600 or more per hour to treat the privileged, and some top child psychiatrists can charge as much as $2,000 and more for an initial evaluation session for a juvenile under sixteen. Thus, only the rich and famous or children of the rich and famous can afford a pay-as-you-go arrangement – insurance coverage will not cover it.

The switch from talk therapy to medication swept hospital psychiatric wards, leaving many older psychiatrists feeling unhappy and inadequate. A Columbia University study found that between 1996 and 2016, the percentage of psychiatrist visits involving psychotherapy had declined by half – dropping to only 21.6% of patient visits.[6] Patients who once underwent months of talk therapy are now discharged with only pills. The very serious security problem surrounding the safety of doctors in the psych ward is somewhat abated – not by adding security devices, but by simply “doping” the patients into a type of stupor. The psychiatrist who treats the public can no longer limit his or her practice to treating fifty to sixty patients at once, or twice weekly talk-therapy sessions of forty-five minutes each. The same doctor can treat up to 1,200 patients in mostly fifteen-minute visits for prescription adjustments that are sometimes months apart. Too often, patients are no longer cured by conventional therapy — they are simply sedated.

Weapons in the Wards

In general, the few shooting incidents that take place in America’s 4,000+ hospitals each year involve gunmen who are determined and have a specific target – making it very difficult to prevent this type of event. About 150 hospital-related shootings occurred in the United States between 2000 and 2019; 88 shootings have occurred since 2010, 133 of the shooters were male (91%), with a median age of 46. About 77 (53%) shooters were killed, 49 from suicide (34%). Shootings were most frequently motivated by social violence (n = 32, 22%). Escape attempts by inmate patients accounted for 11% of the shootings. No perfect solution is possible, nor is any security system available to prevent this type of violence or mitigate the injuries or deaths. After all, healthcare facilities are open arenas – welcoming all types of people, patients, visitors, and staff. The security staff cannot search or interview everyone. Hospitals can never eliminate the problem, but the staff should receive training on how to respond to an event.[7]

A group of Southern California hospitals developed a Guide for Standardization of Facility Codes, which was summarized by the International Association for Healthcare Security and Safety in that organization’s semi-annual Journal of Healthcare Protection Management in 2005. The Guide recognized that responding to different color codes creates a problem, and mistaking a code could change a normal medical procedure into a life-threatening situation – as shown by an incident that occurred in 1999 at a West Coast hospital.[8] A distraught man, upset over his mother’s death, blamed the hospital staff and became uncontrollably violent outside his mother’s room. No one on the nursing staff realized that the distraught individual had a gun. Since the hospital did not have a specific code for a person carrying a weapon, the staff activated the code for a violent/combative person, an understandable reaction. (The response code for a weapon on the premises is different and involves evacuation from the area.) The immediate reaction to the "violent" code alert signal was to send a response team trained to subdue an unruly person. Three of the staff members who responded were trained to subdue a patient or a visitor but had no training in a confrontation with someone carrying a gun, which resulted in three security officers shot dead before the police arrived.

Following the shooting incident, many California hospitals adopted a color code, now under consideration in hospitals throughout the nation. It recommended just six codes after a consensus of the hospitals' administrators deemed that additional codes would be too difficult to memorize. Additionally, the response might be unpredictable and could conceivably exacerbate the situation. The California group that listed a code for a violent, combative person with a weapon did not have much acceptance until 2011, when a doctor was killed in a patient ward at Johns Hopkins Hospital. This incident spurred many of the larger institutions into developing special training procedures for the staff handling gun violence. Today, hospitals are teaching staff on how to respond to active shooter situations.

Emergency situations relying on the public address system sometimes try to apply proper names to sound as if they are messages to doctors to indicate different medical emergency: Dr Redburn (fire disaster), Dr Coolspot (fire alarm clear), Dr Ethyl (ethylene oxide spill), and so forth. Problems arose when a real doctor "Redburn" would respond to the code announcement without any knowledge of the emergency situation. Hospitals should also avoid using code words currently being used by law enforcement agencies, such as "Amber Alert" or the Homeland Security Code "Orange". A growing number of hospitals are relying on the facility's phone service to transmit an emergency notification by calling the security command center and describing the situation and location of the incident. Periodic testing of any code alert system should be performed only after notifying the staff that it is not a real emergency, since patients have been known to automatically call 911 – not realizing that a drill was in progress.

Hospital Shootings

Location of hospital shootings in the average year:

- Inside the hospital: 60%
- Outside on hospital grounds: 40%
- In the emergency department: 30%

- In the parking lot: 23%
- In patient waiting rooms: 19%

One hospital incorporated an innovative concept that consisted of a small, printed flipchart booklet mounted at all the nursing stations to help employees memorize the codes. The booklet noted each color code on a strip matching the color code. "PINK" was written on a pink strip and "RED" on a red strip. Under each strip was a brief description of the response procedure. Recognition of the "code" announced over the facility-wide public address system is only the first step in a two-step emergency. The code would prove worthless unless all the hospital personnel followed a formal, well-planned, and tested response procedure.

Stun Gun Deployment

Violence in healthcare facilities has grown from a rare experience to a major concern for hospital security staff in recent years. Visitors are attacking staff, patients attack doctors, and staff members are attacking each other. The security staff, if proprietary, may not have been trained to conduct any intervention during a violent confrontation or know how to handle a violent person forcefully. A contract security officer is not paid enough to handle even the most minor disturbance involving patients, staff, or visitors.

In addition to standard security officer training required by most states and municipalities, specialized training in handling sensitive patient situations must be seriously considered to ensure that when force is necessary, all means to handle the situation are used. The few hospitals that allow certain staff members (licensed security officers) to use a gun are rare, but with so many retired police officers on the hospital security staff, the use of a gun in certain situations has become more acceptable. In general, the use of a gun in the hospital setting should be left to the local police department. The use of a stun gun is another matter.

The use of any weapon, be it a pistol or stun gun, lays a great deal of responsibility on the facility – especially on the security staff. Liability exposure could very well discourage any use of a firearm or any other weapon, but this may not always be an option. A deadly weapon should be considered as a last resort. When security officers have the training and proper licenses to use a weapon, they usually do not carry the weapon while on the premises. The gun is usually located in a locked cabinet in the security office and taken out only during very serious situations. A Taser, while considered a weapon, is not a deadly weapon and is the ideal alternative in most healthcare facilities.

Procedural guidelines should be enacted after a hospital decides to allow the use of a new type of weapon on its premises. Administrators should know (before it is used) how it will affect its liability exposure. Many hospitals may have armed security, but there is still the problem of approving the use of a Taser. Many hospitals that use Tasers are often willing to share both their policy and their experience – which is probably the best source of information for introducing this controversial weapon. Training is another topic that must be addressed, and the Taser manufacturer conducts training sessions before deeming someone on the security staff qualified as a certified instructor (with recertification required annually). The instructor certification is usually valid for two years.

Hospitals must also comply with applicable federal, state, and local laws – along with any other regulations or legal requirements. Authorizing the use of stun guns is not accomplished as would purchasing a new CCTV surveillance system – it is complicated. The decision to use force on the premises involves policies based on community standards, and varying levels of the types of responses are available to the security department. Hospital security staff members will need to work with hospital administrators to ensure that any new policy related to the operation of the stun gun meets guidelines set by the owners of the medical facility. There should be a program to train all members of the hospital staff – both medical and security – to recognize the early identification of potentially violent individuals and what the initial approaches should be before allowing the use of stun guns in selected situations.

Psychiatric Emergency Room for Pediatrics

Tradition is to treat children who are brought into the emergency room with psychological symptoms as adults – which is a disservice to everyone. An eight-year-old suffering from undiagnosed attention deficit-hyperactivity disorder who acted up in school by throwing a chair at his teacher (maybe due to frustration or more likely because they are falling behind in their work) might now be held in a psychiatric ward with schizophrenic grown men if the emergency room does not have the resources to treat the child immediately. A suicidal teen brought in by concerned parents might not be able to see a child psychiatrist who can understand the nuances and specific troubles of the developing adolescent brain, which the emergency room physician or psychiatrist is not trained to treat properly.

Emergency rooms struggle to diagnose and treat children who need immediate care. Instead, the children end up being unnecessarily admitted to the hospital – sometimes in the same wards as mentally ill and violently dangerous adults. A hospital in New York City that has, for generations, been associated with "crazy patients" started the nation's first Children's Comprehensive Psychiatric Emergency Program (CPEP). A specially trained team of doctors, nurses, and social workers sees children as young as three and as old as seventeen, with a broad range of psychological problems. The CPEP unit at Bellevue Hospital is intended to exclusively help children by catching and diagnosing their psychiatric problems long before they might be addressed in the traditional admittance process. During their first years of operation, the unit treated more than 2,000 patients each year.

Children are not treated just like little adults, since they have other issues that cannot be treated in the same way as adults. People with mental illnesses, such as schizophrenia, often present the first symptoms as adolescents. The average time between a child presenting symptoms and receiving a diagnosis for that type of mental illness is three to four years – a period during which they get no treatment. The CPEP program has also been successful in putting agitated parents at ease and helping them cope with their child's condition.

Violence against the Staff

Hospitals were once a sanctuary from the outside world, where patients felt secure and believed that they would receive healthcare for any illness – including miraculous cures. This feeling of security (especially in the emergency room) has been breached, as doctors and nurses are attacked by unstable patients and possibly by terrorists (Mumbai, India in 2008). In some hospitals along the northern border in Mexico, when drug wars are killing thousands, some of these are deaths occurring within the medical facilities. Doctors are kidnapped, held for ransom, and threatened with death if a drug dealer dies while under their care. The Hippocratic oath that doctors are sworn to follow has become, "Cure me or I'll kill you".

Violent Crime falls into eight categories (in order of the highest-rated incident to the lowest):

1. Simple assault
2. Aggravated assault
3. Robberies
4. Sexual assaults other than rape
5. Rape
6. Murder
7. Suicide
8. Infant kidnapping

The few trade and professional organizations that collect data on criminal activity in healthcare facilities have produced data indicating that these facilities now constitute one of the most dangerous places to work in the nation. Data published by the U.S. Bureau of Labor Statistics indicates that homicides and physical assaults on employees occur more frequently in healthcare and social service facilities than in any other industry. Another report, from the Bureau of Justice Statistics, found that healthcare workers accounted for 73% of all nonfatal workplace injuries and illnesses due to violence in 2018. This number has been steadily growing since the tracking of these specific events began in 2011. According to the International Association for Healthcare Security and Safety's annual crime survey for 2023, hospitals reporting assaults by category, type two (violence directed at employees by nonemployees) attacks were, by far, the most common, accounting for 83% of aggravated assaults and 93% of simple assaults. In 2021, the results were 73% and 86%, respectively. Nurses are more likely to be attacked at work than prison guards in a prison or police officers anywhere. Reports issued by several reliable sources indicate that, in any year, more nurses are killed or injured while on duty than workers in any other hospital occupation.

Screening Identification (ID) at the Lobby Entrance

Security staff need constant training to remind them to be persistent in asking visitors and patients for their identification credentials, including when the request involves an employee who is uncooperative and threatening. Some of the hospital staff feel that they should never be challenged (including doctors and senior administrators) – and in many incidents, an irate employee starts yelling at the security officers, calling them nasty names, and accusing them of being incompetent. Some of the more enraged individuals spit in the officer's face and walk past the officer's post to his or her workplace — completely ignoring the commands of the officer.

Notes

1. Office of Health Policy, Report to Congress, Trends in the Utilization of Emergency Department Services, 2009–2018, March 2, 2021.
2. RA Barish, PL McGauly, TC Arnold, Emergency Room Crowding: A Marker of Hospital Health, *Transactions of the American Clinical and Climatological Association* 2012;123:304–311.PMCID: PMC3540619 PMID: 23303998
3. Seonkyeong Yang, Yulia Orlova, Abigale Lipe, Macy Boren 3, Juan M Hincapie-Castillo, Haesuk Park, Ching-Yuan Chang, Debbie L Wilson, Lauren Adkins, Wei-Hsuan Lo-Ciganic, Trends in the Management of Headache Disorders in US Emergency Departments: Analysis of 2007–2018 National Hospital Ambulatory Medical Care Survey Data, *Journal of Clinical Medicine* 2022 March 3;11(5):1401. doi: 10.3390/jcm11051401PMCID: PMC8910868 PMID: 35268492
4. Urgent Care Association, URGENT CARE INDUSTRY WHITE PAPER: The Essential Nature of Urgent Care in the Healthcare Ecosystem Post-COVID-19, August 2023.
5. PsychCentral, How Many Mental Health Professionals Are There in the U.S.?, https://psychcentral.com/health/mental-health-professionals-us-statistics
6. Columbia University Department of Psychiatry, Talk Therapy By U.S. Psychiatrists Declined By Half Since 1990s, Carla Cantor, January, 2022.
7. Hospital Based Shootings 2000–2019, Published online by Cambridge University Press: 31 October 2024, Nicholas W. Rizer, Alexander H. Chang, Gregory Jasani, Grace Jiang, HSD, Kayla Iuliucci, Edbert Hsu.
8. Los Angeles Times, Hospital Shooter Carried 2 Revolvers, JACK LEONARD and SCOTT GOLD, Sept., 1999.

Chapter 20

Special Healthcare Facilities

Transition in Medical Services

Hospital security directors represent a cross section of dedicated professionals who share similar responsibilities and manage security services at various types of healthcare facilities across the US. The smaller facilities (under 150 beds) and most nursing homes rely on the building manager for security or the senior administrator. They have no full-time person whose only function is managing security personnel and surveillance systems. Security directors are generally paid according to the size of the facility and the salary scale of other staff members. A security director at a teaching hospital in a large inner city is paid about double that of a director at a smaller hospital in a suburban area – especially if the facility does not contain a nursery or an emergency room. A growing number of hospitals are hiring outside contract security guarding firms to staff their security departments with significant cost savings but may be hiring a less-dedicated staff of security officers. In about half the hospitals using contract guards, they also hire a contract security director whose lower salary is usually subsidized by a bonus arrangement that awards the director if the guard force does not exceed a level of overtime pay. Overtime is a cost factor that must be assumed by the contract security service, and overtime can easily eliminate any profit from using that service.

The annual security department budgets can vary from $500,000 (for small staff to minimum security system) to five million (for hospitals employing more than 125 security officers – to protect their facilities and maintain multi-million-dollar complex security systems for which maintenance alone

DOI: 10.4324/9781032630670-20

can cost $350,000/year). The organization and responsibilities of a security director depend on the type and function of a facility, since they can vary from a four-story nursing home to a forty-story medical center (with several buildings spread over several acres – plus a medical school). These facilities fall into ten unique categories:

1. Not-for-profit
2. State owned
3. Prison
4. Physician-owned specialty hospital
5. Teaching medical center
6. Municipally owned
7. Geriatric
8. Federally owned
9. Psychiatric
10. Nursing home

Physician-owned specialty hospitals could be considered a short-lived phenomenon that proliferated in the 1990s and have since sparked an intense debate within the healthcare industry – forcing Congress to impose a moratorium on the construction of new, doctor-owned hospitals that specialize in cardiac, orthopedics, face lifts, and other specific areas. Even the construction of other physician-owned facilities that are not specialty hospitals was halted. Rival medical facilities that fought to have the law enacted included nonprofit community hospitals, along with for-profit institutions without physician investors. The opposition to doctor-owned facilities is based on the contention that the specialty hospitals have an unfair advantage.

They are the first choice of doctor investors referred to as "cash cows", since they typically focus on highly profitable services and healthier and more affluent patients, avoid the less-profitable medical services, and often lose services offered by municipal and nonprofit hospitals – such as emergency departments and burn units. Fewer than half of the specialty hospitals have emergency rooms, according to the Department of Health and Human Services – which greatly reduces overhead.[1]

Corporate Practice of Medicine (CPOM) laws are regulations that prohibit standard corporations (or other non-physician entities) from practicing medicine or employing practicing physicians. Governed by each state, a state's CPOM restrictions typically apply to any standard corporate entity that seeks to provide medical or licensed healthcare services. This includes corporations, limited liability companies (LLCs), and other business entities. The primary goal of these laws is to ensure that medical decisions are made solely based on patient care and not influenced by corporate interests. These laws vary by state, but they generally aim to protect the physician-patient relationship from commercial influence. The goal of CPOM laws is to ensure clinical decisions are not influenced by corporate pressures.[2]

Replacing Doctor-Owned Practices

On top of all the added paperwork, the many HIPAA restrictions, the cost to upgrade files to meet federally mandated electronic medical record requirements, and constantly fighting with insurance providers over reimbursement schedules, the traditional model of doctors hanging up their own shingles or investing in a doctor-owned facility is rapidly losing its attraction for newly anointed and veteran MDs. The lure of having private practice has steadily been replaced by the desire to work directly for a hospital that will assume much of the back-office effort that has begun to overwhelm the medical profession. Many of the older and more established doctors became frustrated with the duties involved in medical practice ownership, including wrangling and dunning patients for their out-of-pocket fees and acquiring new costly technology to conform to new rules and regulations. Some young physicians choose to avoid the paperwork and the time-consuming business side of a private practice altogether – and at the same time seek the more regular hours offered to salaried hospital employees, who happen to be doctors.

A survey conducted by the Medical Group Management Association found that hospital-managed medical practices have increased by about 5% every year since 2005.[3] Another survey by a physician recruiting firm found that the share of its doctors seeking positions within hospitals rather than private practice rose significantly each year, causing the number of searches requested by physicians for partnerships and physician group practices to drop steadily in the same period.[4] Younger doctors – half of whom are now women – are reluctant to take over the smaller practices and are usually seeking a better lifestyle, shorter workdays, and weekends free of the beepers, cell phones, and patient emergencies that have long defined doctors' lives. Doctors are weighed down with debt and want regular paychecks instead of the risks that are part of the opening of private practice. Banks understand the uncertainty of establishing a new medical facility and are far less likely to lend the money needed than they once were.

A doctor with private practice (contemplating retirement) previously found it easy to sell the established practice to younger doctors – a procedure that was a traditional rite of passage in the medical profession. The transfer of ownership from one generation to another generation is no longer as easy as it used to be. The private practitioner, working long hours with patients on round-the-clock schedules, is not an attractive lifestyle for a less-dedicated younger generation. If a doctor had tried to sell a practice at the turn of the century, it would have been possible to persuade another doctor to pay about $500,000 or more for a typical practice of approximately 4,000 patients.

By the year 2012, most retiring doctors could not give a practice away – not only because of the unattractiveness of its schedule demands – but because large group practices can negotiate higher fees from insurers, which translates into more money for doctors. Most of the available data on the cost to operate a private practice, with all its paperwork and negotiations with insurance companies, indicates that expenses amount to about $200 an hour – with Medicare and private insurance paying approximately $69 for each consultation. At that rate, the doctor breaks even by seeing three patients an hour and needs a fourth to turn around any profit. There is no time for small talk or to get friendly with a patient – unless it can be achieved in ten minutes or less. Less than 30% of the active physicians in the United States deliver primary care, as of 2024. This group makes less than half as much money as specialists.[5]

Virtual House Calls

Another twist in the replacement of traditional medical practices is the internet, where entrepreneurs brought new meaning to the phrase "house calls". Online companies, such as MDLiveCare and RingADoc, diagnose and treat common conditions over the internet or on the phone – forcing state regulators to revisit decades-old rules about what constitutes a doctor/patient relationship. People seeking medical advice or a prescription are paying anywhere from $25 to $40 to speak on the phone with a doctor (or nurse practitioner) or chat online with one. These services were intended not to replace the primary care physician, but to replace the hassle and expense of visiting a doctor's office or emergency room for a minor problem.

Individuals can now get medical advice online, while sitting on their couch with a laptop, requesting a virtual consultation by typing in their symptoms and a credit card number. Within an hour, a doctor will appear on screen and will look at the patient, ask questions, provide a diagnosis, and e-mail a prescription to the local pharmacy. The same forces that have made instant messaging and video calls are now being adapted for basic medical care. Some large insurers are starting to pay for the virtual service. UnitedHealthcare, the nation's largest insurer, covers virtual visits for most of its 26 million members – citing the shortage of primary care doctors and a cost of less than $50 per virtual visit. Another advantage to this newly adopted procedure is that it is much more comfortable than having to sit with a bunch of other sick people in a waiting room.

The more traditional sectors of the medical world have pushed back. These doctors contend that hands-on exams are more effective and warn that the potential for misdiagnoses through video is great. Another obvious drawback to internet medical care is the lack of the familiar communication developed in a patient-doctor relationship that comes with sitting opposite one another. Studies have clearly shown that poor or missing communication between providers and patients can lead to patient harm or even death. Ineffective communication has become such a major concern that both The Joint Commission and Joint Commission International (JCI) have incorporated recommendations relating to communications into National Patient Safety Goals (NPSGs) and International Patient Safety Goals (IPSGs) respectively to address the problem. Joint Commission data indicate inadequate handovers are a factor in 80% of all adverse events, which include wrong-site, wrong-procedure, or wrong-patient surgeries; treatment delays; medication errors; and falls. Some degree of physical harm occurred to 49.2% of the patients with limited English proficiency, but to only 29.5% of the patients who spoke English well. Effective communication between health care providers and patients and their families is essential to safe, quality care.[6]

State medical boards have been slow to react to the internet doctor and have not adequately addressed the changes in communication technology. They will have to revise their rules to either embrace or reject the new way people get an instant resolution, rather than having to wait a week to get a doctor's appointment. One rule, followed by a growing number of state medical boards, is the strict requirement that there be an appropriate prior exam before allowing the writing of a prescription. Internet doctors seem to believe that they comply with the face-to-face examination provision if technology, such as videoconferencing or Zoom, can provide the same information. However, this assumption must be tested in court. Since 1995, U.S. medical students have been required to get training in communication skills.

Then, in 2005, the United States Medical Licensing Exam began to include testing on interpersonal and communication skills. These skills, and high patient satisfaction scores, can help give a hospital a competitive edge while reducing malpractice claims.[7]

Divided Loyalty

A problem arises when an increasing number of doctors become hospital employees rather than practice on their own. Doctors' duty to heal their patients can be compromised when the hospital (employer) expects that their medical staff avoid sending patients to providers unaffiliated with that hospital. Guidelines that doctors have always followed state that treatment and referral decisions should be based on the best interests of their patients. Furthermore, patients should be told whenever a hospital provides financial incentives that encourage, discourage, or restrict referrals or treatment options. This policy is not always followed.

This loyalty dilemma became more pronounced in recent years. Recent surveys conducted by physician and hospital organizations, and national recruiting firms indicate that between half and two-thirds of current physician practice opportunities or searches are for employed positions. Further, the number of physicians employed by hospitals grew by 34% between 2000 and 2010, indicating the trend's progression. A recent survey conducted by Jackson Healthcare, a staffing firm that also conducts research on physician practice and other industry trends, found that, between 2012 and 2013 alone, hospital-employed physicians increased from 20% to 26%.[8] The trend continues to accelerate, in part because federal policies encourage doctors and hospitals to band together to coordinate care. The decade-long decline of independent physicians rolled on in 2022 and 2023 with a new high of 77.6% of doctors employed by hospitals or other corporate entities as of the new year, according to a new report.[9] The divided loyalty exists since doctors have to follow hospital procedures. Yet, they have committed by their medical oath to provide the best care to their patients and should retain their right to exercise independent professional judgment in caring for and advocating for patients. Reported incidents include instances in which a hospital told doctors not to place defibrillators in Medicaid patients, because it was a money-losing proposition for the hospital. In other cases, hospitals have informed doctors on their staff that they must use the hospital for laboratory work and certain imaging procedures – even if doctors believed that they got better results or better service elsewhere.[10]

Hospitals often set a goal for doctors that can result in a bonus – but if the doctors fall short, their salary may be reduced the following year. Another issue that affects the doctor-patient relationship is when the doctor leaves the sanctuary of the hospital environment and enters private practice or goes to work for another hospital. Hospitals frequently seek agreements to ensure that physician employees will not work for a competitor if they part ways. Such agreements typically prohibit a doctor from practicing medicine within a certain geographic area for several years after the doctor's employment ends. Most American medical associations discourage such policies and advise doctors not to enter into such an agreement. Patients should always be given a choice to continue to be seen by the physician in his or her new practice setting.

Concierge Medicine

An alternative to former President Obama's national healthcare program and Medicare is in the new world of concierge doctors who are paid a yearly retainer fee. The concierge concept first appeared around 2009 to provide medical services for the very wealthy. It has gradually grown under the radar to become an important segment of the healthcare industry by allowing individuals to ignore health insurance and pay doctors a fixed fee that goes from $38 to $1,500 a month or higher – sometimes extra for office and home visits. This arrangement guarantees each concierge member will give personalized attention and care twenty-four hours a day, seven days a week and then try to get money back from a private insurance provider or Medicare.

Concierge medical care first started in places such as Florida, with its high concentration of Medicare patients. It allowed upper-middle-class retirees to see a doctor for an affixed annual fee – whenever they needed to – rather than waiting two weeks for an appointment through Medicare. Nonprofit hospitals created largely to serve the poor are adding concierge physician practices, charging patients annual membership fees of $2,000 or more for easier access to their doctors. It's a trend that began decades ago with physician practices. Thousands of doctors have shifted to the concierge model, in which they can increase their income while decreasing their patient load.

Northwestern Medicine in Chicago, Penn Medicine in Philadelphia, University Hospitals in the Cleveland area, and Baptist Health in Miami are among the large hospital systems offering concierge physician services. The fees, which can exceed $4,000 a year, are in addition to copayments, deductibles, and other charges not paid by patients' insurance plans.[11]

Under a concierge program, doctor's appointments start on time, last as long as necessary, and can be made the same day. Regular patients are waiting an average of twenty-six days for a scheduled appointment with a doctor, according to a study of commonly used specialty physicians in fifteen major U.S. cities.[12] The annual fee is for extended care and a comprehensive annual physical and wellness plan, but doctors still bill the patient's insurance company for procedures that are separate from the concierge service – since insurance companies and Medicare will not pay twice for the same service. Doctors know each patient's health conditions intimately and can discuss the patient's issues with another doctor anywhere in the world.

One of the more expensive services charges from $20,000 to $75,000 a year by claiming that their clients will receive better care than that provided by a traditional primary care doctor and have access to top specialists when needed. The service also claims that they locate the right doctor, which people outside the service plan would have trouble doing on their own. According to a marketing service survey, between 2013 and 2016, the number of doctors practicing concierge medicine increased sevenfold. The concierge physician receives financial rewards and can earn $500,000 to $700,000 annually, compared to a successful internist in a major city who might earn $200,000 to $300,000 per year.[13]

One concierge practitioner reduced a 3,000-patient general practice that was served under conventional insurance reimbursement to 300 patients who pay $1,800 a year in membership fees for unlimited office visits. The doctor then billed the insurance provider for services not covered under the basic concierge agreement. The biggest concern for the doctor under the new arrangement is running afoul of insurance regulations that prevent doctors from billing twice for the same service. Some insurance companies bar doctors from offering concierge services, and Medicare will not allow a charge to a patient in addition to what the government pays. There is the risk of losing the practice and medical license and being penalized by the government for doing so. Any fee would have to be for services Medicare does not cover – and many doctors opted out of the insurance coverage altogether to eliminate the paperwork and arguments with providers about the fee schedules.

One of the criticisms directed at concierge doctors is that unlike most professions, where money is the primary goal, doctors are obligated by their ethical code to provide care for people in need – which can become an issue when their practices are confined to the wealthy. Some complain that concierge medicine caters only to the rich and famous. Some of the doctors in the plan defend their participation by claiming that this type of care is affordable for people who are not wealthy. The American Medical Association's policy on concierge care (or retainer practices) states that it is part of the changes in the delivery and financing of healthcare – even though the practice raises ethical concerns that warrant careful attention. Meanwhile, the questionable retainer practice is growing, and it seems to eliminate all the problems of the socialized medicine plan passed by Congress in 2012 – for those willing to pay the fee.

Innovative Healthcare

Another method for providing primary healthcare uses the internet or phone, transforming the way patients are treated in this age of digital technology. Experts claim that the explosion of the web and telephone-based medical services will eventually transform the delivery of primary care. It will give patients access to inexpensive, around-the-clock care for most routine problems – without the need to leave home or the workplace. Logging onto an internet site twenty-four hours a day will connect a patient with a doctor who may be 3,000 miles away. A patient reports his or her medical condition to the physician via instant message and then by phone. The doctor diagnoses the ailment and prescribes an antibiotic that is picked up at the local drugstore, where the doctor sent the prescription. The doctor's "visit" costs about forty-five and is paid for by credit card over the phone.

Even as more people are struggling to pay medical bills and are being rushed through five-minute office visits with their doctor(s), an elite group of citizens created another option: exclusive medical care, around the clock and anywhere in the world – including on a yacht or a private plane. One individual who pre-paid for medical care had his yacht outfitted with a medical suite almost identical to the one that serves the president of the United States. The so-called "ready room" lets doctors especially trained for that environment perform basic medical care remotely if something should go wrong while the patient is on the high seas. The cost for this on-call service ranges from $6,000 a month – plus the $700,000 to install the state-of-the-art ready room on a yacht or airplane or in the client's home (or all three for two million).

Urgent Care Walk-In Clinics

According to the Urgent Care Association of America, there are currently over 14,000 Urgent Care centers in the U.S., and the current growth rate for new centers is 7%.[14] Urgent Care is a bridge between the hospital emergency room and home care, treating patients who need to be seen right away. These immediate care facilities are appearing in storefronts in many cities, and they are proliferating by competing directly with the hospital emergency rooms. They focus on treating injuries such as lacerations or illnesses such as a cold (or similar, non-debilitating sicknesses) by employing a staff of doctors trained in emergency medicine. While they can do most things that fall within the realm of urgent care, they also need to recognize when to send patients to a hospital emergency room when a serious, life-threatening event falls outside their venue.

The typical urgent care center should be able to do X-rays and other diagnostic evaluations normally done in an emergency room. It should also offer patients an alternative to traditional primary doctors who are typically unable to make scheduled visits. Immediate care centers have filled a serious need, and some estimate that they have grown to become a fifteen-billion-dollar-a-year industry, annually, by competing directly with the hospital emergency room facilities. There may be many differences between these outside walk-in clinics and emergency rooms – but in many situations, they provide better care. For example, hospitals prioritize patients who have long waits after entering the emergency room, whereas doctors in clinics see patients immediately. Also, going to the hospital is not always a pleasant experience. In contrast, a great number of clinics look similar to a boutique hotel rather than using the décor found in most crowded emergency room environments.

Besides the storefront clinics, many retail chains of drug stores – such as CVS and Walgreens – have opened clinics within their stores to offer the same immediate care as independent clinics.

The cost factor is another consideration, since patients can be treated at a clinic by paying about $150 instead of incurring hospital charges that can start at $800. Clinics are not designed to replace primary care doctors who treat disease prevention and chronic problems such as diabetes, thyroid issues, and provide colonic and breast examinations. If an individual is experiencing chest pains or shows signs of a heart attack or stroke, then an ambulance should be called, and the patient should go to the hospital emergency room. It becomes a little tricky when people have chest pains that are due to stress or indigestion. The EKG at a clinic can indicate that the patient is not having a heart attack, but most people will choose a hospital – especially if the patient has a history of heart problems. An urgent care doctor deals with new, acute problems such as a bad migraine, rash, or sore throat.

Unlicensed Medical Spas

States have few rules or regulations that separate beauty treatment from the practice of cosmetic medicine – leading to the fast-growing "medical spas", which function between the traditional day spas and doctor's offices. These spas offer Botox injections, facial peels, laser skin treatments, and other minimally invasive cosmetic procedures. Some have expanded to include breast implants, tummy tucks, along with chin, face, brow, and eyelid lifts. The International Spa Association listed a network of 21,510 spas in 2021.[15] Some of this growth came from dermatologists and plastic surgeons adding services and amenities to their normal practice – but most medical spas operate without physician supervision.

State regulations vary widely, and some allow spas to perform procedures ranging from laser hair removal to liposuction by non-physicians if there is a medical doctor to oversee the service – though the doctor does not necessarily need to be on-site or even in the same state. There has been a push for more regulations, driven in part by dermatologists who claim that allowing non-physicians to perform cosmetic procedures puts patients at risk. They justify this statement by pointing out the difference between their four years in medical school and five years in residency versus a few months at a beauty school. Supporters of non-physician medical spas counterclaim that their industry is often unfairly accused of giving patients injuries without mentioning that there were more deaths in hospitals related to medical errors by licensed physicians. Meanwhile, if there is a rare death at a spa, it is on national news.

Only a few states require medical spas to report injuries – a fact that has made it difficult for patients to compare safety records at these upgraded beauty treatment centers to the injuries and complications that occur at doctors' offices. The interest in spas has attracted the attention of doctors. Additionally, some doctors who are medically licensed in an unrelated field are opening medical spas, with little experience in dermatology. In New Jersey, only a doctor can perform laser treatments – but that physician can be a psychiatrist or a heart specialist. Several groups have arisen since 2012 to educate doctors from other fields in cosmetic medicine procedures. The National Society of Cosmetic Physicians advertises two-day workshops in laser liposuction, breast augmentation, and tummy tucks.

Meanwhile, an increasing number of states are passing legislation to control the operation of medical spas better and upgrade their mostly out-of-date and confusing regulations. The medical spa law in New York, for example, requires doctors advertising themselves as "board certified" to specify which board. New York also requires anyone who wears a white coat and treats patients to list their credentials on a name tag. Fourteen other states are passing "truth in advertising" laws and require spas to list their personnel's training and credentials in all marketing material. Other laws adopted since 2013 relating to medical spas include the following:

- Maryland mandates that their state health department oversees cosmetic-surgery facilities.
- Florida now requires liposuctions that remove more than two pounds of fat be performed in a state-licensed surgery center, with emergency equipment on hand.

In California, it is a felony (punishable by up to five years in prison and a $500,000 fine) for a corporate entity to own an unlicensed medical facility.

Notes

1. Centers for Medicare and Medicaid Services, Study of Physician-owned Specialty Hospitals, https://www.cms.gov/Medicare/Fraud-and-Abuse/PhysicianSelfReferral/Downloads/RTC-StudyofPhysOwnedSpecHosp.pdf
2. Permit, The Corporate Practice of Medicine 50-State Guide, January 16, 2025, https://www.permithealth.com/post/the-corporate-practice-of-medicine-50-state-guide

3. Medical Group Management Association, Overview & Mission MGMA serves members, customers, and the healthcare community as a trusted partner by delivering insights, solutions, and advocacy to achieve medical practice excellence, https://www.mgma.com/overview-mission.
4. Timothy M. Smith, 3 Top Reasons Why Doctors Are Selling Their Practices to Hospitals, *American Medical Association*, August, 2023.
5. National Center for Health Workforce Analysis, State of the Primary Care Workforce, November 2024, https://bhw.hrsa.gov/sites/default/files/bureau-health-workforce/state-of-the-primary-care-workforce-report-2024.pdf
6. Joint Commission International, Communicating Clearly and Effectively to Patients: How to Overcome Common Communication Challenges in Health Care, 2018.
7. Web Paper, A model for communication skills assessment across the undergraduate curriculum, Elizabeth A. Rider, MSW, MD ,Margaret M. Hinrichs, Beth A. Lown, Published online: July 3, 2009, https://www.tandfonline.com/doi/full/10.1080/01421590600726540#d1e113
8. The New England Journal of Medicine Career Center, Understanding the Physician Employment "Movement" July 23, 2014.
9. Fierce Healthcare, Nearly 80% of docs employed by hospitals, corporate entities in continued shift away from independent practice, Dave Muoio April, 2024.
10. Robert Pear, Doctors Warned on Divided Loyalty, *The New York Times*, December, 2012.
11. ABC News, Hospitals cash in on a private equity-backed trend: Concierge physician care: Hospitals are increasingly offering "concierge service" to affluent clientele, Phil Galewitz, KFF HEALTH NEWS, March, 2024.
12. Bruce Japsen, Doctor Wait Times Average Almost Four Weeks In Big Cities, *Forbes*, September, 2022.
13. Nelson D. Schwartz, The Doctor is In. Co-Pay $40,000, *The New York Times*, June, 2017.
14. Urgent Care Association, The Essential Nature of Urgent Care in the Healthcare Ecosystem Post-COVID-19, August 2023, https://urgentcareassociation.org/wp-content/uploads/2023-Urgent-Care-Industry-White-Paper.pdf
15. The International Spa Association, Now you have the advantage., 2022 ISPA U.S. SPA INDUSTRY STUDY, https://experienceispa.com/wp-content/uploads/2022/08/2022-Industry-Study-FINAL.pdf,

Chapter 21

Nursery Neonatal Intensive Care

Security Misapplications

One of the biggest challenges for security directors in the nation's largest healthcare facilities is that far too many security integrators (alarm installers) and consultants recommend conventional alarm systems for non-conventional facilities – those with twenty-four-hour-accessible emergency rooms and birthing units. Certain systems are appropriate for a medical facility, but very few alarm installation companies seem to address the unique challenges found only in the hospital environment. This section concentrates on controversial security systems indigenous to healthcare centers – particularly as they relate to access control, fail-safe fire-exit door locks, digital recorders, and abduction-preventative infant protection systems. This last subject is a perfect example of how security manufacturers earned the dubious reputation of having almost every system sold and installed but failing so often that their failure rate is legendary – even in an industry not known for its equipment reliability.

The one single factor common to birthing facilities throughout the nation is the lack of shared communication among medical facilities, resulting in the repeated installation of defective security systems – particularly the infant protection system. Professionals in the field estimate that more than 60% of all infant protection systems must be replaced with another defective system within two years of the first installation. This cycle will continue until security directors start to share their experiences and eliminate

DOI: 10.4324/9781032630670-21

the overzealous alarm salespeople who probably have less than two years' experience in the security field – with no understanding of how to alarm the open environment that defines a hospital.

National Center for Missing and Exploited Children

The National Center for Missing and Exploited Children (NCMEC) is a well-known private, nonprofit organization that was established in 1984 and operates under a Congressional mandate in cooperation with the Office of Juvenile Justice and Delinquency Prevention (Department of Justice). Officials from public and private sectors participate in efforts to break the cycle of violence that historically perpetuates crimes against children. This important organization serves as a clearinghouse for information about missing and exploited children by providing data and offering technical assistance to public and law enforcement agencies in areas concerned with child abuse and infant kidnapping. NCMEC has handled more than 400,000 missing child cases and circulated billions of photos of missing children. We've produced thousands of age-progressed photos of long-term missing children and hundreds of facial reconstructions to aid in identifying unidentified children.[1]

Infant Surveillance. Approximately ten incidents of kidnapping are reported in the United States each year, according to the National Center for Missing and Exploited Children. These incidents all occur within seemingly secure, well-staffed maternity areas. Sometimes the abductor has dressed like a healthcare worker, brazenly taking infants from the arms of their parents – a tragic experience for both the families and the medical staff. It brings a feeling of helplessness, disbelief, and violation – as well as a great deal of negative publicity. And last but not least, the inevitable litigation. There is also frustration in finding out that most of these abductions could have been prevented with an affordable technology solution.

Infant abduction is a serious concern to the Joint Commission on Accreditation of Hospitals (JCAHO) surveyors. The possibility of abduction is considered a "sentinel event", requiring a root-cause analysis. Commonly, JCAHO surveyors ask in-depth questions regarding the implementation of infant safety and security plans and carefully review the security controls in the nursery – such as the locking system and procedures used to transport infants to and from the mother's room. While they do not mandate the installation or recommend a specific infant protection system, JCAHO does encourage establishing safety standards and upgrading security procedures in the nursery and labor and delivery areas.

The potential for large monetary judgments awarded by the courts for every confrontation in a hospital is another strong justification for the huge expenditure involved in installing and maintaining a sophisticated, building-wide security system. Many court decisions involve infant abduction concluded with jury awards of more than $100,000. For some hospitals, the amount of the penalty caused the hospital to eliminate the maternity and labor and delivery departments, and tarnishing the hospital's reputation. While no accurate statistics are available to indicate the effectiveness of an infant protection system in eliminating the threat of abduction, the majority of hospitals nationwide have installed such systems.

The number of hospitals with infant protection systems doubled between 2004 and 2010. Hopefully, the systems chosen in the future will be based on proven technology, rather than the recommendations of overzealous salespeople who helped cause the many mistakes made by administrators and security directors over the past decade. These mistakes resulted in about 50% of the original systems needing replacement. Sometimes, the salesperson who sold the second system was the same person who sold the initial defective system. Salespeople in the infant security system industry are known as "job jumpers" since they change jobs semi-annually. All too often, they get hired by rival infant protection system manufacturers.

Built-in obsolescence is a fact of the alarm system life in the security industry – particularly in the infant detection sector. Every hospital surveyed by security organizations had replaced the initially installed infant protection wireless RF system within a four-year period, because of a combination of false alarms and inadequate maintenance. This constitutes the shortest life cycle for any security system, regardless of the application. No simple solutions would alter this replacement trend, nor is there any one outstanding abduction system out of the five major manufacturers that control 95% of the industry. There will never be a perfect system, and no security will eliminate the kidnapping of infants from a hospital nursery.

Approximately 840,000 children are reported missing each year, and the FBI estimates that between 85% and 90% of these are children. While most reports of missing or abducted children are resolved within hours, many involve situations where a child goes missing permanently or for an extended period of time.

Every Forty Seconds, a Child Is Missing or Abducted in the United States[2]

Infant Abductions

The National Center on Missing and Exploited Children (NCMEC) indicated that there were 336 confirmed infant abductions that occurred between 1964 and 2022. This report showed that Texas and California have the highest prevalence of infant abduction, with 44 incidents occurring in each of these two states. Additionally, the NCMEC report found that 140 of these infants (42%) were abducted from healthcare facilities, and the abductor impersonated a nurse or other healthcare worker in nearly 73% of these cases.

Typically, an infant abduction is committed by a female perpetrator of childbearing age who is married/cohabitating and lives within the community where the crime occurs. The abduction itself is frequently planned, sometimes for months, with the perpetrator visiting maternity wards or nurseries at more than one facility to become familiar with the routines of healthcare staff and the parents of potential abductees. Approximately 59% of hospital abductions occur from the mother's room with the abductor impersonating a nurse, lab technician, social worker, or photographer, using deception and manipulation to gain access. Though these events are often premeditated, specific infants are infrequently targeted, and many abductions are crimes of opportunity in which the perpetrator exploits situational vulnerabilities when they arise. Some abductors are male, unmarried, have accomplices, are a parent or family member of the child, and employ no impersonation or other deception.

The following statistics include all U.S. cases documented by NCMEC, the International Association for Healthcare Security and Safety (IAHSS), and the Federal Bureau of Investigation (FBI) concerning abductions by non-family members from healthcare facilities, homes, and other places with newborns/infants (birth to six months). "Non-family members" are individuals who are neither parents nor legal guardians.[3]

Typical Abductor Profile (no guarantee that the infant abductor will fit the description):

- Between the ages of twelve and fifty, (childbearing age).
- Selects infants from newborn to six months of age.
- Appears normal but probably acts compulsively and suffers from low self-esteem.

- Abducts infant of same race – gender is not a factor.
- Visits nursery frequently and usually leaves through the fire stairwell to escape.
- Plans the abduction, but not the specific infant – seizes an opportunity.
- Frequently impersonates a nurse or other healthcare staffer.
- Is often overweight.
- Most likely abducts infant from nursery and the mother's room – rarely from the Nursery Neonatal Intensive Care (NICU).
- Frequently indicates that she has lost a baby or is incapable of having one.
- Often married or cohabiting – companion's desire for a child or the abductor's desire to provide her companion with his child may be the motivation for the abduction.
- Usually lives in the community where the abduction takes place.
- Asks detailed questions about procedures and the maternity floor layout.
- May also try to abduct from the home setting.
- Often becomes familiar with healthcare personnel and even with the victim's parents.
- Demonstrates a capability to provide "good" care to the baby once the abduction occurs.

Further assessment of available data indicates that 69% of the infants abducted are children of color, and most of the abductors are also people of color.

Traditionally, hospitals were suspected of resisting public reporting of certain events, fearing the information might be inaccurate, misleading, or might make the facility look bad and expose it to possible lawsuits. In recent years, hospitals and other public institutions have realized that they need to earn the public's trust by operating more openly. If a hospital appears to conceal information or is reluctant to share or disclose information, it may give the impression that the hospital has something to hide.

To gain a more in-depth understanding of the hospital's obligations in areas relating to reporting events and other relationships with the Joint Commission on the Accreditation of Hospitals (JCAHO), every security director in the healthcare field should obtain a copy of two NCMEC publications (single copies are free). The titles:

- *An Analysis of Infant Abduction* (seventy-six pages) – order #66.
- For Healthcare Professionals: Guidelines on Prevention of and Response to Infant Abduction.

Address: NCMEC, 699 Prince Street, Alexandria, Virginia 22314-3175.

The Jimmy Ryce Law Enforcement Training Center offers a technical assistance program through the NCMEC, named in memory of an abducted and murdered nine-year-old in 1995. Its purpose was to establish and enhance investigative response to missing and exploited children's cases.

Vanished Children's Alliance

An important, but lesser-known organization dealing with missing and abducted children was the Vanished Children's Alliance (VCA), formed in 1980. The VCA addressed the need for victims' parents to obtain credible, effective, and compassionate assistance in the location, recovery, and reunification of their missing and abducted children. VCA literature claimed that it was the oldest and most experienced missing children's organization in the nation and assisted in the location, recovery, reunification, and reintegration of more than 32,000 missing and abducted children. VCA provided training sessions and workshops to hospitals and other facilities on local, national, and international levels. It was the oldest organization devoted to missing children in the United States, and the National Center for Missing and Exploited Children recognized it. As of September 30, 2009, the organization is not operational. The VCA's website claims that the organization "has been unable to recover from the recent recession".

Notes

1. National Center for Missing and Exploited Children, Celebrating 40 Years of Hope, Emma Henderson Vaughan, December, 2024, https://www.missingkids.org/blog/2024/40-years-of-hope#:~:text=Their%20hard%20work%20paid%20off,child%20has%20a%20safe%20childhood.
2. Child Crime Prevention & Safety Center, website, https://childsafety.losangelescriminallawyer.pro/missing-and-abducted-children.html#:~:text=Every%2040%20seconds%2C%20a%20child,percent%20of%20these%20are%20children.
3. The Sam Houston State University Institute for Homeland Security, Infant Abduction from Healthcare Facilities: Prevalence, Explanation, and Risk Mitigation, Peter S. Lehmann, 2024. Report No. HIS/CR-2024-1004.

Chapter 22

Infant Abduction – A Shared Concern

A Common Scenario

A large New York City hospital employed the services of a respected security consultant engineering firm to design the security system for their new nursery area, including the wireless infant protection and tracking-tag system. A few months after the nursery was occupied, the system underwent testing and experienced frequent breakdowns, persistent false alarms, and a complete lack of service from the installation firm. The original system was removed from the nursery ward without ever being used because of inherent technical deficiencies – a fact the manufacturer neglected to share with the consultant or the facility. The system was eventually replaced by a system selected by the security director, who did not allow any salespeople to visit his office during his investigation of available systems – which involved visiting several hospitals to evaluate various operating systems.

The scenario described above is repeated several times a year in many of the nation's birthing hospitals. Such a change wastes about $250,000 each time the hospital replaces an infant protection system. Unless security directors (regardless of the industry they work in) share their experiences and communicate with one another, hospitals will continue to purchase faulty systems – and the same inept consultants will continue to design and promote ineffective systems.

DOI: 10.4324/9781032630670-22

Too Many Tag Systems

Based on sales estimates supplied by the manufacturers for infant protection systems (IPSs), about 75% of the nation's birthing hospitals have installed infant protection systems. While each system operates essentially the same (using an RF sensor attached to the ankle or wrist), each system claims to offer several unique features. All still suffer from false alarms and a lack of an ongoing maintenance program. This section objectively describes some of the important developments in the infant protection system field and is probably the first to compare the history of infant protection systems in detail.

The descriptions are based on comments from healthcare security staff members, who are involved in managing the wireless tag systems, along with manufacturers' comments and observations from several major installation firms. Some systems seem to be more effective than others, but they all exhibit two characteristics that have made the selection of an infant abduction security system the most difficult task confronting hospital administrators:

- Selecting a reliable local alarm installation company that will provide a proper response to service call requests is almost impossible.
- Having a security consultant recommend a system that is not obsolete before it is installed is also almost impossible.

Before wireless-transmitter tags were introduced to the nursery, retailers used them with great success, attaching them to garments and other items in the retail store environment. Then, nursing homes and dementia facilities used them with moderate success. The technique then gradually moved into the hospital nursery without much marketing success. Hospitals were understandably reluctant to purchase untested and expensive systems – especially if they did not consider the threat of infant kidnapping an urgent priority. Before 1986, an observant nursing staff provided all the security that was needed until the abduction of infants became a "sentinel event", according to Joint Commission on Accreditation of Hospital Organizations (JCAHO) statistics starting in the mid-1980s. This caused hospitals to lock stairwell doors and start to consider the installation of more sophisticated methods. At this point, a new industry of sensor infant-tag RF technology slowly evolved.

Nursing homes offered a bigger market for the wireless sensor tag systems in the decade before the manufacturers modified the technology for the infant protection system market. Wandering dementia patients are difficult to monitor and supervise, allowing individuals to wander freely around their floor areas – sometimes exiting the building completely bewildered regarding their whereabouts. Since 2018, more than 2,000 people have wandered away from assisted living and memory care facilities, according to The Post's investigation.

The sensor tag nursing home model is a much simpler system than the infant protection system, since it does not have to be protected against a third party (abductor) removing the sensor tag. The nursing home tag sensors operate at the same frequency, so the sensor does not have to be individually coded. The purpose of the system in this situation is only to alert the staff that someone is at the exit door. In many situations, it will lock the nearby exit doors. The name of the patient is not as important as the location of the attempted departure from the premises. The infant abduction security system is a more sophisticated system than the single frequency adult wandering system, because the infant abduction has more lasting effects than the repercussions caused by the wandering of a dementia patient.

Healthcare facilities that experience an infant abduction can destroy the hospital's reputation for decades and possibly bankrupt the institution due to the inevitable lawsuit. Once an infant is reported missing, facilities have suffered as much as a 50% loss in the number of deliveries made in the years following the abduction. This reaction, along with the lasting consequences, were the impetus for the development of an electronic-based infant abduction security system that can identify the infant based on its distinct coded frequency and can detect if the attached band holding the sensor is tampered with or removed.

The lack of an enthusiastic response from the healthcare community was not because the criminal act of infant abduction was non-existent in the nation's approximately 3,207 birthing hospitals. Hospitals were reluctant to spend the money to install and maintain these systems, and the nursery staff was reluctant to take on another task in an already hectic schedule. The hospital staff shared a concern about the threat of abduction. However, they did not accept it as a major problem and considered the problem a matter that fell under the responsibility assigned to the security department – which had little experience in or knowledge of these tag sensor systems. It was very difficult to get the marketing message from the factory to the nursery because of limited funds, and the relatively small healthcare market did not justify the use of a large, trained sales force.

There was no simple way to sell security concepts to the scattered healthcare facilities, as no one on the hospital staff was trained to understand the unique differences between each of the dozen systems available. Most senior administrators were reluctant to be responsible for purchasing a questionable alarm system and had some concern that the mere act of placing a "tag sensor" on an infant might scare the parents. That fear has completely abated with the public, given each attempted or successful abduction. The public is now aware that security is of prime importance in any facility and accepts the tagging of infants as a normal medical procedure in the nursery. The biggest drawback that has followed the infant protection system from its very inception is that a relatively complex electronic system requires a competent alarm system installation firm in each city to properly program, install, and maintain the system. This problem is a persistent one that most manufacturers in the security industry have not been able to solve. In some situations, the manufacturing firms have used their technicians to install the system – but the cost of travel and the constant need for prompt service makes this approach impractical.

Doctors are encouraged by the medical facility to arrange their schedules to be present in the hospital before the mother arrives, since it will attract more expectant mothers to select their nursery. One large facility (5,000 births a year) has found a way to ensure the public that they are concerned about the welfare of the mother during the entire birthing process. Included in their literature is, "There's none of this 'call me when she's pushing". Pregnancies are never treated as an illness, and in 2023, the number of live births in the U.S. was 3,591,328.[1]

The Good, the Bad, and the Ugly

A highly publicized incident involved a medical aide in a Miami hospital who, while attempting to remove the infant protection system tag from the newborn's ankle with scissors, inadvertently cut off the infant's small toe. The resulting lawsuit practically eliminated the nursery unit from the facility.

In 1988, these tag transmitters moved gradually from the nursing homes to the labor and delivery nurseries, where they were not an overwhelming success. The initial sales were accompanied by a lot of technical problems – mostly due to radio frequency interference caused by nearby hospital testing devices and cleaning machines, such as floor polishers. The initial firms that entered the infant protection industry had limited resources and absolutely no name recognition or experience in the healthcare sector of the security industry. They had no national distribution channels and focused their efforts on large urban cities once they realized that the threat of infant abduction was not treated as a serious concern by hospitals located in suburban and rural areas. The abduction problem was a well-kept secret until data were collected and published by some of the growing numbers of organizations – such as the National Center for Missing and Exploited Children, the Office of Juvenile Justice and Delinquency Prevention, and the Vanished Children's Alliance.

In the first five years after their introduction into the nurseries, only a small number of systems were installed in the nation's hospitals with nurseries. In the early 1990s, as more emphasis was placed on security in our nation's hospitals due to publicity and subsequent lawsuits following infant abductions, hospitals began to consider using the untested and false-alarm-prone infant protection systems. Over 40% of infant abductions take place in a healthcare facility, according to a nationwide data analysis by the National Center for Missing & Exploited Children between the years of 1964 and 2021. Even with the expense and high failure rate, the potential threat of abduction can be a catastrophic event to the parents, the medical staff, and the security officers. Furthermore, the potential threat of a lawsuit may be the most important factor that adds urgency to the situation – since an abduction can bankrupt a medical facility.

The infant protection system is a wireless radio frequency system specifically designed for the nursery and pediatric floors. It is an upgrade of the "anti-shoplifting" garment-protection tag systems used in retail stores. When nurseries use the tag, it needs to be more sophisticated and less prone to false activation. The false alarms acceptable to a retail business are not so in a nursery. This wireless tag technology has had a very controversial history since its introduction in 1985 – when nurses strapped miniature transmitters around the wrist of a dementia patient in a Chicago nursing home. Those early "pilot program" systems were purchased overseas and sold under a U.S. trade name.

Note

1. National Center for Health Statistics, Births and Natality, Data are for the U.S., https://www.cdc.gov/nchs/fastats/births.htm#:~:text=Number%20of%20births:%203%2C667%2C758,age%20at%20first%20birth:%2027.4

Chapter 23

Kidnapping from Unsecured Nursery

Evolution of Tag Technology

In criminal law, kidnapping is defined as "the taking away of a person against the person's will, usually to hold the person in false imprisonment (confined without legal authority) for ransom or in furtherance of another crime" – which can refer to taking persons against their will from one room to another within the same premises. For some unexplained reason, the terminology of kidnapping in common law in many jurisdictions defines the crime of kidnapping as abduction if the victim is a woman. Furthermore, infant abduction has never been a crime of epidemic proportions – but any abduction by a non-family member of an infant from a healthcare facility has understandably become a subject of concern for parents, maternal child-care nurses, healthcare security staff, the risk management administrator, and law enforcement officers.

> *No accurate statistics indicate that the installation of an electronic tag tracking system will eliminate the problem entirely – but hospitals use important factors to justify the expense of such systems.*

The infant abduction security tag sensor systems use some of the technology of the card reader access control system that has become one of the fastest-growing segments of the security industry. An English firm introduced their card access system to this country in the mid-1980s and claimed

DOI: 10.4324/9781032630670-23

a certain level of uniqueness when it introduced a patented "divided signal protocol" technology for a transponder system. The transponder sent a signal at a set frequency, activating the transceivers encapsulated in the sensor tag. The transceivers then transmitted a lower frequency captured on receivers located near each protected door. This system was developed primarily for use as a livestock detector, parking lot control, vehicle access control, and so forth. Some U.S. dealers saw the potential for a new market and adapted the components for use as an infant protection tag/sensor system. The first installation in a healthcare facility occurred around 1986 and has grown into an important industry.

Abduction Prevention

Initially, security staff paid little attention to using this relatively new infant "tag system" – but that changed in the early 1990s. Two major manufacturers in the garment tag retail store industry entered the nursery with their highly motivated sales force, greatly impacting the evolving infant protection business. Many hospitals purchased the garment device from either Sensormatic or Knogo and attached the tags to the garment the infant wore. After a few years, both companies left the industry when their modified retail store tag systems failed in the nursery environment due to false alarms and the lack of detection. An array of small firms with improved infant tag systems filled the marketplace void created by the exit of Sensormatic and Knogo.

Today, much confusion surrounds the infant protection marketplace, and many systems have come and gone. About eight systems are still competing for the 4,200 hospitals in the nation that have a birthing unit. One system employs single-use disposable tags/sensors. Another has a rechargeable sensor tag that can be reused for many years by simply replacing the battery. Others rely on reusing the tag for the battery life of about six to nine months before discarding it. When tags were first introduced, the systems were programmed to activate when the sensor band was "cut off" the infant before abduction was attempted – and only a few systems were designed to transmit an alarm signal if the band slipped off the infant without being cut. The occurrence of a band slipping off the wrist or ankle is far greater than the cutting of the band.

During the two decades of this century, several major manufacturing firms changed ownership and their marketing methods. The changing of ownership, along with selecting new dealers throughout the nation, contributed to the instability in the infant protection industry and its poor reputation during the early years following its introduction. About eight manufacturers control what is still considered a "cottage industry" – as most seem to be one-product companies with annual sales of less than five million. The infant protection system marketplace constitutes a very limited market within the overall security industry, and there is no such thing as "name recognition" for any of the systems. Compounding this marketing problem is that these manufacturers are competing in a limited market involving only hospitals with birthing units.

First Generation: Passive Transmitter

Regardless of the origin or manufacturer, early systems shared the same operating principle, which relied on a tuned transmitter operating at a single frequency. When the tag sensor approached an exit door, the receiver detected the radio frequency (RF) energy – activating an audible alarm. The location (door) was identified – not the person with the tag, since all the tags operated under a single frequency. The systems were copies of the retail garment tag systems that relied on floor-mounted six-foot antennas used with the early installations. These were so large that they created obstacles to free-flowing traffic (wide rolling stretchers), which violated most building codes. As a consequence, the system was limited to oversized door openings and very wide hallways – until the development of a loop antenna that wrapped around a protected portal. This antenna was an advancement, but it also produced new problems as the installation was extremely difficult. A continuous loop had to be created around the entire door frame, including the floor level. The antenna loop had to be extended eighteen inches into the hallway (under the floor surface) to complete the loop effect. It formed a type of "L" configuration with a radiation field designed to detect movement near the door.

The floor material in front of the door jamb had to be lifted to accommodate the loop wire, which posed no problem if the material was carpet. Burying the cable under a concrete or terrazzo floor took hours, and hospitals did not relish the appearance of a trench in the hallway made by alarm technicians who rarely displayed any talent for carpentry. Trying to create a loop effect around the door jamb proved to be impractical for two reasons:

- It formed a radiation field around the door, much like a donut with a hole in the middle. This opening would allow a sensor-tagged infant to go undetected through the hole if the movement were perfectly aligned in the center.
- Most door jambs are made of heavy gauge metal, which forms a radiation barrier – disastrous for RF transmission. Sometimes, someone requested to cut an opening in the jamb to allow more RF signals to pass through. It was unsightly, and the hospital always discouraged it.

Initially, the introduction of this "divided signal transmission" was a definite advancement because it resulted in a much lower false-alarm rate in an application that experienced a high rate of false alarms. However, once hospitals began to increase their use of electronic devices (computers, brush motors in waxing machines, electronic noisy door closures, and other medical equipment that threw off electronic RF noise), the infant protection system became less effective due to the level of sensitivity lowering. The use of coded signals in all access control systems was very effective – but when applied to egress-control types of systems (such as those used in nurseries), it displayed serious shortcomings. With access control card reader systems, the card user has an interest in being detected to open the door – and this person will move the sensor/card patiently around the reader's head until it "reads" the card. When applying the same transmission principle to detect an abduction at the same door opening, it may not always detect movement. Sometimes, the movement was too rapid, too far from the reader antenna, or the would-be abductor was not standing around while waiting for the system to detect the presence of the infant. Eventually, the abduction system had to use the marginally acceptable coding system, even when it produced a high rate of false-positive signals rather than missing a real detection. In other words, even after ten false alarms, the eleventh could be caused by an abductor.

Passive Tuned Coils. These low-power radio frequency fields are passive systems, since the sensing coils have no power to "actively" transmit a RF signal. The last passive tag system that was still in operation was at a Manhattan hospital, with antennas at the street exit doors – none on the nursery floor. In 2005, the hospital replaced it with a system that detected the "slipping" band. In 2010, the hospital was sold – and it is now a condominium.

Nurses in the nursery were unhappy with the persistent false alarm rate and would often turn the system off because of the false signals. It was state-of-the-art in the late 1980s, when a few manufacturers modified the short-range card reader access control systems. The manufacturers increased their range and placed the electronics embedded in the card into a thicker, watch-shaped tag sensor. The sensor could be attached to an infant or a dementia patient to detect movement near a wired portal. But the major shortcoming remained: if someone cut the band off the infant's wrist, the cutter would discard the sensor – rendering the system useless.

False alarms are the most significant reason for user complaints and the reluctance from many healthcare facilities to install an infant protection system. Most false alarms are due to unreliable tamper detection mechanisms and poorly designed tags. Other causes are the proximity of egress points to patient rooms and patient ambulation. It is important for vendors to work closely with hospitals to understand their workflow and provide a system design that minimizes or eliminates these types of alarms – but this is rarely done.

Nuisance alarms. Much controversy surrounds the definition of a false alarm since many administrators classify events as false alarms – even when the technology is performing as it was designed to do. Also, all systems in use today use the band that employs skin-sensing. This mechanism is prone to alarm when water gets in between a band and the baby's skin during a bath. In this situation, the technology had correctly identified that something was between the band and skin, which is what it was meant to do. While it may be identified as a false alarm, it is a "nuisance alarm". The Emergency Alert System (EAS) generation was a step backward since it was a copy of existing shoplifting devices and did not rely on any advanced technology of the infant protection system on the market. In 1992/93, the relatively small market of infant abduction prevention attracted the attention of the major manufacturers of the wireless tag retail store shoplifting systems. These passive systems proved to be less than 70% effective when protecting merchandise – so the idea of using these same systems to protect newborn infants was not a sustainable solution to prevent infant abductions from the nursery.

EAS manufacturers entered the market with greater marketing budgets than the small infant protection system manufacturers could hope to duplicate. Sensormatic and Knogo were, at the time, the two largest retail store/garment tag system manufacturers that used a non-coded passive anti-theft system. The tag was not very sensitive, since passive systems used a tuned coil of wire instead of a battery-powered active transmitter. They simply redesigned retail store clothing tags directly from the retail store and embedded the same electronics into a watch-shaped tag attached to the infant.

These new firms then reassigned their salespeople to the healthcare market, using the same aggressive sales approach that was successful in the retail store marketplace. By contributing funds to help support the National Center for Missing and Exploited Children (NCMEC), the firms supplying retail store EAS systems were allowed to apply the agency logo to their advertisements – which made it appear as if they were recommended by NCMEC (similar to the Good Housekeeping seal of approval). In a brief two-year period during the early 1990s, the passive systems were installed in more nurseries than any other infant protection system – even though a passive sensor could not be detected if shielded by the body or covered with tin foil.

This type of system was also susceptible to false alarms with a so-called "pick-rate" of 60%. This means that 60% of the tags moving within the field are detected. This rate is acceptable if the object is a jacket in a Gap Store, but it is unacceptable in a nursery. After many lawsuits, the retail-passive systems firm left the hospital marketplace in 1995 and turned all its resources back into the retail store market. The last unit in a New York City hospital was replaced in 2006 – after ten years of neglect, because the hospital believed that the six-foot antennas served as a deterrent (even if the system were dormant). The battery-powered second-generation tag system replaced the retail store passive systems, but they still shared one major shortcoming with the retail system. If the tag were cut off the infant and discarded in a wastebasket, the infant could freely move through any portal undetected. What the industry desperately needed was a "redundant" system that would detect the sensor near an exit and activate an alarm if the band were cut off the wrist or ankle of an infant.

Homemade-Customized System. Before the industry found a way to detect the cutting of a band, one security detector in the largest hospital in New York City developed a unique technique to overcome this shortcoming. The hospital's older retail EAS antenna was in place, but it had been abandoned when the first-generation, battery-powered tag system was installed. To overcome the obstacle of not being able to detect a cut band, the retail store system was reactivated. However, the coil was not attached to the infant – since each infant already had a battery-powered tag sensor. The small, flat, tuned coil from the EAS system was instead sewed into the infant garment that all newborn babies wear. The coil was camouflaged, hidden under the hospital logo placed on all the infant garments. In effect, two redundant systems were now in use.

If the sensor tag on the wrist were removed (pulled off or cut off) by a would-be abductor, the abductor (believing the basic system was compromised) would then set off the alarm as the infant was moved between the upright, freestanding antennas placed at each exit door. It was the first time that an infant protection system was able to prevent abduction when the band was cut off (even though it did not detect the actual cutting). It was a success for about a year until the third-generation system became available – which was able to detect the cutting of the band.

Note: The only problem that arose from the coil-in-garment configuration was when the garment was thrown into a laundry bin on the nursery floor. When leaving the floor with a basket filled with dirty, coiled-garment laundry, the coils would set off the alarm at the exit – locking the door. This problem was corrected, and the system proved that security directors are just as innovative as the manufacturer. The leftover coil in the garment can be purchased on eBay.

Manufacturers of Infant Tag Systems

Companies listed below include many tag systems that are no longer available because they were ineffective, false-alarm-prone, accidentally slipped off the infant – or, in many cases, the installation company disappeared (or the manufacturer left the industry) leaving the system abandoned. Many infant protection system companies evolved gradually after 1990, when the infant protection system was first attached to infants in nurseries. Only about a half dozen have survived through 2018. Of those still available, each provides similar models for the newborn infant, mother-matching management, breast milk storage, pediatric protection, and monitoring dementia patients wandering unsupervised in nursing homes.

- HUGS – STANLEY Healthcare; also, Wonderguard and PEDZ (Pediatric)
- Prosec – introduced tags on umbilical cords instead of wrists
- Hollister – familiar name in healthcare; one of the first IP; lasted a short time
- Sensormatic – store garment tag placed on infants in 1990; failed
- RF Technologies – also known as SafePlace; very active in infant protection system industry
- Elpas – owned by Tyco Industries; out of infant protection system production

- My Child – owned by McRoberts Security
- AngleTrac – tag used only once; very costly; out of production
- Safe Alert – not popular
- Secure Care – also KinderGUARD and Match Maker
- Executone – short life cycle
- Stork – owned by Executone
- Dynaflow – Code Alert dealer/integrator substituting own software; failed
- Instatel – not successful
- Accutech/Cuddles – one of the oldest and most popular
- Halo – popular system made by EXI
- CoTag – foreign-made and used under other U.S. trade names
- VeriChip – microchip with a unique ID implanted in human beings, not infants
- Knogo – passive tags; competed against Sensormatic
- KinderGUARD – by Secure Care

PROSEC is an infant protection security system that uses a completely different concept in the design of the sensor tag. It is not strapped to the wrist or ankle – it is wrapped around the umbilical cord. Many religions reject this attachment method – as do many parents. There are strong opinions on the advantages of using the umbilical cord to support the sensor tag. Some medical personnel claim it is a more secure practice, while others feel that it is unsightly and unreliable – since the cord will fall off along with the tag, rendering it useless. Congress is considering the creation of a national registry for umbilical cord donors for bone marrow transplants. Each year, more than 20,000 people are diagnosed with fatal diseases that require a bone marrow donation, but most people die waiting for a match. Blood from umbilical cords helps because of its source, which contains certain important cell material for transplants. It is not as controversial as stem cell research since the cord is thrown away after birth – turning medical waste into medical miracles.

ANGLETRAC entered the infant protection system market in 1997 and remained for a very short period with its one-use concept. This system eliminated any sanitation concerns about a tag that was removed from one infant and attached to another newborn. If a typical healthcare facility has 3,000 annual births, the cost for the disposable AngleTrac sensor tags would be about $100,000 a year – while a reusable tag system (used one hundred times a year) would cost $24,000 a year. While this cost differential appears significant, a typical birth/maternity expense (without complications) can run anywhere from $7,000 to $12,000 per birth (hospital fees plus obstetrician, midwife, testing lab, etc.), according to various insurance brokers and health experts. This makes the added cost for the disposal (twenty-seven dollars) appear insignificant. However, budget-conscious hospitals resisted justifying the cost differential for a sterilized tag. The company is no longer in business.

DYNAFLOW is the trade name of an innovative integrator who purchased the infant protection system from a leading manufacturer and then replaced the software with his software and changed the name of the system. This deception meant that servicing and expanding had to be done by the integrator – eliminating the need for the services of the original manufacturer. Lawsuits followed, and the customized unit was taken off the market – resulting in the integrator leaving the industry.

VARICHIP is about the size of a grain of rice and is implanted between the shoulder and elbow area of an individual's right arm. The chip responds with a unique sixteen-digit number that can then be linked with information about the user held on a database for identity verification and medical records. The system was very controversial – especially for an infant. There was also an ethical dilemma posed by the technology. People with dementia could benefit the most from an implanted device that contained their medical records, but issues of informed consent are the most difficult in this population. In 2006, a Cincinnati company became the first company to implant microchips into their employees as part of their building access control and security system. The workers needed the implants to access the company's secure videotape room. In 2007, the American Medical Association declared that implantable radio frequency identification (RFID) devices may help to identify patients, thereby improving the safety and efficiency of patient care. These devices could be used to enable secure access to patient clinical information. However, in that same year, news reports linking similar devices to cancer caused in laboratory animals had a devastating impact on the entire concept. In 2010, the company withdrew the product from the market due to poor sales. In 2012, the chip assets were sold to another company, and in 2016 they were sold again. For all practical purposes, it is no longer available.

Evolution of Passive-to-Active Tags

The unique features of each major protection system may be divided into four separate generations that cover the twenty-year history of infant protection systems. There is no accurate way of confirming the exact number of systems sold by individual manufacturers. Some of the systems were sold as replacements, so the same hospital recorded two or three systems – even though each one replaced the previous one. Manufacturers are either reluctant to give accurate figures or exaggerate the number of their systems in existence.

During the relatively short time that infant protection systems have been on the market, major changes in the RF technology used to control the nursery exits and the identity of the infant have occurred. Though the models changed, not all were successful:

- First-generation transmitters similar to PROX card access control systems.
- Second-generation retail store type of anti-shoplifting system (big six-foot antennas).
- Special infant protection system designed by a New York City hospital security director.
- Third generation detected a cut band and changed the technology.
- Special mother-child matching security system to prevent accidental baby switching.
- Fourth generation detects cutting or slipping of the band.

Second Generation: Cut-band Innovation: In 1995, one manufacturer developed a system that would solve the most serious shortcomings shared previously by all manufacturers. Until that time, the entire infant protection industry provided the same type of RF technology to detect a would-be abductor at a nursery exit and either activate an audible alarm and/or automatically lock the exit with the fail-safe electromagnetic lock. Once the abductors realized that the sensor tag was the device that could prevent the abduction of the infant, they could disable the sensor tag attached to the wrist or ankle of the infant by cutting the band and disposing of the sensor. The third generation relied on a special band and emitted transmit dual frequencies.

The first transmitter was "on" all the time and tuned to activate an alarm when the sensor moved near an exit door (similar to the function of the basic first-generation system). A second transmitter, mounted inside the same tag as the first transmitter, remained in a "quiet" mode until the cutting of the band activated this second transmitter – which transmitted a higher frequency signal to the ceiling-mounted antennas scattered every 400 square feet throughout the nursery floor. When the band was cut or removed by sliding a loose-fitting band off an infant, the location was instantly displayed on a screen at the nurses' station, and all the exit doors on the nursery floor automatically locked. It was a revolutionary improvement over the previous standalone antenna tower of the retail store passive tag system that could not detect any fast-moving object between the upright antennas or the cutting of the band on the active battery-powered tag sensors.

While the concept rendered all previous tag sensor technology obsolete (particularly the retail garment tag system), it was inherently defective. No one properly tested it before introducing it to the marketplace. On the first production models, the sensor was "tuned" to the common frequency shared by hospital devices, and the system detected extraneous false alarm RF signals emitted from waxing machines, flickering lights, and computer terminals. It caused so many false alarm signals that it was useless, and Queens Hospital removed it from their installations. It should have been treated as a "beta test", as the system was not ready for prime-time applications.

While this premature system had inherent defects and needed more testing, later models of the cut-band technology operated more efficiently. It changed the mindset of the entire infant protection system community. After 1996, all future systems provided a cut-band feature in order to remain competitive in the infant protection industry.

Third Generation: "Skin-sensor" Band Technology. This advanced type of bracelet sensor eliminated the weakness in the previously designed tags that did not detect the removal of the band by slipping it off the wrist or ankle without cutting it off. While it was an advanced technology and solved a major shortcoming in older bands, it also created some unique problems. For example, the infant's constant movement often resulted in the band falling off (sometimes in the bassinet). This event was corrected by the nurse responding to the alarm signal.

It also became a nuisance alarm when the band became loose without falling off the infant, causing a tag-off-body alarm to sound each time the band and the skin became momentarily separated.

Today's Next Generation Systems: Wi-Fi. Today, infant protection systems utilize Wi-Fi in order to communicate between devices and nursing staff. This revolutionary idea was developed for easier installation because of less wiring of devices. It also reduced the cost of the system. However, this innovation has been a nightmare for the hospitals who ventured to purchase and install this new technology. Generally, this technology was forced upon many hospitals since their existing system was considered obsolete and was being phased out by the manufacturer. Although cheaper, most hospitals that purchase this new innovative system spend tens of thousands of dollars upgrading their networks in order to support communication between devices for the infant abduction system. Keeping in mind that hospitals are generally older buildings with thick walls and solid wood doors. Even newer hospitals require two-hour fire-rated hallways with the same rating for fire partition doors and patient room doors. Walls and doors absorb Wi-Fi signals, making transmission difficult. Even after spending a fortune on network upgrades, the infant systems are still ineffective when there is a glitch within the hospital's network. These glitches create alarm conditions that add to the even greater number of alarms initiated by the infant protection system from transmitters not turned off, transmitter bands not fitting properly and nurses who forget to take off transmitter bands on the baby creating an alarm when mothers and fathers are discharged from the hospital with their baby and try to leave the nursing unit.

Fortunately for some of these innovative hospitals, they have been able to spend the money to remove these new systems and return to the old-wired device systems which work more effectively. However, others are still struggling to make their newly purchased systems work, especially when they have spent thousands of dollars to upgrade their wireless networks to support these innovative systems.

Chapter 24

Elopement Deterrents

Evolving Technology

Case #1: Based on the recommendation of their outside consultant, a major healthcare network with more than 11,000 annual births investigated state-of-the-art protection systems after experiencing failures with the installed systems. Their evaluation process was a classic exercise in how to evaluate the changing technology before making a final selection. After visiting many sites and witnessing demonstrations of the most popular infant protection systems available, the security staff from various sites within the network selected two sites where different infant protection systems were installed for a one-year test at the manufacturers' expense. After a year of operation, data was developed based on interviews with the nursing staff, false alarm reports, and response to service calls from the two local installers. Then, they invited each manufacturer to make a presentation before a group of security staff members and senior administrators who would vote on the winning system – much like the American Idol TV show. One system was then selected for installation in all the network facilities. The rejected system was removed and returned to the manufacturer. An employee of the winning system, who was formerly with the rejected system, made the presentation on behalf of the rejected system. The presentation was so insulting that the winning manufacturer instituted a lawsuit. Salespeople have a strange set of loyalties that seem to change on an annual cycle.

Case #2: One of the eleven Health and Hospitals Corporation (HHC) facilities moved its nursery into a newly constructed building. Instead of moving the infant protection system from the old location, it purchased an entirely

 DOI: 10.4324/9781032630670-24

new system. The justification for changing the system was mainly due to persistent false alarms and a failure of the vendor to provide adequate service. The manufacturer realized the problem and completely severed all relations with the original installation firm. The new local, factory-authorized representative demanded that the hospital use his service and pay his fees, because he was now the only factory-trained and authorized representative in the city. The hospital refused this almost-threatening attitude and purchased a replacement system for the new nursery. This is a typical case in which a manufacturer, located thousands of miles from the hospital, tries to control the selection of a local installation firm. The market in any one city is very limited. There would be no justification to authorize and train more than one firm for each manufacturer. This creates an entirely new problem and illustrates how difficult it is for a hospital to choose the local vendor – instead of leaving that responsibility to the manufacturer, who does not always make wise choices.

Case #3: This example is very sad and demonstrates that hospitals can become their own worst enemy unless they survey the field carefully and do not follow the advice of other hospital administrators – people who are not trained to make an intelligent decision on technology that has more failures than successes. It is like the blind leading the blind.

A famous HHC Brooklyn facility selected an infant protection system based on the recommendation of an administrator at a private Staten Island hospital, who claimed to have installed a system with significant cost-saving advantages. The installation cost was about the same as that for competitive systems – but the most impressive fact was the thirty-five-dollar cost for each sensor tag that was attached to the infant. It was also one of the smallest tags in the industry, and the nursing staff agreed that the computer program was user-friendly. The HHC purchasing department was impressed, because the cost for comparative tags from the other seven manufacturers were about one hundred per reusable sensor. The installation cost of $150,000 was about average for a New York City facility, and its other features included an alarm activation whenever the tagged infant approached an exit door along with an alarm if the band was cut anywhere in the nursery causing the activation of the exit door locks. These security features and the low cost of the sensor seemed ideal to the engineering department of the hospital, which was authorized to select the system (rather than the security director). Involvement of the engineering department in security matters is no longer a rarity in the healthcare field. Once installed, the system performed as promised.

This particular hospital averages more than 5,000 births each year – a fact known to the security manufacturer before the sale, but one it conveniently forgot to mention to the hospital engineering department. The relatively inexpensive sensor tag was the only one in the industry that could be used only once. The manufacturer considered this one-time-use sensor to be an advantage, as every tag was guaranteed to be completely free of any contamination. The standard hundred-dollar tags are reusable, with a battery life of about six to nine months. It is conceivable that fewer than one hundred tags were required each year to protect 5,000 infants – equal to a total annual tag cost of $10,000. Infants can share the same hundred-dollar tag, as long as it is washed between attachments and the battery stays active.

The supposedly cost-effective $35 tag worked very well. Yet, it was disconcerting to realize that each of the 5,000 infants required a new tag. The annual tag replacement cost was an astounding $150,000. The system was replaced, along with the system on Staten Island and the engineer who selected the system. The rationale behind the one-use sensor was that thirty-five dollars is not very costly when the average bill for a maternity stay is almost $10,000. Since that firm started production in 1997, they installed only fourteen systems nationwide – including the two systems noted above. By 2008, hospitals replaced all these systems. About 35% of these birthing facilities have installed one of the eight infant abduction security systems still being made. All have mixed results – some with poor results, but none with excellent ones. While there is no intent to recommend any system in particular (since they function on similar technical concepts), the information is a balance between the experience of the end user (New York City security directors) and the claims made by manufacturers.

Chapter 25

Mother-Child Matching System

Preventing Infant Mismatches

The responsibility of the hospital is to inform each new parent about the rare possibility of infant abduction from the nursery, the recovery room – and especially – the mother's place of residence. At the beginning of this century, three out of eight infant protection systems' manufacturers added a feature to their basic system to activate an alarm if a nurse carried a newborn infant and left the infant with the wrong mother for feeding or before discharge. The mother might not easily recognize her infant, if the baby were of the same race and sex and covered with a blanket. This type of error occurs in every nursery – regardless of any claim by the staff that such an event can never happen in their efficient nursery. It remains a serious concern to hospital administrators who have instituted preventative measures to eliminate the possibility of a mismatch. Infant care professionals are well aware that they have a much higher risk of presenting a child to the wrong mother than of an infant abduction – but the problem has been underreported for many years. The crime of baby kidnapping may overshadow it, but delivering the wrong baby is still considered a very serious event – even if it may not be as devastating as a kidnapping.

The impetus for the public's interest in baby switching was due to an incident that occurred in 1998 in Virginia, which was extensively covered on TV. Two mothers left the hospital with the wrong baby girl. The hospital discovered the switching error three years after the birth. The incident publicized the fact that baby "switching" was not such a rare occurrence. According to the DNA Diagnostics Center, an Ohio-based genetic testing

DOI: 10.4324/9781032630670-25

laboratory, of the up to 500,000 babies born each year in the United States, only 18 may be switched at birth and most of them are caught immediately following the incident. Between 1995 and 2008, the laboratory's statistics found that eight newborns were switched in the United States, though this figure might be higher because there is no national mandate for hospitals or individuals to report such incidents.[1] It is a well-kept secret and rarely reported as a sentinel event – unless someone on the staff or the parent reports it to authorities. When the incident is made public, someone on the nursing staff is usually fired – and an inevitable litigation ensues.

This problem has caused concern for all parties involved – even if the error is discovered before the infant is discharged from the hospital with the proper parents. With infectious diseases such as HIV and hepatitis, a temporary switching could potentially be a death sentence to the baby if the baby were to be breast-fed by an HIV-positive mother. The risk of infection can be disastrous for all concerned – the mother, the child, and the hospital staff. While the problem related to HIV is of national concern, it is a more serious problem in larger cities – such as New York, where one-fifth of 160,000 Americans infected with HIV reside (since 2001, according to the Centers for Disease Control). The study focused on HIV diagnoses between 2001 and 2004 in thirty-three states.

The risk of mix-ups increases when the nursing staff is overwhelmed and understaffed, yet still expected to add the responsibility of programming and monitoring infant protection systems and mother-child matching technology. The Virginia switch was a mistake that caused a great deal of harm to all concerned. It also cost the hospitals millions of dollars in damages, awarded by the jury as a result of the inevitable lawsuit. The likelihood of an accidental switch of newborn infants is higher in hospitals that have a birth rate exceeding 3,000 babies a year and have nursery rooms and NICUs that hold more than a dozen babies at a time. Infants are kept in close quarters and are moved several times a day for feeding. Under these conditions, baby mix-ups are a realistic threat. Not only is the mix-up devastating to the family, but it will cause long-lasting damage to a hospital's reputation – exposing the facility to lawsuits and placing the institution in Jeopardy of losing its accreditation.

Switching an infant, even for a brief period, falls into a category shared by wrong surgery (removing the left foot because the X-ray plates were held in a reversed position by the surgeon) and the dispersing of wrong drugs or the wrong amounts of drugs prescribed for patients. These seemingly diverse events are considered sentinel events by the Joint Commission and can place the hospital on probation or eventually result in having its license revoked. Some of the actions instituted by many hospitals to protect against handing the mother the wrong infant include but are not limited to the following procedures:

- Continuing to train the nursing staff on the importance of checking the ID bracelets on both the infant and the mother.
- Placing ID tags on both wrists and both ankles, totaling four tags.
- Transporting only one infant at a time to a room. Many unhappy cases may arise when two infants are brought in at the same time by one nurse – and when she is interrupted, she gives the infant to the mother in the wrong bed.
- Making sure the mother's room is clearly marked on the bassinet.
- Trying to arrange the nursery area so that the infant and mother are on the same floor.
- Checking the ID bracelet continually, so they do not come loose as the weight of the infant fluctuates.
- Moving infants in a crib between rooms, so that a baby will not inadvertently be carried by a nurse and placed in the wrong bassinet.
- Somehow identifying the mother's milk bottle in the refrigerator either by a barcode attached to the formula or clearly labeled with a magic marker.

Technology Versus Training – Conflicting Solutions

The debate lies between those that feel that installing an electronic mother-match system would solve the problem and those who feel the proper training of the staff is a far more effective solution. In an informal survey taken of members of the New York City IAHSS chapter and several nurses assigned to the labor and delivery floors, the groups split on how they would solve the switching problem. The arguments can be summarized by the following:

- About 70% felt the problem could be solved with better training. Staff diligence in checking name tags on the infant and mother is more secure than relying on electronic devices that break down and have inherent defects. Instituting an electronic system places an additional burden on the already overworked nursing staff. Programming the electronic matching system is time-consuming, and some of these systems are not user-friendly.

- The study group also felt that if the electronic system did detect the mix-up, any explanation to the mother would only create anxiety – since it highlights a serious flaw in infant-care procedures. "How could the nurse make such a mistake?" A public relations problem is caused when automation backfires.
- Electronic tag systems have a shortcoming in that they will not always alert the staff if the wrong infant is brought to a mother's room. Several other techniques are used to verify a mother-child match. Some systems place coded tags on both the mother and child. When the tags are held near the frequency, they must match, or an alarm is activated. Other systems match the tag sensor on the infant to the reader on the entrance door, and the infant must be matched to the frequency on the door before entering the room.

It appears that most nurses and security directors feel that the conventional method of visually matching the Hollister bands is the most reliable method, since the electronic tag match approach is not foolproof and may encourage the nursing staff to take a more active role in checking to see that the infant is brought to its birth mother.

Proponents of using electronic technology to ensure proper mother-child matches more than nurse responsibility insist that the older method of training the staff may be 99% effective but feel the procedure has been in place forever – and every time a mix-up occurs, the hospital staff makes the same comments that the incident was an "isolated event". The staff is then retrained, and a few months later another isolated incident occurs. The scenario is repeated again and again.

An alternative to the electronic match system is a simpler device that operates exactly like the barcode reader used to record the price of the item at the checkout counter. The same ID system comes with a packet of ten bar codes (all using the same number) and a handheld barcode reader. The nurse tapes the coded strip on the name tag on the wrist or ankle of all newborn infants. The same bar code is then placed on the mother's wristband (and the father's and relatives', if requested). When the infant is brought to the mother's room, the attending nurse scans the barcode of both the mother and child. The built-in program in the scanning device will alarm if the codes do not match. It costs about ten dollars for each packet of bar codes, and there is a one-time cost of $1,000 for the reader. Another advantage of this system is that it can be applied to the bottle holding the mother's milk, when it is stored in the refrigerator.

Separated at Birth

A clothing store salesman mistook a customer in 2000 for someone he knew, but the customer convinced him that it was a case of misidentification. Out of curiosity (and the strong resemblance to the salesman's friend), he arranged for the two women to meet. They were both twenty-eight years old at the time, born on the same day in 1972, and born at the same hospital. The ensuing meeting was unsettling, as the women discovered their similarities extended well beyond physical resemblance – down to the smallest gestures (despite not growing up together). DNA tests confirmed they were monozygotic (identical) twins, developed from a single fertilized egg. The mother of the twins assumed she had given birth to fraternal twins (dizygotic) from two eggs that were therefore not identical. There are only seven known instances of identical twins being switched at birth.

It is highly unlikely that the error would have been discovered was it not for the fact that the twins were monozygotic, thus having a striking resemblance. There are probably thousands of solitary children growing up with no biological parents, because of hospital switches. This fact argues for an urgent need to improve the existing rudimentary hospital systems of baby identification. The reunion of separated twins is inevitably an emotionally exhausting event. The truth may be so painful that it would be better not to have discovered a sibling many years after the switch. The problem is compounded when twins are separated, and one is still raised as a twin without being biologically related to the assumed twin brother or sister. The two families that brought up the biological twins were awarded about a million dollars each. However, there was no way to equate the real cost of the emotional turmoil endured by the individuals in this thought-provoking dilemma.

Babies can look alike – except for skin color and eyes – and mistakes from a nursery ward who has to supervise dozens of births a day is a security nightmare, the new mother must be attentive and observe who enters her recovery room with the newborn. Nurses and the infant should wear name tags, and the stored mother's milk bottles should have ID tags on it. Further ways to prevent switches from happening:

- Question people who are unfamiliar who seem preoccupied with questions about the baby.
- Do not place announcements about the birth in newspapers.
- Do not carry a baby in one's arms when leaving the room – use a crib on wheels.
- Never leave an infant alone in a room.
- When a baby is brought in for feeding, keep the bassinet beside the bed – on the side furthest from the door.

Banning Pictures in Delivery Rooms

Nationwide, photography and videography have been allowed in many delivery rooms for decades. In recent years, advances in technology have encouraged some hospitals to alter their policies. The hospital community is now trying to balance safety and legal protections against the desire of some new mothers to document all aspects of their lives – including the entire birthing process. No national standards exist regarding cameras in the delivery room, so each hospital sets its own rules (creating a patchwork of conflicting policies). No national organization, including the American College of Obstetrics and Gynecology and the American Hospital Association, keeps track of how many hospitals allow and even encourage recording – because modern cameras are so unobtrusive.

Ubiquitous cellphones have exponentially increased the ability to take a high-quality picture in any setting. As a result, it can be assumed that a camera is always present in every delivery room. About 20% of all hospitals ban cameras in the delivery room – but there is not a nationwide crusade for doing so. Military hospitals use Skype to connect mothers with soldier-fathers overseas, eliminating the need for a camera.

Parents believe that since it is their child, they have the right to take pictures – regardless of the policy of the hospital. For the hospital, the issue is not about "rights", but the health and safety of the baby and mother, along with protecting the privacy of the medical staff (many of whom have no desire to become celebrities on Facebook or YouTube). Hospitals' concerns come against a backdrop of medical malpractice suits in which videos play a big role. Many hospitals have lost malpractice because the juries exposed in videos are so vivid that some of them faint in the courtroom (even if the scene is showing a normal childbirth procedure). Scenes of a mother screaming with the staff responding (or not) to what may look like an emergency can be edited to misrepresent what took place. Doctors contend that deliveries are complicated – and no one on the medical staff wants to be distracted, since it is essential that the doctor be 100% focused on medical care. In a litigious atmosphere, where TV ads are on every thirty seconds about suing, physicians become more than just camera-shy when the subject of cameras in the delivery room comes up for discussion.

Some landmark malpractice lawsuits occurred where the father of the newborn recorded nurses' complaints that a doctor would not get off the phone to attend to the delivery. Another case involved a father who taped a complicated delivery and then pretended to be congratulating the clinicians while recording their responses to the complications – this information was later used as evidence against them.

Note

1. J. Kocher, Switched at Birth: Decades After Discovery, Gillette Woman Forges New Life (Part 1), *The Wyoming Truth*, November 2023.

Chapter 26

Locked Exit Doors in Maternity Ward

NFPA Life Safety Code 101

The National Fire Prevention Association (NFPA) essentially wrote all the fire codes used in municipalities throughout the nation since the 1920s. The most referenced of their hundreds of codes is the Life Safety Code 101. It is also probably the most misunderstood code, but it is the standard followed by the Joint Commission. The complete ninety-eight-page Life Safety Code 101 contains five basic sections, separated into thirty-two chapters that deal with various areas relating to the fire-alarm system sector. The section "Special Locking Arrangements" describes the fail-safe electromagnetic locking systems. These systems lock perimeter exit doors leading to the street at all hours, every day, and lock the entrances and exits to the nursery when an infant is moved near an exit door and the infant protection system detects movement.

The original Life Safety Code was amended in 1980, and it revolutionized how public assembly buildings could now lock their secondary exits. Many architects and consulting engineers are reluctant to accept this code change and still insist that, unless exit doors have unobstructed egress and ingress, they are illegal and in violation of the fire code. JCAHO has not adequately addressed this subject and always adds the disclaimer that the doors shall operate in conformance with the code as defined by the agencies having jurisdiction (AHJ).

DOI: 10.4324/9781032630670-26

Code Surveyors: With the lack of understanding of the various codes, hospitals may very well be in violation of them, so JCAHO added a fourth surveyor to the "team" to ensure that hospitals follow safety codes and fire regulations. Some of these part-time code surveyors are full-time safety directors or facilities managers, with less understanding of codes than the personnel in the hospital whom they were hired to survey.

A JCAHO survey was conducted at a large Manhattan hospital, within a medium-sized birthing unit. The code surveyor (in real life) was the safety director at a small 200-bed nursing home and a very small hospital that did not have a birthing unit, surrounded by little crime or car traffic. This surveyor never was exposed to fail-safe locking systems, did not understand the problems found in a typical nursery, and was unfamiliar with the NFPA Life Safety Code 101. He wrote in a report to the hospital safety director that the locking systems in the nursery were illegal, because they did not have an automatic button release on the interior side of the door to allow immediate exit. He compounded his confusion by submitting a copy of the Life Safety Code, highlighting the referenced paragraphs to justify his interpretation of the code. The surveyor submitted the following comments: the lack of fire-code knowledge is typical of surveyors. The facts are outlined in the following letter (printed with changes, to disguise the identity of the surveyor).

From: John Smith
Sent: Tuesday, July 9, 2005
To: Mary Jonesy
Subject: Infant protection system

I have completed my report to JCAHO and noted a reference to the NFPA Code related to the infant protection system and the need for a "kill switch". Please review NFPA 101 section 2.1.6.2 Access-Controlled Egress Doors. Paragraph (c) refers to a manual release. There are also other criteria including connection to the Fire Alarm System. I will try to become more knowledgeable on the NFPA Code before I meet with our Infant/Child Abduction Prevention Program Committee.

Emergency Voice Codes

A select group evaluated the same list of emergency codes. These 3,000 hospital security directors came to a consensus but were concerned that they could not reach unanimous agreement among the more than 4,000 hospitals regarding which emergency codes should be used in all healthcare facilities. Code RED has traditionally been used to announce a fire situation, and Code BLUE is the accepted standard for a medical emergency. A growing number of hospitals have adopted Code PINK for infant abduction. Some facilities use six to nine codes, with the three codes above being the only codes generally accepted. Code RED has in recent years, been discarded. It was agreed upon that during a real fire emergency, the activation of the fire alarm system replaces the need for a Code RED signal – given the response is significantly faster.

Hospitals Use Some Variation of Four Basic Codes:

RED: fire
BLUE: pediatric medical emergency
PINK: infant abduction
PURPLE: pediatric child abduction

Optional Codes:

YELLOW: bomb threat
GRAY: a combative person (rarely in use)
SILVER: a person with a weapon or a hostage situation
ORANGE: hazardous material release

Obsolete Codes:

TRIAGE INTERNAL: internal disaster
TRIAGE EXTERNAL: external situation

Infant Abduction Response Plan

POLICY: to protect all newborn infants from abduction and unauthorized removal.
PURPOSE: to establish security department procedures if an infant is removed from the nursery floor without proper authorization.
PROCEDURE: department procedures are established, as detailed in section C.

Child Abduction – Code Pink... Alarm Sounds

When a member of the security department receives a code pink notification, this person will immediately relay information to all security personnel through a secure radio transmission, including a description of the alleged abduction (if known). When a child-abduction investigation is conducted, all radio traffic will be limited to that situation. "The director of security and the nursery supervisor will be notified immediately". The Security Control Officer, emergency room psychiatrist, and nursing home desk officers will remain at their posts. The officer will immediately notify the police department via 911.

There are no standards as to the codes to be used by hospitals for the announcement of an emergency. So code designations can be different at each hospital, even if the hospitals are located within the same neighborhood or city. The State of California conducted a national survey, published in 2020, on state-mandated emergency codes for hospitals. Their study indicates that since 2000 there has been a trend to standardize emergency codes, with an increased focus on the adoption of plain language announcements. At least 23 hospital associations have recommended the use of standardized emergency codes, and several have advocated using "plain language" codes based on federal and other recommendations. Plain language codes eliminate the need for hospital staff to learn different code designations as they move from hospital to hospital.[1]

Color-Coded Wristbands

A color-code trend started in 2009 and focused on the bracelets wrapped around the wrists of patients treated in the hospital complex. The color of the band designated the patients' conditions to the medical staff. If the color of the waistband were purple, for example, it meant "Do Not Resuscitate". Bands with other colors indicated different medical needs, which could prevent dangerous mistakes – such as giving the wrong food to an allergic child or allowing a patient with a balance problem to walk unescorted down a freshly waxed hallway. The series of band color codes could create serious problems, which happened when a Pennsylvania hospital almost had a patient die during cardiac arrest because a nurse thought that a yellow band meant "Do Not Resuscitate". This misreading of the color band was because at the hospital, where the nurse formerly worked, a yellow band indicated a different medical response. While these wristbands will never replace medical records, they may often be the first line of communication for those seeking medical help and can often provide an extra safety net in a chaotic setting.

Hospitals have long tagged every patient admitted to their premises with a standard-issue clear or white wristband – made of reinforced paper or plastic, with identifying data such as the patient's name and birth date. Some have added bar codes that staff can screen to verify identity and check medication against a patient's medical record. Radio frequency (RF) identification technology will enable hospitals to use wristbands embedded with special chips – both to track patient movement in a hospital and to access important information about allergies, medications, and special orders.

To address color wristband confusion, some hospitals have formed groups to standardize color designations in their states and regions. They strongly recommend a limited number of color bands to avoid confusion. Hospitals are also purchasing bands embossed with preprinted messages to reinforce the meaning. Some groups endorsed three standard wristbands: red for allergy alerts, yellow for fall-risk patients who may be weak from an illness after surgery, and purple for patients who have signed forms requesting that no one administer cardiopulmonary resuscitation (CPR), if their heart stops or they stop breathing.

In general, color waistbands used throughout the medical environment are chosen based on historical precedent. The language of colors that most people are familiar with is the following:

- Yellow is commonly understood as a symbol for caution.
- Red is used for allergies, as it is associated with a command to stop for danger.
- Blue was once used for DNR (Do Not Resuscitate) – but it was confused with Code Blue, which is often used to call for resuscitation. Ironically, this was the opposite of what DNR patients requested.
- Pink has been adopted to indicate that a patient's limb is somehow compromised and should not be used for drawing blood or inserting an intravenous line.
- Green could mean "no blood transfusion" – usually at the request of a patient with religious beliefs. In some hospitals, it indicates a latex allergy. Green is sometimes worn by Chinese patients, who believe it wards off arthritic pain.

While many hospital officials embraced the wristband color code idea (about 60% of states are using the coded band symbols), there remains a great deal of resistance from vast sections of the medical community regarding accepting a universal code. They have little objection to the red and yellow wristbands – but there is a growing hesitation in using the DNR color purple. This color has been controversial, since it brands patients as being in an "end-of-life" condition, which inadvertently broadcasts that choice to family and friends who may not have been consulted. Some hospitals believe that the "purple" band is too harsh, because any bracelet indicating a do-not-resuscitate order could be demeaning to patients. It may make the patients feel that they would receive a lower quality of care than patients without the band. The hospitals concerned with this symbol modified their bracelets by marking a plain wristband with a purple "jewel" small enough that no one can see from thirty feet down the hall. Other hospitals have embossed the purple bracelet with a white dove carrying an olive branch, rather than the initials DNR. In another reported case, a hospital chose the initials A.N.D., for "allow natural death", as a gentler alternative to spelling out the medical phrase that the DNR signifies.

A state hospital association found nine different colors used to denote patients with DNR orders. Five separate colors indicated allergies, and other colors denoted the risks of falling. Many hospitals have cautioned their staff that for patients, wearing the color-coded bracelets is voluntary. Patients are allowed to opt for other methods instead, such as colored dots or just old-fashioned notations on medical charts. Another problem (not fully addressed) is caused by children who do not understand the system and are prone to trade the wristbands like baseball cards.

Another important factor to consider when using coded wristbands is that the entire hospital staff must be trained in the medical meaning of the bands so that staff (including janitors, housekeepers, and transport personnel who wheel patients between units) recognize the colors. That way, if someone is mopping the floor and they see a patient with a yellow bracelet trying to get out of bed, they know they should immediately contact the nurse. Hospitals are also educating patients about the wristbands' color codes – explaining the meanings of different colors at admission, emphasizing the importance of wearing wristbands during their stay, and pointing out the risks associated with not wearing their wristbands. Hospitals provide refusal forms to patients who do not want to wear color-coded bracelets and provide the option to take off their social-causes bracelets and wear a hospital bracelet.

Healthcare Employment

The health care industry employed over seventeen million people in 2023, making it the largest employment sector in the United States. A total of 933,788 physicians are professionally active, of which 800,355 are reported as patient care practicing physicians. Across all physician specialties in the United States, there is a projected shortage of 187,130 full-time equivalent (FTE) physicians in 2037. Non-metro areas will experience greater shortages of physicians than metro areas. There are over four million registered nurses (RNs), licensed practical nurses (LPNs), and advanced practice registered nurses (APRNs) as of 2023. The number of RNs

increased by 5.3% between 2019 and 2023. During that period, the number of nurse practitioners (NPs) grew by 35.5%, while the number of LPNs and nurse midwives declined by 8.4% and 2.8%, respectively.[2]

Survival of the Unfittest

Hospitals throughout the nation are competing for patients, and they are under increasing pressure to reduce costs. Yet, they continue to spend heavily on certain luxurious areas, such as maternity wards – since the nurseries are profit centers and hospitals have to make a good impression on moms-to-be and their families in order to develop lifelong loyalty. Some major hospitals have added a children's library, where expectant siblings can play, and offer free massages and Jacuzzi amenities for the mothers to be. These inner-city hospitals are in stark contrast with hospitals in areas of small populations and low occupancy rates that are fighting for survival. Installing Jacuzzis is not on their agenda.

Many hospitals operate with empty beds, facing drastic cutbacks or closures under cost-cutting plans. In 2024, New York City had 37,004 licensed beds for patients.[3] However, on any given day, the occupancy rate can be low. This is due to advances in medical care, along with patients avoiding hospital beds by using outpatient clinics. In rural areas keeping hospitals open despite huge losses is fiscally unjustifiable, causing closures leaving residents without local healthcare.

Catholic Medical Centers in New York City constitute the largest church-related hospital chain in the State of New York – controlling several large hospitals, clinics, and outpatient healthcare facilities in the metropolitan area. The system had revenues of approximately $1.6 billion, with a staff of about 12,000. It served around 600,000 patients annually and provided about $104 million in charity care in an average year. In the early part of the 1990s, merger mania swept the healthcare industry (Presbyterian, Mt. Sinai, and Lenox Hill), and the philosophy spread to include the Catholic Medical Centers that merged. However, the expected results in cost savings did not materialize. The strongest hospitals (financially) in the chain began to underwrite losses of the weaker institutions. Eventually, some of the facilities were sold to better-funded healthcare providers. One hospital closed. The centers sought bankruptcy protection as the only alternative to keep the more profitable facilities from closing. Of the several mergers completed in the 1990s, only two survived and then expanded by collecting "affiliated hospitals" that were allowed to keep their names and certain accounting departments, then becoming part of a chain. As an example, Booth Memorial Hospital was an independent facility that fell under the umbrella of the largest New York City hospital that then changed its name to "Queens Hospital of New York Presbyterian".

When bankruptcy was finally sought after, every vendor was affected – particularly those having anything to do with security. The hospital paid for essentials such as salaries, utility bills, and maintenance on complex medical equipment – but would not purchase security alarm installations. They did not maintain existing surveillance and monitoring systems, and the guard force was concerned about being replaced by a lower-cost contract guard service. Most of the alarm-integrating security firms found that to maintain a goodwill relationship with the hospital, they would have to maintain the existing security alarm systems – without being paid. Some firms disappeared because they could not survive as creditors with the expectation of eventual payment of 50% of the true debt. Other principals affected by the bankruptcy included bondholders. Since the hospital chain was self-insured, hundreds of plaintiffs with pending injury and wrongful-death claims are caught up in the bankruptcy proceedings, and their lawsuits may never receive proper judicial consideration. Collection firms approached all debtors with offers to pay 10% to 20% on the debt. Any large institutions seeking bankruptcy protection should attempt other solutions, because the aftereffects are long-lasting – and the morale of the employees will probably never be restored.

Aftershocks were immediate, and every department was affected – particularly the security department. Since security and fire system vendors were not paid for completed work, they were reluctant to service the critically needed life safety systems. After the date of the bankruptcy filing, vendors were promised prompt payment for any new work. Some reluctantly returned to the premises, knowing that old debts would be paid very slowly and would only amount to about 50% of the total debt. Each vendor agreeing to service the hospital required some form of down payment or promise of payment not affected by the court-ordered bankruptcy. In many cases, vendors refused to return, and the security director had to solicit a new set of service companies.

Network hospitals were forced to carefully review all contracts to eliminate frivolous purchases and seek more competitive bids. Contracts supporting computer stations and the IP network suffered a loss well into the millions of dollars. In one facility, the fee for servicing the computers was more than $180/month/unit, involving hundreds of computers. That fee also included all service and maintenance and a new computer terminal every two years. The hospital started to study the possibility of establishing an in-house service team and purchasing terminals directly from manufacturers with a two-year service agreement. They also replaced the entire security force with a contract guard service for annual savings of about three-fourth of a million dollars.

One noteworthy aspect of the bankruptcy proceeding (and a dire warning to some of the nation's many financially troubled healthcare facilities) is that legal fees for bankruptcy filing under Chapter 11 can be very expensive. While the facility might recover from debts incurred in providing medical services, it may never recover from the legal fees that the bankruptcy lawyers charged. The legal fees are not common to other sections of the nation – but they offer a perfect example of how a healthcare institution can fall prey to costly legal expenses that are far beyond their wildest expectations.

After declaring bankruptcy, the hospital network obtained new financing (some for added security systems). Once the poor-performing hospitals were divested from the Saint Vincent Catholic Medical Centers network, the surviving hospitals were forced to operate more efficiently than they did before filing for bankruptcy. Some of that debt was paid by the firing of the executive director of the centers and the replacement of the entire in-house security staff with a contract guard service. The way the hospital chain survived while operating under the terms of bankruptcy may be the beginning of a wave of the future, as other marginally performing hospitals seek protection under Chapter 11 (while trying to be more fiscally responsible). An old proverb guided alarm installation firms in seeking customers: "Hospitals, such as most municipal funded facilities are notoriously slow payers, but they never go out of business". The alarm installation industry has found this proverb to be out of date, since five major hospitals closed their doors in New York City in 2009 and 2010 – and the remaining facilities are paying more slowly than ever.

St. Vincent's Hospital closed in 2010, after 160 years of being the busiest healthcare facility in the West side of Manhattan and was demolished in 2013. The site is now a high-rise condominium.

Notes

1. Iroquois Healthcare Association, Hospital Emergency Codes Standardization and Plain Language Recommendations and Guidance, January 2020.
2. National Center for Health Workforce, Analysis in State of the U.S. Health Care Workforce, 2024 November 2024.
3. New York State Web Site, Covid-19, Hospital Bed Capacity.

Chapter 27

Geriatric Care – A Challenge

The "Baby Boomer" generation, procreated at the end of World War II, has resulted in what is often referred to as "The Silver Tsunami". According to the U.S. Census Bureau, the U.S. population aged sixty-five and over grew nearly five times faster than the total population over the hundred years from 1920 to 2020.[1] With the benefit of miracle drugs, balanced diets, an obsession with exercise, and the introduction of Viagra, Americans are not only living longer – but they are also enjoying a relatively good sex life well into their late eighties and nineties.

Eventually, they will still need special geriatric care facilities in greater numbers than previous generations, and the people entering nursing homes and assisted living facilities demand more luxurious accommodations than their predecessors. "Old Age" is now a rather vague term, with seniors running in marathons and joining the 70+ Ski Club or the UFO association for active licensed pilots (United Flying Octogenarians). People are not only flying their own planes in their nineties but are also playing golf (sometimes without taking a single milligram).

The anticipated age of death has significantly and steadily risen over the past half century. The original estimate was issued by the Social Security Administration in 1935 (the year it was created) and based social security payments on its prediction that most people would die by the age of sixty-five. The prediction proved to be false, and healthcare providers are treating the growing elderly sector of the population, consisting of people who have stayed healthy for over nine decades. However, their mental health may not always keep pace with their physical condition.

DOI: 10.4324/9781032630670-27

Each year someone is alive, the risk of dying increases by 10%. People in their thirties have a one in 1,000 chance of dying, compared to those at the age of ninety whose odds of not making it to the next birthday are roughly one in six. There is ongoing research to extend life, which is referred to as "health span," not lifespan. The goal of longevity is to not reach the age of 130 if it includes a fifty-year stint in a nursing home. Healthcare for older people relies on treating individual diseases. If an unusual lump appears, a person will go to a primary care doctor, then to the oncologist who attacks the cancerous cells. However, at this advanced age, a patient is already suffering from diabetes or cognitive decline at the same time.

Nursing homes and other healthcare facilities dedicated to the nation's growing class of seniors often ignore the fact that "elder security" is a greater challenge than the traditional problems found in conventional healthcare facilities like hospitals or assisted living. During the 2020/21 pandemic, twenty states exempted nursing homes (both nonprofit and for-profit institutions) from lawsuits due to coronavirus deaths.

Note

1. US Census Bureau, U.S. Older Population Grew From 2010 to 2020 at Fastest Rate Since 1880 to 1890, May, 2023, Zoe Caplan.

Chapter 28

Assisted Living and Long-Term Nursing Care

Eldercare – An Often Neglected but Growing Population

Even though eldercare-type housing likes to advertise itself as a vacation site in the Caribbean (while providing a viable solution to everyone's fear about old age healthcare), the image of the couple holding tennis rackets and swinging golf clubs in front of the clubhouse is a fantasy that doesn't exist. Eldercare facilities are being overwhelmed by applicants whose family members are seeking a real solution for long-term care for their parents. The aging public would like to believe that assisted living was designed for people who are mostly independent. Yet, it is now an industry that has nearly tripled in number in the years between 2000 and 2020. It is also a completely unregulated industry – lacking the regulations and inspections that are mandatory for hospitals and nursing homes which were exposed during Covid.

Assisted Living caters to "residents" who voluntarily seek admission, which is unlike "patients" treated in a hospital facility. This situation poses a unique challenge to the nursing home security staff, because residents are free to wander around the facilities and often leave the premises undetected due to some form of dementia. More than three million nursing home residents are currently diagnosed with Alzheimer's disease and related dementias.[1] In most states, there is no requirement that these assisted living units be staffed with enough people or that they be properly trained. While nursing homes are regulated, inspected, and graded for quality of care, the

DOI: 10.4324/9781032630670-28

federal government does not license or oversee assisted living facilities. In addition, nursing homes are required to have medical directors on staff who review patient medications regularly, while there is no such requirement in the assisted living environment.

Sixty-two years and over usually marks a senior citizen, as it is the age when people become eligible for social security payments. Unlike other specialized hospitals (such as psychiatric or children's hospitals), long-term care hospitals do not treat any specific types of illness. They also do not offer services that meet the standards associated with the traditional hospital. Senior citizen care is a small sector of the healthcare community and is usually defined by the fact that they keep residents longer than the traditional hospital. They are also typically smaller, averaging about sixty beds. Furthermore, categories of living arrangements within the eldercare community keep changing, with new special-needs care centers being introduced every decade.

Hospital intensive care units were designed to serve patients who survive acute illnesses, heart attacks, and traumas. However, they are not intended to treat patients for weeks or months. Under Medicare payment rules, traditional hospitals lose money on patients who stay for long periods, and this economic consideration provides a financial incentive to discharge patients from hospitals as quickly as possible – and then receive new Medicare payments for re-admitting other patients.

Although many adults in the United States do not feel prepared for the cost of providing for long-term care for themselves, when asked about the prospect of needing living assistance as they age, four in ten adults (43%) say they are "not too" or "not at all confident" that they would have the financial resources to pay for such care, while 37% say they feel "somewhat confident" and a much smaller share – one in five – say they are "extremely" or "very confident." The group that does not feel confident is household incomes less than $40,000 (58% "not too" or "not at all confident"), Hispanic adults (53%), and those between the ages of thirty and forty (48%) or fifty and sixty-four (51%). In contrast, adults aged 65 and older (77% of whom report that they are retired), 30% say they are not confident about affording such care, while 31% say they are "extremely" or "very confident. However, the overwhelming majority of adults say that it would be impossible or very difficult to pay the estimated $100,000 needed for one year at a nursing home (90%) or the estimated $60,000 for one year of assistance from a paid nurse or aide (83%).

There is also confusion about how long-term care is financed within the United States. Although Medicaid is the main source of coverage for these services and Medicare coverage of them is limited, 23% of adults to 45% of those ages 65 and older – assume that Medicare would pay the bill for their own or a loved one's time in a nursing home if they had a long-term illness or disability. Four in ten adults incorrectly believe that Medicare (rather than Medicaid) is the primary source of insurance coverage for low-income people who need nursing care or home care over a long period of time.[2]

A general list of these facilities includes the following, which specialize in care for the elderly and the infirm:

- In-place living
- Independent living
- Senior living/gated community
- Continuing care retired community
- Assisted living (the fastest-growing category among the facilities for the aged)
- Home healthcare
- Independent living apartments
- Rehabilitation or short-term
- Acute care centers
- Long-term healthcare centers
- Long-term acute care hospitals
- Nursing homes
- Respite care
- Day care
- Adult day services
- Memory care

In-place living is the least intrusive of the choices for healthcare for the aging population, as it allows individuals to remain in their familiar home. Medical aides visit the home for part of the day or move in for 24/7 assistance. Usually, "long-term care" insurance policies will cover the cost for either in-place home care or healthcare arrangements in a facility. Long-term care policies are expensive and are provided to the policyholder only after the person loses control of at least two specified functions. The cost for these policies varies by the age of the holder when payment starts and depends on annuity tables that predict the age of death. The average recipient is expected to live less than three years after the policy starts payments.

Independent Living describes apartment complexes for people over the age of sixty-two (often just over fifty-five) that rent or sell studios along with one- and two-bedroom suites (including full kitchens). The facility offers restaurant-style dining, social activities, and educational programs – plus housekeeping privileges and transportation to physicians and places of interest. Many of these facilities have a nurse on-site.

Senior Living/Gated Communities consist of low-rise housing complexes, limited to people over the age of fifty-five. In addition, there are many high-rise elevator buildings dedicated to the same age group. Occupants can be either owners or renters. Some operate in a way similar to any other private condominium or cooperative housing complex, with a trend toward offering daily meals within the same building or nearby. Medical assistance is available, though not as visible as in a nursing setting. These communities are generally occupied by active people jokingly referred to as a group interested in discounted early dinners so that they can eat by 4:30 and be in bed by 6:00. Many have clubhouses, golf courses, restaurants, and gymnasiums. These are apartments or separate homes owned by the occupants, who can sell their property like any other homeowner. Homeowners who hire property managers control the complexes.

Continuing Care Communities are more regulated than some of the other options. People purchase the right to live on the property with a one-time initiation fee, but they do not own their homes and cannot sell the property if they leave. They retain no equity in the apartments. A monthly maintenance fee is required for certain services, and occupants can live in their homes/apartments until death or relocation to a nursing home. Meals are available as well as medical assistance – both provided at an extra cost.

Assisted Living is the fastest-growing housing community that is specifically designed for seniors – both the infirm and the healthy. This type of facility has proliferated since the 1980s, mainly due to advancements in the medical treatments of the elderly that have extended life expectancy into the mid-1980s and beyond. Assisted living tenants typically are seventy-five or older and are generally healthy and can take care of themselves. The facility provides services such as nurses, aides, dining, and memory care. Assisted living has the potential for rapid growth, as it allows residents to live independently in their own apartments, with their own furniture if they so choose. The facilities have a built-in societal network, since meals are available in a central dining room. They may also offer several levels of care to meet occupants' requirements.

Independent Living Apartments do not provide any of the services associated with assisted living but offer a more controlled environment than many of the age-restricted, senior high-rise apartments and over fifty-five gated communities – especially Florida. The housing staff provides more watchfulness than just cutting the grass, as they do in continuing care or senior living communities. In recent years, many have added nonmedical services such as transportation, meals, and concierge desks. Some of these facilities are available and include rent plus three meals a day.

Home Healthcare is a well sought-after alternative to Assisted Living and even Independent Living. This scenario involves trained medical assistants (or people who claim to be trained medical assistants) visiting the homes of senior citizens on a part-time or full-time basis. The cost for this type of service can be twice as much as the cost of living in an Assisted Living Residence. However, if the care given is four hours or more during the work week at $15/hour, the cost is reasonable and covered by most long-term medical care insurance plans. This service is for homebound seniors who have a medical condition that calls for the attention of highly qualified caregivers, such as registered nurses and housekeepers. The goal is to ensure independence and dignity for those wanting to remain at home but are unable to care for themselves.

Rehabilitation or Short-Term Acute Care Centers involve post-surgical attention, usually for fewer than twenty-six days. Under Medicare regulations, patients must be admitted to a hospital for immediate or emergency treatment – and after seven days, they can be discharged to an approved rehabilitation facility or long-term care facility. Hospital and rehabilitation center occupancy will be covered under a medical plan, but after thirty days in rehabilitation, a patient is transferred to assisted living and pays out-of-pocket for any further stays.

Long-Term Healthcare Centers are a specialty type of hospital, sometimes defined as a small medical center that specializes in treating chronically ill patients – usually the elderly. These facilities have no doctors on staff – and in emergencies, they must call in physicians from outside. They are defined solely because they keep patients longer than other hospitals and are generally smaller than a typical hospital, averaging about sixty beds. They also do not have emergency rooms. Only a few long-term care hospitals existed in the 1980s, while more than 400 existed in 2020. The number of such facilities will continue to grow. Government studies suggest that the reason these institutions are popular is driven mostly by the Medicare rules that a hospital can only keep patients for twenty-five days and then must discharge the patient–usually to a long-term care facility. Each state has a federally funded long-term care ombudsperson, who acts as an advocate for nursing home residents and can offer information about state rankings or surveys on nursing homes or long-term care facilities in the state. The same office maintains records of complaints about specific nursing homes and the nature of those complaints in addition to Medicare ratings.

Long-Term Acute Care Hospitals. This is the fastest-growing segment of elderly care, with more than 400 locations opening since 1985. They accept patients requiring more medical help than specialty hospitals. Few have doctors on staff, and most are owned by for-profit companies.

Intermediate Care Facilities for the Mentally Ill. These facilities provide services for developmentally disabled people from youth to old age.

Nursing Homes are the symbolic places where life seems to end at the entrance door. The public considers these facilities to be loveless and lonely places, with death hovering close by. People project their terror of death onto the aged, if fear and depression must stalk the final years of every life. There is a cost to this myopic view of aging, which impacts the treatment of the pains associated with late-life ailments. This impression distracts from the fact that even old people still enjoy new pursuits, which relatives of nursing home residents often fail to understand. Rarely has a nursing home staff member ever heard a resident say that he or she was afraid of death – almost as if there is an acceptance of impending death when reaching a certain age. Most of the time death is not of great concern to a patient who shares the belief held by others that life goes on. Long-term nursing home residents often seem to embrace the wisdom and meaning that only old age can bring.

Respite Care is not exactly a separate entity. It is usually associated with a rehabilitation home or long-term care facility that will accept a patient (usually diagnosed with dementia or Alzheimer's) from children who need a few days of relief or "respite" for the sometimes overwhelming responsibility of caring for the mentally impaired.

Adult Day Services provide health, social, and therapeutic activities in a group setting for people with functional and cognitive problems. Some are housed within nursing homes, assisted living facilities, or hospitals. The average charge is a daily rate of around $120. This setting is for patients who can sleep through the night at home.

Day Care will foster independence for patients who wish to remain living in a community. Usually, these services are provided for part of a day for seven days a week – but the hours may vary from full time to set hours.

Memory Care facilities are specifically designed for residents with memory-impaired conditions that include early to mid-range Alzheimer's/dementia and other memory-related impairments. There remains a stigma with dementia-related illnesses. People do not want to discuss this, causing the government to be stingy about funding research on a problem that costs the nation more than any other medical condition. This stigma is much like the word "cancer" was at one time – when people would only whisper the word or call it the "big C". There is a lack of Alzheimer's spokespeople who are cured and can tell their stories, like those with cancer or HIV/AIDS, to help promote federal research funding.

An estimated 6.9 million Americans age sixty-five and older are living with Alzheimer's dementia today. This number could grow to 13.8 million by 2060, barring the development of medical breakthroughs to prevent or cure AD. Official AD death certificates recorded 119,399 deaths from AD in 2021. In 2020 and 2021, when COVID-19 entered the ranks of the top ten causes of death, Alzheimer's was the seventh-leading cause of death in the United States. Official counts for more recent years are still being compiled. Alzheimer's remains the fifth-leading cause of death among Americans age 65 and older. Between 2000 and 2021, deaths from stroke, heart disease, and HIV decreased, whereas reported deaths from AD increased by more than 140%. More than eleven million family members and other unpaid caregivers provided an estimated 18.4 billion hours of care to people with Alzheimer's or other dementias in 2023. These figures reflect a decline in the number of caregivers compared with a decade earlier, as well as an increase in the amount of care provided by each remaining caregiver. Unpaid dementia caregiving was valued at $346.6 billion in 2023.[3]

Nursing Home Costs Varies

The national median cost of assisted living in 2024 is $4,995 per month, according to A Place for Mom's 2024 proprietary data. Many communities have a base fee that doesn't include the cost of care. Instead, care services are added based on how much assistance a senior needs. Other factors affect the total monthly cost too, such as location, chosen room size, amenities, and added-on services.[4] The median yearly cost of in-home care in the United States in 2023 was $75,504 for a Home Health Aide and $68,640 for Homemaker services. The hourly rate for a Home Health Aide ranged from $22 in Mississippi to $42 in Maine. The median yearly cost of a private room

Table 28.1 Hourly Wage Comparison for Home Care Health Staff

Service	*National Median Hourly Rate 2023*	*National Median Hourly Rate 2022*	*Year-Over-Year percentage Change*
Homemaker Services	$30	$28	7.14
Home Health Aide Services	$33	$30	10
	National Median Daily Rate 2023	National Median Daily Rate 2022	
Adult Day Health Care	$95	$90	5.56
Assisted Living Facility	$5,350	$5,278	1.36
	National Median Monthly Rate 2023	National Median Monthly Rate 2022	
Nursing Home Care Semi-Private	$285	$273	4.40
Nursing Home Care Private	$320	$305	4.93

in a nursing home in the United States in 2023 was $116,800. The daily rate for a private room in a nursing home ranged from $215 in Missouri to $1,137 in Alaska. The median yearly cost of care in an Assisted Living Facility in the United States in 2023 was $64,200. The monthly rate for assisted living facility care ranged from $3,800 in Mississippi to $9,563 in the District of Columbia.[5]

Assisted living typically averages about half of the cost of a nursing home, and the rates are likely to be higher for residents seeking specialized memory care or requiring special considerations for disabilities. Rates in 2023 compared to 2022 include (see Table 28.1):

Home Healthcare

Home healthcare may be less expensive than assisted living or nursing home care, but it is also one of the most emotionally demanding and worst-paid jobs out of the options available. Traditional home healthcare aides assist seniors with daily activities of living, light housekeeping, and medication reminders – all while also serving as companions. The hours are long, with periods of grueling activities and many hours of isolation and boredom.

The workday (when the patient gets up and finishes the day) can stretch for fourteen hours or more for over twenty-seven days out of the month. Elder boomers are not only living longer but tend to seek "age in place" after they get infirmed. Choosing to live at home rather than in an institution has created a demographic explosion. Despite an increase in-home care workers, there remains a serious shortage of workers. With a high turnover rate, many home care workers leave the job every year.

The alternative to hiring an outside aid is for family members to become caretakers for their ailing parents – which becomes a growing burden to all concerned. Americans who reach sixty-five will need long-term care, spending their resources until they become indigent enough to qualify for Medicaid – a program that pays over one-third of the country's long-term care costs. This cost typically covers two years, according to government projections. A little more than half of long-term care will come out of pocket of the person receiving the care, and the family will pay the rest unless they qualify for Medicaid.

Nursing Homes vs. Home Care

The Boomer Generation is turning seventy years old at a rate of 10,000 per day and living years longer than most experts had anticipated in 1936 (when Social Security was enacted by the federal government, which did not cover Medicare for long-term nursing homes, assisted care living, or home care expenses). Nursing homes provide nursing care for the elderly around the clock, with twenty-four-hour medical care available. These types of care are also referred to as skilled nursing care and convalescent care. While seniors typically transition into a nursing community on a permanent basis, some homes also provide short stays for those in need of rehabilitation after an injury, illness, or surgery that may require skilled nurses and/or therapists. Whether one uses these services part-time or full time, nursing home care does come at a premium price compared to other healthcare options.

Medicare coverage is limited, will only cover skilled nursing care expenses in very specific situations, and is not designed to pay for nursing home or custodial care costs long-term. One such situation is when a senior has been hospitalized and released but still requires a bit of specialized care. Medicare pays for short-term stays in nursing homes if residents:

- Were admitted to the hospital for a minimum of three days as an inpatient.
- Have been admitted to a Medicare-certified facility within thirty days of the hospital stay.
- Need skilled care such as physical therapy, speech therapy, or other types of rehabilitation.

An excellent option for low-income patients is the state and federally funded program known as Medicaid. This coverage assists individuals with many types of medical care, including doctors' visits, hospital stays, and long-term care services like those offered in a skilled nursing facility. Often, this program covers 100% of these costs – but there may be copayments for certain beneficiaries. For those who qualify for Medicaid, this is the best choice for nursing care coverage.

Long-term care services for veterans with service-related injuries and disabilities enjoy full coverage from the Department of Veterans Affairs (VA) at specified locations or through certain providers approved by the department. Those without service-related disabilities may also qualify for Veterans Affairs benefits if they meet certain qualifications. Depending on the veteran's household income, there may be copayments required.

Notes

1. Health Affairs, Dementia Care Is Widespread In US Nursing Homes; Facilities With The Most Dementia Patients May Offer Ways To Better Care, Dana B. Mukamel, Debra Saliba, Heather Ladd, and R. Tamara Konetzka, June 2023
2. KFF, The Affordability of Long-Term Care and Support Services: Findings from a KFF Survey, Liz Hamel and Alex Montero, November 14, 2023.
3. The Journal of The Alzheimer's Association, 2024 Alzheimer's disease facts and figures, Alzheimers Dement. 2024 April 30;20(5):3708–3821. doi: 10.1002/alz.13809, PMCID: PMC11095490 PMID: 38689398
4. A Place for How Much Does Assisted Living Cost in 2024? Factors and Price Structure, Melissa Bean, May 8, 2024
5. Genworth, Cost of Care Trends & Insights, Website: https://www.genworth.com/aging-and-you/finances/cost-of-care/cost-of-care-trends-and-insights

Chapter 29

Five-Star Federal Rating

Dementia Fog

Medicare has been assigning hotel-style ratings to nearly every nursing home in the country since 2009, and only one out of five of the more than 15,000 nursing homes nationwide holds a five-star rating. Medicare ratings have become the gold standard across the industry, but they are highly suspect since the number of "stars" given to a facility is based on self-reported data supplied by the nursing homes that the government does not verify. Only one out of the three criteria used to determine the rating (the results of annual health inspections) relies on assessments from independent reviewers. The other measures (staff levels and quality statistics) are reported by nursing homes and accepted by Medicare at face value. The final rating ignores complaints from inhabitants and lawsuits by their families to state officials. Some patient groups consider the rating so inflated that they no longer support their use and have found them helpful only in weeding out the worst-performing homes.[1]

Many of the nation's nursing homes received a one-star rating in the federal government's Centers for Medicare and Medicaid Services (CMS), the lowest level on a five-star scale. None of the institutions had put any effort into improving their status over a three-year period. Low overall ratings are awarded to homes that fall below the average assigned to other nursing homes in the same state. Among the problems that can drop the rating are the following: consistently dirty equipment and linens, mistreatment, and unlicensed caregivers or specialists. Having a low rating can be detrimental to the survival of the nursing home. Receiving a high star rating has become

 DOI: 10.4324/9781032630670-29

very important, since nurses and doctors often use the ratings in referral decisions, and insurers consider them when setting up preferred networks.

With all the flaws in the five-star rating system, Medicare changed it in 2015, for hospitals, dialysis centers, and home care agencies.

Emergency plans for nursing homes are overlooked in the rating system, even though the federal government requires them. Nursing homes often do not institute specific steps during an emergency – such as coordinating with local authorities, notifying relatives, or even pinning name tags and medication lists to residents in an evacuation. This means that plans may not be worth the paper on which they are written. Nearly eight years after Hurricane Katrina devastated New Orleans and exposed the vulnerability of nursing homes, serious shortcomings persist. After tornadoes, hurricanes, or floods, nursing homes are woefully unprepared to protect frail residents in any natural disasters, according to government findings in a 2012 report by the Department of Health and Human Services.

One of the largest nursing home chains paid $38 million, the largest settlement ever received by the Justice Department after being found guilty of providing substandard care to residents (2014).[2] The seventh largest nursing home chain had received a five-star rating a year before federal prosecutors claimed that the homes' operator did not hire enough trained nurses, leading to serious health-related problems for many of its patients. The total settlement, which exceeded ten million, went to resolve claims brought by a whistleblower who claimed the nursing home operator exaggerated the amount of therapy a patient needed to inflate their Medicare reimbursement. The federal government successfully argued that the quality of care was so poor in most of the 150 homes that Medicare and Medicaid should not have paid for the services, as they were essentially worthless. It was not the only strike against nursing homes in the last two decades – all of which were based on violating the False Claims Act that allows the government to go after people or companies who defraud government programs.

After many years of complaints concerning the reliance on nursing homes' self-reported, unverified data used to create the five-star rating system, the federal government revised it. Nursing homes must report their staffing levels quarterly (since 2015) using an electronic system that can be verified with payroll data. Although the federal healthcare law, passed in 2010, required that nursing homes' staffing data be collected electronically, the provision was never adopted. Instead, nursing homes reported their staffing levels on a form during their rarely audited annual inspection. Congress passed a law in 2014, the Improving Medicare Post-Acute Care Transformation Act. It requires more frequent inspections of hospice facilities. Many of the 3,600 for-profit facilities went years without any inspection – despite claiming responsibility for over 1.2 million patients. The government will also collect data on topics such as whether patients who are bedridden or need a wheelchair develop bedsores or have had serious falls. Another condition required to be reported is the percentage of residents given antipsychotic drugs. These drugs are often used to sedate residents with dementia, even though they can prove to be dangerous and result in dementia fog.

National Alzheimer's Project

The National Alzheimer's Project was enacted in 2012 with the stated purpose of preventing and effectively treating Alzheimer's by 2025, by following the successful government approach to the wars on heart disease and cancer. Dementia is the only disease among the top killers for which there is no prevention, cure, or treatment that will slow its progression. In 2022, 4.0% of adults aged 65 and older reported a dementia diagnosis. The percentage of adults with a dementia diagnosis increased with age, from 1.7% for those ages 65–74, 5.7% for those ages 75–84, and 13.1% for those aged 85 and older. The costs of dementia care in 2023 in the United States have been estimated to be 345 billion dollars.[3] Fear of the disease has always been high – and in the United States, it is the second most feared disease, after cancer. Although this fear remains high, denial lessens it. As recently as 2006, most studies found that people did not understand what Alzheimer's was, nor that it was fatal.

Most people don't know the difference between dementia and Alzheimer's disease.

- **Dementia** is the general term for the decline in mental ability severe enough to interfere with everyday life.
- **Alzheimer's** is a degenerative brain disease that can lead to dementia.

Aside from finding a cure, one of the goals of the National Alzheimer's Project is to remove the stigma associated with the disease. Back in the

1990s, studies indicated that people did not talk about it, because they were ashamed of it and wanted to hide it. When Ronald Reagan announced his affliction with the disease, the public did not see much of him, and the disease stayed under the radar. This is slowly changing with the high-profile faces of people living with Alzheimer's in recent years (Glen Campbell, for one) — and many hope that the publicity will bring about more effort for a cure, as Betty Ford did for breast cancer.

Scientists have had some success in discovering the disease's biomarkers through a variety of tests, potentially making possible diagnoses years before the disease causes damage. Before this discovery, the only way to identify Alzheimer's was through an autopsy of the brain. The aim is to identify drugs that treat risk factors for Alzheimer's, much in the same way that drugs lower cholesterol levels – a primary risk factor for heart disease. Currently, the only drugs available are to treat the symptoms. Once the symptoms appear, it is too late – the disease will keep progressing and killing more brain cells. With the government funding research, it is hoped that eventually a cure will be found.

Government and private research facilities continue to spend more money on breast implants and Viagra than on Alzheimer's research. By 2022, there will be a large elderly population with perky boobs and huge erections but absolutely no recollection of what to do with them.

Home care is one of the most desirable options for the aging population, since it allows seniors to maintain their independence while remaining in a place where they feel most comfortable. In any given city, dozens of competing companies offer what appears to be the same service. The questions to ask to separate the better services from the suspicious ones include the following:

- How long has the company been in business?
- Is the caregiver staff bonded or insured?
- How extensive are the criminal background checks?
- Does the agency have a Licensed Vocational Nurse or RN on the staff?
- How are the employees selected?
- Will the agency provide information describing their services and fees?
- What are the financial procedures, and are the rates negotiable?
- Are references provided?

- Is the home care agency a small independent company or part of a large conglomerate?

Early Signs of Alzheimer's

- While it is normal to forget telephone numbers and remember them later, those with dementia may forget things more often and not remember them later.
- Preparing a meal – and not only forgetting to serve it, but also forgetting that they made it.
- Forgetting simple words and making sentences incomprehensible.
- Becoming lost on their own street, not knowing where they are, or how to get back home.
- Dressing inappropriately, wearing several shirts or blouses.
- Putting things in inappropriate places: an iron in the freezer or a wristwatch in the sugar bowl.
- Having rapid mood swings – from calm to tears to anger for no apparent reason.
- Changing drastically – becoming extremely confused, suspicious, or fearful.
- Becoming very passive, requiring cues, and prompting to become involved.

Alzheimer's is a debilitating disease with no prominent survivor or patient who has recovered and can personally campaign for more federal funding. Memory-care nursing homes cannot cure the condition, but they can make the patients more aware of their surroundings through therapeutic programming.

Living in a Dementia Fog

Security considerations for any of the homes or medical facilities described in this chapter are far different from those found in a conventional hospital setting – even though both types of healthcare institutions fall within the same community. All facilities provide some level of medical care to patients and residents but have vastly dissimilar threats and security problems. There are some similarities, since many hospitals also house nursing homes on their campuses – and every nursing home, or assisted living facility, relies on the services of a physician at one time or another.

In general, hospitals have serious security requirements associated with people constantly moving in and out of the facility – plus the chaotic atmosphere in departments such as the emergency rooms along with the special needs of a psychiatry ward and nursery care. The typical nursing home, by comparison, is not as busy. There are no emergency rooms, obstetrics and gynecology, ambulance docks. Their main concern is patients wandering aimlessly around the building and eventually out one of the exits (where they could be injured or killed).

It is difficult to get a physically healthy, elderly citizen with dementia to voluntarily remain within the confines of the ward or section of the building without resorting to physical restraints – which has been illegal for the last forty years. Many people in assisted living or long-term care facilities have only occasional bouts of dementia and may leave the building, intending to find a shopping center or visit friends who have long ago died or left the region. When patients become confused or disorientated, they can fall into out-of-the-way ditches or gullies and freeze to death before someone reports them as missing. The facility will then be accused of having lax security and face a lawsuit brought on by the distraught family.

Nursing-home facilities have difficulty defending themselves against any lawsuit unless they have installed some acceptable level of security at each exit and a surveillance system throughout their facilities. In selecting the appropriate security system, building owners should avoid creating a prison-like environment. Additionally, locking doors without any fail-safe feature would violate local fire codes. Restraining or chaining patients to a bed is illegal, and simply expanding the security staff is economically unjustified. With all these obvious restrictions, the average nursing home facility must improvise on the general environment to keep the patient within the confines of the facility. One of the simpler solutions is to keep patients from being depressed. If they feel depressed, this feeling can lead to their wandering. Part of the solution is to brighten the lights in dementia facilities. Increasing the light intensity helps patients see better so they can be more active. A brightly lit room significantly decreases feeling of loneliness and depression.

The number of wanderers, mostly made up of dementia patients who have Alzheimer's disease, is growing. Those cared for at the homes of family members present another problem (since the exhausted relatives caring for people living with Alzheimer's may have nodded off or been briefly inattentive, allowing a loved one to slip out). Then, they might feel guilty and will understate when the person disappeared, sometimes by many hours. How long the person has been gone is a crucial variable, as time on the run hugely increases the potential size of the search area. In many cases, the escapee may follow fences or power lines. For some unexplained reason, these people tend to be drawn toward the water.

Alzheimer's disease works backward, destroying the most recent memories first. Wanderers are traveling in the past tense, and conventional search procedures are often totally useless. A medical journal published a list of behavioral patterns that could be useful in finding the wanderer:

- World War veterans are known to travel huge distances, believing they need to report to an army base camp or try to return to their buddies at the front lines.
- Determine which door the person exited from and then concentrate first in that direction (because wanderers tend to walk in a straight line).
- Do not bother calling out the person's name, which the patient has often forgotten.
- Use the person's previous occupation. Farmers have tried to get to farms in time for the morning milking of their cows.
- Wanderers follow strict routines. If a patient never leaves a facility or house without his or her hat, then hide the hat.

More than four in 10 U.S. adults grade nursing homes negatively for overall quality of care – 36% give them a "D" (poor) and 6% an "F" (fail). Another 33% grade nursing homes as satisfactory, a "C", while few rate them positively with an excellent "A" (1%) or good "B" (8%) grade. These ratings average out to a D+ grade for nursing home quality of care overall.[4] These ratings are based on an analysis done by oversight agencies, after visits to the premises and complaints from patients and family members – plus other pertinent data collected by the Centers for Medicare and Medicaid Services. A star rating is used to compare facilities, drawn from a combination of the quality of living conditions, the staffing, and the general healthcare. For-profit corporations usually own nursing homes that repeatedly receive low overall stars (one or two) while publicly sponsored facilities receive higher ratings. The lowest-rated homes must still meet baseline Medicare standards to receive federal funds. The rating system places pressure on an individual facility to improve its operations and upgrade its treatment of patients by alerting the public eye about how the facility compares to others in the area.

The idea behind the rating system was to create two types of homes (the excellent and the nonexistent) – but this did not work out as planned. The ratings of the nation's nursing homes are available on the internet.

Nursing homes and long-term care facilities have proliferated throughout the nation. However, the rapid growth has occurred without much oversight or scrutiny by organizations that provide a similar service for hospitals. Fewer than ten hospitals dedicated to long-term care existed in the 1980s. Medicare rules fueled the phenomenal expansion of these facilities that offer high payments for hospitals that treat patients for an average of twenty-five days or more. In 2023, about 66.7 million Medicare patients received assistance from the U.S. government and, only thirty-seven new facilities opened their doors. This is compared to seventy-three new facilities that opened in 2020; seventy-one in 2021; and fifty-five in 2022. So far in 2024, only seven new facilities have opened, and few of them have doctors on staff.[5] Most are owned and operated by for-profit companies, with the largest of these firms having over fifty long-term hospitals under their control. Other companies with fifty or more facilities all share the same shortcomings, as indicated by the growing number of lawsuits and state inspection reports. As a result, these facilities present a troubling image. The situation is not improving, and more government oversight is beginning to address the shortcomings and complaints.

Elderly people who suffer from some form of dementia will wander from their homes or medical facilities, creating a growing problem for healthcare security professionals. Some estimate that one of the "wanderers" will die each month after leaving a facility without authorization or permission. A patient at a long-term acute care facility who is physically able to move about the premises means he or she can also wander off the property just as easily and often undetected. This situation poses a hazard for both the patient and the facility. If this occurs, the nursing home faces a liability lawsuit and a loss of accreditation – meaning no federal funds, if they ignore the wandering problem. There are almost daily reports of patients wandering onto the street, getting into a car, and disappearing, or being found dead many days later.

The Alzheimer's Foundation of America estimates that 6.9 million Americans aged sixty-five and older are living with Alzheimer's dementia in 2024.[6] Of that number, more than three million will wander away at some point, since they are not necessarily bedridden. Many enjoy short periods of seemingly cognizant communicative skills. Currently, eleven million people care for Alzheimer's-afflicted relatives at home.[7] Far too many families who have relatives suffering from Alzheimer's living with them will hide when a person is first noticed to be missing – since it indicates that they were not doing their job 24/7. Of course, living in a long-term institution is no safer than living at home, since two-thirds of nursing homes have residents with some form of dementia and must be monitored constantly.

Leaving Undetected to Go to Nonexistent Home

A nursing home in Germany addressed this common problem by erecting a fake bus stop right outside the facility to attract residents who stray off the premises, unobserved. Residents frequently walk out of the nursing facility, intent on returning to their nonexistent homes, and head directly to the familiar-looking bus stop. Some residents try to leave almost daily, undetected by the TV cameras mounted throughout the premises. Five minutes after capturing the escaping desperado, the resident has completely forgotten how he got to the bus stop or where he or she was going. Replicas of the bus stop are found throughout Europe and are beginning to appear near a few American nursing homes – mostly in the Northeast of the country.

Another issue that is increasing in frequency in Long Term Care (LTC) institutions is something popularly called "Sundown Syndrome", which usually occurs for nursing home residents toward the end of the days as the sun begins to set. Sundowning is the reaction of our internal clocks or circadian rhythm that affects people – mostly those over a certain age, who become accustomed to doing certain things at certain times of the day. An example is the lifelong routine of working during the day and returning home to eat and go to bed. After decades of establishing this repetitive routine, it becomes etched in a resident's circadian rhythm for them to seek out. In their minds, it's time to go home, hence finding the exit.

Locking of fire exits is essential in nursing homes and other long-term care facilities for the elderly, but the locking hardware must be fail-safe and installed in compliance with local and national fire codes issued by the National Fire Prevention Association (NFPA). Even though locking fire exit doors have been legal since that year, the architectural community has traditionally been reluctant to incorporate such a locking arrangement due to the unfounded belief that it could conceivably expose them to a liability suit if someone dies due to the exits being locked. This reluctance ignores the fact that shootings in schools and many other public assembly locations have resulted in more deaths and injuries from active shooters who enter the building through the unlocked fire exits than the deaths from fire in the last hundred years.

Wandering is a universal problem that can often lead to serious injury (death by freezing, getting hit by a car, or being attacked due to their strange behavior). Complicating the growing problem is that it is illegal to restrain residents by chaining them to a bedpost or randomly locking the perimeter or room doors without receiving permission from the local fire marshal. The fire marshal and others from Agencies Having Jurisdiction (AHJ) can cause a problem, because they are not familiar with the fire code changes that allow the fail-safe locking arrangement. Furthermore, the residents in the nursing home cannot be treated as prisoners. They were admitted either voluntarily or by a close family member and cannot be physically restrained.

A lawsuit against a psychiatry clinic for drug addicts and alcoholics of famous celebrities had a resident voluntarily admitted for long-term treatment and slept in a padded cell since she would hit her head against the wall during periods of detoxification and was always monitored as she walked the hallways for meals or visits to the therapist's office. She was considered a persistent wanderer and required close surveillance on the CCTV system. If she tried to leave the premises through one of the many exits required by fire codes, the staff would immediately and calmly try to get her back into the clinic. Since she volunteered to be admitted and was not forced or sentenced to live in the clinic, the staff could not legally retrain her. One day, she wandered off the premises undetected – and after walking in pajamas in the cold for a short distance, she fell into a ditch and died before her disappearance was noted. The resulting lawsuit almost bankrupted the facility, and a consultant was hired to find a way to lock all the fire exits while meeting national and local fire and building codes in which the doors would release only after an emergency in the building occurred.

Notes

1. J Silver-Greenberg, GR Maggots, Rape and Yet Five Stars: How U.S. Ratings of Nursing Homes Mislead the Public, *The New York Times*, August, 2021.
2. CBS News, Nursing Home Chain To Pay $38M In US Settlement, October 10, 2014, CBS Minnesota, Website: https://www.cbsnews.com/minnesota/news/nursing-home-chain-to-pay-38m-in-us-settlement/
3. National Health Statistics Reports, Diagnosed Dementia in Adults Age 65 and Older: United States, 2022, Ellen A. Kramarow, Ph.D, Number 203, June 13, 2024.

4. M Brenan, Americans Give Nursing Homes D+ Grade for Quality of Care, *Gallup*, September, 2023.
5. American Healthcare Association, Report: Access to Nursing Home Care is Worsening, August 2024.
6. Alzheimer's Association, 2024 Alzheimer's Disease Facts and Figures, Alzheimer's Dement 2024; 20(5).
7. CDC, Caregivers of a Person with Alzheimer's Disease or a Related Dementia, September, 2024.

Chapter 30

Monitoring Resident Movements (24/7)

Hiding Fire Exits

The wandering situation described above is a common event in nursing homes, and about six in ten dementia victims will wander at least once from either a nursing home or while under home care supervision. There is no perfect alarm or surveillance system to prevent wandering, but the existence of one means a nursing facility will be in a better position to defend itself in any lawsuit — even if the security system failed. A failed system is easier to defend in court than having ignored the problem altogether by having no system at all. In any event, when a patient is not located within a reasonable period, law enforcement must be notified to assist in initiating a wider search. The tendency to avoid bad publicity by delaying notification to authorities regarding a missing patient could prove disastrous.

Preventing freedom of patient movement sometimes creates a no-win situation, since restraining a patient may cause injury and a lawsuit from the family. If the wanderers venture off the building's premises without being detected and are injured by a car or freeze to death while trying to get to their home that probably no longer exists, relatives can initiate legal action.

One of the more effective security systems used in nursing homes is the so-called fail-safe perimeter exit door electromagnetic locking arrangements, which meet the National Fire Protection Association's (NFPA) Life Safety Code 101 and, most likely, the local municipal codes. Since 1980, when the NFPA amended its Life Safety Code, exit doors can be locked with a special

DOI: 10.4324/9781032630670-30

locking arrangement that keeps the door in a locked position if power is provided to the magnetic lock installed at the door. However, during power failures or the activation of the building's fire alarm system, the lock is released immediately. Adding closed-circuit television (CCTV) surveillance systems with cameras facing the exits and nearby corridor areas usually helps gain approval from the local authority with jurisdiction to install the fail-safe locking arrangement. Under HIPAA regulations, cameras should not be installed in private rooms or bathrooms – but they can be installed in most of the public areas.

Dementia patients can have periods of full comprehension and may be aware that by simply pulling the fire alarm emergency box, it will immediately release power to the magnetic lock on the door (allowing them to leave the premises). Of course, if a resident can figure out the connection between the locking system and the building fire alarm system, they should be able to find the nearest bus station to take them to the home they still believe exists without falling into a ditch or getting hit by a car. Less cognizant residents may never figure out the function of the fail-safe lock but will be smart enough to ignore the locked secondary exits and leave the premises through the main entrance of the facility, which is often unattended. Most of the smaller facilities rely on the one-person receptionist desk to monitor incoming or outgoing people. If this desk is left unstaffed, residents walk out of the facility alongside visitors and staff members – completely undetected by the staff or by the cameras.

Home care for the elderly and infirm has created a major market for handheld wireless "alert" transmitting systems (which operate like a modified garage door opener), carried by individuals who elect to live alone in the familiar setting of a home rather than in a nursing home. The strong possibility of falling and being unable to reach the telephone to call for assistance is the reason for the popularity of portable radio frequency (RF) alert systems, which are provided for a monthly fee. Many variations of the system exist, but they are mostly made up of a small transmitter that is worn or carried by an individual. The RF receivers are attached to a preprogrammed telephone with an automatic dialer. If people fall, they can seek outside assistance by simply pressing a battery-powered transmitter to activate the telephone to call a central station operator with a pre-recorded voice message or a digitally coded signal, giving the location of the emergency – which is then used in the 911 call.

Newer systems for the homebound patient include wireless sensors under the bed that detect movement off the bed. Scattered motion sensors in the bedroom and bathroom register that the individual has not left the area in an unusual pattern or within a programmable timeframe. If this happens, the system goes into an alert status with the information relayed to an off-site monitoring service (paid for with a monthly fee). A call is made to the home of the individual to inquire if everything is alright and to check if the signal was accidentally triggered. If there is no answer, a call is made to a neighbor, building manager, and finally, 911.

For centuries, the prototypical search-and-rescue case in America concentrated on children and adolescents lost in wooded areas or gigantic shopping malls. That ritual has changed since 2010 when, for the first time, public safety officials reported that search teams were summoned more often to find wandering and confused dementia patients of a certain age than for any other age or class of people. Individuals suffering from a form of cognitive impairment, such as Alzheimer's, often feel a restless urge to head out the door. Unpredictable journeys are often dangerous and frequently fatal. Some studies indicate that one nursing home patient wanders off the nursing home premises and is killed monthly in the United States.

Many alarm-monitoring devices are directed specifically to the "wanderer market", including a GPS device that looks similar to a wristwatch. There are even shoes with GPS monitors embedded in the heels. A nonprofit organization equips people living with Alzheimer's with wristbands after contacting the local police department to set up the service that works somewhat like a LoJack. The Alzheimer's Association offers a group for victims and their families. They established a twenty-four-hour emergency response line in conjunction with local law enforcement, which includes an ID bracelet program to identify an Alzheimer's patient. Sometimes, residents are no longer able to even identify themselves.

The security professionals assigned to evaluate long-term care facilities that house dementia patients must understand that the resident is mentally impaired, not physically impaired. The resident will often wander for exercise or to overcome loneliness – especially after a holiday during which no friend or close relative visited. Installing CCTV cameras is only a Band-Aid solution, since there is no assurance that anyone is viewing the monitors. Other techniques to make the premises more pleasant and to discourage wandering are the following:

- Installing a large, emphatic sign on every door saying "STOP". This can often deter the wanderer.

- Installing a black, rectangular-shaped carpet in front of the dementia unit elevator bank, as residents appear to interpret it as a cliff and will walk along the edge but will not step into the "black hole". People with dementia have visual-spatial problems and become so wary of the black obstacle that a nurse has to put down a white towel to cover the black carpet in order to get the person to move.
- Encourage keeping residents out of diapers and taking them to the toilet to preserve their feelings of independence.
- Adopt a policy that patients can eat at any time. Increase the number of tasty foods, such as chocolate. Comforting food improves behavior and mood, and it sends messages that the patients understand: "This feels good; therefore, it must be a place where the patient is loved".
- Instead of group events such as bingo (in which few residents participate), there should be more one-on-one activities such as block building, coloring, and simple conversing.
- Consider giving the resident a type of security blanket, such as a doll. While this may be considered undignified and demeaning, for a lot of parents with dementia, it gives them joy to care for "children".

Hiding Fire Exit Magnetic Locks within Wall Murals

A large nursing home complex in South Florida, with over 300 beds in eighteen different types of eldercare nursing units, has found a way to be in conformance with fire codes that require fail-safe electromagnetic locking arrangements on its 250 exits. The multi-building complex accomplished this challenge by hiding the exits in plain sight. The local and state Agencies Having Jurisdiction (AHJ) required doors to be locked in accordance with related local building and fire codes but allowed floor-to-ceiling colorful murals on the egress doors to disguise the exits. The covered doors had to meet the following safety conditions mandated by the code change:

a) Staff can readily unlock doors, at all times, in accordance with code requirements.
b) The door releasing hardware, where provided, is readily accessible for staff use.
c) Door leaves, windows, and door hardware (other than door releasing hardware) shall be permitted to be covered by the murals.
d) Murals shall not impair the operation of the doors.

In some healthcare occupancies, especially nursing homes, the use of murals to disguise doors has been found to be beneficial for certain residents' populations – especially those that show signs of Sundowning behavior. Murals will not affect the ability of residents (or visitors) to escape because in a locked area, the doors can always be unlocked by staff. It does not reduce the level of safety intended by Life Safety Code 101 Amendment adopted by NFPA in 1980. These camouflaged door locations are known by staff members and can readily be opened at any time. The painted murals on doors do not reduce the level of safety. The mural variance has not been adopted for nursing homes in all jurisdictions, and the wording may be different – but the use of disguises at exit areas is a growing trend throughout the United States.

Sex and Nursing Home Residents

The most highly regulated healthcare facilities are nursing homes, but they have lacked rules regarding sexual encounters among residents – until a few homes introduced guidelines around 2012. The rules usually involved the preservation of privacy, while recognizing that senior citizens were actively pursuing sexual pleasures (just like everyone else). It seems that sexual relations know no expiration date. Only about a quarter of facilities had policies on intimacy and sexual behavior by 2015, according to the Society for Post-Acute and Long-Term Care Medicine. The newly developed regulations were not only to protect consenting adults but also to protect residents from unsafe, unwanted, or abusive situations. Sexual expression in nursing homes was usually defined as anything from compliments to hugging, flirting, fondling, and, of course, intercourse. Social connections and human touch help ward off the depression and loneliness that old age institutional living can bring.

Allowing sexual encounters, in all their diverse forms in a nursing home setting, is a controversial subject considering that the people involved may be unable to balance a checkbook or barely speak. The general attitude toward the sex issue is that it is more an impulse akin to eating, a pleasurable appetite that one retains the ability to indulge in – even if the participant has Alzheimer's disease or another form of cognitive impairment. In a place that is not very exciting, residents may be looking for ways to have fun and have something to look forward to each day. A person with dementia is essentially a new person, and it is unfair to judge them by their old self

– since this treatment may be denying them one of the few pleasures in life that they have left.

A former resident in a state-operated nursing home was arrested and charged with third-degree sexual abuse for having sex with his wife, who was also a resident in the same nursing home. The facility claimed that she (the wife) was incapable of giving consent – a claim shared by her daughters. Others who were involved in the situation believed that accusing a spouse of a crime for continuing his relationship with a spouse in a nursing home seems to be incredibly illogical and unnatural, as well as incredibly hurtful. The case went to trial, and the husband was found not guilty.

Some nursing homes have a policy of offering double beds, rather than two singles. Married couples have mattresses placed on the floor and use "do not disturb" signs. They may provide Viagra, personal lubricants, porn magazines, or Fifty Shades of Grey on the desk. Staff members are taught to knock and pause before entering a room. A resident with Alzheimer's finds new companionship with a fellow resident, as happened with the Supreme Court justice's husband who forgot he had a spouse. That spouse was the first woman to be appointed to the Supreme Court.

Residents in a nursing home or living in senior citizen communities have resorted to ingenious arrangements to find privacy without renting a motel room or renting a golf cart and taking it into the out-of-bounds wooded area of a senior citizen community golf course. This golf course rendezvous is highly suspicious and used only as a last resort, since the reservation for a cart did not include the scheduling a tee time, nor did the couple show up with clubs. A more affordable location was discovered by an ingenious couple living on Social Security – and it was free and safe.

The older couple visited their doctor and asked if he will watch them have sex. The doctor agreed, though confused, and the couple went at it. When they were both done, the doc said, "I can't see anything physically wrong with either one of you, since you both seem to be enjoying yourselves and it doesn't look like you were in any distress or in pain. The couple thanked him and left without a prescription but continued to visit with the same request every week for a few weeks. Finally, the doctor had to ask why they were coming to his office to have him watch them have sex, since there was nothing that required medication. "Well, doc," the man responded, "she lives with her daughter who is a stay-at-home mom with a young child, so there's no privacy. I live in a nursing home, but just got a roommate, so there's no privacy. A hotel is too expensive, but Medicare or Medicaid takes care of your bill".

Besides the sexual encounter just described, it should be noted that humor is shared by people of all ages. The debilitating health problems that residents in nursing homes anticipate does not mean that they lose their sense of humor, which is often displayed on bulletin boards within the facility. Two samples of nursing home humor are as follows, but there are hundreds more on social networks and on Google.

- Some politicians had complained that during the 2020 pandemic the number of victims had spiked only because more people were being tested for COVID-19. That ridiculous statement and its illogical conclusion are the same as claiming that if more people took the IQ test it would result in a spike of morons.
- There was an invention developed for nursing home residents in the form of a Senior GPS that not only gets the resident to the proper destination in the shortest amount of time, but it also informs the user as to why they went there in the first place.

Thefts against Residents

Thousands of elderly patients, often suffering from some form of dementia and living in a nursing home or long-term care center, are the most vulnerable to having their trust funds or lifetime savings stolen by the very staff entrusted to care for them. These thefts are from bank accounts that are easy to steal from, and it can be difficult to detect any errors in the bank statements. Usually, receipts back up every transaction, so the victims and their families are unaware of the theft – until all the money is gone. A typical example of a shady transaction is when designer jeans and expensive shoes were paid for from a trust fund, and there were receipts to back up all charges – so audits found nothing amiss. Little may be said about the Ugg boots and jeans until a family member questions the expense – since the patient who owns the trust funds had her legs amputated ten years before the purchase. Additionally, thefts involving more than $100,000 have become common and mostly undetected, especially when the money is slowly embezzled over a long period from the accounts by a nursing staff member or senior administrator.

In scores of cases involving nursing-home-trust-fund thefts, employees and administrators siphoned huge sums of money from the helpless and feeble patients under their care, with the thefts of more than jeans and shoes. The stolen funds went toward shopping sprees and gambling debts and have involved numerous staff members and dozens of patients. Officials at the Centers for Medicare and Medicaid Services, the agency that regulates the nation's nearly 16,000 nursing homes, acknowledge that trust-fund thefts and mismanagement, along with forged checks, are a growing problem that gets insufficient attention. State and federal inspections of nursing homes and long-term care facilities typically focus on resident health and safety, devoting little scrutiny to the security of residents' trust funds. With more people ending up in nursing homes and the fact that only one administrator oversees the bookkeeping, there is little chance that the thefts can be stopped completely. Adding more security guards at the entrances will not have any effect on the security of the trust funds.

Silver Alert

This notification is the senior citizen's version of Amber Alert, a system to notify the public of missing children since the early 1990s. As the population of aging citizens increases, more patients suffering from Alzheimer's disease and other symptoms associated with dementia will be admitted to nursing homes every year. About half the states have instituted a Silver Alert system, and the federal government sponsored the Silver Alert Grant Program Act of 2008 – which awarded a grant of $100,000 as an impetus for establishing an alert system.

The International Association for Healthcare Security and Safety developed the definitions of various categories of patients who are unauthorized to leave medical treatment premises:

- Elopement (or absconding) is defined as patients incapable of adequately protecting themselves and departing from the healthcare facility without the knowledge and agreement from the clinical staff.
- Wandering refers to patients who stray beyond the view or control of clinical staff – causing concern, but without the intent of leaving.
- Leaving against medical advice is determined by the patient's decision to leave the facility after being informed of and understanding the risks of leaving without completing treatment.

Evacuation of Residents during a Hurricane Threat

This is a particular and serious problem to senior care facilities located in Southern states, where hurricanes and high-temperature weather conditions require emergency evacuation. Florida, the mecca for retirees and senior living facilities, has experienced periodic devastation from hurricanes like Matthew in 2016 that flooded St. Augustine, and Irma that caused many deaths in Hollywood, Florida, in 2017 – followed two years later with the Dorian hurricane of 2019. These events have focused on the security staff who need to be trained to ensure the orderly evacuation of nursing homes and assisted living facilities. These facilities become flooded or lose their air conditioning power source during weather-related tragedies. The staff must help in any evacuation, and the lack of such effort in the Hollywood incident resulted in the deaths of residents who died from heat – which led the medical examiner to rule the deaths as homicide.

This ruling came two years after the deaths, but the event shocked Florida lawmakers enough to pass laws that required nursing homes to have backup generators and enough fuel to maintain comfortable temperatures during power failure. No state has more retirees than Florida, where they make up more than one-fifth of the population, according to AARP. Some 190,000 in that sunny state live in 687 nursing homes or in one of the 3,063 assisted living centers – most of them in the state's southeastern tip.

In 2017, after Hurricane Irma in Florida, at least twelve nursing home residents died of heat exposure after their facility lost power to its air conditioning system. This led to state legislation in Florida requiring all nursing homes and assisted living communities to have generators or other sources of power to maintain cool temperatures. In Texas, in 2021, dozens of nursing homes and assisted living communities were required to evacuate because of freezing temperatures when Winter Storm Uri caused near-statewide electrical blackouts.[1] These scenarios exposed the grave consequences suffered by the most vulnerable residents due to poorly planned relocation policies followed by nursing home administrators who had mandated evacuation of all the patients. There are 66.7 million patients in the nation's nursing homes, and they all face more harm by following conventional evacuation procedures than if they had been subject to the "Settlement-in-Place" policy. The three-year study focused on patients with severe mental health issues such as dementia, depression, and Alzheimer's. The study included 21,255 residents living in 119 nursing homes over three years of observation. Relative to the two years before the storm, there was a 2.8% increase in death at 30 days and a 3.9% increase in death at 90 days for residents with severe dementia who evacuated for Hurricane Gustav, controlling for resident demographics and acuity.[2]

Evacuation plans for most nursing homes are now believed to compromise health and safety by forcing the evacuation of mentally ill patients. Sheltering-in-place is not a new concept, but it has been steadily replaced with "evacuation" guidelines for the last half century – many of which may change because of the study that showed a fourfold spike in deaths due to drowning between the 2005 Katrina and the 2008 Gustav hurricanes evacuations.

Medicare and Medicaid-certified nursing homes are required to have written emergency preparedness training. However, a report issued by the Office of Inspector General of Health and Human Services cited various problems found in a sample group of twenty-four nursing homes – especially in their preparedness plans that covered both evacuation and shelter-in-place policies in all the homes in the study. For example, the homes sampled did not have the required amount of water needed to ensure a sufficient supply to support the patients and staff for a week, as required by governmental guidelines. This was only one of the many shortcomings the report found.

Notes

1. Journal of American Geriatric Society, Protecting Nursing Home Residents in Disasters: The Urgent Need for a New Approach Amid Mounting Climate Warnings, Lindsay J Peterson, PMCID: PMC10023326 NIHMSID: NIHMS1864767 PMID: 36807117.
2. American Journal of Alzheimer's Disease and Other Dementia, The Effects of Evacuation on Nursing Home Residents With Dementia, Lisa M. Brown, David M. Dosa, Kali Thomas, Kathryn Hyer, Zhanlian Feng, Vincent Mo, PMCID: PMC3711109 NIHMSID: NIHMS477935 PMID: 22930698.

Chapter 31

Coronavirus – Deadly for Elderly

Nursing Home Vulnerable Population

According to the *New York Times* database, at least 184,000 coronavirus deaths have been reported among residents and employees of nursing homes and other long-term care facilities for older adults in the United States. As of June 1, 2021, the virus has infected more than 1,383,000 people at some 32,000 nursing home facilities. While 4% of the country's cases have occurred in long-term care facilities, deaths related to COVID-19 in these facilities account for about 31% of the country's pandemic fatalities. Deaths in long-term care facilities accounted for more than a third of all COVID-19 deaths in the United States for much of the pandemic – at one point, rising to about 43% of all coronavirus deaths – but this number has declined since the vaccination rollout began.[1]

Even in normal times, nursing homes are cauldrons for infections, and each year, over 380,000 residents die from infection, according to the Centers for Disease Control and Prevention. Infected patients with all types of bacteria-based illnesses are seldom separated from other residents, and caregivers go from one bed to the next without using disposable gowns and gloves. A quarter of all nursing home residents contract dangerous drug-resistant bacteria, and consequently, these homes become the riskiest place during a pandemic. Far too many states and federal agencies often treat the frail elderly as an afterthought.

DOI: 10.4324/9781032630670-31

People living in nursing homes and all other long-term care facilities were known as residents, never patients.

The American nursing home industry, as it was in 2020, came to fruition as a result of federal laws and regulations that go back eighty-five years. No matter how well instituted, no one was able to foresee the magnitude, speed, and disaster that defined the deadly results that followed the COVID-19 rampage. The laws not only allowed but encouraged the placement of 150 people in their eighties together in tight quarters – two to a room, sleeping four feet away from each other. As the pandemic proved, this was the worst living condition that a nursing facility could offer. The law that created Social Security in 1935 established many of the regulations that nursing homes had to operate under. To keep the elderly out of poor public houses, the Social Security Act prohibited payments to residents of public institutions that helped launch the rise of private nursing homes. That steady rise was unpredictable in 1935, when a lifetime was defined as sixty-five years.

The next law directed at nursing homes was passed in 1954, known officially as the Hill-Burton Act, which funded hospital construction and was expanded to provide loans and grants to build nursing homes to provide low-cost care. It was not a very good law, since it set the medical model of nursing homes to resemble a hospital environment rather than a college dorm or an apartment. This model is still in effect throughout the nursing home industry. Another and even more influential law was the creation of Medicare and Medicaid in 1965, which covered healthcare for the elderly. It was set to pay for doctor and hospital visits as well as short-term stays in nursing homes. Medicaid primarily covers the poor and is funded by matching states and federal funds for long-term care in nursing homes.

Prior to the establishment of Medicare and Medicaid few families struggled to pay for nursing home care. In those years, nursing home care was relatively inexpensive, and few people lived long enough to require it. The great takeoff in healthcare prices didn't start until the early sixties – and by 2021, a nursing home could charge $100,000, and assisted living facilities often charge more than $80,000 a year.[2]

Nursing homes are not good places for anyone, except in situations that require short-term rehab. Despite the flawed reaction to the virus spread, lives could have been saved if state and federal officials had acted quickly to make nursing homes a priority in the early stages of the coronavirus outbreak. The total lack of testing doomed facilities to become incubators of high-risk infection by unknowing spreaders of the virus. Since the discovery of the cure for the world's deadliest virus this threat has been abated. However, the pandemic exposed the mostly hidden fact that geriatric care has long been neglected, ignored, and poorly regulated. When doctors and staff members became overwhelmed, they chose between treating the younger infected people first or the elderly. These decisions have never been fully investigated, but it is suspected that ER personnel often gave preference to treating younger arriving patients.

It should be noted that nursing home residents, during the pandemic years, were dying alone. As no visitors were allowed, this neglected group was the perfect population for any sort of tests. Even getting the attention of the drug industry and scientists involved to consider the elderly was considered short of a small miracle.

Shameful Conditions in Nursing Homes

COVID-19 deaths in long-term care facilities make up at least 23% of all COVID-19 deaths in the United States.[3] Despite this disheartening statistic, the federal government has maintained a long-term practice of avoiding testing any anti-virus drugs in nursing homes and other extended elderly care environments even though they house the people who need treatment most. The nation's older population, susceptible to a range of complicated conditions, makes it difficult to tell if a newly drug developed is working. Additionally, nursing facilities are governed by a raft of complex regulations regarding privacy and access.

Through the end of 2020, the death rate for non-nursing home residents was about 87 per 100,000. The death rate for nursing home residents is more than 108 times that number at roughly 9,200 per 100,000. The death rate in nursing homes is 23 times larger than the death rate for those 65 and over outside of nursing homes, which we calculate to be about 390 per 100,000.[4] The disproportionate number of fatalities could have been much lower if the federal government hadn't left the individual states, cities, and institutions to set social distancing policies, secure needed equipment, and effectively test and trace enough people to stop the virus from spreading. Nursing assistants make up the bulk of nursing home workers and have one of the most dangerous jobs in America – especially during the pandemic, yet they make minimum wage or close to it. The work was and still is more deadly than logging or deep-sea fishing. Some changes were made after the pandemic ended, and nursing homes are now under more regulation than they were prior to 2020.

Another problem endemic to long-term facilities is that 70% of the nation's long-term facilities are operated by for-profit companies, including private investment firms. A report issued by the Government Accountability Office found that almost 82% of American nursing homes routinely violate infection control standards, and the pressure instituted by the nursing industry convinced Congress to pass a law granting nursing homes total immunity from wrongful death and other malpractice lawsuits through 2024.[5] The industry claimed that such protection was necessary to prevent struggling homes from collapsing under the weight of excessive litigation.

Compounding the problem in long-term facilities is that drug companies and the federal government have a history indicating that they try to avoid testing drugs that include senior citizen volunteers because, as they claim, the elderly have a range of existing health-related conditions that make it difficult to tell if the drug is working. Consequently, senior citizens generally do not get access to innovative new drugs and trials. There was one exception to this policy involving drug tests conducted by Eli Lilly and the National Institutes of Health that focused on the elderly in 2020. The drug test was assigned to randomly selected residents, with some receiving a placebo. The results were encouraging – and in some cases, they helped in developing the successful drugs in use today.

False Positive in Rapid Virus Tests Can Be Deadly

During the virus rampage in 2020, the federal Department of Health and Human Services (the agency that has overseen U.S. testing efforts) issued orders for states to stop using rapid coronavirus "antigen" tests. The order was based on the growing number of false positives reported that were threatening the health of nursing home residents. About 14,000 long-term care homes around the country had been using equipment that performed the so-called antigen tests that did not require them to be evaluated by an off-site laboratory, which delayed the results for days. Antigen tests focus on virus proteins, while "molecular" tests look for the genetic material in the virus. While this method takes longer for results, it is a much more reliable indicator than the antigen rapid on-site test.

The real problem with the rapid test is the large number of "false positive" results, which pose a particularly significant risk in a nursing home environment. A resident wrongly believed to have COVID-19 would normally be placed in an area dedicated to infected residents, potentially exposing uninfected persons to the virus.

Nursing Homes Protected against Lawsuits

Nursing homes had so many deaths due to COVID-19 in 2020 that the possibility of family instituted lawsuits for lack of due diligence in caring for their residents forced many states to pass laws protecting long-term healthcare facilities from liability and the subsequent civil suits for negligence, malpractice, and wrongful or neglectful treatment. The law also shielded nursing homes from being accused of the effects directly related to the lethal coronavirus.

The American Health Care Association led a lobbying effort to protect nursing homes and other long-term care facilities from legal liability during the COVID-19 pandemic. About twenty states granted lawsuit protection to these facilities by issuing laws or by governors' orders. While the state laws of protection vary, they usually protect nursing homes from simple negligence for injuries, deaths, and care decisions throughout the pandemic. Suits are generally allowed for gross negligence, malice, and willful misconduct, according to what became known as the Bloomberg Law.

The first group of states that enacted lawsuit protection laws includes Alabama, Arizona, Connecticut, Georgia, Illinois, Kentucky, Massachusetts, Michigan, Mississippi, New Jersey, New York, Nevada, Rhode Island, Vermont, and Wisconsin, according to the AP. Some states have enacted laws and executive orders that protect health care providers but don't specifically mention nursing homes. For example, the law in New York protects hospitals and nursing homes from claims of ordinary negligence for providing care throughout the COVID-19 crisis. The *New York Law Journal* reported that the facilities are also immune from criminal liability.

Immunity does not apply to "willful or intentional criminal misconduct, gross negligence, reckless misconduct, or intentional infliction of harm". The law specifies that any actions taken due to staffing shortages or supply shortages are entitled to protection. Critics claimed that nursing homes should be held accountable for deficiencies, such as staffing shortages and poor infection control, which were problems even before the pandemic. Those same critics also contended that providing blanket immunity to nursing homes for any kind of substandard care, abuse, or neglect is an extremely poor and dangerous idea – anytime, and particularly regarding COVID-19.

The few long-standing safeguards against abusive care in nursing homes had been rarely used before the pandemic in 2020. The following safeguards were mostly ineffective before the protection laws were passed and practically disappeared as a result of the law, as listed below:

- Family members who visit the sites report mistreatment to authorities. Visitors were no longer allowed to visit.
- Regular inspection by government regulators > Regulators stopped inspections.
- Lawsuits (used as a last resort) that can hold negligent homes accountable > States began passing laws protecting nursing homes from legal action.

Counter Measures Compensation Funds – Vaccine Injuries

In 1990, the National Vaccine Injury Compensation Program (VICP) was established. The program was designed to specifically cover harm resulting from vaccines for flu, pandemic, or for drugs to treat an anthrax or Ebola outbreak. In 2020, this was expanded to cover coronavirus injuries or death. This program was created in the 1980s, after lawsuits against vaccine companies and health care providers threatened to cause vaccine shortages and reduce U.S. vaccination rates – which could have caused a resurgence of vaccine-preventable diseases. Any individual of any age who received a covered vaccine and believes that they were injured as a result can file a petition. Parents, legal guardians, and legal representatives can file on behalf of children, disabled adults, and individuals who are deceased.

According to the CDC, from 2006 to 2022 over five billion doses of covered vaccines were distributed in the United States. For petitions filed in this time period, 12,499 petitions were adjudicated by the Court, and of those 9,075 were compensated. This means that for every one million doses of vaccine that were distributed, approximately one individual was compensated. Since 1988, over 28,085 petitions have been filed with the VICP. Over that thirty-year time period, 24,464 petitions have been adjudicated, with 11,564 of those determined to be compensable, while 12,900 were dismissed. Total compensation paid over the life of the program is approximately $5.3 billion.[6]

Vaccines save lives by preventing disease, and most people who get vaccines have no serious problems. Vaccines are generally safe, but they can cause side effects including shoulder injuries related to injections, allergic reactions, fainting, and certain neurological conditions like encephalitis. Some health problems that follow vaccinations are not caused by vaccines. The National Vaccine Injury Compensation Program (VICP) may provide financial compensation to individuals who file a petition and are found to have been injured by a VICP-covered vaccine. Even in cases in which such a finding is not made, petitioners may receive compensation through a settlement.

Notes

1. The New York Times, Nearly One-Third of U.S. Coronavirus Deaths Are Linked to Nursing Homes, June 1, 2021.
2. The New York Times, Extra Fees Drive Assisted Living Profits, November 20, 2023, https://www.nytimes.com › long-term-care-assisted-living.
3. KFF, Over 200,000 Residents and Staff in Long-Term Care Facilities Have Died From COVID-19, Priya Chidambaram, February 03, 2022.
4. Journal of Health Economics, Nursing home quality, COVID-19 deaths, and excess mortality, Christopher J. Cronin, William N. Evans, PMCID: PMC8776351 PMID: 35104669.
5. US Government Accountability Office, Infection Control Deficiencies Were Widespread and Persistent in Nursing Homes Prior to COVID-19 Pandemic, May 20, 2020.
6. Health Resources & Service Administration, HRSA Data and Statistics January 2025, https://www.hrsa.gov/sites/default/files/hrsa/advisory-committees/vaccines/vicp-stats-01-01-25.pdf.

Chapter 32

Palliative Care Killing Granny

Death Sites

Most people are unfamiliar with palliative care and often confuse this treatment with hospice care, treating palliative care as the last resort when a loved one is about to die. However, palliative care is one of the fastest-growing fields in medicine and focuses on helping residents with their pain and symptoms. It offers counseling to help people who are still fighting their disease. This comprehensive service aims to relieve suffering in people with serious illnesses through practitioners who counsel terminally ill patients. These practitioners receive training in how to talk about accepting death, making it as comfortable as possible. The palliative care practice was encouraged almost as a backlash against the highly impersonal medicalized death prevalent in American hospitals. Palliative care focuses on relieving pain and recognizing that, after a certain point, aggressive treatment is not only a waste of money but may also prevent patients from enjoying what life they have left. Palliative care is not limited to deathbed counseling and has gradually become a standard practice in many hospitals across the nation.

Often, residents assume their doctors will take care of their pain and do not realize that in the nation's specialized medical system, oncologists and cardiologists are not well-trained in pain and symptoms management – nor do specialists have a lot of time to spend on quality-of-life issues. When patients are treated for serious illnesses, they are referred to a specialist who focuses on his or her organ or disease. This expert is not trained to treat the whole person. Palliative care takes a team approach by providing a doctor, nurse, social worker, and chaplain who work together to go beyond medical

DOI: 10.4324/9781032630670-32

issues to address all of a patient's needs. This could include managing nausea associated with a disease, as well as counseling or providing help in navigating the healthcare system. While palliative care has become the standard of care in large hospitals, gaps in access remain in for-profit and rural hospitals. Eighty-three point six percent of U.S. hospitals with 50 or more beds report having specialty palliative care services, and this prevalence climbs to 96.2% for hospitals with 300 or more beds. However, the proportion of for-profit hospitals and rural hospitals with palliative care lags behind significantly, at 49.0% and 34.5% respectively.[1]

A study conducted by the New England Journal of Medicine in 2010 confirms the positive effects of end-of-life care.[2] Terminally ill residents were not only happier, more mobile, and in less pain as the end neared – they also lived three months longer than expected. The approach used in palliative care is not just to keep the terminally ill alive but to help the patient have the best quality of life. The study could not determine why patients lived longer under palliative care – but experts strongly believed that depression shortens life. In addition, residents whose pain is treated often sleep better, eat better, and talk more with relatives.

The nursing home industry is the biggest user of Medicaid claims collected about $39 billion in the 2019 fiscal year, which is expected to increase by approximately 4% or $1.4 billion by 2024.[3] Government auditors find thousands of cases of overcharging for so-called skilled services that were not performed, and the inspector general of the Department of Health and Human Services documented a serious number of bills paid to the nation's roughly 15,000 nursing homes for services not performed or, if performed, were unnecessary, inappropriate, or fraudulent. These bills amounted to somewhere around 1.5 billion annually.

Palliative Intervention

Over seven in 10 Americans, 71%, believe doctors should be allowed by law to end the patient's life by some painless means if the patient and his or her family request it.[4] Most of these assisted suicides are done by prescribing large doses of morphine. The groups that oppose medically assisted suicide point out that some patients who suffer from depression have been given lethal overdoses without being referred for a mental health evaluation. When consultations indicated competency concerns, these opinions were ignored. Furthermore, some suicidal residents report being concerned about being a burden to their family, and there is a potential for death by overdoses administered by "loved ones". In addition, health plans concerned with keeping down expenses have become subtly coercive. In some cases, cancer patients were denied treatment coverage by the state Medicaid program yet offered full coverage for assisted suicide.

Palliative sedation (a comfortable death) has been added to the controversy surrounding assisted suicide. However, it should not be confused with euthanasia. When death is imminent, sedating a patient (if nothing else can be done to ameliorate severe suffering) is a legitimate medical intervention. Any medical intervention may have some unintended lethal side effect. However, the fact remains that palliative sedation is more closely related to a resident dying during heart bypass surgery than to euthanasia. In a landmark U.S. Supreme Court decision in 1997, the Chief Justice writing for the majority opinion stated, "Just as a State may prohibit assisting suicide while permitting patients to refuse unwanted life-saving treatment, it may permit palliative care related to that refusal – which may have the foreseen but unintended 'double effect' of hastening the patient's death".

Most resident deaths during the first year after Washington State legalized assisted suicide in 2009 were cancer sufferers.[5] Prescribing doctors, who are required to submit forms to the state department of health, said that all who died cited "loss of autonomy" as a reason for seeking the lethal drug. Most also said they could no longer enjoy life and feared losing their "dignity". Rarely was the reason due solely to finances. Some critics of the law claim that assisted suicide could prompt disproportionate use by lower-income people who worry about being a financial burden on their families. A further study of the Washington State group found that almost all had private insurance, Medicare, Medicaid, or some combination. None claimed they had no insurance.

There remains a medical myth that pain relievers and sedatives hasten death, but sufficient research exists to contradict these concerns. Even further, research suggests that such interventions appear to have a neutral effect on survival and may prolong life while relieving suffering.

A resident with uncontrollable pain is under severe cardiovascular stress from the pain itself. A rapid heart rate, shallow breathing, and agitation will shorten life as death nears. Relief of the pain calms the heart and helps the resident breathe more effectively and, in effect, extends life for the individual.

A strong legal penchant seems to override the common human acts of decency throughout American culture. In 2011 in the Bay Area around San Francisco, a dependent man walked into the chilly (but not fully freezing) waters to commit suicide – in broad daylight, in front of dozens of bystanders on the shoreline. Police and firefighters got there with plenty of time, but they all just stood there and watched. Due to union-backed rules, firefighters and police officers simply declined to save the man's life for fear of being sued. A bystander, amazed at the inaction taken by people who usually save lives, asked the fire chief on the scene what he would have done if the person in the water were a child instead of a suicidal adult. The chief responded, "If I were on duty, I would have let the child drown – but if I were off duty, I would have saved the child".

Hospice Care

Some residents – and even many doctors – treat palliative medicine and hospice as the same. Yet, there are differences in treatment. Hospice care is a form of palliative care for people in their last six months of life who no longer need or want to treat their condition but want help for managing their pain. Hospice care is intensive palliative care and differs by allowing home nursing to be covered by insurers and Medicare, when a resident abandons medical treatment and two doctors certify that death is less than six months away. An important factor in treating terminally ill residents is that when pain is controlled, people not only feel better, but they seem to live longer after receiving the appropriate drug protocol.

Another positive result is that residents feel well enough to leave the confines of the hospital or nursing home environment and return to their home. This change in atmosphere is important, as hospitals are not only depressing but dangerous places for very sick people. They may get fatal blood infections, pneumonia, bedsores, or simply be overwhelmed by some of the powerful drugs and radiation used to attack their disease (most often, cancer is the focus of palliative and hospice care).

Medicare costs for hospice care have increased more than any other healthcare sector, and government records show for-profit companies continue to gain a larger share of the end-of-life medical market. Some of the nation's largest for-profit hospice companies are paying multi-million-dollar settlements for fraud claims and are facing investigations from state and federal law enforcement agencies. Costs for hospice care have increased so rapidly because for-profit organizations have cherry-picked patients who live the longest and require the least amount of care – such as those with dementia or Alzheimer's, rather than those with cancer.

End-of-Life Choices

Some states passed laws making it easier for seriously ill residents to voluntarily make their wishes known about end-of-life care by creating an electronic database that first responders can quickly check during a medical emergency. The data is taken from the information on signed forms (known as Physician Orders for Life-Sustaining Treatment or "POLST") and is supposed to direct all healthcare providers on the type of care a resident wants to receive in the event of an emergency. The paper forms are still used in thirty-three states, and people take the forms home and put them on their refrigerators or place them another prominent location in their homes. Nevertheless, paper forms are often lost or simply overlooked. Several states have created electronic databases to make it easier for the seriously ill to voluntarily make their wishes known about end-of-life care in a format that can be checked during a medical emergency on the internet, by fax, or via smartphone. Oregon, in 2009, was the first state to develop and use a format that can be checked during an emergency. New York and West Virginia started similar databases in 2011.

The information on the POLST form will eventually be phased out by digitally stored information, shared by all fifty states that instruct responders as to whether a patient wants a feeding tube or to even be taken to a hospital at all. Whatever form these instructions take, the end-of-life care directives are controversial. Critics argue that elderly or sick residents could be persuaded to choose less care to save money – even if it is not in their best interests. Some of the opponents also liken it to physician-assisted suicide – since in the long run, many of these choices will significantly hasten death.

Oregon registered more than 50,000 people in three years, using the electronic database. These residents had gone through a two-minute process to fill out the POLST form during a consultation with their doctor. Before the electronic registry, if emergency personnel could not find a form, they would provide any life-saving measures possible – which might conflict with a patient's request. Being able to check a form via a digital network will quickly help determine the method of treatment during a very stressful event.

POLST forms are different from living wills, as they are medical orders signed by a physician and are meant to be used by patients who are elderly or very ill. In contrast, living wills can be completed by healthy individuals and typically name a proxy who will make decisions about end-of-life care. POLST forms usually offer three primary options: comfort care, limited care intervention, and full treatment:

- Comfort Care includes administering medicine and oxygen, but no hospitalization.
- Limited Intervention includes the previous measures, plus intravenous fluids and hospitalization – but excludes mechanical ventilation and intensive-care treatment.
- Full Treatment is everything above plus mechanical ventilation and intensive-care treatment.

Doctors in England used to administer terminally ill cancer residents an elixir known as the "Brompton cocktail". This drink was a blend of cocaine, heroin, and alcohol (which formed a very potent cocktail). The results were gratifying, not only to the recipient, but also to the relatives of the stricken resident. It drew life to a close with a drug-induced orgasmic bang instead of the standard pathetic, painful whimper. This drink may eventually be accepted as a civilized advance in the process of dying. Some of the Brompton-cocktail practitioners have plaques on the front office door with the following motto:

SINCE ONE IS CONCEIVED IN PLEASURE – THEREFORE, IT IS REASONABLE TO EXPECT THAT THE INEVITABLE ACT OF DYING SHOULD ALSO BE CONSUMMATED BY ANOTHER PLEASURABLE EVENT.

A great controversy arose after Congress passed the Affordable Care Act that went into effect in 2011. One of the items in the act concerned a so-called "death panel", the name of the guideline that reimburses doctors under Medicare for the time they devote to voluntary end-of-life consultations with residents during annual medical examinations (also called "wellness visits.") These doctor-patient talks generally cover palliative, hospice, and other services that would cost less than an all-out effort to prolong life. Opponents had criticized the language of the first draft of the end-of-life discussions as pressuring residents into making a living that would cut off care if they were incapacitated. The guidelines in the law that Congress eventually passed did not include any reference to how the doctors would conduct the discussion but authorized (for the first time) reimbursement for the discussion.

Medicare insures fifty-five million older and disabled Americans. Regulations were criticized for setting up a so-called "death panel" that supposedly cut off care for the terminally ill. The government, to eliminate that criticism, passed a law in 2015 that reimburses doctors and qualified professionals, such as nurse practitioners and physician assistants, for any face-to-face meetings with residents, relatives, or caregivers regarding whether and how they would want to be kept alive if they became too sick to speak for themselves. The plan was created because residents, families, and health providers sought to give people a greater say in how they die – whether that means trying every possible option to stay alive or discontinuing life support for those who do not want to be sustained by ventilators and feeding tubes.

Medical Assistance in Dying – Euthanasia

Medical assistance in dying provides options to patients who may be experiencing suffering and pain due to a grievous and incurable medical condition. This option involves ending life with the assistance of a doctor or nurse practitioner. Medical assistance in dying is provided only to legally eligible patients. "Physician-assisted suicide" is a familiar term that has been called upon for many years – mainly because it was illegal. It was also made famous by Dr. Kevorkian (Dr. Death). Suicide is still an illegal act in all but very few states.

A terminally ill individual, who wishes to have someone's help in ending life to avoid pain and suffering caused by illness, falls under what is now termed "Aid in Dying".

Organizations with names such as Final Exit Network, Death with Dignity, the National Center, and Compassion and Choices advise on legal ways to reduce end-of-life suffering. In an average year, about 3,000 terminally ill patients contact one of these advocacy groups for information to hasten their deaths. These groups are careful to avoid legal conflicts by insisting that they only offer guidance and may witness suicide, but do not assist in the performance of what almost all states consider a criminal act. The Supreme Court ruled in 2006 that states can set their laws on suicide assistance, but it never clearly defined the term "assistance". The guidebooks distributed by organizations in this suicide assistance community suggest that it is legal to hold a dying person's hand for support – but not in restraint. Final Exit Network is a New Jersey-based non-profit that spreads the word on how to assemble a homemade "exit bag" – a plastic hood that fits over the head and is fed by lethal helium, resulting in a quick death. The organization will even supply an exit guide during the procedure but denies that these volunteers prevent people from removing the hoods if they have last-minute doubts.

Opponents of suicidal assistance claim that offering to help in the commission of suicide is either illegal or unethical. One state defines assisted suicide as "direct and physical involvement, intervention, or participation" and carries a sentence of five years of imprisonment. A case that became controversial involved a man who had suffered from mouth and throat cancer. By the time he sought assistance and did commit suicide, he had overcome the disease and was instead just embarrassed by a facial disfigurement. The debate concerning assisted suicide is probably unending. One side claims that people have a right to decide for themselves, and the other believes that assisted suicide should never be allowed. The people against assisted suicide formed a group called "Not Dead Yet".

State Laws on Medically Assisted Suicide

The U.S. Supreme Court ruled in 1997 that there was no constitutional right to physician-assisted suicide and upheld a prohibition against it. It was an ambiguous ruling since the justices conceded that terminally ill patients were entitled to aggressive pain management – even if the opiates or barbiturates had the "double effect" of hastening death. Using that fuzzy description, Oregon voted in 1998 to become the first state to allow physician-assisted suicide. Its law was upheld, and in 2009, Washington State joined Oregon. The state court in Montana found that it was not illegal for physicians to prescribe lethal medication to terminally ill residents in certain situations. Vermont joined the group of assisted-suicide states in 2013. In 2008, California (in a close vote) rejected the proposition to allow assisted suicide – but in 2015, it passed a law to allow it. No other state or municipality has passed similar laws and attempts in Michigan, Maine, and

Massachusetts failed when voters rejected the policy. More than thirty states explicitly criminalize assisted suicide, and right-to-life groups maintain a vocal opposition to assisted suicide.

In 2009, the state of Washington reported that in the first year after passing the law, at least thirty-six terminally ill people died after taking lethal medication prescribed by doctors. A total of sixty-three people filled prescriptions for lethal medications, but not everyone took it. All those who took it died. Eleven people who did not take it died from other causes. Oregon issued a report in 2009 that said fifty-nine people had died in the last year from lethal medication prescribed under the law out of the ninety-five who filled prescriptions.[6]

Jack Kevorkian became infamous as a result of his rallying cry for assisted suicide. He was subsequently found guilty in the assisted suicides of seventy-five people between 1990 and 1999; 72% of them were women and three-fourths of the women were not terminally ill. It is still a crime in most states and countries to actively participate or physically assist in a suicide.

Kevorkian was successful in avoiding prosecution in his home state of Michigan for many years, simply because he videotaped each suicide to prove to the law enforcement agencies threatening prosecution that, while he may have been present during the suicide ritual, he did not get involved in the actual suicide process. The process was performed by the victim completely, and Kevorkian never charged for his consultation and advice. His downfall occurred when he appeared on the popular TV show, 60 Minutes, and allowed the program to show a suicide in which he injected the lethal dose of the drug. He was convicted and sentenced to ten years in prison and lost his medical license. Kevorkian was released from prison in 2007 but was barred from assisting anyone in committing suicide. He died a natural death in 2011.

Residents in the nine states that allow assisted suicide can request a lethal prescription from their physician. They must be mentally competent and have six months or less to live, as verified by two physicians. Then, they must wait fifteen days and repeat their request orally and in writing. The law also mandates that the patients must be at least eighteen and a resident of the state. The patients cannot have a mental disorder – including depression, which may impair judgment. They must be capable of administering the medication themselves and agree to attend counseling if their physician requests it. Patients must also be told about alternatives. The usual prescription is for a lethal dose of barbiturates. A physician can be present when the drug is taken but cannot help physically in any way to administer the drug

— which would be considered euthanasia and is illegal in all fifty states. Most die within ninety minutes of taking the medicine, though a few live as long as 224 hours.

Thus far, the law does not justify suicide for debilitating diseases such as Parkinson's, multiple sclerosis, or Alzheimer's. While they may be painful, they are not considered fatal diseases.

New Jersey passed right-to-die measures in 2019 that included certain stipulations:

- Patients who wish to end their lives would first have to request a lethal prescription verbally.
- After that request, there would be a fifteen-day delay, followed by another verbal request.
- The second request would be in writing and signed by two witnesses.
- After that request, a doctor would have to offer the patient a chance to rescind all requests.
- A second doctor would then have to certify the original doctor's diagnosis and affirm that the patient is acting voluntarily and can make the decision.

A would-be suicidal individual is forewarned that taking out an insurance policy, specifically to have the surviving family members collect the principal value of the policy, is not advisable. Desperate individuals may consider a life insurance policy when a career ends abruptly, they are diagnosed with a terminal disease, or the stock market crashes. Most life insurance policies contain a disclaimer that the policy does not cover suicides if the event occurs within two years of the policy taking effect. Rarely are suicides the result of long-range planning by the person attempting suicide.

Hippocratic Oath

Ancient Greek physicians were tempted to help desperate patients kill themselves. While many probably did, just as many refused to do so. Those who refused were following the dictates of the Hippocratic Oath, which forbids such an act. Assisted suicide is contrary to the basic concept that doctors must work to benefit the sick, as stated in the Hippocratic Oath. Using the same reasoning, doctors have traditionally refused to participate in capital punishment and, if inducted into the military service, refused to bear arms. Hundreds of doctors in the state of Oregon (where assisted suicide is legal) will not participate or assist in the process.

Under a physician-assisted suicide, many people besides the terminally ill could be affected. Those suffering from depression or those who are demoralized and bewildered might die before their time. Palliative care by doctors and nurses offers a better and more humane alternative to suicide – whether assisted or not.

Psychiatrist and Resident Suicides

Suicide is a serious matter, and some jurisdictions consider it a criminal event – one that has become the eighth leading cause of death in the United States. Taking one's life often inflicts grave emotional damage on surviving families, especially children and spouses. Americans have had a national fixation on suicide prevention for more than a half century, and it has transformed psychiatric care – often at the expense of other aspects of resident well-being. Not too many years ago, patients left hospitals on day passes as a crucial step in the road toward recovery from suicidal thoughts because fresh air and sunshine work wonders for many thinking about ending their lives. In the 1970s, depressed patients leaving the hospital for short periods (sometimes unsupervised) were no less likely to harm themselves than if they they weren't under medical care.

Psychiatry practitioners are not always willing to take the risk of unsupervised release for the sake of the few residents who would benefit. Psychiatry has radically changed in many other ways in the last thirty years. The fact still remains that most residents are still involuntarily admitted to the hospital psychiatric ward, which is a "threat to self", a catchphrase used to hold residents against their will. The current attitude, held by many psychiatrists, is that it is safer to have 1,000 patients lose their short-term freedom if one potentially suicidal resident is kept safe. This philosophy has no valid or historic justification, and the opposite effect may result since there is ample evidence that involuntarily held residents often resent their loss of freedom or fear future confinement. These feelings often compel patients to hide self-harming thoughts from their therapists to avoid a return to a locked ward. While it may sound shocking, the present system allows no space for the patient whose suicidal thoughts are genuinely healthy – a reassuring outlet that lets him or her know that there is always an escape from their suffering, even if they never choose to use it.

A growing number of experts in the field believe that the obsession with suicide is suffocating psychiatry, and some therapists in private practice will no longer take patients with histories of suicide attempts (as they are afraid of a lawsuit if a future attempt succeeds). Thus, the vulnerable individuals most in need of mental healthcare have the least access. At the same time, far too many psychiatric wards are increasingly populated by antisocial malingerers who have no pressing need for hospitalization, but they know that if they claim they are contemplating suicide, they will be guaranteed a comfortable bed and three hot meals a day. It is estimated that 20% of those purported to be suicidal in the emergency room are there solely for the hot meal – a better choice than a homeless shelter.

Psychiatrists should not be blamed for events that they could do nothing about. Oncologists are not blamed if their residents die of cancer, despite heroic efforts because some cancers cannot yet be cured. If society were similarly able to accept that some suicides are inevitable, psychiatrists might take risks that would save and improve other lives. Under the present circumstances, they are discouraged from trying to help people who are desperate for treatment of their mental illness.

The Right to Die: Foreign Countries' Experience

Japanese people (living in Japan) commit suicide (hara-kiri) at double the rate of Americans. A recent study compiled by the World Health Organization indicated that there were about 35,000 suicides in Japan every year in this century. This would make the suicide rate in that country the ninth highest in the world. Japan has long practiced a suicide culture, based on the history of Samurai warriors disemboweling themselves rather than surrendering. In modern times, hundreds of kamikaze pilots killed themselves during the infamy of World War II. Among Japanese suicides in recent years, nearly 71% are men, with more than 73% aged forty or older, more than half being unemployed. Unlike their American counterparts, when a man commits suicide in Japan, his beneficiaries can still collect the life insurance – and the policy even carries options that pay off the house mortgages. When the head of the household dies (for whatever reason), the rest of the family gets money. If the same man had decided to live (without a job), the family would lose their house.[7]

Why did the Japanese kamikaze pilots always wear helmets?

Point of Interest: Death-row inmates in Japan's prisons are isolated from other inmates, and the method used to prevent suicides is a little unusual and has been condemned by human rights organizations. The reason is that once the appeal process is complete, a death-row prisoner may wait for years or even decades before execution. During these extremely lengthy periods, the prisoners are not told the date that they are going to be executed. They are only told a few hours before they are led to the gallows, which has lowered the suicide rate to zero. Their families find out only after the hanging.

Another strange characteristic of the Japanese culture surrounding suicide is that a growing number of people choose to jump to their deaths in front of trains. Some Japanese railway operators have installed special blue lights above station platforms that they believe will have a soothing effect and reduce the urge to commit suicide. The illumination comes from blue-emitting diodes (or LEDs) in the main train stations, which are used by eight million passengers daily. No scientific proof exists that these lights help to reduce the number of suicides, but experts in the field of color psychology claim that the color blue has a calming effect on agitated people – since it represents the sky and the sea and may prove to make people pause and reflect. Of the 35,000 people committing suicide each year, more than 2,000 jumped in front of a train – with one particular station becoming the resting place for almost seventy suicides in 2010. The station hangs the eerie blue lights, which are brighter than standard fluorescent bulbs, at the end of each platform – a spot from which people are most likely to throw themselves in front of a train. While there is no scientific proof that blue lights will help deter suicides, they cannot make the situation worse. It is too early to tell if the lights are effective, as this type of statistic requires a ten-year study.[8]

Germany's highest court ruled that it was not a criminal offense to cut off life-sustaining treatment for a patient. The decision distinguished between "killing with the aim of terminating life" and the action that lets a patient die with his or her consent. The ruling was similar to the practice sometimes called voluntary euthanasia. Up until the ruling in Germany, German citizens traveled to Switzerland to die – but the issue became very controversial in Germany because of its past in which the Nazi regime used the term "euthanasia" as cover for a mass extermination program of disabled people. The German law can lead to controversy, as it did with a well-publicized suicide in 2010. Someone helped a woman kill herself at home, though she was not sick or dying – she simply did not want to move into a nursing home.

India pays $2,000 to the family of any farmer who commits suicide due to the threat of foreclosure on his family farm. European countries, including the Netherlands, Belgium, and Sweden, allow assisted suicide. The British Parliament, in 2015, voted down a measure that would have permitted physicians to help terminally ill people end their lives.

Notes

1. Cision PRWeb, Center to Advance Palliative Care Releases 2024 Serious Illness Scorecard: A State-By-State Look at Palliative Care Capacity, Center to Advance Palliative Care, December 2024, https://www.prweb.com/releases/center-to-advance-palliative-care-releases-2024-serious-illness-scorecard-a-state-by-state-look-at-palliative-care-capacity-302321056.html
2. DG McNeil Jr., Palliative Care Extends Life, Study Finds, *The New York Times*, August 2010.
3. CMS.gov, Fiscal Year (FY) 2024 Skilled Nursing Facility Prospective Payment System Final Rule - CMS-1779-F, July 2023.
4. R Yi, Most Americans Favor Legal Euthanasia: Smaller Majority Support Doctor-assisted Suicide, Slim Majority Say it Is Moral, *Gallup*, August 2024.
5. The New England Journal of Medicine, Implementing a Death with Dignity Program at a Comprehensive Cancer Center, Elizabeth Trice Loggers, M.D., Ph.D., Helene Starks, Ph.D., M.P.H., Moreen Shannon-Dudley, M.S.W., L.I.C.S.W., Anthony L. Back, M.D., Frederick R. Appelbaum, M.D., and F. Marc Stewart, M.D., April 11, 2013.
6. The New England Journal of Medicine, Implementing a Death with Dignity Program at a Comprehensive Cancer Center, Elizabeth Trice Loggers, M.D., Ph.D., Helene Starks, Ph.D., M.P.H., Moreen Shannon-Dudley, M.S.W., L.I.C.S.W., Anthony L. Back, M.D., Frederick R. Appelbaum, M.D., and F. Marc Stewart, M.D., April 11, 2013.
7. J Lamar, Suicides in Japan Reach a Record High, *BMJ* 2000 September 2;321(7260):528.
8. The Associated Press, Tokyo Train Stations Use Lights to Stem Suicides, *NBC News*, November 4, 2009.

Index

For Product Safety Concerns and Information please contact our EU
representative GPSR@taylorandfrancis.com
Taylor & Francis Verlag GmbH, Kaufingerstraße 24, 80331 München, Germany

www.ingramcontent.com/pod-product-compliance
Ingram Content Group UK Ltd.
Pitfield, Milton Keynes, MK11 3LW, UK
UKHW050057200926
475702UK00019B/2892
* 9 7 8 1 0 3 2 6 3 0 6 5 6 *

Healthcare Safety and Security

Navigating a Service in Crisis

Charles Schnabolk
Bernard Scaglione

Routledge
Taylor & Francis Group
A PRODUCTIVITY PRESS BOOK

Designed cover image: Shutterstock

First published 2026
by Routledge
605 Third Avenue, New York, NY 10158

and by Routledge
4 Park Square, Milton Park, Abingdon, Oxon, OX14 4RN

Routledge is an imprint of the Taylor & Francis Group, an informa business

ISBN: 9781032630663 (hbk)
ISBN: 9781032630656 (pbk)
ISBN: 9781032630670 (ebk)

DOI: 10.4324/9781032630670

Typeset in ITC Garamond
by Deanta Global Publishing Services, Chennai, India